The Statesman's Science

The Statesman's Science

History, Nature, and Law in the Political Thought of Samuel Taylor Coleridge

PAMELA EDWARDS

COLUMBIA UNIVERSITY PRESS
NEW YORK

Columbia University Ppress
Publishers Since 1893
New York Chichester, West Sussex

Copyright © 2004 Columbia University Press
All rights Reserved

Library of Congress Cataloging-in-Publication Data
Edwards, Pamela, 1956–
The statesman's science : history, nature, and law in the political thought
of Samuel Taylor Coleridge / Pamela Edwards
p. cm.
Includes bibliographical references and index.
ISBN 0–231–13178–X (cloth : alk. paper)—ISBN 0–231–13179–8 (pbk. : alk. paper)
1. Coleridge, Samuel Taylor, 1772–1834—Political and social views.
2. Political science—Great Britain—History—19th century. 3. Coleridge,
Samuel Taylor, 1772–1834—Knowledge—Natural history. 4. Coleridge,
Samuel Taylor, 1772–1834—Knowledge—History. 5. Coleridge, Samuel Taylor,
1772–1834—Knowledge—Law. I. Title.
PR4487.P6E23 2004
821'.7—dc22
2004047825

Columbia University Press books are printed on permanent and durable acid-free paper
Printed in the United States of America

c 10 9 8 7 6 5 4 3 2 1

CONTENTS

ACKNOWLEDGMENTS

F OR THOSE COLLEAGUES, friends, and family who have offered support and encouragement throughout this long journey with Coleridge, I offer my profoundest gratitude. Particular support, intellectual, moral, and editorial was given in the later stages of this project by James J. Sack and Joseph M. Levine. I am also grateful to those scholars who read, or with great forbearance listened to, substantial portions of the work in progress. Kevin Sharpe, David Leiberman, James Bradley, Jonathan Clark, and John Pocock have all at various stages of the project offered thoughtful assistance on questions pertaining to the religious and juridical discourses of the long eighteenth century. I must also offer heartfelt thanks to those friends who provided intellectual, emotional, and often material sustenance along the way. Lori-Anne Ferrell, Tony Claydon, Jeremy Gregory, Tom Auffenberg, and Katherine Clark have all helped to keep various wolves and doldrums from numerous doors and windows. Thanks also to my parents, Yvonne and James Edwards, for years of encouragement. Finally, to James Caudle, who has offered every kind of support and is due every kind of gratitude, love and thanks.

ABBREVIATIONS

Some of the works of Samuel Taylor Coleridge are referred to in the text and the notes by the following abbreviations. Two refer to writings unpublished during Coleridge's lifetime:

CL *Letters of Samuel Taylor Coleridge.* Ed. E. L. Griggs. 6 vols. Oxford: The Clarendon Press, 1956–71.

CN *The Notebooks of Samuel Taylor Coleridge.* Ed. Kathleen Coburn. 4 (of 6) vols. London: Routledge and Kegan Paul, 1957.

The other abbreviations all refer to volumes of *The Collected Works of Samuel Taylor Coleridge.* Bollingen Series 75. 14 vols. London and Princeton, N.J.: Routledge and Kegan Paul and Princeton University Press:

Lects. 1795 Vol. 1. *Lectures, 1795: On Politics and Religion.* Ed. Lewis Patton and Peter Mann. 1971.

W Vol. 2. *The Watchman.* Ed. Lewis Patton. 1970.

EOT Vol. 3. *Essays on His Times in the* Morning Post *and the* Courier. Ed. David V. Erdman. 3 vols. 1978.

TF Vol. 4. *The Friend.* Ed. B. Rooke. 2 vols. 1969.

LS Vol. 6. *Lay Sermons.* Ed. R. J. White. 1972.

BL Vol. 7. *Biographia Literaria.* Ed. James Engell and W. Jackson Bate. 2 books. 1983.

CS Vol. 10. *On The Constitution of Church and State.* Ed. John Colmer. 1976.

M Vol. 12. *Marginalia.* 3 books. Books 1 and 2 ed. George Whalley. 1984. Book 3 ed. George Whalley and H. J. Jackson. 1992.

L Vol. 13. *Logic.* Ed. J. R. de J. Jackson. 1981.

TT Vol. 14. *Table Talk.* Ed. Carl Woodring. 2 books. 1990.

The Statesman's Science

The Politics of Reputation, or, the Myth of a Modern Apostate

Party, Faction, or Critical Ideology?

C OLERIDGE CLAIMED THAT he was "ever a man without a party."[1] Others, including contemporary friends and associates from Robert Southey[2] to Henry Crabb Robinson, have viewed Coleridge's portrait of himself as a lifelong "independent" as disingenuous. But careful examination of the political thought of Coleridge from his earliest writings on politics and religion in 1795 to his last and most coherent work of political thought, in *On the Constitution of the Church and State* in 1830, confirms that neither a "Young Radical" nor an "Old Tory," Coleridge contributed to what Mill himself termed a second school of liberalism.[3]

"Liberal" is a term at least as problematical as "radical" and "conservative." All three of these terms entered the British political lexicon during or immediately after Coleridge's lifetime, and he was a key participant in the debates that shaped their origin and meaning. In considering Coleridge's life and thought in terms of these ideological categories, one invariably challenges and thereby clarifies those categories. Liberalism has, from its origins in the works of John Locke (as described by both C. B. Macpherson and Richard Ashcraft), been associated with atomistic visions of individual liberty, the doctrine of natural rights, the fiction of an "original social contract," and the discourse of jurisprudence. But more recent notions of liberalism have tended to emphasize its connection to questions of social welfare and moral freedom. One might garner a more useful assessment of the term "liberal" from that greatest exponent of the classical republican paradigm, J. G. A. Pocock. He observes, with an eye to a twentieth-century context, that "the rise of the social to preeminence over the political (to denote which is at present one of the cant usages of the term liberalism) seems to have rested on a psychology of sentiment, sympathy, and passion better equipped to account for politeness, taste and transaction than was the rigorous individualism of private interest."[4] In considering a political thinker such as Coleridge, whose conception of the social was both determined by and in turn determined the political, one may hope to avoid cant while considering the source of a strand of liberalism that comprehended the interests of both citizen and commonwealth.

It was certainly Coleridge's view that the pursuit of ideas of "sympathy," "virtue," and "rigorous individualism of private interest" were not incompatible goals. Indeed, Coleridge believed that recognition of the interdependency of these values was essential for the constitution of a sociopolitical state. This interdependent moral and political force in what amounted to a social and cultural matrix could only be cognized as science. Coleridge attempted explicitly to set out the principles of this statesman's science in his work *The Statesman's Manual*, but the synthetic intersection of history, nature, and law as essential and defining principles behind virtuous government was a thesis implicit in all of his political writings.

Coleridge's approach to the idea of the "State" sought to integrate the principles of organic nature, the philosophy of history, and the science of the legislator.[5] The principles of organic nature he derived from a combination of the works of Bacon, Cudworth, Kant, and Schelling. His own view of organicism, whether associated with history, nature, or law, was expanded in reference to these ideas through his ongoing interest in medicine and chemistry. This "medico-philosophical" approach, as he described it, was developed and indulged in the lectures on chemistry and magnetism that he gave for Humphry Davey at the Royal Society and through the lectures on anatomy that he gave at King's College London. These he delivered at the insistence of his friend and amanuensis, J. H. Green. Coleridge also developed his own account of life for his friend Dr. James Gilman and dictated large portions of his *Hints Towards a More Comprehensive Theory of Life* to Green in 1816. It was published posthumously. His "Lectures on Philosophy," which were also delivered at King's, suggest much of the connection that Coleridge invariably made between natural philosophy, natural law, and organic nature.

The idea of organicism was also the basis of Coleridge's conceptions of historical change, and in this he had considerable sympathy for Burke. He believed that the history of society was a record of a living process of growth and decay, of mutation and regeneration. The institutional form that accompanied and in some instances unnaturally constricted this process was the law. Coleridge believed that the common law and the ancient constitution revealed, through an ongoing adjustment and accommodation of social and political will, the workings of reason and providence. He believed that reason and the common-law were fundamentally related ideas. In this view, providence was the (Kantian) "cunning of reason"[6] or the (Coleridgian) "science of history"; it was a providence of second causes. Coleridge's conception of "organic nature," his under-standing of "philosophy of history," and his belief in the "science of the legisla-tor"[7] are interdependent ideas, all of which point towards the development of a sociological jurisprudence.[8] For Coleridge, as for Kames or Smith, the bridge between the moral and the commercial discourse was to be found in the law.

The young Coleridge was certainly more "conservative" than his "radical" critics have suggested. The old Coleridge was far more "radical" than his Tory supporters could have imagined. As Mill observed, Coleridge's real opinions on society, politics, and religion were, even under Lord Liverpool's patronage, "sufficient to make a Tory's hair stand on end." Continuity based on a com-mitment to the idea of liberty is the distinguishing mark of a career that "res-cued from oblivion truths which Tories had forgotten and which the prevail-ing school of liberalism never knew."[9] It may be useful to take Mill's lead in this and consider that the "prevailing school of liberalism" was not the only school of liberalism. Coleridge's perspective as a social and political critic, his concern for a constitutional polity that could promote communal goods with-out obviating personal agency, his interest in a sociological jurisprudence that could compass history, power, and law in terms of natural organic processes, are all suggestive of this second liberal party that at once paralleled and op-posed the "prevailing school" of the Benthamites.

Beyond being a man of no party, Coleridge was, from first to last, a great classical scholar. His understanding both of the oratory of the greatest expo-nents of classical rhetoric and their principles was extensive. He had read the classic texts of English civic-humanist thought, such as *Cato's Letters* and *Oceana*. But his acquaintance with the discourses of virtue, corruption, liberty, and tyranny was rooted far deeper than those shallow recensions. Coleridge read his Machiavelli first hand, rather than through neo-Harringtonian intermediaries. He had read in the Greek and Latin the political texts of Cicero, Seneca, Plato, and Aristotle. He also read broadly in the "moderns," reading Descartes, Rousseau, Spinoza, Leibnitz, and Kant. While it is true that his distaste for "Scotchmen" became legendary, he read Adam Smith, Adam Ferguson, Sir James Steuart of Goodtrees, and Andrew Fletcher of Saltoun. His preoccupa-tion with Hume was so vivid and lively that it amounted to a virtual, although necessarily one-sided, editorial engagement in *The Friend*. While attacking Smith, by way of undermining Malthus and Ricardo, there is much in Co-leridge's later writings to suggest that his understanding of the social, political, *and* moral significance of the new Scottish economic science was considerable. Through these considerations, most evident in *Church and State*, Coleridge united, or at least considered in tandem, aspects of the thought of Montesquieu and Kames, Rousseau and Smith. In the political thought of Samuel Taylor Coleridge, the language of classical republicanism and the language of jurisprudence found a certain accord.

Coleridge scholarship has passed through a number of recognizable phases since the poet-philosopher's death at the age of sixty-two. One must begin by saying that Coleridge "studies" began largely with an informal, discipular tradition, relatively uncritical in its admiration for the "Sage of Highgate," in the nineteenth century.[10] The amount and variety of Coleridgiana and the number and variety of both single and collected editions of Coleridge attest to his popularity among the "Victorians." Coleridge, like Samuel Johnson[11] and Walter Scott, was erroneously thought to provide justifications of "Tory" principles and a "Tory" way of life in general.[12] Yet he had a more important and influential status beyond his position as a Tory saint. Coleridge's statements on the formative power of ideas in society influenced the mid- and late-nineteenth-century political theorists, even those who did not think of themselves as within the "Idealist" or "Tory" traditions. His writings received respect and attention from John Stuart Mill[13] and T. H. Green[14] not merely as artifacts in the history of ideas but as a vital rethinking of persistent problems of politics.

Alongside this tradition of praise, of course, there arose a parallel tradition of criticism that saw Coleridge as an "Apostate" from the cause of democracy. Implicit in this critique was the suggestion that Coleridge's treason inherently demoted his thought to a second-rate category. Coleridge's contemporary and critical adversary William Hazlitt was the first to refer to him as an "apostate,"[15] and Hazlitt and Thomas DeQuincey both attacked Coleridge in editorials and reviews during the early nineteenth century.[16] They accused Coleridge, as well as the other Lake Poets (William Wordsworth and Robert Southey), of turning their backs on the cause of parliamentary reform, spurning the principles of the French Revolution, and betraying the "Radical" ideas and loyalties of a Jacobin youth in favor of the comfortable haven of Anglican piety and Tory patronage.

Hazlitt and DeQuincy were not the last to view Coleridge or the language of political affiliation during the critical years after 1793 in simple and defamatory terms.[17] The theme of betrayal and disappointed promise, both political and literary, has survived in many of the accounts of Coleridge that literary scholars have produced. It is most striking in Norman Fruman's *Damaged Archangel*,[18] which emphasizes Coleridge's personal vices and failures, his addictions and plagiarisms.[19] But it also became a stalwart interpretation of political and social historians like Edward Thompson, who revived the charge of "apostasy" in his paean to the 1790s radicalization of plebeian and artisan London, *The Making of the English Working Class*.[20] Thompson's work exercised a considerable influence on the analysis of romantic "Radicalism" that literary and cultural critics of the 1960s and 1970s produced. Most notable amongst Thompson's contemporaries was the work of Raymond Williams,[21] although more recently Marilyn Butler's slight but now standard volume, *Romantics, Rebels, and Reactionaries*,[22] has continued this tradition. Thompson, Williams, and Butler have all, in their different fashions, approached the cultural politics of this period through the lens of Marx-influenced ideologies, whether economic reductionism or Gramscian hegemony theory.[23] In the pursuit of what Butler has described as a radicalized and politically self-conscious "urban subclass,"[24] certain questions of incongruity have been ignored. Butler has established a new industry in the historicist study of romanticism, and many of the most recent accounts of Coleridge's work have been undertaken with a more careful eye to the contexts of their production. Yet, we find the idea of context to be itself a hotly contested concept, and while the best of the new historicism is oddly reminiscent of the best of the old historicism, the worst of it is curiously unhistorical in its historicity.[25]

The historically uncritical treatments which followed from these assumptions of class formation and consciousness failed to take heed of John Cannon's careful discrimination of the various factions, languages, and styles of reformers that were characteristic of the opponents of the Unreformed Constitution during the last decade of the eighteenth century.[26] Nor did they consider the strategic development of "oppositional" rhetorics during the long eighteenth century from 1688–1832. The ideological considerations which must follow from H. T. Dickinson's careful charting of the changing significance of eighteenth-century oppositional languages of corruption and virtue—marked by the transition from "Whig" versus "Tory," to "Court" versus "Country," and finally to "Radical" versus "Conservative" rhetorical dichotomies—suggest the need for caution when reading "Radicalism" out of all reform rhetorics.[27]

Beyond the contextual problems of ideological and rhetorical analysis by which some of the less historically careful of the literary accounts have been plagued, there is the problem of Coleridge himself. Thompsonite advocates of "Apostasy" have also failed to reconcile the striking continuity of Coleridge's political, moral, and social thought—and his persistent assertions of political independence in matters of conscience and party—with the problem of "Radicalism" as an ideological category during this period. "Apostasy" is a term loaded with religious sentiment, and, in the case of Thompson and those

Marxist social historians who followed him, it was the religion of political radicalism that Coleridge had betrayed.

More recent scholarship has considered both Coleridge and "Radical" ideology with an evener temper. J. G. A. Pocock's treatments of the ancient constitution and the classical republicanism of James Harrington and his disciples has provided a subsequent generation of scholars with a new understanding of the rhetorical and ideological strategies of Georgian Britain.[28] Caroline Robbins's careful examination of the agrarian-gentry classical republicanism of what she termed the "Commonwealthsman" described a world of gentlemen politicians who were as concerned with issues of virtue and the corrupting influence of excessive property (luxury) as they were with the use of liberty as a strategy for protecting their own property.[29] Robbins's thesis was countered by the liberty-as-rationale-for-property possessive individualism of C. B. Macpherson's Lockean urban-bourgeois "man of property."[30] The Lockean thesis produced its own wider influences, particularly in accounts of the politics of the American Revolution. Overturning the idea of a "Lockean Liberal" revolution, Bernard Bailyn reconstructed Robbins's commonwealth thesis, tracing the language of republicanism across the Atlantic and considering its impact on the "Patriot" faction in the thirteen colonies of British North America who subsequently evolved into American "revolutionaries."[31] It is arguable that those scholars who have more recently enlisted under the banner of the classical and communitarian model pioneered by Robbins, Pocock, and Bailyn have as much of an "ideological" axe to grind as the disciples of Thompson or Macpherson . The Robbins/Pocock/Bailyn thesis, which began its life as a fresh new "heresy" against the monolithic vision of a single tradition that recognized only "Lockean liberalism" and the Whig-versus-Tory dichotomy from 1688 to 1789, has itself hardened into a rigid orthodoxy as stultifying as the paradigm which it unseated.

In this new humanist and communitarian synthesis the language of individual property, liberty, and natural rights was eclipsed by the agrarian republicanism and civic virtue that Pocock has associated with the Catonian and Florentine Republics. It is this "Classical Republican paradigm" which has been providing the theoretical assumptions for the most recent accounts of the political thought of Coleridge.[32] In this manner, the post-1968 Marxist accounts of radical consciousness were overturned in favor of the competing languages of Old Whig/Country Tory politics versus the religious and political significance of rational dissent. Radicalism in the 1790s was constructed anew; the model based on class struggle and artisan consciousness gave way to a paradigm of Unitarianism and the Good Old Cause.

It is striking, however, that with several notable exceptions, the work that was produced on Coleridge's politics in literature departments failed to keep pace with the changing face of debate in historiography and political theory on eighteenth-century rhetoric, ideology, and party. Some of the best works on Coleridge have, arguably, been produced by the meticulous editors of the Bollingen collected works. R. J. White,[33] who was the first to edit Coleridge's writings on political thought, annotated *The Lay Sermons* for the series.[34] David Erdman produced the volumes comprising the journalism of the Napoleonic years originally issued as *Essays on His Own Times*.[35] John Colmer, who understood the unique and independent quality of Coleridge's political and social thought, presented him as a "critic of society" in both his own work of that title and his edition of *Church and State*.[36] These are only a few of the editors of the series whose work combined extensive explications of allusions in the texts themselves with perceptive and subtle readings of the works in their introductions. Significantly, they were also those who, along with the general editor, the late Kathleen Coburn, have produced the best interpretative works on Coleridge as a political thinker.[37] Unlike those of their colleagues who have emphasized the broad ideological significance of Coleridge's thought, they remained scrupulously within the boundaries of the texts that they explicated.

J. T. Miller was likely the first to reconsider Roberta Brinkley's evidence for Coleridge's debt to seventeenth-century thinkers.[38] Brinkley had examined how, in addition to his uses of seventeenth-century divines like Ralph Cudworth and Robert Leighton, Coleridge drew heavily on the writings of Locke, Milton, Sydney, and Harrington. Miller argues that Coleridge's appropriation of Harrington and the "neo-Harringtonians," Trenchard and Gordon, established him within the parameters of Commonwealth and Country Party ideology. But, in view of Robbins's careful distinctions between the differing political views of the Commonwealthsmen, it is important that Coleridge's republicanism is not too hastily inferred from his laudatory references to "Milton, Sydney, Harrington, and Locke." Miller contends that Coleridge undertook "radical ends through conservative means." His comment is a provocative and appealing way of arguing for some degree of continuity in Coleridge's thought. But his study is an interpretation that continued, in some degree, the problems of ideological "lumping" that blighted the earlier accounts by Thompson, Butler, and, most recently in that tradition, Nicholas Roe.[39] It is not useful to demolish Coleridge as a "Radical," if he is only to be resurrected as a "Classical Republican." The question becomes how "Radical" was Coleridge's "Republicanism"?

John Morrow has produced the most recent, and in many respects the most satisfactory, account of Coleridge's political thought to date.[40] Like Miller, Morrow emphasizes the importance of Commonwealth and Country Party arguments in Coleridge's writings from 1795 to 1830. He charts a shift in Coleridge's views of property and its moral and political significance after the Peace of Amiens in 1802. He echoes Miller's focus on Coleridge's equation "Property is Power," a formula strikingly similar to that of Harrington. The question begged by both Morrow and Miller was, what kind of property[41] and what kind of power?[42] Morrow sustains the old myth of Coleridgian "Apostasy." However, he believes that Coleridge's concerns after 1800 shifted away from the more "Radical" appropriations of republican language that characterized his youthful writings, through the politics of the Napoleonic era, toward a conservative classical synthesis in the later years of *Aids to Reflection* and *Church and State*.

Morrow's account is persuasive, and it is a careful attempt to explain the development and changes that attended Coleridge's maturation as a political thinker. However, it is possible to consider change, growth and development, without returning to the old songs of apostasy and betrayal. Coleridge did change, as did the world in which he lived, but he did not recant. R. J. White's early assessment, made in 1939, stands very well: "Coleridge was never a radical nor a Tory. He was a liberal philosopher and a great Christian seer."[43]

Coleridge's conviction was, from first to last, that political liberty was secured by independence of conscience and reason, that this independence was undermined by party allegiance, that positive institutions and the Common Law rather than an encoded charter of natural rights was the best hope of a just and lasting polity, and that virtue and voluntarism were the prerequisites required for a free and liberal society.

Perhaps the most striking deficiency in Morrow's otherwise measured and careful account is that in the service of the civic humanist/classical republican paradigm, he failed to consider adequately one of the central aspects of Coleridge's thought: the philosophical significance of his constitutional theory. Coleridge's persistent concern with constitutional and Common Law arguments separated him from both the radical/Tory dichotomy and, more interestingly, from the civic humanist paradigm, at least in its Harringtonian incarnation. The philosophical underpinnings of Coleridge's late political theory suggest a far more "radical" view of state and society than any he compassed in his early career.

One aspect of Pocock's early conceptions of the discourse of *virtú* is that it was a language incompatible with the language of *ius*. Philosophically, Pocock argued, rights and virtues cannot be the same thing; therefore, theories that emphasize the one must invariably devalue the other. For this reason, the classical republican paradigm is inevitably antagonistic to the juridical one. Quentin Skinner and Richard Tuck have both suggested instances where the juridical and humanistic discourses allied rather than clashed.[44] In particular, Richard Tuck has devoted considerable attention to the juridical–civic humanist syntheses in the political thought of the Dutch Republic. Pocock chose to treat this discovery dismissively, describing the writers rediscovered by Tuck as obscure and marginal: "some Dutch contemporaries of Spinoza's."[45] But beyond these examples of parallel discourses, some of the most interesting connections to be made recently between ideas of liberty, law, commerce, and virtue have come from those scholars who work on the Scottish literati.

Donald Winch, in particular, has argued with regard to the "Adam Smith problem" that the bridging discourse between *Theory of Moral Sentiments* and *Wealth of Nations* may be found in the "Lectures on Jurisprudence."[46] Indeed, Pocock himself has described the Scottish Enlightenment to be the partial respondent and partial heir to the Commonwealth tradition. In the case of Scotland, Pocock argues, the Addisonian conception of civility and urban virtue, so popularized by the proliferation of Spectator Clubs in Edinburgh, engendered a Ciceronian (as opposed to Machiavellian or Catonian) conception of classical republicanism in the Scots.[47] This more urban and urbane conception of virtue promoted a temperate sociability that made Scotland more conducive to a legal and commercial world of professionalism than did the military and agrarian view that Harrington, Trenchard, and Gordon celebrated.

Coleridge was certainly aware of and admired aspects of the works of Harrington, Trenchard, and Gordon. Although retaining a conviction that something in the permanent value of landed property anchored social values and constitutional principles, Coleridge also conceived a role for the moral significance of commercial property in the development of what he called "an expanding liberty."[48] While his earliest conceptions of the political and moral importance of property suggested more than a passing debt to the republicanism of the seventeenth-century Commonwealthmen, he also focused on the idea of liberty as a function of the ancient constitution and the Common Law. He produced his final synthesis of these parallel discourses, which ran throughout his writing, in *Church and State*. This treatise was an institutional theory of government and society predicated on an understanding of dynamic "equipoise."[49] This dynamic was to be understood as the fundamental and integrative fusion between land and commerce as active forces driven by "lived experiences," in short, by human, moral, and social agency. Both landed and commercial interests were sustained by and regulated by the law. Accordingly, Coleridge's juridical assumptions as to the nature of liberty and law were historical and sociological in nature. His political thought owed as much to the arguments of Hooker,[50] Coke, Montesquieu,[51] DeLolme,[52] Blackstone, and Burke[53] as it did to the republicanism of "Milton, Sydney, and Harrington."

More than any other political thinker of late-eighteenth-century England, Coleridge provides a unique opportunity to examine the rhetoric, ideology, and, beyond that, the political ideas of his age. His complexity as a political and moral thinker was such that John Stuart Mill believed that Coleridge and Bentham were the two keys to the intellectual life of the nineteenth century.[54] Coleridge's impact throughout the nineteenth century on figures as varied as Mill, John Sterling, Frederick Denison Maurice, Thomas Carlyle, John Henry Newman, Hurrell Froude,[55] and Thomas Hill Green has yet to be adequately considered.[56] His ambiguous reputation as a Tory philosopher who was "more liberal than liberals"[57] underlines the central role that Coleridge certainly played in the development of definitions of "positive liberty" by later twentieth-century thinkers such as Isaiah Berlin[58] and Charles Taylor.[59]

A "positive" conception of liberty, or the idea that freedom as moral choice was the foundation of duty and citizenship, was certainly the point of origin for all of Coleridge's political ideas.[60] He detested the corruption and abuse that he associated with the unreformed constitution and was a persistent critic of the excessive encroachment by government on the liberties of its subjects. However, Coleridge believed that the state had a positive role to play in the betterment of social conditions and, through the right institutions, such as the Common Law and the church, the moral improvement of individual citizens. In this regard he developed arguments that paralleled as much as they derived from those advanced by Kant on questions of morality and law. Coleridge emphasized that rights were a subset of duties, stressed the importance of public and private virtues, and advocated a government founded upon active and living institutions. Throughout his writings, he always returned to the central importance of voluntarism, of human agency, and of the free discourses of commerce and opinion. It is possible that in considering the political thought of Coleridge, certain of Professor Pocock's questions and challenges may be advanced.

CHAPTER I

Romantic Radicalism

THE PROBLEM IN considering Coleridge's political trajectory has largely been the consequence of attempting to read his various early works
and private utterances as though they were all of one piece. This same error
has been replicated with respect to his later writings; however, the superim-
position of order has tended to reverse the focus on political questions. That
is to say, critics have searched for the radical tones in the early writings and
sought out the most conservative aspects of the later work in their search for
apostasy, or indeed even consistency, in Coleridge's life. While I would argue
for coherence and continuity in Coleridge's career, I would resist the impulse
to "tidy" Coleridge up. I would also suggest that any assessment of Coleridge's
overarching principles must be made in terms of balance over time and that
such a balance depends on a reading of his underlying principles as they pertained to a complex network of ever-changing political realities.

Like most people, Coleridge's opinions on various subjects tended to
present themselves in terms which suggested an ambivalence towards reductionism and the doctrinaire. Human conviction is harder to educe than the
simple utterance of a single text. The specific principle or event in light of its
consequence, the particular audience for the work, the immediate emotional context of a letter: all of these must be considered in order to judge an individual's overarching principles as they pertain to any given moment in life.
If these various expressions of belief are passionate and contradictory, or fragmentary, the problem is exacerbated. In Coleridge's case this is unusually
true. Nonetheless, there have been numerous efforts to categorize Coleridge's
political sensabilities. "Apostate," "mime," "glacier," and "unconscious man"
are the epithets associated with four classic theories of Coleridge's political
development that have attempted to delineate a pattern for his thought from
1794 to 1834.

The crucial years of 1795 and 1802 have often been presented as two possible loci for Coleridge's "apostasy" away from "radicalism" toward "conservatism."[1] Many critics suggest that in the early months of 1795, Coleridge's writings reflected an active support for popular "radicalism." Coleridge abandoned the "radical" cause, these interpreters contend, when the tide of popular counterrevolutionary fervor and high-handed government muzzling of the "radicals" mounted in the closing months of the year.[2]

There seem to be four major schools of thought on the issue of the changes, if any, in Coleridge's political ideas in 1795. The first school is that of "self-conscious apostasy," as suggested by E. P. Thompson and his acolytes, a quick and Judas-like about-face that took place in either 1795 or 1802. The second school is that of the "mime," which claims that Coleridge possessed a chameleon-like habit of shifting his opinions to conform to what he perceived to be the beliefs of his audience, in the same way that a weather vane turns to indicate the direction of the fresh winds. Given this propensity, Coleridge appeared to be in constant change and alteration, when in truth all that was changing was the audience to whom he conformed his ideas in search of better rhetorical effect. The third is that of a slow but sure evolution away from "radical" toward "Tory," a sort of "glacial" change. The fourth and oddest is that Coleridge was not at all political during this segment of his life, the theory being that Coleridge was "inert and unconscious" in his youth and, indeed, throughout his career as to matters of practical politics. Each of these theories—the "apostate," the "mime," the "glacier," and the "unconscious man"—has specific weaknesses; all tend to ignore the fundamental continuities in Coleridge's work throughout his lifetime.

The "mimetic" thesis had an early articulation in Crane Brinton's 1926 study of *The Political Ideas of the English Romanticists*.[3] Brinton described this chameleon-like behavior as Coleridge's "obliging way of adapting himself to the views of the person with whom he was dealing."[4] The interpretation continued to win adherents as recently as the work of Thomas McFarland in the mid-1980s.[5] Its value was that it recognized that Coleridge was a complex and rhetorically sophisticated writer who did not speak with one voice and could not be successfully analyzed by those who presumed he did. McFarland believes that the suggestion that Coleridge was a young "Jacobin" is misleading because Coleridge used certain prorevolutionary idioms and locutions in order to reach his audience with a non-Jacobin message. In studying Coleridge, McFarland suggests, one must consider audience and context rather than simply pointing to the use of certain isolated phrases. Both Brinton and McFarland argue that Coleridge, in dealing with a wide diversity of audiences during some of the most politically supercharged decades in British history, used a variety of lexica in an attempt to reach various groups of readers. This suppleness of idiom, they agree, has led to unfair and inaccurate readings of Coleridge as "changing his mind" when all he was "changing" was his rhetorical strategy.

Pocock has contributed to the "glacial" thesis in his location of the romantics. He describes Coleridge as being a "republican" in youth and a "Tory" in his middle and late career, a pattern which Pocock also saw in Wordsworth and Southey.[6] Pocock has analyzed this change as a major shift in opinions without employing E. P. Thompson's morally supercharged and fundamentally negative term of "apostasy."[7] Pocock's examination of Coleridge's career has been shaped by his opinion that the discourse of "classical republicanism," to which he thinks Coleridge subscribed, was an alternative, communitarian political language of *virtu*.[8] This "republican" language, according to Pocock, was the masquerade costume of choice for those "citizens," from Niccolo Machiavelli to John Thelwall, who aped antique virtues (which they imagined to have existed in the incorrupt and manly polities of the ancient Spartans and late-republican Romans) in the service of moral and political *rinovazione*. According to Pocock, this language of the stalwart citizen protecting his civically constructed rights through the dutiful exercise of *virtù* and *rinovazione* was opposed to and fundamentally incompatible with the rival language asserting God-given claims to individual natural rights (*ius*). The language of *ius* was employed by proponents of cosmopolitan and Continentally based jurisprudential theory (Jurieu, Grotius, Pufendorf), a discourse which spoke of the "Universal Rights of Man" rather than the virtues and duties of citizens of a particular realm. The pagan/classical language of citizen-virtue among the republicans was also a contradiction to the Christian/medieval discourse of Tory paternalism, patriarchalism, staunch churchmanship, high monarchism, and *noblesse oblige*.

A fourth strand of thought contends that not only was Coleridge not an apostate in 1795 or 1802, nor a mime, nor even a glacially paced evolver-away from youthful ideas, but was instead politically "unconscious." Jonathan Mendalow argues that Coleridge's ideas during 1795 and, indeed, throughout his career, were aimed predominantly towards "religious and metaphysical speculation" and never turned specifically towards "questions of constitution, law, and practical politics."[9] While Mendalow's thesis may be dismissed as the weakest of the four, it is finally the "apostasy" thesis, with its concomitant model of "disappointed radicalism," which has continued to dominate literary and historical accounts, both of Coleridge's political thought and the cultural and political realignment of party politics in the 1790s.[10]

Coleridge has long been viewed as one of a group of English romantic poets whose political careers can be conveniently divided into three distinct political stages: "Jacobin radicalism," "apostasy," and "Tory conservatism." In the first stage, the "radical" period, the poets in question are supposed to have uncritically and wholeheartedly embraced the principles of the French Revolution and the cause of parliamentary reform and served with distinction on the polemical barricades of democratic revolt against the old regimes of Europe. In the second stage, the moment of "apostasy," they are described as having turned tail and deserted the Jacobin cause in the hour of its greatest need, in a series of sudden and traitorous acts of defection. In the third phase, the "Tory conservative" period, they are presumed to have settled into a long and profitable senescence in which they enjoyed the fruits of their apostasy as lackeys of the counterrevolution. In these final years, they are thought to have obsequiously defended the same values of landed hierarchy, titled nobility, and feudal chivalric tradition that they had so recently marked out for destruction.

Like all myths of betrayal from Brutus and Judas through the Duke of Marlborough to Benedict Arnold and Charlotte Corday, the "apostasy" model offers the tempting high drama that is absent from so much political history.[11] The dagger blow to a great politician or cause, if it comes from the hand of a recognized enemy, only has the status of a detestable murder. The dagger blow attains the height of the horror and power of tragedy if (and only if) the stab in the back comes instead from the unsuspected hand of a trusted friend: then it partakes of the sin of betrayal as well as the sin of assassination. The anguished cry, "Et tu, Brute? Then fall, Caesar," is not so far from the style and tenor of the mythicized description, in conventional historiographical accounts of the 1790s and 1800s, of the execrable "apostasy" of the great romantics from their early and admirable devotion to democracy.

Historians such as E. P. Thompson have charged Coleridge, along with Southey and Wordsworth, with a dramatic "apostasy" of this sort against British Jacobinism, the political movement that Thompson saw as having offered Britain a narrowly fumbled opportunity for a true democratic revolution in the 1790s.[12] Thompson and those who followed in his footsteps harnessed the rhetorical power of the myth of betrayal to their equally powerful myth of lost opportunity through which they depicted the English 1790s. Given that Thompson's *Making of the English Working Class* was Marxist historiography's own mythographic *Acts of the Apostles*, Coleridge and the romantics were ably and dramatically cast in the roles of its Judases.

Literary critics such as Meyer H. Abrams added to this myth of treason against the cause a biological and sociological explanation based on another myth, that of "idealistic youth" and "cynical old age." The romantic poets' process of disenchantment and retreat from their youthful idealism, argued Abrams, represented the universal experiences of maturation, encroaching cynicism, and despair.[13] Coleridge's experience, Abrams believed, reflected a common human process, the disillusionment attendant to age and experience. Simply put, young men are radical and old men are conservative.[14]

One naturally begins to ask when reading these works on Coleridge's "apostasy," whose radical? whose Tory? whose apostasy? One also begins to suspect that the apparent retrograde movement of "apostasy" was merely the optical illusion produced by Coleridge remaining constant in his principles even as his associates moved rapidly forwards into even more (contextually) "radical" positions than those he could support.[15] If one is interested in seeing Coleridge as more than the stock villain in the tragedy of the death of the British Revolution, one must question this myth of "apostasy" and see how far it corresponds to facts. For one begins after any extended study of Coleridge and other thinkers of this era to question the value of these terms— "radical," "conservative," "Jacobin," "Tory"—as they are so often uncritically and polemically applied to the politics of the 1790s. Obviously, in order to judge sensibly whether Coleridge was once a "radical" and then became a "Tory," it is necessary to understand the meaning of those terms as they have traditionally been used in studies of Coleridge and his time. Beyond the observation that a radical/Tory dichotomy comprises a mixed metaphor of ideological category and party political label, the question of change must be addressed not only to Coleridge but also to the meaning of those terms. Radical or conservative, the problem of using nineteenth-century political vocabulary in analysis of the 1790s (or indeed the entire eighteenth century) remains confused by the failure to use either ideological or party political labels with any degree of consistency or with any establishment of relative benchmarks.

During the last decade, considerable debate has addressed the nature, vocabulary, and taxonomy of the political ideology of "radicalism" during the 1790s. Discussion of 1790s "radicalism," generally speaking, tends to divide scholars into three camps. The first one is that of the reconstructors. The second is that of the debunkers. The third and final position is that of the pantheon builders. Much of the misunderstanding and rancor that characterizes scholarly debate on this era is due to the incompatibility of these three approaches.

Obviously, the divergent goals of these groups—to reconstruct mentalities, to debunk cant, or to find one's political ancestors—result in different approaches to the problem of "radicalism" in the 1790s. Although few scholars are pure examples of any of these three "types," most researchers into the marginal political movements of the 1790s *do* tend to undertake study of the "radical" movement either by seeking to discover how that term was used in the 1790s *or* by rejecting the lexicon of the period and evaluating "radicalism" by political deeds rather than by words *or* by presuming a "radical tradition" and looking for its earliest members.

The first group is that of the "reconstructors" of the political discourse of the 1790s. Their work owes much to the Annales school of the *histoire des mentalités*, as well as to the works of Michel Foucault on the archaeology of knowledge. The historiography of reconstruction is based on the theory that a given society's political lexicon constructs and bounds the perception of what is "possible" in that society. It follows from this contention that the political vocabulary used by that society to describe itself will more accurately mirror the "real world" of that day than terms borrowed from later eras with different *mentalités*. This style of historiography, therefore, focuses its efforts on discovering what sorts of terms people living in that period used to describe their political parties and political actions. It tends to discredit and condemn all interpretations of a period that use concepts that were nonexistent in the lexicon of that period (such as "Puritan" in the 1550s, "middle class" in the 1640s, "petite bourgeoisie" in the 1750s, "Tory" in the 1770s, or "radical" in the 1790s) as "anachronistic" and therefore wrong. Therefore, if scholars are to be strictly "chronistic" in their use of political vocabulary appropriate to this age, they must eschew the term "radical," however much they may like it. They must choose other terms to describe the movement.[16]

Jonathan Clark has found himself in the position of attacking the historiography of "radicalism" in the 1790s on reconstructionist grounds. Clark argues that if we are ever to understand the politics of the 1790s, we must cease applying anachronistic terminology to them. Although "radical" developed recognized meanings by the 1790s, he argues that radicalism emerged in the 1810s and 1820s, its component parts from earlier and limited uses assembled "in novel and unexpected ways." He concludes that only if we can reconstruct or "date and analyze" that "conceptual innovation" can radicalism be "recovered as a valid term of historical analysis."[17]

The second approach is that of "unmasking" a given political lexicon, the approach of the "debunkers." This second variety of work is based on an assumption that people use language generally to conceal rather than to communicate reality. Knowing that political labels and party rhetoric consist mostly of what Lewis Namier famously described as "names and cant," such historians act in sharp contrast to the lexicon reconstructors. Where the reconstructors tend to accept and embrace the lexica of the past as valid, the debunkers almost always end up rejecting the political language of the past as failed models of reality that were inaccurate in their own time and misleading to historians in subsequent periods, particularly our own. The tribe of Geoffrey Elton, Lewis Namier, and Ian Christie tend to be profoundly skeptical about the utility of study of wifty political discourse that does not root itself in the hard-headed and eagle-eyed study of how the politicians of the era *actually* acted, as opposed to how they *said* they acted. Ian Christie's well-known book *Myth and Reality* expresses the fundamental belief of Christie and his ilk that a scholar may only hope to learn as much about the truth of politics by studying its rhetoric as a medical student could hope to learn about pharmacology from the patter of a snake-oil salesman.

The "debunkers" invariably discover that the radicals were not really so radical after all. To their opponents, of course, they were beyond the pale and introduced novel ideas. But once one examines their writings under the cold light of the comparative history of political thought, they do not seem so "radically" different from Whigs of the era. The major difference between a fiery radical and a staid reformer, according to the "debunkers," was the speed and degree of change they desired rather than the direction of that change.

Two major expositors of this view of the "radicals" as a more daring set of Whigs have been H. T. Dickinson and Gunther Lottes. Dickinson has suggested that the French Revolution had its greatest impact on the "new and more radical societies that sprang up in London and the provinces in the early 1790s."[18] These British Jacobins adopted the "more extreme political program of the earlier reformer."[19] Dickinson suggests that something qualitatively different in platform and approach characterized these popular reform societies during the period of the French Revolution.

British radicalism during the 1790s was, in Dickinson's view, the more daring brother of Whiggism. The radicals in their audacity adopted a more extreme and innovative ideology than that espoused by those Whigs (like Burke and Portland) who favored a moderate constitutional or economical reform. Indeed, for Dickinson, the British Jacobins only evinced a more extreme position than that held by the association and petitioning movements of the late 1760s and early 1780s (i.e., Christopher Wyvill or even James Burgh and Major John Cartwright).[20]

Gunther Lottes has tended to agree with Dickinson's vision of the radicals as the more daring customizers of standard-issue Whig political ideology. Lottes has described radicalism as embracing a very broad agenda indeed—one in keeping with traditional reform arguments which reached back to 1688 and beyond.[21] Nonetheless, Lottes, who argues for the constitutional nature of this radical polemic, acknowledges that during the revolutionary period, "some theorists like John Thelwall, Thomas Spence and William Godwin went far beyond this frame of reference."[22]

The third major approach is that of pantheon building. This branch of historiography sees history as a model for and inspiration to political action. It therefore interests itself in building up a "radical tradition" that it can use to evangelize followers into political action of the sort that they praise in past times.[23] The pantheon builders tend to be unconcerned that their uses of terms such as "radical" in the description of the 1790s are anachronistic, since their goal is to show how the "primitive radicals" of those days and before evolved into the sophisticated radicals whose inspirers they strive to be.

The most famous exponent of this approach has been E. P. Thompson, whose *Making of the English Working Class* still exerts its gravity on scholars more than forty years after its first edition. But the reification of a radical and a conservative tradition into something that is far more than just hyperactive Whiggism or a false and anachronistic use of nineteenth-century terms is not entirely the province of Marxist labor historians. Philip Schofield has examined conservative ideology during the period with a view to understanding the polemical range of the 1790s. He has interpreted the conservative position as consisting of "theological utilitarianism, social contract theory, and natural law tradition."[24] According to Schofield, conservatism constituted a "whole moral and political theory that undermined the intellectual foundations of radical theory."[25] Schofield sets this ideology against the rights-of-man theorists, and in terms of the "more solid ground of economic prosperity and social happiness."[26] For Thompson and Schofield, the "radicals" of the 1790s are aptly named, in a fundamental way that they are not in Clark's or Dickinson's accounts of extremist politics in the period.

My argument for the most part accepts Dickinson and Lottes' basic premise that radicals were the "hotter sort of Whigs." On the other hand, it does not enter into the camp of the "debunkers," since it contends that there were recognizably radical approaches to politics in the 1790s that escaped the traditional boundaries of Whiggism. Although the "radicals" were not called by such a name at the time, they were in their own time recognized as different, novel, and extreme. In my reconstruction of what "radicalism" meant in 1795, I have avoided both the excessive verbal niceties of the "reconstructors," suggesting that the convenience and relative accuracy of post facto terms such as "radicals" outweighs the dangers of their abuse by anachronistic pantheon builders. Thus, my own solution to this persistent and probably insoluble puzzle of political categorization in the 1790s is that there were indeed "radicals" of a sort, notorious for their "Frenchified" egalitarian-democratic ideas and far-ranging, novel proposals for innovation in government and society, but Coleridge was never among their number. The hallmarks of "real" radicalism—antimonarchism in some cases leading to a republican intent to dethrone all kings; anti-aristocratic sentiment in some cases leading to an egalitarian desire to abolish all hereditary titles; strong anticlericalism in some cases leading to a desire for disestablishment; proposals for the immediate or rapid expansion of the electoral franchise to the lower orders; consistent philo-Gallicism in many cases until and even after the Terror; and (in many cases) suggestions for the redivision or redistribution of property to offer greater economic power to the disenfranchised—appear in Paine and Spence, but not in Coleridge.

The traditional grouping of Coleridge amongst the radicals, I argue, is due to at least four factors. The first factor is the assumption that all romantic poets "transgressed" social norms of elite hegemony, since poetry is a liminal art form, and that therefore Coleridge, since he was a romantic poet and therefore "transgressive," must have been a radical. The second factor is the persistent misreading of his nonpartisan friendships with those radicals with whom he openly associated. The third factor is a naive acceptance by scholars of contemporary critics' claims that Coleridge was a rabble-rouser. The fourth factor, perhaps the most important of all in recent years, is a decontextualized reading of certain difficult and hyperbolic passages in the lectures that isolates "radical" phrases while ignoring reams of moderate phraseology and argumentation.

Coleridge's earliest political thought may best be considered within the context of those works that, over the course of his entire lifetime, contributed to a theory of human societies as dynamic, living, social, moral, and economic matrices. He did not, of course, publish a full-dress version of his systematic moral and political social theory until his late work of 1830, on *Church and State*.[27] However, one may detect assumptions as to the nature of history, power, and public opinion of the sort that Schofield defines as quintessentially "conservative" in Coleridge's earliest writings of 1795, when he was supposed by conventional accounts to have been a fiery radical.

Coleridge's first forays into politics were not at all characteristic of British "Jacobinism" as practiced by Thelwall, Paine, Spence, the Scots Martyrs, or the Conventioneers.[28] His political vision was consistent from 1795 to 1830 in its moderate, pragmatic constitutionalism. In his earliest writings on the liberty of the press, party spirit, Pitt's "ministerial treason,"[29] revolution and reform, Coleridge displayed a respect for organic moderation, disgust at all governmental policies of terror, dislike of politicians' exploitation of the passions of the moment, and mistrust of paper constitutions. The above are all traits that are so atypical of British Jacobinism that they are usually seen as hallmarks of Burke's counterrevolutionary writings of the same period. Coleridge consistently adhered to this perspective, grounded in his fundamental religious and ethical principles, in the face of the rapidly shifting political realities of these years and the changing reader response which those shifting realities brought about. No less an authority on English reactions to the French Revolution than Albert Goodwin once noted that the chaos of the Revolution so warped responses to politics that political opinions which had been approved of in the 1770s and 1780s suddenly became regarded as scandalous or dangerous after 1792.[30] Such was Coleridge's fate. With respect to the charge of Jacobinism, the so-called self-indictment of Coleridge's youthful exuberance, "when first" he "squeaked" his "tinny trumpet of sedition," must be set against the overwhelming evidences against.

Knowing that Coleridge himself had always rejected the charge of Jacobinism, it remains to be seen, "in any of [Coleridge's] writings,"[31] whether charges of his having espoused a French Jacobin–style, democratic republicanism in 1795 were justified. It is true that he admired (and rhetorically made use of) the *classical* republicanism of the past. He had little but praise for the historic defenders of freedom among the ancient Greeks and Romans (such as Lycurgus and Cicero), the Commonwealthmen of the Civil War era (such as Milton and Harrington), and the first Whigs (such as Locke and Sidney). But this generic love of the "great tradition" of fighters for liberty did not, on its own, betoken admiration for the *avant-garde* anti-monarchial republicanism so favored by the radicals of the 1790s.[32] Nor did it entail admiration for Robespierre and other Jacobin leaders.

Three major aspects of Coleridge's thought make theories of his early "Jacobinism" unlikely and probably unsustainable. First, Coleridge rejected the Jacobin languages of the natural rights of man and the equality of the people as mechanistic fallacies, "half-truths" that missed the deeper reality of political ideas. Second, he supported the influence of the national clergy and religion in the activities of the state, whereas most Jacobins tended to be anticlerical. Third, by his assumption throughout his life of the role of a nonjoiner and a critic, he deliberately excluded himself from the world of party politics and refused to accept any political creed, whether Jacobin, Foxite, or Pittite.

Coleridge varied from the "patriot politics" of the British Jacobins because he consistently articulated a "conservative" social theory that was incompatible with the "radical" political rhetoric grounded in the language of abstract general principles and natural rights on which Jacobinism rested. Coleridge consistently derided Jacobinism as narrowly mechanistic, even in his earliest writings. In this respect, his condemnation of the French Revolution was not so different from Burke's well-known denunciation of the new regime in France as the work of "sophists," "economists," and "calculators," or Samuel Johnson's famous quip that he found most philosophical "schemes for improvement" to be very laughable things. The "mechanism" to which Coleridge so frequently alluded was a conception of ideas and, more pointedly, political and social institutions, which was formalistic, positive, or utilitarian. Such an account of society, predicated as it was on a narrowly mechanical model of the world, could only produce the fatal moral nescience born of false science.

Mechanistic philosophy, to Coleridge's mind, put into full force the worst aspects of the empiricist epistemology of Locke, which ignored the underlying truths of reality while focusing on the phenomena and ephemera of the sensory world. Such ideas constituted "half-truths, more dangerous than lies."[33] The conviction that "half-truths" were more dangerous than lies became one of Coleridge's most persistent themes. He warned against such theoretical fallacies as late as his 1830 publication, *On The Constitution of the Church and State*. He believed that all theoretical maxims were by their very nature imperfect and fragmentary assertions of truth; as such, they could not stand the test of common sense.[34]

Half-truths, while providing less than satisfactory explanations of the moral and metaphysical world, were especially dangerous as grounds for pragmatic decisions in politics. Adherents of these false philosophies ignored the living, organic nature of human polities, treating the dynamic matrix of society as if it were a machine in which unsatisfactory parts could be torn out and replaced with new designs with no regard to the original configuration of the machine itself. Such vulgar materialism, even when expressed by "friends of liberty," suggested a mind sealed off from the study of the "real," transcendent world of ideas and forms and the telos of government, the study of which alone could lead to true political wisdom.

The French Revolution was, for Coleridge, an important example of imperfect and fragmentary theory applied as wholesale remedy to a practical crisis. He would later describe Jacobinism as "monstrum-hybridum," a grotesque and sterile conjoining of the most beautiful parts of existing creatures that resulted in a hideous freak.[35] In its lack of common sense, in its inability to compromise, the French Revolution had been grounded entirely in "half-truths." When institutionalized into a system for action, it had proven far deadlier than a lie. Such a system, of mechanized morality, was fundamentally at odds with Coleridge's own moral and political philosophy.

The second idea to divide Coleridge from the "Jacobins," whether English or French, was his conventional religious piety.[36] Coleridge was never at ease with the often anti-Christian and anticlerical tone of the Revolution in France, which in its more violent phases among the strictest sansculotte "radicals" aspired to do away with all priests and churches and place a generic Cult of Reason in their place.

Throughout his life, Coleridge's philosophy was consistently underscored by his own deeply personal religious conviction and his persistent commitment to freedom of conscience in matters of religious belief as the critical driving force behind political "independence": in short, the autarchy of the individual will was the essence of the free moral citizen. Although Coleridge may have mulled over alternative Christologies or even prefigured some of the vague, impersonal ideas of the Godhead that would later appear in the American transcendentalists, he never renounced his lifetime commitment to a fundamentally Christian system of belief. Indeed, he abhorred atheism and seems to have considered one of the successes of his life his convincing Godwin to at least become a theist rather than an outright atheist.[37] His language in his early years showed a pervasive Anglican evangelical vocabulary of personal redemption and repentance.[38] Whatever ideas on the relationship of the Father to the Son his anti-Trinitarian speculations may have led to, his soteriology appears to have been that shared by Anglicans such as Cowper and More. Coleridge represented that unfortunate Christian strand of reformism characterized by Price and Priestley. Loyalty to traditional theism made extreme anticlerical "radicals" denounce it as a prop of the Old Regime. But its reconsideration of Athanasian formulae of Christ's nature made "Orthodox" Christians attack it as an enemy to that same old establishment.

Coleridge's career as a political writer began with six lectures at Bristol on "Revealed Religion" in 1795, and ended with his conception of the social and political significance of a National Church in *On The Constitution of the Church and State According to the Idea of Each* in 1830. Throughout his lifelong attempts at forging an ethical system that would be a ground for political action and social reality, Coleridge insisted upon the need to "bottom on fixed principles" and his philosophical adherence to moderation and compromise were always in mind. His Broad-Church sensibilities and his love of moderation and toleration for their own sake were as incompatible with Jacobinism's quest for unity and ideological purity as were his philoclericalism and his Christian belief.

Coleridge's image of himself as a true political independent and therefore the critic of all things was a third aspect setting him apart from the "Jacobin" party. It excluded him from the increasingly sectarian and factional interests of the reform societies of the late 1790s, which demanded the "citizen's" close loyalty to the group. It also made him an enemy of the rhetoric of Pittite law, which maligned all who criticized the government as "seditious" or "unpatriotic." Coleridge's political writings throughout this period reflected his life-long belief in the cult of the political independent. Coleridge often skirted absurdity in his attempts to be an "independent" man, a critical voice who stood outside the petty groupthink of slogans, parties, and factions. As John Morrow has argued, the vocal rejection of party spirit by Coleridge was an echo of the rhetoric of the "outsider" used to such effect in the Country Party polemic of the 1720s.[39] Indeed, a contemporary from Bristol who contributed to *The Monthly Magazine* attested to the "independence" of Coleridge's early politics. Writing under the designation "Q," he recalled Coleridge's politics from the Bristol days as "anti-Pittite *and* anti-Foxite" (my italics). "Q" continued that far from siding unreservedly with opponents of government, Coleridge had once delivered a "philippic" against Fox.[40]

In this regard it is best to view Coleridge's writings as generically critical and polymorphously "oppositional" rather than factional, as independent rather than party-minded. His vision of himself as a public intellectual who fought only on the side of truth resembles the Socratic role of gadfly that Leo Strauss later defined as essential to the true political philosopher.[41] Both saw the true political philosopher as a man of vision able to see through the exoteric cant of party rhetoric, and who dared to plumb the dangerous depths of true esoteric wisdom without fear of the criticism he would incur for doing so. Arguably, Coleridge's end-of-career scheme for the clerisy was designed to produce a sort of Straussian elite who would be trained in criticism rather than in creed and who would provide an objective voice that could clearly articulate the foibles of society.

Contemporary friends such as Hazlitt, Cottle, and Southey and twentieth-century critics of Coleridge such as Holmes and Jackson failed to make a convincing case for locating Coleridge within a tightly factional framework of party politics.[42] It is very hard to conceive of a man as being a traitor to a political party to which he never belonged; similarly, a man cannot be deemed a heretic for diverting from a creed that he has never confessed. Coleridge's temperament precluded him from professing a creed (whether political or religious) on the grounds that creedal allegiance to party or church would erode his critical independence. This habit of mind anchored his judgment to a criterion of fidelity to his own personal cult of outsidership. This same self-professed independence makes Coleridge extremely slippery when measured by political-party categories. He invariably evades any critical attempts to pin him down as easily as he evaded his contemporaries' attempts to categorize him.

If one rejects the view that regards the Coleridge of the Bristol Lectures period as a Jacobin or radical, what becomes of the myth of "apostasy'? The charge of "apostasy" to the cause was the natural response of those friends who falsely assumed that Coleridge's affiliations and sympathies were the same as their own and who were shocked to discover that this was not the case.

Southey's accounts of his early friendship with Coleridge provide much of the evidence for the claims of "apostasy" and "betrayal" maintained by Edward Thompson, Nicholas Roe, and others. Southey wrote of Coleridge's early politics that

> It is worse than folly [for Coleridge to deny that he was ever a Jacobin], for if he was not a jacobine in the common acceptation of the word, I wonder who the devil was. I am sure that I was, am still, and ever more shall be. I am sure too that he wrote a flaming panegyric of Tom Paine, and that I delivered it in one of my lectures.[43]

Unfortunately, Southey is open to charges of hypocrisy in his criticisms of Coleridge. Such tu quoque charges, if they do not precisely rid Coleridge of the charge of apostasy, arguably sully Southey's credibility as a witness. Lewis Patton, one of the editors of Coleridge's works, used his introduction to *Lectures 1795* to examine Southey's motives for calling Coleridge a turncoat. Pointing out Southey's bias, Patton wondered whether Southey maintained the tone of virtuous indignation, of radical scorned, in the presence of his neighbors and patrons, Sir George Beaumont and Lord Lonsdale. Southey's advancement to poet laureate by 1813 was itself accompanied by a reasonable degree of political inconstancy, if his pantisocratic youth is to be viewed as a polemical marker. Oddly enough, Southey in 1795 had claimed authorship of the "panegyric to Tom Paine" which he foisted onto Coleridge in his 1809 denunciations.[44]

Coleridge addressed the issue of his own supposed Jacobinism in an 1803 letter to Sir George Beaumont. He complained that he had been forced into "retirement" from active political life in the year 1796 at the age of twenty-four, "disgusted beyond measure by the manners and morals of the Democrats."[45] This hardly suggests someone who was socially or intellectually suited to the social world of promoting liberty, equality, and fraternity. It also implies that there was a fundamental elitism that Coleridge felt in the presence of the "Democrats," whom, he felt, exhibited the degraded mores of those who they wished to elevate into franchise.

Because he did not see himself as belonging to the "party" of the democrats, Coleridge was typically dumbfounded when less careful intellects (who saw even the mildest reformists through the lurid, blood-colored "spectacles of prejudication" in the wake of the Terror) associated him with that sect. A violent swarm of critical opprobrium arose in response to Coleridge's 1794 publication *The Fall of Robespierre*, a mordant condemnation of the late chief of the Jacobins, the dictator Maximilien Robespierre.[46] In a heartfelt 1794 letter to his brother George, Coleridge bemoaned the fact that *"People have resolved that I am a Democrat"* despite the burden of evidence to the contrary. He realized that those who had already lumped him in with the arch-Jacobins would continue to do so no matter what his doctrine or conduct, simply because they "look at everything I do with the spectacles of prejudication." He wrote much of this bigoted reaction off as the inevitable result of the upper ranks' paranoia in the wake of the Terror: "In the feverish distemperature of a bigoted Aristocrat's brain some *phantom of democracy* threatens him in every corner of my writings."[47] Even at this early stage, Coleridge saw his status as a "democrat" as given to him by his enemies rather than his friends. It is certainly significant that even before the traditional date of his "apostasy" he saw the label of "democrat" not as a badge of honor, but as a denunciation pinned on him by those imbeciles who saw a "phantom of democracy" in his writings. Coleridge mocked their belief in his Jacobinism as "feverish distemperature," the same sort of paranoia that made small children create bugbears from the shadows in their bedrooms late at night. Referring to the book against Robespierre specifically, he continued,

[Because my polemic on Robespierre's fall] is an anti-pacific one, I should have classed it among the anti-polemics—Again are all who entertain and express this opinion [deriding the war against France] Democrats? God forbid [that it were ever the case that all who opposed the war were necessarily Democrats, for then] they would be a formidable party indeed! I know many violent anti-reformists, who are as violent against the war on the ground that it may introduce that reform which they (perhaps not unwisely) imagine would chant the dirge of our constitution.—Solemnly my brother! I tell you—*I am not a Democrat.*[48]

Several things become clear in this passage. First, Coleridge stressed that his opposition to the war against France did not make him a pro–Democrat; he decried this linkage with a shudder of "God forbid." Second, unlike the true "radicals," who tended to see a natural, broad support for their work amongst the dispossessed, Coleridge did not believe there were many "democrats" at all. Indeed, he could not envision the democrats seriously as "a formidable party" unless they could be (wrongly) redefined as consisting of anyone who for any reason defied the hawkish strategy of the Pittite War Party. Third, he considered his distaste with the war analogous to that of the "anti-reformists." Both he and they, for different reasons, disliked the war against France because it would unintentionally bring about alterations that would end by destroying the "constitution."[49] He hated the war not from a wish to protect the French system of government but from a desire to preserve the English system. Coleridge's outrage at the conflation of all criticism of government policy with democratic principle is suggestive of his own political neutrality. He viewed himself even amidst the heat and fury of 1794 as a moderating voice: moderate and, most significantly, independent.

Coleridge's political independence owed more to the ancient and tradition-bound British "country" tradition of criticism in politics than it did to the new doctrines of radical anarchism which some have associated with William Godwin's writings.[50] The idée fixe of a freely critical political intelligence and autonomous voice, which Coleridge held at the heart of his self-conception of his role as a political actor, made him prone to use the "language of the outsider" in his politics. The great language of political "outsidership" in the England of 1794 was still the "country" tradition. The "country" tradition in politics had been perfected in the seventeenth century as a strategy for denouncing the political misdeeds of the "court" and "administration" from the allegedly more objective and more ethically pure stance of those not on the ministerial dole.[51] Coleridge's lectures and pamphlets of 1795 borrowed from critical geniuses of all parties, from the great "Whig" Shaftesbury, the great "Tory" Bolingbroke, the great "reformer" Burgh, to the great "conservative" Burke. But he was especially drawn to the critical acuity of the "country" tradition, which, after all, was Britain's own home-grown and authentic reformist movement rather than a graft from a foreign tree.

John Morrow argued in favor of the affinities that Coleridge had for Godwin rather than Burke, despite the moderate tone of *A Moral and Political Lecture*. But if Coleridge was also influenced by Godwin the constitutional historian, and not only by the author of *Political Justice*, then the affinities that Coleridge felt for Godwin and Burke should not prove to be incompatible. While Coleridge did hold certain views in common with Godwin in these early pamphlets, he disagreed most emphatically with Godwin's view that a disinterested benevolence that treated all men as one's neighbors and brothers was attainable and desirable. Godwin was, of course, famous for expounding the doctrine that a proper and true moral agent would consider all humans equally as objects of his care. The perfect Godwinian benevolent man would refuse to ration his charity on the traditional basis of preferring family and friends to strangers in deciding whom to help and would instead extend his bounty equally to all. Coleridge, although he favored an expansive vision of charity on a Gospel-based model, found Godwin's proposition that humans should completely give up their ties to locality and family an inhuman and preposterous scheme.

Given Coleridge's fundamental breach with Godwin on this issue, Morrow is inaccurate in arguing that Coleridge's view was "quite consistent with the rationalism of writers such as Godwin, who started from the 'grand and comprehensive truth' of universal benevolence."[52] Coleridge did use the phrase, "some grand and comprehensive truth," in *A Moral and Political Lecture*. However, when he used the phrase he was not referring to Godwin's concept of benevolence. Coleridge saw "grand and comprehensive truth" in the context of the need to "bottom on fixed principles."[53] His choice of words may have intentionally echoed Burke's proposition that "opinion [should be] . . . bottomed upon solid principles of law and policy."[54] At any rate, Coleridge's and Burke's concepts of "fixed principles" were kindred formulations of the same problem in a way that Coleridge's and Godwin's concepts of "grand and comprehensive truth" were not. Coleridge's "fixed principles," since they belonged to the only partly knowable world of ideas, were seen as through a glass darkly. Only "half-truths" could be so foolish as to parade about in the dress of mathematical certainty that Godwin and other system-builders assumed for their work. The "fixed principles" of which Coleridge spoke could not be defined with a geometer's precision because they always remained obscured by the contingencies and particularities of history. Only the active historical process, not any system of positive formulation, could hope to achieve the ideal of "political justice" that Godwin hoped to reach through pure principle.

Coleridge attempted to reconcile what he perceived to be opposite camps in a political crisis of ideology and rhetoric. To Coleridge, the conflict of the 1790s was at its root a battle that set "French theory" against the "science of history." This crisis accelerated and became more violent due to the British reaction to the revolution in France and Pitt's need for a strong set of executive powers to conduct the war as he wished.

The success of the Jacobin hunts of 1794 to 1795 had pushed the reform movement into a more "radical" opposition to the government: "radical" in the Dickinsonian sense. Coleridge contended that the set of "constitutional abuses" of the years 1792 to 1795, which, he believed, Pitt had forged as a gauntlet for crushing "Jacobins," were every bit as severe and grave in their own way as the destructive forces which had been let loose by the French Revolution.[55] Pitt's Terror, it was argued, mirrored Robespierre's. The two men's policies of repression were the same phenomenon in looking-glass variants. The only difference was that while in the French "side" of the mirror the iron gauntlet of Terror appeared to be worn on the dictator's left hand, on the British side of the mirror it appeared to glove the dictator's right hand.

By Coleridge's estimate, during the years 1792 through 1795, the Crown and administration had eroded or suspended the stabilizing effects of constitutional balance and the just operation of the courts and public opinion. In a healthy polity, claimed Coleridge, the gradual bringing-about of political justice through the courts, the constitution, and the "public will" allowed the continued development of the nation through an organic and historically evolving social process. He contended in his anti-Pitt writings that this social process must be defended as the best means of both developing and exploring the "fixed principles" ("the grand comprehensive truth") that he believed existed in the realm of ideas. Only Providence, or the teleological "science of history" as he called it, could reveal these "fixed principles" as valid.

The critique of Pitt rested on Coleridge's personal development of his own theories of three crucial social phenomena: ethics, historical development, and enlightenment. Coleridge charted the relationship between these principles through a criticism of political "function" and an analysis of the "agency" of public opinion. Through a better understanding of politics and power as historical processes, he believed that moderate reform could be achieved and, more importantly, violent revolution avoided.

Having considered the evidences against Coleridge as a youthful radical it remains to be seen whether there was any degree of merit to the characterization of him as a late-life Tory. While he was hostile to much of the policy associated with the rising school of political economy and consequently felt a greater degree of sympathy to the Liverpool government than to its opposition, there is much evidence to weigh against the view of Coleridge as a conventional Tory supporter. Most ideologically based interpretations of Coleridge's political thought have tended to focus on his early career and the question of his "radicalism." Less has been written about the "conservatism" of his later works, such as *Church and State*. This is presumably because although Coleridge ceases to be useful as a subject for the scholars of "radicalism" after his assumed "apostasy" in about 1800 gives him the taint of the turncoat, he does not tend to be adopted into the pantheon of subjects for scholars of "conservatism" in the nineteenth century because of his checkered past and his presumed (and largely undocumented) Unitarian heterodoxy.[56]

The notion of Coleridge as a quintessentially reliable and dependable "Tory philosopher" was a standard assumption of the Victorian editors after the mid-nineteenth century. It was they who created the myth of Coleridge as a hot-headed, controversial youth who had held the torch of revolution high in the 1790s, but who finally grew old and settled back into a drowsy reactionary dotage in the 1820s, which he supposedly spent espousing the values of church and king from the comfort of a well-upholstered armchair. Coleridge was not so easily "domesticated" by his contemporaries and by the generation of philosophers immediately following his death.[57] Among those who actually knew him or read his works, the "Sage of Highgate" was held in an almost superstitious awe for his ability to force his readers to reconsider standard problems of religion, philosophy, and politics in unusual and unconventional ways. Like all deeply critical intellects, Coleridge did not make a good party hack; he could not resist the urge to be unique or innovative even when he defended traditional institutions.[58]

One central question is persistently begged in the party-political analyses of Coleridge's later "Tory" years. It has never been explained why a Tory philosopher, given that we presume Coleridge to have been a Tory partisan after 1809, wrote *Church and State* when he did. Why would a true-blue Tory write a treatise in favor of a deep and total reform of the church and the clergy on adoctrinal lines in an era when the party of church and king was doing its best to *resist* reformist attempts to clean up the church's political structure, place its clergy under the management of politicians rather than prelates, and expand the church's toleration? Like so much in the young Radical/old Tory mythology of Coleridge's life, the vision of Coleridge in his middle and old age as the apostle of Toryism does not bear the weight of a close reading of documents such as *Church and State*. Indeed, his work on *Church and State*, according to John Stuart Mill, was so far from typical Tory formularies of the 1820s that it could be depended upon without fail to "set a Tory's hair on end."[59] The problem, as Mill recognized, is that one may introduce as many pieces of evidence that suggest that the "old" Coleridge was a conservative liberal—the founder of what Mill famously called a "second strand" of liberalism——as one can introduce to prove that Coleridge in old age was the chief of Tories.

Coleridge from 1802 to 1830 definitely exemplified the "Tory" tradition in many writings. His respect for land, hereditary primogeniture, and hereditable titles as a basis for the values of honor and permanence was "Tory." His advocacy of the retention of a state-supported and enlarged national clergy was "Tory." His support of Peel's paternalism in the instance of the 1818 Factory Acts was "new" Tory, but Tory all the same. His despite for Benthamite and Malthusian "scientific" solutions to complex social problems was generically "conservative," but specifically Tory. His ascription of a large compass for the influence of the education of citizens into virtue and morality in the state owed much to "Tory" polemic. Finally, Coleridge's contention that moral reform needed to precede extension of the franchise showed a Tory lack of faith in the disenfranchised in their native state of illiteracy and immorality.

However, during the same years of 1802 to 1830, Coleridge exemplified the "liberal" tradition in as many venues. His high esteem for commerce, the rise of fresh talent and ingenuity, and increasing capital as a basis for the values of liberty and "progression" (in the technical sense as it was used in *Church and State*) was "liberal." His suggestion that a national clergy would transcend the classical limits of the Anglican confessional state and become a trans-Protestant "clerisy" that would include paid Dissenting pastors was "liberal." Also liberal was his idea of the clerisy (as opposed to the clergy as a subset of the clerisy), which professed that the clerisy drew their inspiration from the best that the general community of moralists and thinkers had to offer rather than the specific traditional formularies of the Athanasian Creed. His attack on the excessive influence of the landowning classes in both houses of Parliament was "liberal." His suggestion that the government had no business legislating morality and ought to allow each individual citizen the right to do as he pleased as long as he did not damage the rights of others was outrageously "liberal." His belief that liberty was as important a value in the state as community and virtue and order was classically "liberal," as was his suggestion that the franchise ought to be enlarged as soon as the subjects could be educated into their proper performance of duties. This list could be broadened far more, and indeed most of these contentions are made at length in the final chapters of this study. Essentially, Mill was correct in suggesting that Coleridge's "Toryism," if we wish to call it such, was far more "liberal" even than that of Peel on many fronts. In the end, the "old" Coleridge truly had attempted to forge a middle path for liberalism that would reconcile the "Tory" values listed in the preceding paragraph with the "liberal" values elucidated in this paragraph. It was Coleridge's consistent belief that such a synthetic approach was only possible through the pursuit of deep philosophical or "underlying" fixed principles.

Having considered the ambivalences of Coleridge's political opinions as they relate to conventional uses of modern ideological categories, it remains to explain the substance of those views of politics which reveal continuity in Coleridge's principles. I would argue that the serious reintegration of Coleridge's philosophical thought into his political principles suggests such deep continuities. Through his revival of an indigenous British Platonism, Coleridge used Bacon's doctrine of the double truth to established the foundations of his statesman's science. His essentially metaphysical approach to the underlying "fixed principles" of political and moral society must be understood in terms of this "double vision." In short, Coleridge pursued the very practical science of the science of practice in politics. In doing so he revealed the interconnected unities of the principles of history, nature, and law as the empirically structured instruments of an ever-unfolding providence of agency and design.

Coleridge was preoccupied from his earliest writings—long before he encountered the German revival of the dialectic—with the cooperative relationships between opposed dualities of meaning. He constantly endeavored to balance, or moderate, opposing forces: reason and understanding, subject and object, theory and practice: to create a model of ideas in which, to use Blake's celebrated phrase, the *opposition* of *contrarieties* led to *progress*. Isaiah Berlin evocatively pictured this duality in Coleridge as existing between an "ideal" or "higher" self, who inhabited the world of ideas, and his benevolent rule over the "lower," "empirical" self in the material and moral world. Berlin described this phenomenon as "Coleridge's great I AM over less transcendent incarnations of it in time and space."[60]Coleridge's own language for this "double vision" focused on the distinction between subject and object, between ideal and actual, between philosophic "reality" and practical morality. Even as Coleridge concerned himself with the formal validity of institutions as "Ideas" he maintained a belief that such institutions invariably contained or incorporated the activities of material forces and historical agents.

Coleridge's reading of Kant and other German idealists from 1800 to 1817 gave him access to a rich vocabulary of "synthetics" and a teleological framework in which to embody his ideas.[61] However, one can easily locate an earlier source for these "synthetic" ideas in Coleridge's eager and enthusiastic readings, by 1796, of the seventeenth-century Cambridge Platonists, or "Plotinists" (as Coleridge called them), such as Cudworth and More.[62] The link with the English tradition of "Platonism," which is missing from so many accounts of Coleridge's intellectual influences, is crucial. Without knowing of Coleridge's link to "Plotinism," it is difficult to explain how Coleridge had developed so many concepts that we normally think of as "Kantian" and "Hegelian" before he had ever read any books by Kant or Hegel. Without understanding his feverish embrace in his youth of the native-born Neoplatonist doctrine, it is difficult to see the rationale for Coleridge's later devotion to the formation of a wholly English Platonist canon and tradition. English Neoplatonism suffused his earliest writings and provided him with the basic concepts for his "synthetic teleology." His later encounter with the German idealists only refined and improved these ideas.[63]

Coleridge conceived of all change, whether historical, cultural, or moral, as resulting from the linked and mutually dependent interaction of opposing forces. This has led to suggestions that he lacked the courage or integrity to be on one side of a question or another. It must be reiterated that Coleridge's dualist view of dynamic relations was not a throwing in of the towel. Nor was it the sign of an intellect too lazy to see which of the two contrarieties in a pair—land and money, church and state, ideas and concepts—was the "important" or "formative" one. Coleridge's effort to combine analysis of all major factors in a system (rather than isolating one factor, labelling it "the important one," and bracketing out all other data, as he alleged Malthus and Ricardo did) was a decision of considerable audacity. His forging of a novel system of "ideas" was a pursuit of intellectual autonomy and independence that was more costly in time and effort than the advocacy of an existing system would have been.

Coleridge's theory of ideas, like his *Theory of Life*, was foundational to all his other work.[64] One cannot afford to ignore his doctrine of ideas and their relations because it is "about" metaphysics rather than "about" politics. That is certainly a distinction which Coleridge himself would not have made. Like the Cambridge Platonists he emulated, he was at heart a monist, who believed that an accurate system of metaphysics was the golden key to an accurate theory of physics and an accurate theory of politics. Indeed, Coleridge's philosophical work on dualities and synthesis was basic to all of his later writings on any subject. Therefore, a comprehension of Coleridge's "metaphysics" is and will always be essential for any true understanding of Coleridge's aesthetic, religious, and political ideas.

From the "young" Coleridge's earliest writings, "On Politics and Revealed Religion" (1795), to the "old" Coleridge's most complete and mature political synthesis in *On The Constitution of the Church and State According to the Idea of Each* (1830), he presented a persistent and complex argument for the centrality of individual agency and free will in political and social life while at the same time arguing cogently for duty and community. Coleridge's researches in the pursuit of this system were, as I have emphasized elsewhere, authentically eclectic to a degree that most nineteenth-century philosophies were not. It is certainly the case that Coleridge was not a disciple, propagating and elaborating the ideas of a "master" such as Kant. Nor was he a magpie (as Fruman has alleged),[65] tearing up bits and pieces of the systems of others and slopping them together in his nest without any personal contribu-tion.[66] If Coleridge was one of the most careful students of the works of Locke, Hartley, and Godwin, he was also one of their most careful critics. Any study of "influences" on Coleridge's intellectual development will show that Coleridge rejected as much as he retained from those authors whom he read.

In general, Coleridge's theories of politics from 1795 to 1830 predicated themselves on moral constants of "conscience," "right reason," and "duty," all three of these being ideas that he perceived as providing the essential organs of good government and a just society.[67] Yet his reliance on transcendental "Ideas" never made him a utopian, as some have claimed. To categorize Coleridge as a utopian is to misread his doctrine of ideas. Although Coleridge believed ideas to be ultimately perfect and universal in their transcendence, he insisted through-out his career that they were always filtered through the imperfect and local con-tingencies of the material world. In his writings on liberty, he attempted to rec-oncile the universal and pure idea of liberty with the quotidian need for stable, efficient, and practicable government in "the moral world."[68]

This phrase of Coleridge's, the "*moral* world," was his technical term for what is now typically termed "the *real* world." His phraseology is somewhat confusing; on the surface, he seems to have argued that the "real world" of everyday life is "moral," when what he actually meant was that everyday life was "imperfectly moral" and always uncertain in its moral decisions. Co-leridge's use of the term "moral world" evokes the now-classic distinction be-tween "mathematical certainty" and "moral certainty." "Mathematical cer-tainty," the absolute conviction of the correctness of a solution, can only exist in the realm of purely rational systems such as numbers. "Moral certainty," a general belief in the appositeness of a solution short of absolute conviction, is the more usual degree of certainty attainable in the real/moral world. For Co-leridge, the complexity of the moral world required a science of great subtle-ty and great precision. Such was the science of history, such was the philoso-phy of nature.

Metaphysics was the foundation of Coleridge's statesman's science, its fun-damental doctrine of ideas considered as active and formative realities. That is, ideas were real and transcendent and yet still gave shape and meaning, gave structure, to things in the material world. In short, they were for Coleridge the word made flesh. They gave cause, they gave form, they gave purpose. Coleridge suggested, in *Aids to Reflection* and in several other works, that the sort of conflicts most philosophers cited as questions of idealism versus mate-rialism were better stated as questions of subject-observer versus object–thing observed.[69] Materialism was exceptionally useful as a conceptual model for studying the material world: the world of sensible and detectable objects, objects which could be weighed, measured, and counted. Idealism, for its part, provided a deeper explanation of causality and teleology and was, consequently, better for studying the immaterial aspects of that material world. The idealist model of the world could accommodate and so explain the *properties* of objects, which could not be measured and which were not available to empirical scrutiny but which were, nonetheless, available to human reason and open to rational debate.

Coleridge discussed his Conception of the "Idea" throughout his career and perfected it in his last and most important political text, on *Church and State*. His distinction between subject/observer/idealism and object/thing observed/materialism may not suit all readers as a solution to the battle of the methods between the two long-warring schools, but it was innovative for its time.[70] Coleridge's metaphysics was a creative solution to the dilemma of whether to privilege idea or matter, because it chose to reify the central conceptions of both materialism and idealism. In doing so, Coleridge's new system honored the claims of those who argued that matter was important and the claims of those who argued that ideas were important, while denying the typical claims of each of the two views that matter was so important as to make ideas of scant significance, or vice versa. Coleridge suggested instead that matter and Idea existed in a dynamic pairing in which neither had an absolute primacy or self-sufficient centrality. For Coleridge, Ideas were real, but they were embodied in the world of matter. Here, they were perceived and sensed, construed and measured. On the other hand, the changing configurations and "habits" of worldly institutions in the world of matter embodied themselves in the realm of Ideas. For Coleridge, even as Ideas "constituted" material objects, at the same time material objects "constituted" Ideas.

The minds of observers/subjects generated these Ideas, and Coleridge stressed that they did not exist in a pure transcendence independent of whether anyone considered them or not. Ideas, he asserted, were always predicated on and anchored in the circumstances of the "real world." Yet, these Ideas, he claimed, were more real than the sum total of all observers'/subjects' opinions of the meaning of ideas. Thinking, or simply "conceiving" of the world to be a mere material place did not make it so. Although the rationalizations of individual human minds and the solid matter of everyday life were the building blocks of ideas, ideas for Coleridge gained a transcendent life of their own above and beyond the net of matter and concepts.

This distinction between matter and idea was the basis of one of Coleridge's most important epistemological distinctions, his study of the psychological differences between the faculties of understanding and reason. Like other aspects of his metaphysical and scientific study, Coleridge's faculty of psychology defined and shaped his political theory, to such a degree that it formed an indispensable groundwork both for his conception of British political institutions and his critique of the French constitution. Coleridge wrote extensively about the divide between the faculty of "Understanding," as outlined by Locke and the sensationalists, which produced "Conceptions" in the mind, and the faculty of "Reason," as analyzed by the Plotinists, which was able to partially comprehend transcendent "Ideas" that maintained a life of their own outside of the minds of their perceivers and shapers. In Coleridge's psychology of faculties, understanding is the facility for organizing experience and perception. It is the faculty that allows the mind of an individual observer/subject to develop an individual and partial apprehension, what Coleridge termed a "Conception," of the Idea. For Coleridge, reason is the faculty that allows deeper (but still partial) comprehensions of this realm of ideas In this sense, Coleridge's theory is different from Kant's. Whereas the faculty of understanding keeps the mind rooted in "facts" and material data, the faculty of reason coaxes the observer outward from that data towards the formation of abstractions, or "laws" or "theories," of the broader meanings and significances of things. Therefore, the Idea of a given class of objects depended on more than intense observation and low-level (taxonomical or commonsense) generalizations. Reason depends on the slow and gradual apprehension of broad, abstract patterns of the value, the meaning, and the end goal of a thing rather than its number, weight, or dimensions. Reason entails "seeing through" an object to its underlying reality. The understanding, then, perceives and organizes sensory data, while the reason perceives the intuitional and theoretical and abstract categories for that knowledge.[71] The Kantian view is in the end a more Aristotelian and, finally, materialist view. Coleridge's account is Platonic and idealist. But unlike Plato, for whom the appearance of an object of sense was no more than fleeting shadow, Coleridge believed the world of sense to be the concretization of Ideas.

The arena for this cross-fertilization of ideas and material life was what Coleridge termed the "moral world." Coleridge's use of the term "moral" here is counterintuitive; it denotes not a "moral world" in the sense of "a good and just world," but a "moral world" in the sense of "a world where only moral certainty rather than mathematical certainty can usually be reached." For Coleridge, the moral world was the imperfect world "here below" in which ideal and material realities intersected and influenced one another. The deep ordering principles of the reality of Ideas were valid independent of individual experience, in the same sense that the validity of mathematics did not depend upon the mathematical acuity of all humans, or even more than a handful. However, those "fixed principles" from the realm of ideas "constituted" themselves in the material world in ways which were infinitely variable. This interplay between material circumstances and the two levels of thought used to interpret those circumstances was the pivot of Coleridge's entire political system. Coleridge's 1795 plea that constitutional reformers adhere to some "fixed principles" greater than their technical schemes for short-term improvement based only on material circumstances of the moment was essentially rooted in his theory of Ideas. This theory later matured under the influence of Kant, branching into Coleridge's campaign for a theory of Ideas that would portray them not as desiccated and impotent imaginations, but as living, active agencies, performing important "dirty" work in the material "moral" world. If his scheme was correct, Coleridge argued, it meant that politics could not be reduced to a science of simple algorithms allocating who got what, where, and when. The new political economy constituted just such a system. It was based on the amoral uses of statistical sciences; of social biology (Malthus), economics (Ricardo), and franchise reform (the "radical" reformers). It was crude and superficial at best, morally nescient at worst. A true and virtuous reform, Coleridge claimed, was the ongoing search for "fixed principles"—the effortful entrance of the fallible human reason into the transcendent realm of Ideas. That the ultimate objectives and purposes of this reform be undertaken with vision was even more crucial than that more popular and immediately practicable search for the best political tools for "reform" be accomplished. The French, in their haste for change and only dimly understanding their purpose, had employed the wrong tools and achieved the wrong ends. On that rock the revolution had foundered and the moment for enduring change had been lost.

In making such unusual claims, Coleridge offered the startling suggestion that metaphysics was a basic science of statesmanship, too important to be parceled off to decrepit Oxbridge dons as if it were an amusing but unimportant puzzle and too important to be shunted off to clergy, as if clergy were to be considered a dustbin where politicians could toss the "higher" moral concerns in the state. Since the concept of the Idea intruded at all times and in all places into the "material world" and indeed, Coleridge stressed, *shaped* and *molded* that material world, only an imbecile could claim that a government could succeed by privileging material and economical schemes for reform while ignoring entirely the ethically based Ideas that must inevitably undergird such systems.

It is impossible, argued Coleridge, to sever "everyday realities" from "transcendental Ideas," either in political thought or in political action. The two are so intertwined that to disconnect one is to obviate the other. Thus, a political pragmatism that bracketed out the higher concerns of morality and teleology (as Coleridge believed the utilitarians had done) was doomed to fail. This was not statesmanship he argued, and certainly no science. Coleridge concluded that without the long-range vision and moral anchor of the "fixed principles" provided by the Idea, such blinkered, narrow-minded and mechanistic schemes for reform would invariably fail. There was no Machiavellian bargain to be made wherein one could succeed in politics by eschewing moral ideas sticking to pure amoral strategy. According to Coleridge, the proper understanding of political circumstances required deep thought on the ends and uses of government beyond mere plotting and strategizing. In the Machiavellian bargain of utilitarianism, he argued, lay both moral nescience *and* material failure. To move beyond the superficiality of such a crude political functionalism required, Coleridge argued, that government be grounded in an active Idea. Such an Idea required a formative institution. The state, then, must be understood as both active idea and formative institution.

Coleridge's *Church and State* was his final articulation of the very old theme of the constitution as an Idea. Throughout his career, but especially in *Church and State*, his political theory envisioned governing institutions as living forms of power and action rather than as mere territories or machines over which political ideologies fought for possession. Emphasizing the ideal and formal nature of institutions, the first chapter in *Church and State* began with prefatory remarks on "the true import of the word, IDEA" and what the author meant by "according to the Idea."[72]

Coleridge understood the state through the same philosophical perspective by which he considered the world, as an expression of successive opposing dualities. These dualities constantly and actively mediated between the ideal and the actual, between persons and things, between institutions and the particular historical objects of those institutions. Through this "double [i.e., dualistic] vision," Coleridge first defined and then reconciled the purportedly antithetical interests of landed and commercial society through his constitutional philosophy in *Church and State*. The constitution, as conceived by Coleridge, was an active institution that synthesized and directed the contradictory elements of social and political life. The "STATE," which Coleridge (like most others of his day) considered in its broader sense as church and state combined, became a dialectical and teleological idea.

The relative novelty of Coleridge's dialectical "double vision" in the British "ancien régime" of 1828 is often lost on modern readers who were either weaned on William Blake's literary doctrine of contrarieties engendering progress or Hegel's philosophical concept of the hybridization of thesis and antithesis resulting in a vivid synthesis. The idea that the opposition of social forces might be bracing and vivifying rather than corrosive was still relatively novel in 1828. The "double vision" was especially novel among those Tory circles who still envisioned normative politics as a consensus under one king and one church, and for this reason feared Dissenters, papists, and reformers as the representatives of social fragmentation of unity. Archibald Foord's work on the development of ideas of a "loyal opposition" in the eighteenth century showed that the concept of political struggle as beneficial to the state developed late in the eighteenth century and was slow to gain respect.[73] Most sixteenth- and seventeenth-century political theory had argued that opposition and conflict between segments of society was inherently destructive. Therefore, it viewed contradictory social or political forces as mutually exclusive and diagnosed conflicts of land versus commerce, church versus state, king versus Parliament, or Whig versus Tory as signs of illness and dysfunction in the body politic. Coleridge, in sharp contrast, believed that opposition was desirable because it was progressive and creative.

Coleridge's "Prefatory Remarks" on the Idea begin:

> By an *idea*, I mean, (in this instance) that conception of a thing, which is not abstracted from any particular state, form, or mode, in which the thing may happen to exist at this or that time; nor yet generalized from any number or succession of such forms or modes; but which is given by the knowledge of its *ultimate aim*.[74]

An Idea, then, might exist in the world of theory and reflection, although no state in the real world (past or present) had ever fully realized its "ultimate aim." The idea of a church was more than the sum of the jumble bag of all of the various churches that had existed in human history for Coleridge. It was, rather, the expression of the "churchness" that all of those organizations had (often unconsciously) striven for, with varying degrees of success.

Coleridge defined "Idea" teleologically, by reference to goals and substance rather than current externals and accidents. The Idea, for Coleridge, existed by virtue of some "final," real cause that preceded and was greater than the "material" or formal cause of a thing. Ideas could not therefore be adduced or extrapolated out of the experience of things as they existed in the world of the present or even in the "bank" of history. They were instead formed out of reflections on how things *might* exist, were they able to realize their aims. Things as they were and had been invariably reflected some imperfect instantiation of an Idea. They were fragmentary.[75]

Coleridge continued by describing how an individual's knowledge of "ultimate aim" might be experienced:

this knowledge, or sense, may very well exist, aye, and powerfully influence a man's thoughts and actions, without his being distinctly conscious of the same, much more than his being competent to express it in definite words. This indeed is one of the points which distinguishes *ideas* from *conceptions* being used in their proper significations. The latter *ie.*, a conception, consists in a conscious act of the understanding arranging any given object or impression into the same class with any number of other objects, or impressions, by means of some character or characters common to them all.[76]

Ideas, for Coleridge, had an objective and transcendental independence above and beyond the Conceptions of subjects. Individuals constantly learned and formalized certain things and relations between things in the world and gave names and taxonomies to these formulations. But the sortings-out of accumulated experience were Conceptions, Coleridge argued, and not Ideas. In his ranking of Ideas over Conceptions, Coleridge expanded on a tradition of philosophical realism that may be traced backwards to the Platonic forms and laterally to Kantian conceptions of rationality.

This distinction between Ideas and Conceptions was not an exercise in high-theoretical logic chopping for its own sake. The definition of Ideas and Conceptions was foundational to Coleridge's politics, since it determined the relative weight he gave to experience and reflection as guides to political action. A proper understanding of Coleridge's metaphysics is, therefore, an essential first step in any attempt to understand his view of Ideas as being superior to Conceptions of politics, power, and the state. R. J. White[77] and John Muirhead[78] have both emphasized the centrality of metaphysics to *Church and State*. But more recent scholarship would seem to share in a modern disinclination to take such philosophical inquiry as anything other than woolly and speculative mysticism.[79]

By treating the subject of the constitution in the context of his concept of the Idea, Coleridge was able to discuss the obvious discrepancies between the sought-after true object or goal of power in the state, as opposed to the day-to-day, fallible manifestation of its workings. Coleridge's distinction between the "ideal" and the "quotidian" served as a useful means of comprehending the difference between pure political principles and their imperfect operation when plunged into the myriad contingencies of everyday politics.

According to Coleridge, constitutions (whether written or unwritten) existed on the level of *Conceptions* of power and governance rather than on the level of Ideas. Like rulebooks for games, constitutions were contingent and constantly changing formulations based on accumulated experience. If they were to be of any true value, if they were to be just and enduring, then the Conceptions had to be aimed towards the attainment of the Idea. Formulations of Ideas in a given polity's constitutions must, as far as was possible, approximate the Idea of the (just) state in reality. Coleridge believed that there had been many attempts by different governments at different times to formulate just and lasting constitutions. He added that such efforts had failed or succeeded according to the degree to which, as active institutions, they allowed that polity to achieve the "true" Idea of a constitution.

Coleridge believed that all "true" Ideas, whether of constitutions or other things, were necessarily teleological and transcendental. It was therefore essential, Coleridge argued, to think very carefully about how society operated and which institutions most perfectly allowed it to progress and change, to adapt towards its ultimate aim or telos. A constitution put into concrete form the Conceptions of a set of institutions that the constitution makers had designed to allow society to evolve toward its *real* (pure, transcendent) self as an Idea.

The mistake that many governments—but most notably the misconceived republican and imperial governments of France—had made was in confusing the Conception (the rules of the game) with the Idea (the object of the game). The French Republic and Empire had erred in their attempts to construct a government because they had built institutions that were ideologically pure in terms of voguish Conceptions rather than institutionally sound in terms of lasting Ideas. This led to constant squabbles as to what constituted ideological purity, and horrific abuses and compromises in the pursuit of that purity. For Coleridge, a just and well-framed *institution* was far more dependable as a vehicle for travelling towards the Idea of the state than was an ideologically purified Conception of rights, such as the "Declaration of the Rights of Man and the Citizen." The French, although they had believed that they had founded their new regime on Ideas, had (so Coleridge claimed), become trapped in the shadows of the cave of Conceptions of liberty. They had doomed their quest for freedom to failure because they had plotted their journey toward liberty without first considering the meaning and nature of freedom or the Idea of a constitutional monarchy or republic. Ironically, whereas Burke despised the French revolutionaries because they were *excessively* obsessed with theory

rather than practice and experience, Coleridge pitied the revolutionaries because they had been *insufficiently* theoretical and had in their quibbles over the
means of government forgotten to meditate upon its ends.

At no time a "Painite" radical, the "young" Coleridge is more accurately
classified among the numbers of the "moderate" or "reform" timocrats of the
decade than among the truly "radical" democrats who were his contemporaries and in many instances friends. Independence, and a view of reform based
on historical pragmatism and constitutional balance, characterized his early
writings. Coleridge's career as a political thinker may be characterized in terms
of two central obsessions. The first of these was his conviction that the moral
and political natures of liberty were essentially intertwined and could not be
severed through some Machiavellian or, indeed, Benthamite calculus. The
second of Coleridge's twin obsessions was with the perfection of what he
termed his "medico-philosophical" theory of statecraft. His view was that society, as well as the state that expressed its intentions, was a living organism
and as such must be understood systemically. The capacity to hold these considerations, both of the substance and of the institutional forms of political society, in parallel tension with each other was the essence of the statesman's science. Coleridge's political thought did develop from 1795 to 1834, but
through the expanded *formulation* rather than the *recantation* of the principles
present in his earliest writings.

Understanding the fundamental science of statecraft was Coleridge's answer to the faction of sect and party. Both those who enlisted him under the
radical banners of revolutionary France from 1794 to 1801 and those who
wished to line him up, from 1802 onward, as a "Tory" who defended the
British ancien régime against its reformist opponents missed the significance
of his central preoccupations. Attacking the simplistic dichotomy of "radical
and Tory," or indeed "left and right," Coleridge looked for a solution which
offered the statesman a third choice, a visionary middle ground, where integrative compromise and innovation moved political and social change beyond the deadlock of both the long entrenched interests and their modern
radical critics.

Against those arguments based on a rhetorical zero-sum game, Coleridge's
view, expressed most completely in *Church and State* (1830), emphasized the
natural and organic maturation of political society through a progression regulated by structure and system. *Church and State* was more than an eccentric
religious tract. Indeed, it is a mistake to consider the work in religious terms
at all. Religion, as a matter of doctrine, is incidental to *Church and State*. Nor

was it a simple response to the political crisis of Catholic emancipation and the reform controversy that surrounded it. Ultimately, *Church and State* was a work of constitutional theory. It was a treatise on the idea of the modern state and a political- and economic-systems analysis of the relationships between Britain's landed and commercial interests. It was finally the culmination of a lifetime's thinking on morality, history, law, and society. It was Coleridge's most complete cultural and political synthesis, his *chef d'oeuvre*—in short, the final articulation of his statesman's science.

~~~~~~~~~

CHAPTER 2

Attacking the State

THE CLOSE OF 1795 provided Coleridge with the occasion to apply certain of his *general* political principles to *specific* questions of policy and legislation. During his Bristol Lectures in February 1795 and throughout his revision and publication of those lectures as *Conciones ad Populum* in December 1795, Coleridge methodically anatomized the connections between historical process, public opinion, and political change. As a consequence, he was able to set his attacks on the Pitt administration, charged as they were by the crisis of the war, within the context of the long-standing Whig tradition of oppositional loyalism. This "patriot" loyalism, pairing the attack on government with the defense of the realm, constituted Coleridge's first efforts at distinguishing between the uses of a small "s" state, connoting government, and a larger idea of the "State" as nation and realm comprising the activities, interests, and communal histories of the commonwealth.

A close reading of the antiministerial pamphlet *The Plot Discovered* (1795) suggests it was precisely this characteristically Whig preoccupation with the constitutional crisis of the moment that characterized Coleridge's early career as a journalist, social critic, and political thinker. The constitutional crisis, which began with the State Treason Trials of September 1794 and culminated in the passage of the antisedition laws in December 1795 implied, in Coleridge's estimation, a threat to British juridical freedoms through the creation of what amounted to a form of ministerial prerogative. Coleridge described Pitt's wartime creation of emergency powers as "Ministerial Treason." Portrayed in this light, the prime minister's treachery consisted of transferring the executive power from the Crown to the cabinet. By doing so, Coleridge argued, Pitt exerted an increasing and unconstitutional legislative control in the House of Commons over King George's Crown authority. But beyond the parliamentary usurpation of the king's constitutional role in the house, Coleridge also regarded the tentacles of Pitt's conspiracy as reaching beyond Parliament. The passage of the two acts against seditious practices extended legislative despotism (in the form of corrupt statute) out of doors, beyond the Commons, to regulate thought and to censor the voice of public opinion expressed in print and in the speech of public lectures such as Coleridge's own. Such censorship amounted to more than mere legislative tyranny. In Coleridge's estimation, Pitt's plot operated on a deeper level by gagging the "authentic" voice of the people of which the monarch, or *lex magestis*, was the purest constitutional embodiment.

Coleridge's neo-Polybian analysis of the British Constitution was not an inherently radical one. Rather, it worked well within the mainstream of an older Whig polemic portraying the constitution as a sublime and ancient instrument of historical and organic refinements. While the ancient constitution had suffered recent perversions and deformities and was in need of remedy for these corruptions, extending the democratical powers of the British parliament was not, in Coleridge's estimation, the proper remedy—not the proper means of restitution and reform.

Like Montesquieu and Bolingbroke, Coleridge was an advocate of a system of checks and balances moderated by gradual adjustments. While his oppositional writings were hostile to the "aristocrats" they were vehemently protective of the landed interest. Certainly this was the case where the term "aristocrat" stood as a factional label for despotic baronacy corrupted by money and the term "landed interest" was identified with virtuous and independent gentry. While these distinctions may have contained "radical" associations in a seventeenth-century context, they must be placed within a more moderate and far less "revolutionary" framework in later eighteenth-century political discourse.

Coleridge's earliest political debt was to Burke's revolutionary writings on the American War. Although his own antiministerial writings of 1795 were decidedly antiwar and so parted company with Burke's position on the French Revolution, Coleridge's opinions were strongly Burkean with regard to the proper course of English parliamentary reform. This would require a delicate tuning of the existing powers of king, Lords, and Commons and not some comprehensive, far-reaching democratic republican reform founded on the unchecked popular power of a single unicameral assembly. The British Constitution could only be tempered by gradual and organic (or natural) historical change and through the mediating force of traditional institutions such as the Common Law. One could not tune such a sensitive instrument by severing the monarchy and aristocracy, as Robespierre had done in France. But equally, a constitutional balance could not be achieved, as Pitt wished to do in Britain, by stifling and silencing the voice of the common people. According to Coleridge, all efforts to rapidly change the constitution of the realm through "plots" without consulting the mediated consent of its people—whether undertaken by "radicals" such as Robespierre or "conservatives" such as Pitt—were equally heinous.[1] Indeed, both the background to the passage of the "Two Acts" and Coleridge's pamphlet response, *The Plot Discovered,* underline the volatile combination of glass houses and thrown stones in the war-torn and famine-strapped Britain of 1795.

On 16 October 1795, unknown individuals in an immense crowd threw stones at George III's carriage as that monarch rode toward the houses of Parliament in order to open their session.[2] This endangerment of the king *in itself* was nothing new; previous British kings had confronted far greater dangers from trained assassins[3] or well-aimed enemy guns[4] than George III did from amateurish rock-lobbing malcontents. However, in the climate of 1795—in the aftermath of the repeated humiliations of Louis XVI by the Parisian mobs in the years leading up to his execution—the stone throwing took on much larger dimensions than it would have in safer and saner years. The king, whose popularity had soared in the wake of his mental illness and recovery in 1788 and 1789, was now perceived by many to be deeply hated.[5] Indeed, the symbolism of the thrown stone suggested that there was a new and profound disrespect, of national proportion, for the institutions of king, church, and aristocracy. Conservative thinkers depicted this disrespect as emanating from a volatile combination of two elements. The first of these was the French, or Jacobin, theory that was carelessly parroted by the ambitious "radical" intelligentsia and the "revolutionary" rich, the second was the consequence of the hunger and resentments of the angry plebeian mob.[6]

William Pitt responded to, or perhaps used, the isolated episode of the hurled stones as the pretext to introduce two new pieces of legislation. The two bills against "seditious writings" and public meetings passed into law on 18 December 1795. Those oppositional presses and pamphleteers who were the ostensible targets of these laws quickly nicknamed the legislation the "gagging" acts. The first of the bills limited the freedom of the press. The "Treason Bill" expanded the old treason laws of 1336 (25 Edward 3) well beyond the sphere of *overt* actions.[7] The new definition of "treason" would even include works of theory or imagination, either spoken or printed, which *seemed* to cause disaffection between the subject and the monarch. The new treason law aimed to constrain or silence the rising tide of writing, publication, and circulation of "seditious" literature, such as *The Rights of Man.* Such books, which had become popular in their cheap editions, were presumed by conservative critics to inflame the minds and hearts of Britons towards rebellion.

The second bill restricted the right of assembly. The "Convention Bill" stated that no more than fifty people were allowed to be in the audience of any public political meeting.[8] This aimed to put an end to the sort of large, crowded meetings and monster rallies favored by London "radicals," numbers that the Gordon Riots and the French Revolution had proven were essential to form the nucleus of a powerful mob. The law was described as a moderate measure toward the prevention of riot, but the "radicals" considered it to be a strategy for crippling their access to the ears of the people at large and as such an impediment to their purported plans for the mobilization of the unpoliticized masses.

"Radical" organizations, such as the London Corresponding Society, complained that Pitt's legislation constituted a direct persecution of the reform societies and was not the sincere and reasonable response to the threat of revolt that it claimed to be. Significantly, the meetings of *both* the Whig club *and* the London Corresponding Society on 10 November 1795 to protest against the two bills suggest the disproportionate nature of the government response.[9] While the reaction of the LCS was to be expected, even moderate Whig critics such as the Earl of Lauderdale dismissed the theory that there was a clear or present "Jacobin" danger to the realm. Lauderdale maintained that the new legislation was in truth designed for the Pitt government's own nefarious purposes of expanding administration and Crown powers at the expense of the traditional rights of Britons.[10] Whig Parliamentarian Richard Brinsley Sheridan went so far as to contend that the final objective of the legislation was to be the consolidation of what amounted to executive powers in cabinet.[11]

Critics of the Pitt Administration during the winter of 1795 murmured that the government's new legislation laid the groundwork for a grander scheme by the prime minister and his cabal to stifle the popular press. By silencing the press, they claimed, Pitt hoped to dampen the public objections to the war policy that had thwarted, or at the least nipped at the heels of, Crown and administration powers. Coleridge launched his own critique of the bills in the midst of the violent and accusatory paranoia of the debate. Pittites, who viewed those who opposed the bills as Jacobins who would murder the king if they could, clashed with "patriots," who viewed the proponents of the bills as absolutists who would murder the constitution if given the chance.

The pamphlet *The Plot Discovered* was the result of an earlier lecture that Coleridge had delivered on 26 November 1795. The advertisement ran in the *Bristol Gazette* that same morning, giving notice that "On Thursday evening next, seven o'clock . . . , S. T. Coleridge" would "deliver an address to the inhabitants of Bristol on the two bills now pending in parliament." The performance took place in "the Great Room, at the Pelican Inn, Thomas Street" in Bristol. The price of admittance was one shilling.[12] At the time of the lecture, the Treason Bill had passed its third reading in the Lords and its second in the Commons. The Convention Bill had passed its second reading in the Commons and had not yet been heard in the Lords. There was, therefore, a degree of urgency behind Coleridge's intervention. It was essential that the address in Bristol deliver a decisive rhetorical blow to the atmosphere of panic that the government had so carefully constructed. For this reason, *The Plot* aimed at a careful rhetorical balance between moderating reasonability and persuasive passion. Coleridge for his part believed that the bills marked a new attempt by a small self-interested group in Parliament to destroy the British liberties guaranteed in the constitution and to institute a new form of absolute power grounded in the first minister rather than the king.

In his own theory of what was taking place in 1795, Coleridge saw King George as the pawn of the younger Pitt. It was Pitt, and not the king, who had been the target of the mob's stone-throwing fury, who was the true beneficiary of the "Gagging Acts." Coleridge regarded Pitt as a great evil genius, in the tradition of Cromwell, Richelieu, Mazarin, and Robespierre. Like all of those political operators who were capable of leading monarchs and indeed entire peoples by the nose, Pitt was convincing the people's representatives in Parliament to hand over their liberties and rights to his dictatorship in the putative interest of their own safety and well-being. Pitt's bid to centralize parliamentary power through a war cabinet, which allocated to itself extreme emergency powers, spoke in the Jacobin language of the day.[13] Arguing in terms of public safety and the security of the realm, it was in truth simply a plan to gain unparalleled and centralized authority in the state. In the interest of attacking this newly crafted and absolutist Pittite state, Coleridge defended the traditions of the balanced constitution.

Coleridge cleverly dubbed Pitt's shadowy plan "the Plot." The very act of calling it a "Plot" conjured up images of wicked deeds done by cover of night, of muttered whispers by cloaked figures, of secret writings which meant things other than they seemed to mean on the surface, of visible puppets and unseen puppet masters. The term "plot" bore a plethora of connotations, all negative, to the reading public of 1795. The term had been used frequently in popular entertainments, including plays such as Ottway's *Venice Preserved: Or, the Plot Discovered*. English history in particular was riddled with "plots" and "plotters," particularly in the Elizabethan and Stuart eras. The word "plot" almost always connoted evil and treasonous activity. In English history, plots had been levelled, traditionally against the monarch, but sometimes against the nation at large.

They include the "Gunpowder Treason and Plot" (1605), the "Popish Plot" (1678), the "Meal Tub Plot," the "Rye House Plot" (1683), the "Assassination Plot" (1696), the "Atterbury Plot" (1722), and the "Elibank Plot" (1754). The early reign of George III had also seen reference made by the Rockingham Whigs to the "Shadow Cabinet" of the king's evil adviser Lord Bute (see the *North Briton* papers of the 1760s). These are but a few resonant examples for audiences of the 1790s.

The word "plot" carried with it the idea of the normal routines and procedures of governance and change being subverted by clever and demonic men who, unlike quotidian politicians, were willing to transgress any law or standard they needed to in order to grab power. By entitling his pamphlet-rebuke of the two acts *The Plot Discovered or an Attack Against Ministerial Treason*, Coleridge suggested that the very men who claimed to pass legislation designed to stop secret conspiracy and plotting against the constitution by Jacobins were *themselves* the true plotters against the nation. The true English Jacobins featured in Coleridge's *Plot Discovered* were the king's own ministers. This metaphor of "the Plot" and "Ministerial Treason" was artful, not only because it applied the very accusations that Pitt's administration had made against John Thelwall and Thomas Hardy to Pitt himself, but because it did so by employing the well-worn and time honored strategy of blaming the king's "wicked ministers" while absolving the king of any wrongdoing. Thus, it would be read within the limits of the classic trope of Whig monarchial constitutionalism.

The true plot, Coleridge implied, was not Hardy's proreform public meetings with "members unlimited," but Pitt's elite and secret cabal. Secret cabals met behind locked doors. Their proceedings were not subject to spying by the radicals in the same way that the proceedings of the radicals were subject to spying by the government. The true treason, Coleridge insinuated, was not Thelwall's public lectures and their buzz of democratic arcana that would probably never amount to anything concrete, but Pitt's secret machinations that had already resulted in a set of concrete and powerful bills. Such bills would, if passed Coleridge asserted, undoubtedly silence all voices in favour of liberty, present and past. The ideas of "plot" and "treason" played well into Coleridge's own vision of himself as critic and "Watchman." Coleridge, as we have seen, persistently thought of himself as an independent voice that dared to point out the evildoings that went unnoticed by a supine people. Coleridge's identity as a "Watchman" was presumably tied up with his vision of himself as one of the few honest men who dared to venture out to locate and uncover the secret plotting of the "shadow monarchy" with Pitt as its king. In this sense, the worse and more lethal the plot and treason were, the more they made Coleridge's work as a discoverer of them seem an act of importance, heroism, and vision.

Coleridge pointed out to his audience that the "ministerial treason" had two main objectives. The first was to silence the voice of public opinion and criticism that would have ordinarily acted to discover and expose the unconstitutionality of the plot and challenge Pitt's expanded authority. The second goal was to expand the legislative power of the first minister in such a way as to overrun the executive power of the king and the judicial power of the courts. By means of these two strategies, Pitt hoped to achieve unprecedented, extraordinary, and dictatorial powers. This grab for power by Pitt, Coleridge maintained, was the true goal of "the Plot." Coleridge remarked that "in all ministerial measures" there were "two reasons, the real and the ostensible. . . . The ostensible reason for the bill," to combat sedition and rebellion, "we have heard," he noted. "The real" reason for the legislation was hidden from view but not impossible to detect. Coleridge reassured his audience that the secret plans of the cabinet "will not elude the search of common sagacity."[14]

The long-range but hidden grand-strategic rationale for the two acts was far more worrying and ultimately much more destabilizing than Pitt's present tactical efforts at the censorship of books and public meetings, Coleridge argued. Thelwall, the corresponding societies, and "republican thought" were only the closest and most unpopular targets of the bills. Pitt's true goals were far more expansive. Pitt had wisely chosen the extremist "Jacobins" as his first target. He had done so with the full knowledge that he could exploit the "moderate" reformists' and Tory and Whig constitutionalists' fears of the "Democrats." Pitt, argued Coleridge, hoped to hustle the moderates into granting the administration and Crown emergency powers of suppression and prerogative to fight their common enemy. These powers, Coleridge pointed out, were of a height and extent which the moderates who supported the acts out of fear would ordinarily, in a time of peace free from anxiety about sedition, have opposed on the grounds that they were blatantly unconstitutional.

Coleridge identified four pillars of despotism in his analysis of Pitt's architecture of tyranny. In *The Plot Discovered* Coleridge wrote that there were "four things which being combined constitute Despotism." His purpose in writing *The Plot* was to point out how perilously close Pitt was to achieving the goals of his "Treason" and "Plot." "Let the present Bills pass," Coleridge warned, "and these four things will be *all* found in the British government."[15] It is worth examining three of these four factors in depth, since they served as the general definition of "despotism" around which Coleridge built his critique of Pitt's "plot."

Pitt undertook the first ingredient of despotism argued Coleridge, for the true mark of tyranny was "the confusion of the executive and legislative branches." Pitt intended to accomplish this task by silencing public opinion and its embodiment in regal "Majesty." Although Pitt publicly claimed to be acting to defend King George's safety and honor, Coleridge alleged that this served as pretence for Pitt's treasonable stifling of the public's impassioned petitions and prayers to their majesty the king. In separating the voice of the people from the king, Coleridge maintained, the first minister weakened and enfeebled royal power by separating it from its source in the millions of common people.

The second prop of despotism was "the direct or indirect exclusion of all popular interference" in government.[16] This Pitt had done by the gagging acts, which excluded popular "out of doors" participation in government by preventing the previously legal and definitely constitutional privileges of free speech and public assembly. As Coleridge explained, although the "feelings" of the people were not always articulately or coherently expressed, they were nonetheless an important component in the British Constitution. The House of Commons alone was not sufficient to express this public opinion even in an uncorrupted state, Coleridge claimed. Informal, extraparliamentary means such as petitions, lectures, newspapers, and pamphlets were equally "constitutional" as components of the people's representation, or "popular interference," in the polity.

The third component was "A large military force kept separate from the people."[17] This Pitt had done by inventing high ministerial war powers, thereby taking away from the king the time-honored and constitutional royal prerogative of amassing and directing the army and navy and levying war. Coleridge's disapproval of the war against France stemmed in part from his loathing of Pitt's hypocritical crusade against the sort of republic Pitt had once applauded. Pitt, like Edmund Burke, had been an erstwhile supporter of American liberty. Although neither Pitt nor Burke would see much similarity between the French and American cases, Coleridge believed them to be common causes, an insight that must identify Coleridge's French sympathies with the early and constitutional phase of the revolution. However, the deeper anxiety underpinning Coleridge's antiwar sentiment was born of a conviction that the prime minister, as mastermind of the war, had stolen—from the king, the houses of Parliament, and the common people—the power to guide or censure the country's conduct. Since Pitt had essentially defined opposition to his war against the French Republic as a treasonable and disloyal defense of regicide republicanism, he had separated the war powers in the state from the people, from their legislators, and from their king.

The fourth element was a misuse of the judiciary: "when the punishments of state offenders are heavy and determined, but what constitutes state offenses left indefinite, that is, dependent on the will of the minister, or the interpretation of the judge."[18] This Pitt had done by the vague wording of the treason bill, which could theoretically result in the hanging of a man for printing a copy of Plato's *Republic*. Coleridge disliked the granting of heavy prerogatives to judges and ministers, because this traduced the tradition of Common Law.

From Coleridge's sketch of the four pillars of despotism, an ideal type of a bad government, one may easily infer what he thought a free and good government contained. First, he implied that a free government separated rather than confused "the executive and legislative branches." Second, he argued that a free government included rather than excluded the voice of "popular interference" in its deliberations; while it was not directly democratic, it was thereby virtually representative, since it listened closely to "out of doors" opinion. Third, he maintained that a free government kept the standing army small and under the control of the national consensus rather than of the first minister's or king's whim alone. Fourth, he implicitly stated that a free government in its laws carefully and accurately defined a small number of "state offences." Such a free government did not use statute to offer prerogative powers and strong discretion to the Crown or to the bench. Rather, a free government left the greater measure of latitude to the Common Law, in the hands of the jury rather than "on the will of the minister or the interpretation of the judge."

It remains to consider Coleridge's treatment of three of the four pillars of despotism as he analyzed them in *The Plot*. These three principles as problematics follow roughly from the following assertions: first, Coleridge's contention that "the confusion of the executive and legislative branches" was implicit in Pitt's overwhelming of the king and the courts in his grab for power; second, that "the direct or indirect exclusion of all popular interference" was the direct consequence of the censorship imposed by the passage of the two acts; third, Coleridge's construction of the practical weakness of the law "when the punishments of state offenders are heavy and determined, but what constitutes state offences left indefinite, that is, dependent on the will of the minister, or the interpretation of the judge," which means that the weakness of the treason law was implicit in its framing rather than its application, in its theory rather than its practice.

Drawing on the ideas of Bolingbroke and Burgh, Coleridge focused on the ancient constitution as insuring the independence of the legislative power of Parliament from the executive power of Crown and ministry.[19] The "plot" undermined and sapped precisely this independence. Pitt used positive law,

Coleridge argued, conceived and executed by his junto in the cabinet, to corrupt the free representative voice of the House of Commons. Pitt's plot, as
Coleridge depicted it, subverted the formal (virtual) representative voice of the
house and its informal corollary in "out of doors" (direct) public opinion. The
treason, if it succeeded, would create a consolidated cabinet executive that
would unite in the single person of First Minister Pitt the powers that had formerly under the constitution been separated in the branches of Crown (executive), Parliament (legislative), and courts (judicial).

Coleridge held the merging of the legislative power of the first minister
with the executive power of the Crown in the person of Pitt to be the ultimate form of despotism. Pitt's plan was particularly devious as it also intruded
the minister's reach into the system of justice. Coleridge's arguments against
the plot bore a striking resemblance to those of Blackstone whose principles
became axiomatic among theorists of constitutional balance by 1795:

> [Liberty] cannot subsist long in any state, unless the administration of
> common justice be *in some degree* separated from the legislative and also
> from the executive power. Were it joined with the legislative, the life,
> liberty and property of the subject would be in the hands of arbitrary
> judges, whose opinions would then be regulated only by their own
> opinions . . . were it joined with the executive, this union might soon
> be an overbalance for the legislative.[20]

Coleridge had already indicted Pitt for upsetting the balance of the constitution
in the earlier lecture *On the Present War*: "who is this Minister, to whom we have
thus implicitly trusted every blessing?"[21] He contended in *On the Present War* that
Pitt had, for almost two years, conducted his war with France in opposition to
the voice of the House of Commons and the will of the people. Through the
creation of faction and coalition, through the smoke screen of a war against radical agitation fought by treason trials and suspensions of habeas corpus, Pitt had
gathered the reins of all three branches of government into his hands.[22]

Coleridge's criticisms of Pitt's "plot" considered the force of the "Ancient
Constitution" as mediated through the institutional workings of the "Balanced
Constitution." Fusing the traditional accounts of history and law, long invoked by the common lawyers, with the discourses of morality and opinion
favored by the polemic of skeptical Whiggery after 1688, Coleridge attempted to set the case for legitimacy in both the language of juridical science and
customary right. Accordingly, Coleridge argued that the "science of the legislator" was an extension of the "science of history."

Coleridge depicted the British Constitution as the tripartite system that Montesquieu and De Lolme had described. Two houses, one popular and one hereditary, and a king who was the symbolic and historical union of both, generated policy, instituted laws, and appointed and sustained an independent judiciary to interpret and apply those laws as justice. In its mediation between the national interest and what he frequently defined as "the harmony of government," the constitution was at one and the same moment both a stable and disinterested line of traditions and an active interpreter of the immediate needs of the polity. As such, Coleridge considered it to be more than the sum of its parts: more than the division of powers, more than an accumulation of statutes, and more than popular contemporary reflections of political interests. Coleridge viewed the constitution in organic terms as an active living agent, with memory, capacity, and intentions. In his theory of the constitution, Coleridge distinguished between "Constitution" and "Government" and "People." His extended conception of a "State" embraced all three of these elements even as it transcended their limitations.

This distinction was emphasized by Coleridge in his contention that mere "government" alone, in the sense of a clearly recognized authority rather than chaos, was not enough. The state had to be governed by more than iron-handed coercion if a free government was to be markedly different from a slave plantation. Coleridge scoffed at Pitt's excuse that the emergency measures were designed to preserve freedom and "government" from the sedition of English Jacobins. Once the emergency powers of coercion were granted to Pitt, Coleridge complained, there would be no more British freedom to protect from the Jacobins: "A government indeed we should have had: there is not a slave plantation in the world that has not a government!" On the other hand, he pointed out, "a constitution[,] if it means anything, signifies certain known laws, which limit the expectation of the people and the discretionary power of the legislature."[23]

Believing that the distinction between the people and the legislature had been made in the English Bill of Rights of 1689, Coleridge claimed that it was a historically established principle of the constitution that the law was sovereign over the political wills of Parliament or the king. This same principle of law guaranteed "constituted" opinion through the liberty of the press. Dickinson has described the distinction between the arguments in favor of the "Ancient Constitution" versus those in favor of "Revolution Principles."[24] Coleridge, borrowing as it pleased him from both these traditions, believed that both constitutional history and the Common Law had been vindicated and perfected in the 1689 Bill of Rights. The bill, he believed, formally established the sovereignty of law over the political agitations of Crown versus Parliament, agitations that had led to the unlawful absolutist dictatorship of King Charles in the 1630s and the equally unlawful absolutist dictatorship of the Rump Parliament in the 1640s. Still, he emphasized his suspicion of positive law removed from the moorings of historical practice, and also the distinction between law in its broadest sense and statutes that served immediate legislative corruption.

The first axiom that Coleridge drew was from Montesquieu's theory of balances in the constitution. He argued that "the people," represented "by their proxies in the House of Commons," were "a check on the [influence of the] nobility" of the realm, thereby preventing the excesses of aristocratic caballing and oligarchy.[25] Coleridge himself asserted that the government of Britain was intended to rule "by" or "with" "the people" rather than "over" them. Theories that had claimed otherwise, he characterized as inherently despotic.[26] Coleridge used the term "people" to describe three major interests in the nation. He used the word, in his discussions of constituted government, specifically to denote the House of Commons. But he also used it in a broader sense, to include two groups who embodied public opinion "out of doors," beyond the narrow purview of Parliament. The first of these two groups comprised the literate and educated classes. This group made its voice heard through newspapers, pamphlets, and public lectures like Coleridge's.

The second of the two groups considered institutionally significant by Coleridge was that of the lower orders. This group, lacking the literacy, education, and money which would admit it to the true sphere of enlightened public opinion, made its "response" (if not its "opinion") felt through the cruder discourse of criminal activity and mob violence. This broader national sensibility, which included and incorporated social unrest, existed as a diffuse but palpable form of opinion. At the level, therefore, that order may be disrupted and property threatened by this lowest stratum of the people, Coleridge recognized some limited degree of a consensus of the poor. But the lower orders had no claim to *direct* or *unmediated* political presence in Coleridge's conception either of government or of public opinion. Still, Coleridge emphasized, the legitimate needs of the unenfranchised must be considered by those who inhabited the parliamentary constitutional sphere. The opinion of the extraparliamentary elite, *responding* as it must to the needs and tempers of the poor, actively shaped public opinion and government policy.

The "people" then, in Coleridge's use of the term, were dually represented in the constitution. Firstly, they sent over four hundred representatives to the House of Commons, at least a few of whom purported *directly* to represent the local interest of any given citizen through county or borough seats, and the remainder of whom aspired *virtually* to represent them as composing the national interest. Secondly, they were represented as a class, along with all of the subjects of the realm, by the "majesty" of the Crown.

Coleridge reminded his audience that new laws, if not forged in the tempering fires of precedent and the Common Law, were merely arbitrary edicts and were not to be thought of as "the voice of the people" speaking through its representatives. Statutes that broke with the historical traditions of English law in favor of sudden novelty and innovation were to be considered aberrant and perverse. They were, in this regard, as despotic an act of law as any absolute monarch's fiat, even if they were rubber-stamped by Parliament claiming (wrongly) to act as representatives of the people.

Coleridge referred to the political genius of Lord Burleigh, whom he claimed stood as witness that the danger of an unhinged Commons was recognized almost two centuries before Pitt: "England can never be undone except by a parliament."[27] The Common Law, argued Coleridge, trued the balance between the Crown and Parliament. This ultimate sovereignty of law was the defining principle of the good republic. England, he argued, had been in essence a good republic since the guarantee of the Bill of Rights. Underlining his point, Coleridge pointed out that Burleigh's contention that Parliament might undo the nation by acting irresponsibly had been made in a time "before the contract of the Bill of Rights had been entered into by the people and their governors," William and Mary. "But now" Coleridge opined "we cannot [legally] be undone even by a parliament." Placing these arguments in the context of Bolingbroke's constitutional republicanism, Coleridge concluded finally "Parliament cannot annul the constitution."[28]

Coleridge's intrinsically positive critique of magnate oligarchy depended on preserving the role of the nobility in the constitution. The second axiom which Coleridge drew from Montesquieu's theory of balances in the constitution was that "the nobility," represented directly on a one-seat-for-one-noble basis in the House of Lords,[29] were "a check on the [influence of the] people," thereby preventing the excesses of mob rule and demagoguery.[30] The Lords had significant power in the Parliament, not only by virtue of sitting in their own rights but by their exercise of political patronage in those "corrupt" seats in the Commons which they "owned'—and in which they could place pliant eldest sons and other henchmen. Recognizing this double influence in the upper house, Coleridge advocated a strengthened voice in the lower house. In the House of Commons, Coleridge complained, "three hundred and six [M.P.s] are nominated or caused to be returned by one hundred and sixty Peers and commoners with the treasury." These "three hundred and six" members were "more than a majority" in a house of only five hundred and thirteen members. "The majority therefore of the house of Commons," Coleridge concluded, "are the choice, and of course the proxies, of the treasury, and the one hundred and sixty-two [peers]."[31] "The majority" in the Commons, he lamented, "is tipped to the propertied and the aristocratic, and the so-called independent voice in the house is overshadowed by the interested" voices of the sons and cronies of the lords.

Believing that, "Everyman a King," "majesty" was to be understood in terms of the powers of the first magistrate, and Coleridge depicted the Crown powerfully as the supreme representative of the people. Therefore, the third axiom which Coleridge drew from Montesquieu's theory of balances in the constitution was that "the king" and his ministers who composed the corporate person of the Crown served as "a check on both" the potential misdeeds of the nobles and the House of Commons.[32] This idea of the king as providing an important balance in the tripartite constitution was not in itself such an innovative theory.

The monarchical theory of the balanced constitution dated at least as far back as Charles I's Hyde/Falkland-influenced *Answer to the Nineteen Propositions* in the 1640s and had become so widespread among both Georgian Whigs and Georgian Tories that it was hardly a "radical" idea in 1795. Indeed, Coleridge's suggestion that the king was a necessary "check" against the vagaries of the Parliament was a distinctly "conservative" position to espouse since it raised a critical and cynical voice against Painite confidence in the capabilities of an unmediated "people" as makers of law. Even as it attacked caballing oligarchs, Coleridge's suggestion that the king was the protector of the "real" people against the depredations of a perverted and nonrepresentative Parliament had been used by sources as disparate as Charles I in the 1640s and the American patriots in the 1760s. In both of those cases, and in Coleridge's case, the rhetorical "move" consisted of suggesting that the king represented the true will of the people, which had been thwarted by the parliamentarians. By praising the king even as he damned the Parliament's mistakes, Coleridge (like the American patriots before him) essayed to show himself as a loyal subject whose objections to current policy did not diminish his status as a faithful servant of the king.

If the Crown was the focus and representative voice of the people as an order, it must act as the champion of those disenfranchised masses who were not directly represented in Parliament. Kingship, for Coleridge, was the living embodiment of majesty. To this extent, Coleridge frequently referred to the king as the "first magistrate."[33] Majesty was the concentrated political will of the people. It operated, not as an amalgamated incorporation, as in Rousseau's general will, but both individually and collectively, as the aggregate of individual assent. He provided the etymological information that "the word majesty in its original signification" meant "that weight which the will and opinions of the majority imparted." Counterintuitively, the laws regarding "majesty," considered in the context of that word's true signification in ancient times, defended democracy rather than despotism. For in its original meaning, "majesty" "meant the unity of the people; the one point in which ten million rays concentrated." Yet, in that concentration, there remained the distinctive presence of those ten million separate rays of light. Therefore, "The ancient Lex Majestatis, or law of treason[,] was intended against those who injured the people," as well as for those who attacked the person of the king.[34] In this sense, Coleridge argued, a treason against the people was a treason against the king, and a treason against the king was a treason against the people.

The king, in Coleridge's account of "majesty," represented the living law and was the very essence of his organic constitutional model of the body politic, its vibrant, beating heart. Continuing Montesquieu's line, he concluded that the king was "the majestic guardian of freedom." George III was, Coleridge informed his audience, "gifted with privileges that will incline, and prerogatives [such as the royal veto] that will enable him to prevent the legislative from assuming the executive power." For the expansion of Crown into Parliament or Parliament into Crown both meant the same dire outcome. The "union" of legislative and executive powers, Coleridge apprised his listeners, "is the one distinguishing feature of tyranny."[35]

Coleridge's royalism in *The Plot* requires some explanation. The appearance of a democratic-monarchist polemic in the middle of what is commonly thought to be one of Coleridge's more radical "early" works is emblematic of the slipperiness of Coleridge's rhetoric in *The Plot*. For a "radical" to have such high praise for the office of the king in the unreformed constitution violates one's common expectations that "radicals" in the 1790s depreciated the powers of the king and elevated the powers of the unrepresented people. One wonders initially why, in a polemic against William Pitt—who was, after all, the king's own choice to head the ministry in Parliament—Coleridge aspired to depict the powers of King George so vitally and so plentifully. One would have intuited that Coleridge would have taken the usual tack, made famous by Dunning's resolution in 1780, of suggesting that the "ministerial treason" was the result of an expansion of the powers of the Crown over those of the Parliament. Instead, Coleridge did the opposite. He employed a style reminiscent of the polemicists against Sir Robert Walpole and the Duke of Newcastle from

1725 through 1755. He suggested that the evil and designing ministers in Parliament had not only corrupted the Parliament itself through treasury monies, but had gone so far as to put "the king in chains," effectively drawing Crown powers out of the king's hands into their own. Why, in 1795, did Coleridge prefer the strategy of "the king in chains" to that of "the influence of the Crown increasing"?

First, one gathers that the appeal to the king was a last-ditch attempt—an *appello Caesaris*—by which Coleridge hoped to gain the attention of the king and, perhaps, win the veto of the two acts. One must doubt this hypothesis from the start. George III had not publicly displayed dissatisfaction with the Younger Pitt in the same manner that his grandfather George II had publicly and violently objected to the Elder Pitt. It is unlikely that Coleridge imagined that his pamphlet could gain the king's ear and rouse into life the royal prerogative of the veto that was still recognized in the constitution but had lain dormant by tradition since the reign of Queen Anne. Nevertheless, Coleridge does mention in *The Plot* the royal "prerogatives that will enable [King George] to prevent the legislative from assuming the executive power." Appealing to the good will of the king and encouraging the Bristol gentlemen to do the same, Coleridge hoped to stop the acts with the king's veto: the last place where they plausibly could be stopped since they would almost certainly pass in their final readings in the two houses. This was a bold hope, but, at the very least, the appeal to Caesar was a good-faith gesture. It showed Coleridge and the Bristol gentlemen as publicly imploring the king to stop the acts that would abate his power. Such an appeal was, in this sense, probably more than just a mask of loyalism to excuse the violence of the attack on Pitt. While the appeal to the king may have been an honest attempt to convince the monarch to destroy the bills and save the nation, it was a long shot. But even if the realistic chance for George depriving Pitt of confidence and sinking the bills was almost nil, it was a gesture that had to be made.

The second and more likely explanation for the appeal to the king is that, by using the old royalist trope of the king as cynosure of the nation's majesty, Coleridge was attempting to lay a rhetorically complex snare for Pitt. The argument ran as follows: Royalist doctrine said that the king represented not only his own majesty as an individual prince, but "that weight which the will and opinions of the majority imparted . . . the unity of the people; the one point in which ten million rays concentrated." In that sense, the king was not only the first magistrate, but also *was* the people in a mystical sense. He was, claimed Coleridge, a sort of material objective corollary of the "Idea" of a people. Therefore, if one injured the people, one injured the person of the

king: "The ancient Lex Majestatis, or law of treason [against majesty,] was intended against those who injured the people." Pitt had excused the excessive
curtailment of the freedoms of the common people—the freedoms of speech
and assembly—on the pretence that these acts were necessary to protect the
person of the king from the tumultuous people who had thrown stones at the
royal carriage. Coleridge pointed out that the acts, by curtailing the constitutionally granted protections to the press and to free association, materially "injured the people." To injure the people was in truth to injure the king. Ergo,
Pitt's acts, that claimed to protect His Majesty, actually injured his "majesty."
Ergo, Pitt was as great a traitor as the men who threw stones at the royal carriage. Greater, even, because the stone throwers only annoyed and frightened
the king for one day, while Pitt's acts attempted to institutionalize and make
permanent the "treason against majesty" of the acts for all times.

Third, the high-royalist argument accomplished the same "work" that the
Hyde/Falkland doctrine had managed in the 1640s and that the American patriot argument had accomplished in the 1760s and early 1770s. It undermined
and subverted Pitt's claim that the acts represented the will of the British people because they were passed by a Parliament that was the representative of
that people. Coleridge's redefinition of sovereignty and majesty jerked sovereignty away from the hands of Parliament, where Pitt had placed it, and redistributed it among king and people. Thus, he attempted to undermine the
rhetoric of parliamentary absolutism that had been used last to such great effect against the colonists two decades earlier.

None of these three arguments was disingenuous or spurious. Coleridge's
Plot employed plenteous sarcasm and ridicule against Pitt. Still, it is imperative
that the heavy larding of humor, which the work employed, not be used as license to say that the entire pamphlet was written "tongue in cheek," nor that
it possessed an esoteric meaning opposed to that which it put forward, nor that
it hid an essentially "radical" message in conservative clothing. In any event,
the very habit of mind that argued that one *ought* to dress up one's arguments
for reform in the modest garments of the traditional constitution and ancient
authority was, in truth, one of the major traits which separated true "radicals"
from "moderate reformers."

The "radicals" who are so-termed by historians generally earned that post
facto classification because they proposed bold measures for swift reform and set
out their plans for social change in stark and uncompromising images.[36] It de-
preciates the true "radical" tradition of Godwin, Thelwall, Paine, Spence, and
Wollstonecraft and the activist artisans; the "reform" tradition of Wyvill, Burgh,
Cartwright, Rockingham, and Burke and the aristocratic reform societies, and

(one might argue) Coleridge and the Bristol gentlemen; and the shadowy "radical middle" of reform which included Price, Priestley, and (one might equally
well argue) Coleridge and the Bristol gentlemen, to herd them all into either the
pen marked "radical" or the pen marked "conservative." Coleridge's use of
"Tory" strategies such as the royalist polemic set him apart from the "true radicals" as surely as his acid "Whig" critique of the corruption of the unreformed
constitution set him apart from the true "conservatives." The very fact that one
still demurs after analyzing the 1795 writings as to whether to place him amongst
the "reform" or the "radical-middle" partisans of renovation suggests the degree
of difficulty inherent in creating any valid taxonomy for these years. The British
reaction to the war with revolutionary France produced a political atmosphere
not only supercharged with paranoia and rage but also gradually being stifled by
the onset of the censorship acts.

Coleridge gave extensive attention to the stabilizing influence of public
opinion in his lectures and pamphlets of 1795. He believed censorship to be
one of the ultimate causes of faction precisely because it suppressed criticism
and debate. The suspension of public opinion, Coleridge believed, created an
abnormal and polarized tension between social and historical forces and the
political institutions of government. In both his *Bristol Lectures* and *Conciones
ad Populum*, Coleridge had considered the artificial rigidity of legislation that
suppressed, or intrusively altered, the natural course of political, social, and historical process. However, not until *The Plot Discovered* did he apply these considerations to contemporary political crisis and particular English law. The two
bills and the entire Jacobin-baiting campaign were, in Coleridge's estimation,
only a smoke-screen. Pitt had used the "Jacobin crisis" to excuse his inattention to the very real concerns among the populace who resented the depressed
economy at home and the unpopular war on the continent. The mob that had
thrown the stones at the king in October had been expressing hunger, resent-
ment, and disaffection rather than allegiance to Tom Paine or Thelwall. The
prime minister, Coleridge assured his reader, knew this fact perfectly well.
Thelwall was far more useful, unpopular, and visible as a scapegoat than the
nameless "miserable people," who had disrupted the King's procession to Parliament on that October day.[37]

Coleridge contended that the implications of the proposed bill were enor-
mous. The acts were calculated to repress all critical opinion and to hasten the
destruction of the free press. Moreover, through the implementation of arbitrary law and corrupt politics, they threatened to poison the constitution itself.
The fundamental assumption underscoring Coleridge's critique of Pitt's acts
was the belief that the critical opinion of the opposition was essential for the

health of the constitution. This argument was not a justification of capricious or self-interested factionalism; opinion, to be legitimate, had to be reasonable and in good conscience.[38] Coleridge expressed his belief in the centrality of free public opinion to the stability of the nation in a clear aphorism: "to promulge what we believe to be true is indeed a law beyond the law."[39] With this idea in mind, he spent a good part of *The Plot* debunking the "ostensible cause" of Pitt's acts: John Thelwall and the London Corresponding Society. The intention of the convention bill was plain in this respect. The "first" goal, remarked Coleridge, was "that the people should possess no unrestrained right of consulting in common." The "second" aim, he concluded, was "that Mr. Thelwall should no longer give political lectures."[40] But why, Coleridge asked, did the government care so intensely about Thelwall? Thelwall's relative insignificance would certainly appear to mark the desperation of Pitt's gesture. Coleridge wrote that "in proportion that [Thelwall] feels himself of little consequence," then Thelwall could only come to his own conclusion, and "perceive the situation of the ministry is desperate."[41] Coleridge observed that "nothing could make [Thelwall] important [as a target of Pitt] but that [Thelwall] speaks with the feelings of multitudes."[42] Coleridge's most successful technique in maligning Pitt was to point out that Pitt was prepared to condemn Thelwall as an incendiary for saying certain things which Pitt himself had said in different, although similar, circumstances.

Pitt's new laws would have resulted in the younger Pitt's being jailed in 1795 for statements that were ignored by the law in 1781. Coleridge quoted Pitt's own "seditious" words in a 1781 denunciation of the American War: "by this iniquitous and unjust War the Nation was drained of its vital resources of Men and Money."[43] Pitt the "apostate"[44] had mourned the expensive triumphs in the former thirteen colonies over "men struggling in the holy cause of Freedom."[45] "O calumniated Judas Iscariot!," Coleridge wailed: "All this William Pitt said!" in his youth. As prime minister and virtual monarch by 1795, argued Coleridge, Pitt's concerns had changed. The Pitt of 1781 once approved of the battle of a republic in America to protect newly coined American liberties against the invasion of British troops hoping to squelch the infant American constitution and restore monarchy. The Pitt of 1795 now disapproved of the battle of a republic in France to protect newly coined French liberties against the invasion of British and allied troops hoping to squelch the infant French constitution and restore monarchy. Therefore, Coleridge concluded, this newborn crusading zeal must have been engendered by something more heartfelt than his hate of republicanism: namely, his lust for unrestrained power.

Coleridge charged the Pitt administration with deliberately attempting to muzzle the London Corresponding Society and the republican and democratic lectures of "Citizen" John Thelwall. This criticism was not so much a mark of Coleridge's democratic sympathies as his constitutional concerns. For he saw the attack on Thelwall and the LCS as the first step on the government's way to grander things: the muzzling of the entire nation. Having failed to convict the twelve radicals in the State Trials of 1794, the prime minister had decided that the existing legislation regarding seditious writings was insufficient to his purpose. Squelching all opposition, public and parliamentary, was a necessary precondition to his expansion of ministerial power in the state. That purpose, Coleridge argued, was the ultimate goal of Pitt's "plot." Pitt desired, reported Coleridge, to use "Citizen" Thelwall as a scapegoat. The pursuit of Thelwall was Pitt's method of marshalling onto his side the great emotional power of reflexive, fearful anti-Jacobin hysteria. This hysteria and the charged political discourse that it fuelled swept the nation even as rumors of an impending French invasion and a British fifth column began to surface. Pitt's stated objective, for the better pursuit of which he requested extraordinary powers, was the defence of the realm against foreign French enemies and domestic "British Jacobins." Coleridge "unmasked" Pitt's true goal: to gag all opposing voices, stigmatizing even moderate opposition to the war with France as "Jacobinical," and thereby liberate the power of the first minister from the constitutional restraints of public opinion and press criticism. But the construction of "Treasonable Words" as "Treasonable Deeds" amounted to a new interpretation of *acta non verba*.

In *The Plot* Coleridge devoted several pages to the way in which Pitt's new law of treason obliterated what had been an obvious distinction between republicanism as a contemplative Grecian theory as opposed to republicanism as regicidal French practice. He thought that the true madness of the new law was that it would punish those who passively spoke of the merits of a theoretically perfect republic as severely as those who actively plotted to kill the king and create a republic in fact. Coleridge argued that under the existing law "if any man should publish" a republican idea, even if it were only "published" in the narrow venue of "a friendly letter" or "a social conversation," he would be called a traitor. For in the eyes of the law, if any should "assert a republic to be the most perfect form of government" and "endeavour by all argument to prove it so" for *any* reason, he was "guilty of high treason." He was guilty because under the new law of treason, "what he declares," even theoretically, "to be the most perfect form of government, and the most productive of happiness" was a republic, "and to recommend a republic is to recommend the abolition of the kingly name."[46]

The freedom to voice purely theoretical opinions had been upheld by the old Edwardian law precisely because of its clarity in demanding clear evidence of *deeds* against monarchy as well as *words* critical of it. Coleridge maintained that "by the existing treason laws" of Edward, "a man so accused" of speculating that a republic was the best form of government "would plead, 'it is the privilege of an Englishman to entertain what speculative opinions he pleases provided he stir up no present action.'" Emphasizing the long established merits of the ancient law of Edward, Coleridge also recalled the guarantees and liberties provided by the ancient constitution, or "the privilege of an Englishman." His timeless English everyman was here offered in the guise of an innocent though accused man who must rightfully conclude his defense with the maxim: "Let my *reasonings* be monarchial or republican, whilst I *act* as royalist I am free from guilt."[47]

The new legislation proposed by Pitt and Grenville would destroy the ancient privileges of the free-born Englishman. Coleridge "fear[ed]" that "soon . . . such a defense will be of no avail." "It will be in vain," he warned his hearers, "to allege that such [republican] opinions were not wished to be realized" in the government of Britain.[48] Addressing the indefinite character of such a charge, Coleridge saw little protection for his imaginary free-born John, despite claims that his dreams "[neither] could be nor would be nor ought to be realised in the present or the following reign." Even if his reflections were a pure fantasy of utopian proportions and admitted by him to be so, "still he would be guilty of high treason." This was so because "though he recommends not an attempt to depose his present majesty from his kingly name, he evidently recommends the denial of it to some one of his distant successors."[49]

The ministerial treason against the ancient constitution was expressed as a double perfidy, as a treachery against the ancient and sacred traditions of the British Constitution in church and state. Coleridge's account of this treason in the *Plot* points out an act of impiety and sacrilege as well as secular treachery. To this end, the rhetoric of the *Plot* is saturated with mystical imagery—gothic visions of corruption, wizardry, and "Spells of Despotism" against the "Canon of British Liberty." Not only was Pitt's crime treason, it was blasphemy. Coleridge's Pitt was an apostate in the tradition of Julian, a role he would later fashion for another French nemesis, for Bonaparte.

The diabolical nature of "the plot," as described by Coleridge, was not only that it smothered the living voice of opinion, but that it sought to proscribe those parts of the British past that did not conform to Pitt's vision of the national character. Coleridge was mindful that the new calendar of the French Republic established in 1793 had been an attempt to "murder history." He associated the destruction of English constitutional traditions, both in church and state, with the Jacobin erasure of such French Catholic traditions as saints' days and indeed the generically Christian seven-day week punctuated by a Lord's Day.

The destruction of the French ecclesiastical-political calendar was another one of the Terror's cautionary examples. More than a welcome assault on a foreign Romish remnant, it struck at the heart of a British constitutional heritage anchored to a sacred conception of time. As an example calculated to frighten the most conservative elements of his readership into a moderating opposition, Coleridge could not have chosen better. Indeed, in the Jacobin case, the committees had violently erased from public view all reminders of France's monarchial and episcopal past in the name of public safety.

Coleridge was able to employ the fear of Jacobinism, with all its associations of unnatural, anticlerical and antihistorical innovation, against the Pittite regime of revisionist Terror. Robespierre's tyranny had cut away the past and proclaimed the new age of the revolution as the Year One. Coleridge feared that Pitt had similar goals in mind. Pitt, Coleridge argued, intended to extirpate that great plethora of books that *might* tend to encourage people to want a republic or even think well of a republic. This was a far more comprehensive scheme than simply stamping out that small number of books that openly and directly issued a call to arms, advocating revolution in Britain in 1795. Such writing and speaking was already proscribed by the old treason laws of England. Coleridge implied that by censorship, Pitt wanted to erase from the collective memory of the nation the scholarly traditions of theoretical debate on republics and utopias that had exercised so many of the great political thinkers of the previous centuries. The new act, after all, stipulated that "whoever by printing, writing, preaching, or malicious and advised speaking" caused disaffection between the sovereign and the people was guilty of sedition. Moreover, the proscription was extended to cognize "distribution" as a criminal act. The guilt would now be pinned equally to publisher as well as author. How long before it attached its significance to purchaser as well as vendor, reader as well as writer, listener as well as speaker? Coleridge wondered. Both "he who writes against" monarchy and his formerly innocent abettor, "he who prints and publishes against monarchy," would, under the new law, noted Coleridge, "be hanged as traitor[s]."[50]

Coleridge believed that this law must inevitably apply not only to both present and future publications and discourses on politics, ethics, and religion, but also to those past treatments of the subject. Indeed, this single "execrable clause" would "smother" entirely "the exertions of living genius." It would also "equally proscribe" "all names of the past ages dear to liberty!"[51] This carte blanche license for censorship, Coleridge concluded, would stifle not only the hotheaded controversialists of the 1790s, but the formerly anodyne books on republics from previous centuries, including those by purely theoretical republicans and utopia makers.

The list of bannable books was theoretically limitless, insinuated Coleridge, once the old insistence on the book posing a real and immediate threat was discarded and the new criterion of imagining a world or even praising a nation without kings was applied. (The prohibited canon in such a world might imaginably include previously "non-controversial" books such as Sir Thomas More's *Utopia*, Neville's *Plato Redivivus*, Milton's *Free and Easy Way to Establish a Commonwealth*, Thomas Hobbes's [pro-Cromwellian when written] *Leviathan*, James Harrington's utopian *Oceana*; even perhaps Jonathan Swift's *Gulliver's Travels*, Plato's *Laws*, Livy's and Tacitus's antiroyal Roman histories, and the Biblical books of Judges and Samuel.) Once a book was judged to be seditious, "the future editions" of it "will be treasonable" in perpetuity.[52]

Coleridge himself listed some of those authors who might be liable to prosecution under the new law: the great republican writers of the seventeenth century. Coleridge warned that the "cauldron of persecution" was "bubbling" "against the Sages and Patriots that being dead do yet speak to us." These "Sages and Patriots" were the "Spirits of Milton, Locke, Sydney, [and] Harrington," voices that "still wander through your native country giving wisdom and inspiring zeal!." "The spells of despotism," he concluded in a somber finish, "are being muttered" with increasing success against the works of those authors.[53] The Gothic imagery that Coleridge employed—of warlocks' cauldrons bubbling up noxious persecution even as Pitt's wizards mutter spells of despotism in attempts to destroy the benevolent "Spirits" of the great patriots—was pure theatre but nonetheless communicated an important point.

The "spells of despotism" was a very apt image in this context. Coleridge identified Pitt's repression of the lights of the ancient constitution with the entire Kingdom of Darkness once anatomized by Hobbes: a kingdom that, for Coleridge, was governed by the moral equivalents of witchcraft and cabalistic practice. Coleridge saw himself as defending public opinion as the embodiment of reason and the law against all religions of absolute power, including the Jacobin one. For this reason, Coleridge defended the emotional power of popular opinion as a "Mode of Expression Blended with Error." Through this antiegalitarian paean to the "Feelings of [common] Men," Coleridge could attack the arguments of Thelwall, Paine, and the so-called English Jacobins while still defending the liberties of assembly, speech, and press.

Coleridge used Thelwall's expression of the "feelings of multitudes" as the basis for examining the proper sphere of influence for public opinion in politics in *The Plot*.[54] Coleridge suggested that Thelwall's emotional rhetoric provided a cathartic point of focus and release for the "feelings" of common subjects, feelings which, although distorted and confused, were essentially true. By "true," Coleridge meant earnest, sincere, and ultimately constructive of good. He was convinced that "the feelings of men are always founded in truth." The "modes of expressing" those truth-inspired feelings "may be blended with error," Coleridge warned. Indeed, he cautioned that, "the feelings themselves may lead to the most horrid excesses." "Yet still," he insisted, the feelings "are essentially right." The feelings were right because they encouraged a critical awareness, which was superior to supineness in the citizen: "they teach man that something is wanting, something which he ought to have."[55] In considering the veracity of "feeling," Coleridge was careful to distinguish between the authentic "substance" of a sincere intention and the often-distorting "accidents" of its expression in a man such as Thelwall or in a club or crowd. As was the case in his consideration of the "graceful indiscretion" of informed political commentary as opposed to the "whirlwind" of a plebian public opinion, Coleridge suggested that whether civil or vulgar, such opinion must be recognized as genuine expressions of need.

In the end, Coleridge regarded Thelwall as "a mode of expression blended with error." He warned repeatedly that the great emotional tide of a mob was destructive and violent. Emphasizing again the significance and complexity of the deeper human causes of political strife, Coleridge argued that the source of such "feelings of want" must be acknowledged and addressed by governments. The government could not silence the true vox populi, Coleridge contended, nor could the government border and contain that general opinion by classifying it in limited and inaccurate terms, such as "Democratic sedition," "Republicanism" or "Citizen Thelwall." Just and prudent legislation ought to consider the voice of the people, whether that voice came from the jury box or from the press gallery or from a petition,or even from the street. The government and the law had a duty to respond to the political realities of the day, particularly when those realities became manifest in the voices of disaffection and want. Coleridge linked and juxtaposed the legislative power with the "censorial power . . . the exercise of which must be left to the people themselves."[56] His attack on the abusive and coercive powers of Pitt's ministry of the state turned on his defense of the legitimate and sovereign authorities of the people in the constitution. It was a timeocratically *res publican* rather than democratically republican argument.

CHAPTER 3

Defending the Constitution

C OLERIDGE'S CONCEPTION OF the law was that it contained a constituted dialogue between the governors and the people. He did not
expect that any simple legislative solution to social and political crisis existed within the limits of a single positive statute. But he did believe that the
complex of laws attached to certain policies alleviated problems of distress
and suffering, whereas others compounded them. While government may
not solve the problems reflected by the "voice of tens of thousands" it had
a duty to attend to that voice.[1] In this sense, Coleridge's constituted dialogue
between the people and their government suggested a reflexive and organic
mediation of political will and social change over time. Simply put, he ju-
ridically integrated the vital component of public opinion into his conception of government as an institutional form of political and social discourse.
The link between opinion and political will was and is a difficult thing to
chart. But Coleridge believed that it was possible to do so and that through
the harmony of feelings and interests a "harmony of government" could be
ascertained. This "harmony of government" and the national interest were,
Coleridge argued, best sustained by legislative dialogue. The achievement of
a coherent legislative dialogue was the consequence of a "true" science of
government.

Coleridge believed that the rising tide of interest and feeling, that surfaced
as opinion in response to a particular moment of crisis was a genuine sign of
consensus. Where it was not twisted by propaganda, dominated by demagoguery, or the distorted voice of vulgar opinion, such feeling was true and
respectable. Coleridge's distinction between public opinion and vulgar opinion was an important one. The line separating public opinion from vulgar
opinion was consistent with his emphasis on such classical virtues as reason,
conscience, and duty. Coleridge thought that these qualities of virtue which
allowed a true public voice lived in the "hearts and minds" of individuals in

society and were not to be found in the particular doctrines of individuals claiming to "speak for the public."

Central to this distinction between public opinion and vulgar opinion was Coleridge's notion of a "thing of concretion [or] some home born feeling." His constant reiteration that strong feeling in the hearts even of the vulgar often proceeded from transcendentally inspired intuitions of truth was markedly romantic. This Coleridgean link between "home born feeling" and authentic political opinion became increasingly clear as Coleridge perfected his theory of intuition and absolutes. He had referred in his earlier analysis of power and revolution, *Conciones ad Populum*, to the need for constantly "bottoming on fixed Principles."[2] Without this "bottom" foundation of ethically known truth for a solid groundwork in the nation, all revolution and reform was artificial innovation—a perfectly designed house built on sinking sand—and would end in arbitrary despotism.

Coleridge believed that there existed great inequalities of talent and attainment, of education, virtue, and political competence. Yet he also believed in "common sagacity" and "truths available to all." While the people at large were not equally suited to the tasks of formulating and administering policy, they were capable of expressing a form of moral veto. In this respect only the people could perform the task of censure. In Coleridge's contention that all dissent arose through the authentic voice of feelings of want, feelings grounded in truth, he came close to his fixed principle. Coleridgean "Common Sagacity" was something more than Paine's conception of "Common Sense." For Coleridge, "feelings" were complex sensations blended with intuitions: not just rational deductive logic, but transcendental and emotional judgments. As such, "feelings" proceeded from a complex association of sense and memory, structured by intuition and the will.[3]

Coleridge would develop his epistemology of emotion and, finally, intuitive imagination,[4] throughout his mature writings. But even in his earliest analysis of social and political power, his views on human nature and understanding formed a central component of his conception of agency. Already in 1795, Coleridge emphasized personal feelings and affections and their corresponding relationship to intuitive knowledge in politics as well as art.

Intuition, Coleridge argued, expressed itself to the human mind immediately and directly. It did not require reflection, analysis, or association of ideas. He articulated this more completely after 1800 in *Logic*, when he observed that mathematics was based on intuitive reasoning, and he defined "*immediate* presentation *et in concreto*, in contradistinction from the knowing a thing *mediated* by *re*presentative marks obtained by abstraction."[5] Intuition, as Coleridge learned both from the Cambridge Platonists and Kant, existed a priori; that is, prior to any accumulation of "sense-data" or experience. It is the source of what Coleridge considered real knowledge: the light that allows one to see the shadows in the cave. Intuition was a pure form, some human aspect of "the Good," "plastic nature" or the categories of time and space.[6] Intuitive perception was certainly, for Coleridge, a manifestation of the will of God. As such, he considered all intuition to be the recognition, in some form, of an absolute idea, but, as perceived *et in concreto*, he argued that it was feeling and sense.

Feelings, Coleridge implied, surfaced in false ideas as they were rationalized and distorted in fragments and as they were "blended with error." This constant admixture of error with feeling meant that all feelings were not to be trusted equally. Where a common and impassioned expression of want existed, however, Coleridge postulated that some degree of genuine feeling would be found. A polity that habitually surrendered to every mood and whim of the populace, Coleridge deduced, would quickly degenerate into demagoguery. But a polity that totally ignored the impassioned pleas and agonies of the public voice, he added, would equally quickly degenerate into tyranny. Whereas the French Jacobins had gone too far by indulging every folly of the popular emotions of the Paris mob, Pitt was about to go too far by gagging and binding the London mob in order that its voice would never be heard again.

Coleridge considered political virtue to subsist in the recognition and assessment of such honest "home-born" feeling, the recognition by the rulers of the voice of God in the voice of the people. Coleridge separated what he defined as legitimate public opinion from the vulgar cacophony of "opinions" and slogans slung about by the mob. He emphasized that the "swinish multitude" so publicly detested by Burke was not to be confused with the *senatus populusque britannicum* or the vox populi, which was truly, rather than merely rhetorically, *vox dei*.

J. A. W. Gunn has charted the transformation of public service into public opinion over the eighteenth century. He notes a tradition to 1780 by which "everyone knew that in some imprecise sense *vox populi* was held to be *vox dei*."[7] Increasingly after 1760, the question was whether this voice was best expressed through timocratic republicanism or through democracy. Was justice to be achieved through an elite consensus? Were the "best men" in the nation to provide a civilized and temperate form for what they perceived as the demands of the plebeians? Or was government to be trusted to a populist plurality, in which citizens felt a right to instruct their members of Parliament on exactly how they were to vote on certain issues of importance to those constituents? Gunn suggests that after 1780 the County Associations and theorists such as Dr. John Jebb not only encouraged a wider respect for the "opinions" of the "people" (Jebb went so far as to regard "opinion as the sole foundation of power"), but had set up new and innovative out-of-doors organizations such as clubs and associations through which they hoped to present their ideas to Parliament.[8]

While Coleridge certainly believed that in 1795 some had forgotten the "*vox populi*," he would never at any time cut loose public opinion from the anchor of the constitution as Jebb had done. In Coleridge's opinion, the people had no more implicit right to ruin the country than the Crown or the first minister did. All Britons, from George the king to the lowest common subject, were obliged to defend the balanced constitution from attacks from any quarter. In the seventeenth century, these attacks had largely come from the Crown; in the late eighteenth, they came from the first minister's hammerlock on the legislature; in France, they came from the mob and the resultant fall into demagogue-dictatorship. In keeping with the Whiggish perspective of the Bishop of Llandaff and the constitutional theory of DeLolme, Coleridge believed that public opinion must be balanced against the three estates as an element of constitutional government. Before the judgments of the legislative, executive, and judicial branches can be brought to bear on matters of policy, public opinion and criticism, the voices of want and dissention, must be heard. Moreover, they must be heard in their varied and particular circumstances, when and where they surface. In short, while a distinction must be made between popular and vulgar opinion as to actions, both must be recognized before acts of judgment by the governing classes can take place.

Coleridge contended that to ignore the voice of public opinion, or to intentionally misrepresent it through a distorted propaganda, was to concentrate its many voices into one. Thelwall expressed feelings of dissention but did not speak accurately for all opinion. In this respect, it was ironically Pitt who "created" Thelwall as the single face of the many-headed mob. In doing so he dangerously intensified a distorted aggregate of varied individual feelings into the single voice of the mob. Coleridge observed that "William Pitt knows, that Thelwall is the voice of tens of thousands." Knowing this, Coleridge asserted that Pitt "levels his parliamentary thunderbolts against [Thelwall] with the same emotion with which Caligula wished to see the whole of the Roman state brought together in *one* neck that he might have the luxury of beheading it at one moment."[9] The metaphor comparing Pitt to Caligula was, on the whole, no more favorable than that which compared that minister to a devious plotter or a spellbinding warlock or a heartless French dictator. It implied that Pitt was not only overzealous in his prosecutions, but actively and crimi-

nally insane. The "moment" which Caligula-Pitt had chosen for his beheading of the British state's tradition of liberty, Coleridge implied, was the
crowd's stoning of the king's carriage in October. From that moment forward,
Coleridge argued, Pitt had neither ceased nor rested from his plot to sever the
vocal organs of the English state from the body politic.

Arguing that seditious faction did not in reality exist, Coleridge urged the
government to act specifically in its deliberations using the existing law when
and if it applied, both as to treason and in response to the many individual
voices of want. Coleridge demanded evidence of "Where? when? and by
whom have factious and seditious speeches been made, and the public peace
been endangered by assembled petitioners? . . . Unless these questions are cir-
cumstantially answered," Coleridge warned, "and the answers proved by legal
evidence," it could not be certain that the acts were not a confidence game by
which Pitt was deceiving a gullible nation out of its liberties. If the acts were
passed without firm evidence of a crisis, then the public would have enacted
into law a dangerous instrument of "emergency" power for no reason what-
soever. Pitt justified the constitutionality of his assumption of powers, argued
Coleridge, on the strength of a crisis that did not actually exist. If the Commons granted Pitt emergency powers without first demanding that the prime
minister provide some evidence of the emergency, Coleridge admonished,
then "an act for repealing the constitution will have passed on the strength of
a ministerial assertion."[10]

The "Pure Breeze" of public opinion was the foundation of Coleridge's
conception of political stability. Public opinion was centrally important to
Coleridge's constitutional theory because he thought that it, like juries, represented a legitimate venue for popular power in the constitution. Indeed,
Coleridge viewed the freedom of the press as similar to jury freedom because
both allowed criticism by common citizens of the actions of government. He
emphasized that "the Liberty of the Press, (a power resident in the people)
gives us [the people] an *influential* sovereignty."[11] Coleridge argued in the
Bristol Lectures that the artificial silencing of public opinion by the "Republic
of Virtue" and the Committees was the cause of the violent extremities of the
revolution in France. With the issue of security in mind, he considered the
probable impact of the two acts in England. He predicted that under the influence of the new laws "all political controversy [will be] at an end. . . .
Those sudden breezes and noisy gusts [of controversy] which purified the
[political] atmosphere they disturbed, [will be] hushed to death-like silence."[12] It was precisely the suspension of public controversy on the grounds
of "emergency," argued Coleridge, that provoked rather than prevented the

atmosphere of paranoia and violence that the prime minister (purportedly) wished to avoid.

Coleridge maintained that the same air of panic and violence that was the ostensible cause of the two bills had caused the worst mayhem of the French Revolution. With an eye to France, Coleridge characterized despotism as a silence of "cadaverous tranquillity." Public opinion voiced through a free press might be subject to "graceful indiscretions," but it alone produced "generous order." The alternative, Coleridge insisted, was a freedom stifled by "the black pestilential vapour of slavery." Suggesting that to live by the censor's pen was to die by the censor's pen, Coleridge advised the government to take heed of "the example of France." "But beware[,] oh ye rulers of the earth," he intoned, "for it was ordained at the foundation of the world by the king of kings, that all corruption should conceal within its bosom that which will purify." He ended with the prophetic warning that "they who sow pestilence must reap whirlwinds."[13]

This warning suggested yet again to Coleridge's audience the similarity between the prime minister's policies and those of Robespierre. Comparing the two leaders as politicians who sowed the despotic pestilence of censorship, Coleridge noted that both men had subverted representative governments in favor of arbitrary executive rule. Pitt would, as Robespierre had done in 1794, finally provoke the sudden reassertion of the disaffected voice of public opinion, and in its most violent incarnation, the angry and murderous mob. Coleridge argued that Pitt's proposed legislation would do more to further a French-style popular revolt of the masses than the rambling manifesto of the corresponding societies ever could. Broad censorship, Coleridge concluded, produced a backlog of dissention and dissatisfaction which would inevitably break free, not through the gradual working of constitution and law, but "out of doors," in the streets. Coleridge's formula was almost Newtonian in its simplicity: every action of government pushing down the power of public opinion created an equal and opposite reaction by public opinion pushing upwards against government power.

Arguing that the bloom of corruption concealed the seeds of purity and renewal, Coleridge cautioned Pitt's ministry. His seasonal metaphor suggested that the process of purification would be revolutionary. But whether that meant rotation and replanting or the bitter harvest of slash and burn was the choice of legislators. Emphasizing that censorship corrupted, Coleridge accused the government and its fear-mongering of transforming reasoned public discourse into panic and vulgar opinion. Equally, he insisted it was corrupt law that ultimately led to lawlessness. But these were not the only conclusions to be drawn from the proposed bill. Returning to the implicit meaning of the legislation at hand, Coleridge considered the law's impact on the authors of the ages in the publication of books, past and present, and on writers living, dead, and as yet unborn.

Coleridge considered the actions of Pitt in 1795 tantamount to a conspiracy against the constitution and, as such, a *"Ministerial Treason"* against the people and the state. His objections were grounded in his own interpretation of the Common Law, those semi-mythologized congeries of laws, interpretations, and habits of mind that stood as an inveterate opponent of attempts to expand executive prerogative of any sort since the time of Charles I.

Arguments for the sovereignty of the Common Law had traditionally taken aim against the centralization of power in the Crown and its ministers, a centralization, constitutional theory posited, that invariably reduced the power of the judiciary and the legislature to act quasi-independently.[14] During the seventeenth century the common lawyers had fought against prerogative courts and against Crown influence over the decisions of juries and judges. During the eighteenth century, this tradition of suspicion of Crown intrusions into courts and lawmaking expressed itself in a generic attack on the corrupting "influence" of the Crown and its agents in Parliament.

Coleridge believed that the sovereign consensus of the Common Law manifested, through its continuity, the true political will of the people. In doing so, the Common Law revealed its relationship to the process that Coleridge conceived as history. But just as history and law were more than the compilation of statutes, Coleridge regarded sovereignty as more than a simple expression of popular public opinion. In *The Plot Discovered*, Coleridge suggested ways in which sovereignty and law under the British Constitution exemplified and yet remained distinct from the voice of the people.

The core of Coleridge's argument in *The Plot* was that Pitt's real reason for changing the existing law of treason was to obfuscate the concept of treason as it had theretofore existed in the Common Law. Defending ancient legal traditions, Coleridge returned once more to the comparative clarity of the old law as to acts and intentions. He emphasized that "our ancestors were wisely cautious in framing the bill of treason; they would not admit words as sufficient evidence of intention."[15] In light of the ambition to expand the prime minister's power over the nation and laws implicit in Pitt's conspiracy, Coleridge explicitly declared that "the existing laws of treason" were "too clear, too unequivocal!" to be the flexible tools of censorship demanded by Pitt. Edwardian and Georgian treason acts could be compared to reveal the true intent of the new legislation. While the law of Edward III was clear and simple and in keeping with the underlying principles of the Common Law, the new Georgian statute attempted to introduce a discretionary prerogative into judicial interpretations of the law of treason.

The government's proposed legislation was, in Coleridge's opinion, an attempt to tailor the law for the specific purposes of the administration. In this regard, he argued that the existing law was being amended because it did not suit the government's current needs, that it was, indeed, too clear. He distinguished between the statute 25 Edward III and the bills proposed by Pitt and Grenville. The existing law stipulated that "if any person within the realm or without" should "compass, imagine, invent, devise, or intend death or destruction, maim or wounding, imprisonment or restraint of the person of our sovereign Lord the king" or if he "levy war against his majesty or move or stir any foreigner to invasion," he would be "adjudged as a traitor."[16]

In Coleridge's estimation, the Edwardian standard of treason was not unreasonable. Coleridge placed the strength and clarity of the existing statute in the law's focus on actions and intentions to act that were direct and demonstrable. He concluded of the passage, "we object not."[17] But the new legislation, he continued, obscured action and addressed the realms of speculative imagination. This was the vital difference between the two forms of the law. The new law stipulated that "whoever by printing, writing, preaching, or malicious and advised speaking" should "compass," or "imagine," or "devise," either "to depose the king" or even to deprive "his heirs and successors from the style, power, and kingly name, of the imperial crown of this realm," he would be "adjudged a traitor."[18] As Coleridge observed, "here lies the snake."[19]

The old law as it existed concerned itself with immediate spheres of action and intent. It considered the mens rea of individual agents "compassing the death," "levying war," and "stirring foreign invaders." It addressed individual deeds rather than some amorphous construction of a public imagination (as opposed to opinion). The proposed bill referred to the less immediate purposes of "printing, writing and preaching," to "malicious and advised speaking," to "devising to depose" the king and his successors from their "style, power, and kingly name." In short, the new bill was not about treason at all, it was about censorship and seditious libel. Beyond this, Coleridge argued that far from being concerned with any genuine libel, the new bill was the tool of a government campaign of arbitrary repression. It had been drafted broadly in order to allow general and arbitrary applications so that almost any speaking, writing, or thinking that was politically awkward or inconvenient to the ministry could be prosecuted by the government.

This breadth of power violated Coleridge's rule that statute should not place vague or ill-defined crimes in the law. Good law, in the Common Law tradition as Coleridge defined it, was like the Edwardian Law of Treason: concrete, simple, detailed, and fit for centuries of use. Bad law, in the Prerogative Law tradition as Coleridge defined it, was like the Pittite Law of Treason: abstract, complex, vague, and suited only to be the momentary tool of a faction. For the sublunary practice of justice in Common Law to exist, Coleridge believed that there must be some historical mediation of judgment through a union of the all too human faculty of reason and some transcendental "Idea" of *Lex Natura*.

Coleridge's 1795 pamphlet was more than a polemic against Pitt's illegal actions in particular. In *The Plot*, Coleridge also considered the general limits and dimensions of sovereignty as defined in law. His principal concern was whether that sovereignty was constituted by the rule of law or by political will, and indeed whether there was a clear delineation or a close proximity between law and will. Coleridge rejected Enlightenment theories that a transhistorical and universal Natural Law could be discovered scientifically and known in most of its details by men. He objected particularly to the idea that "natural rights" could be codified in newly hatched civil laws such as those in France. Because he refuted the contention that the divine, universal "Idea" of Natural Law was knowable to any detailed extent by mortals, he denied the original-contractarian and natural-rights-based arguments of Locke and Rousseau, which were so popular in vulgarized forms among the French Revolutionaries. Instead, Coleridge imagined law as a socially and historically shaped construction of the universal but only partially knowable "Idea" of justice.

In rejecting natural-rights arguments in his discussion of law, Coleridge did not imply that all power was amoral or that the law ought ever to be used in unjust ways. He attacked the natural-rights theorists for positing a toothless set of "goods" without force or a network of civil duties to maintain them. But at the same time, Coleridge's moral "Watchman," in its indignation at Pitt's "plot," revealed a strong vision of a moral justice that was transcendental and that operated through a general set of universal norms which set "good" laws apart from "bad" ones. In this regard, the complexity of Coleridge's early position becomes clear. He was an intense historicist without ever becoming a moral relativist.

Distinguishing that intuitive and vague form of shared moral common sense that Montesquieu had described as "*raison primitive*" from the rationalized and specific system of natural rights espoused by many, Coleridge emphasized the historical and particular virtues of the common law. In doing so, he never gave up a belief in a transcendent and even divine ethical ground-work for law. On the other hand, he consistently rejected the belief in ab-solute natural rights outside the context of a granting civil government that honored those rights as nonsense. Instead, he contended that reason, consti-tuted through time and practice, provided the only sound ethical foundation for government. Coleridge, like Montesquieu, spent a great deal of effort at-tempting to discern whether the law of reason was a product of nature or time.

When writing on issues that dealt with the concept of constitutional sov-ereignty, Coleridge also leaned heavily upon the works of English intellectual descendants of Montesquieu, relying on the strongly historical arguments of writers such as Blackstone and Burke. At first, this pairing seems odd: the great apostle of *raison primitive* and common, human moral ground juxtaposed with the particularist and historicist arguments of Blackstone and Burke. Yet, as David Lieberman has suggested,[20] Blackstone's strong respect for the authori-ty of custom and tradition as such did not preclude him from a strong belief that there was a universal morality that should shape and define the particular common laws of kingdoms. Common Law judges, such as Lord Mansfield, had long stated the principle that "The law of England is only *common reason* or usage."[21] Coleridge resembled Blackstone and his successors in that he lo-cated the ultimate seat of sovereignty in Parliament.[22] He was unlike Black-stone in that he believed that if Parliament became "corrupt" and failed to pre-serve the checks and balances of a mixed constitution, it was the responsibility of law courts, judges, and juries—the personnel and tradition of the Common Law—to exercise judicial review and overturn the law as contrary to justice.[23]

From its earliest development in *The Plot Discovered*, Coleridge's constitu-tional theory was pragmatic and conservative. It was pragmatic in that it based its conclusions on the tradition of the actual laws observed in the polity rather than on an overarching theory of law. It was conservative in that it tended to think that long-established common laws of realms should not be discarded wholesale and replaced by novel and untried systems of legislation.

According to Coleridge, the moral principle of natural justice—which he regarded as the transcendental "Idea" of Natural Law—could only express and preserve itself through material, fallible, and specific incarnations in historical, national, and local institutions. Thus, although the general idea of justice was the same the world over, argued Coleridge, the actual shape which it would take in Babylon in the time of Hammurabi would be different from that it would take in Bristol in the time of George III. The universal "Idea" of justice, Coleridge asserted, mediated itself through variations in customs, geography, moral standards, and governmental power. In particular, the "Idea" of justice emerged through the everyday give and take of the law courts and juries of a polity as dictated by circumstances over time, rather than through the interminable abstractions written by legal theorists. Particular statutes had a duty to reflect the law of reason as best they could, Coleridge maintained. Still, given his postulate of man's fallible knowledge of transcendental (or divine) ideas such as justice, Coleridge asserted that it was impossible to attempt to write down in full, and thereby fix and codify forever, the principles of Natural Law. Nor was it possible or desirable to use such a contrived code to run actual societies.

Coleridge assumed that general universal principles were so complex and pure as to be unsusceptible to concretion in a single set of particular rules. He offered an example of this disharmony in a marginal note that he appended to the Huguenot natural-rights theorist Pierre Jurieu's historical reflections on church councils. Coleridge wrote that "a general council" of the church "may be the best attainable Judge" of "what is fittest or most expedient for the Church" at any given moment, "at that any one particular time." On the other hand, he asserted, "a general council is not, and without arrogation of a divine attribute cannot be assumed to be, a compet[e]nt judge of the Truth in itself." Such a council made up of fallible human beings was assuredly not a competent judge "of all truths, relatively to all ages, all future times."[24] If such were the case with a purportedly inspired general council of the Catholic Church, it presumably was all the more evident in the instance of the British Parliament, which had (almost) never made the claim to be acting under the inspiration of God.

It was in the light of this distinction between the "Idea" of something aspired to by a government and the fallible customs and institutions by means of which they edged their way toward that goal that Coleridge drew a sharp line between Common Law *custom* and *statutes* such as the Gagging Acts. For Coleridge, the *general principles* of the English Common Law went far beyond the positive rules enacted by the Parliament and printed in the *Statutes of the Realm*. Had law been only a simple matter of statutory algorithms applied to certain facts, Coleridge implied, then the courts could be dispensed with and a simple printed copy of the statutes (along with a single reader of that copy who would act as judge) would be enough to dispense justice. As it was, the Common Law required contextual reasoning by judge and jury. This contextual reasoning included considerations of intent and other mitigating factors in the cause. It demanded thought be given to precedents from similar causes (as remembered in printed books of judgments by famous jurists in the major courts or in unwritten local or judicial memory). It required judicious attention to the habit and repute of the accused. It requested the jury's discretion in judging the value of stolen goods so as to be a misdemeanor or a hanging felony. It allowed judicial offers of mercy from the bench or commutation of sentence in the case of hanging offences. English juries, judges, and lawyers regularly exercised discretion as well as independent action beyond the boundaries of statute. Such discretion was not only tolerated by that legal system, it was actively solicited.

Individual "Judges indeed" might try to warp the law to their own purposes, "might endeavour to transfer to these laws their own flexibility." For, as Coleridge cynically remarked, "what will judges not do?"[25] Judges might bend or even break the law in overzealous and blind attempts to condemn someone for a crime they considered heinous, even if the party in question currently on trial was not guilty. Judges may be honest or not, Coleridge argued, but their counsel should be restricted by custom to specific points of law, written or unwritten, and not indulge in direction as to facts.

British juries had historically served as a brake on the enthusiasms of such hanging judges.[26] Although the practical abuses of British courts had caused Coleridge to distrust individual judges, Braxfield for example, he retained his faith in the English system of law as vindicated by the honesty and power of the average juror. Coleridge had boasted in the wake of the acquittals in the State Trials of 1794 that "English judges might make strange interpretations . . . but English Juries could not and would not hear them." Coleridge emphasized the degree to which an English jury knew what it *felt* to be the truth *despite* any bullying and browbeating which they might receive from the judge.[27] This faith was upheld by the acquittal of twelve radicals in 1794, despite the best efforts of government to convict them. Juries had often blocked the efforts of the judge to convict in centuries of historic cases such as Throckmorton's case of 1554, the Quakers' Case of 1678, and Hardy's case in 1794. Coleridge specifically accused Pitt, Grenville, and Dundas of trying to remove the traditional discretionary power of the jury by their wording of the new law. He charged this ministerial triumvirate and not the House of Commons at large with attempting to confuse and delude English juries by muddling the law beyond comprehension.[28]

Thus, for Coleridge the Common Law system represented the consensus of a cumulative, suprastatutory wisdom of practice and habitude over time. Common Law decisions were derived through practice in the historic courts and were applied in practice to individual cases that occurred in particular and local circumstances. For Coleridge, the Common Law revealed its accord with higher principles of reason and justice through its durability and historical continuity. Particular Statutes of the Realm, taken individually, did not partake of this "cumulative wisdom."

Coleridge considered particular statutes to be too localized and "presentist," too often overtly political in their inception and their execution, to articulate any principle of universal truth in and of themselves. Bad bills, such as the Gagging Acts of 1795, and even good bills such as the *Habeas Corpus* Act of 1678, appeared in order to address the issues and circumstances of the day. A government could only shape long-term legal policy by carefully and discreetly shaping the preexisting complex of rules by interpretation and by improving the education, the moral norms, and the professional habits of those deputized to enforce those rules.

In a given legal system, there were a number of arcane customs, procedures, and norms that each, like the various strands in a spider's web, contributed integrity and strength to the whole. Would-be reformers of a legal system had to be aware that certain aspects of that system that might seem antiquated or arcane actually accomplished important tasks when considered in context. Unless one understood how and why the part functioned within a system, one would be unwise to remove or amend it beyond recognition.

Coleridge dealt with this interrelatedness of the parts of a given system in his lecture of 1795 on Mosaic law, the legal system that in his eyes had the greatest plausible claim to be in accord with divine reason and will. Reflecting on the imagined possibility that "any" individual member of his Bristol audience "had the legislative power committed to [him] for the next hundred years" in the manner that Moses had, Coleridge wondered at the feasibility and outcome of such an experiment. The individual in question would have unlimited authority to write and introduce statute but not to execute them or judge offenders against those laws. Given those terms, the individual in question would be expected to "introduce a pure republic" or "perhaps an abolition of all individual property . . . at the end of [that century]," that is, by 1895. (The achievement of a "pure" republic in England and an end to the ownership of all property, it will be recalled, were two projects that Coleridge saw as inherently difficult, theoretically problematic, and probably not realistic goals given current moral standards.) He concluded that "a variety of laws" in the system would prove "useful only as tending to a better form of things," that is, as means to a more significant end. In the end, the interrelationship of the laws was such that seemingly useless or arcane or imperfect pieces actually accomplished important work within the system as a whole. "We are not hastily to conclude an ordinance or action trifling," argued Coleridge, "simply because at first sight we do not perceive its uses." "Many ordinances [in the law of Moses] which would appear trifling or injurious if considered as universal and perpetual might have been highly useful" in the context of their specific civilization and culture, he concluded.[29]

Coleridge's parable of the legislator with a century to perfect a country by statute alone was, of course, meant to stun his Bristol audience with the sheer impossibility of the task. He thus forced upon them the recognition that civilizations were not made or broken by statute alone, although bad statute more easily and rapidly destroyed a polity than good legislation constructed it. His parable was a thinly veiled argument for the wisdom and complexity of the unwritten constitution, as well as for traditional law, however "trifling" or "injurious" it might seem. Even a good-hearted Bristolian given a century to transform the English people, he insinuated, could not instill universal principles of reason (or cultural habits such as disregard for property) in that people by acts of Parliament alone. For statute, by virtue of its fixity and specificity, was an incredibly awkward and counterproductive method of expressing vague and general moral truths. It was not possible to formulate, without the divine and infinite wisdom that only God possessed, a law code that would be a universal assertion of truth. Legal systems therefore had to fumble along as best they could using the cumulative historical wisdom of their tradition and the grounds of common sense and judgment.

Given the inevitable fallibility of human legislation, Coleridge wondered how the legislation of Parliament could be drafted to *reflect* the general principles of justice and reason in light of the contingencies of historical change and the impossibility of *encoding* them. Coleridge aspired to know how laws could be made productive of or even harmonious with morality. He had already suggested the connection between policies of government, rules of law, and principles of morality in his consideration of the "right" of property. He argued in the Bristol lectures that "the right of landed property *made* [the idea that one might own such property] consistent with the prevailing ideas of justice" (my italics).

Coleridge implied that in politics pragmatic considerations and the lessons of experience were a better guide to practice than pure theory. This was not for Coleridge a distinction between the "bad science" of the French theorists versus the "good pragmatism" of the English traditionalists. It was instead the distinction between that "bad" hypertheoretical science that claimed mathematical certainty and in doing so held onto its theories in the teeth of the evidence and that "good" theoretical science that only claimed moral certainty when and if warranted and which based any "hypothesis" on "phenomena." This Coleridgean pragmatism, therefore, was not irrational, nor was it celebratory of tradition for its own sake. Instead, it was truly scientific. For in the natural sciences ("natural philosophy"), Coleridge asserted, "we scruple not to adopt a hypothesis as true which solves Phaenomena [sic] in a simple and easy manner." He added, "if no other [explanation for the phenomenon] can be produced, that gives a similar solution, the probability [of the hypothesis being valid] amounts to a *moral certainty*. . . . A Rule is given and demonstrated to be the true one, if it solves all the cases to which it can be applied."[30] In this sense the law was more than mere rules. As ultimate sovereign over the king and the houses of Lords and Commons, both transhistorical and the creature of time and place, the law existed as a social matrix.

Coleridge made a clear distinction between particular statutes or rules and law as a larger process. Proceeding from this assumption, he began *The Plot Discovered* with a consideration of the sovereignty of Parliament, which for Coleridge was subordinate to the sovereignty of law. He quoted James Burgh's *Political Disquisitions*: "We have entrusted to Parliament the guardianship of our liberties, not the power of surrendering them."[31]

Implicitly, Coleridge believed that it was not within the power of Parliament to abrogate or abolish the subject's fundamental liberties as defined in basic constitutional documents such as Magna Carta or the 1689 Declaration of Rights. Coleridge was sensible to the fact that most subjects did not understand the nature or the powers of their rights under the law or their position within the Common Law system. He acknowledged the wit of Samuel Horsley's acidic Tory observation that "the mass of people have nothing to do with the laws but obey them."[32] Coleridge nevertheless argued against Horsley that if the "people had nothing to do with the laws" in practice, they had everything to do with them in principle. As Coleridge defined them, the civil liberties of the subject resided within the existing power and spirit of the English law. These constituted civil liberties were the "majesty" of the nation, and Coleridge embodied his opposition to the statute in the melodramatic cry: "Ere yet this foul treason against the majesty of man, ere yet this blasphemy against the goodness of God be registered among our statutes, I enter my protest!"[33] Coleridge considered it a "treason against the majesty of man," the common subject of Britain, a treason which he implicitly saw as the corruption of the laws, if the two acts were "registered among our statutes." Where Parliament created unlawful laws, he argued, Parliament exceeded its sovereignty. Emphasizing this distinction, Coleridge concluded his catalogue of perils with a warning that men of conscience had to act rapidly "ere yet it be made legal for Ministers to act with vigour beyond the law."[34]

Coleridge's distinction between rules and law in the larger sense was consistent with the arguments of common lawyers of the sixteenth and seventeenth century that placed sovereign power in the *law* rather than in any one man or set of men. Coleridge did not dispute that Parliament had the supreme power to enact statutes, but he considered that activity as only a small part of "making law" in the larger sense of refining, shaping, and molding the Common Law to the changing face of English culture and society. Not unlike Coke, Coleridge considered, that unreasonable statutes were "inapplicable" if not "unlawful."[35]

Coleridge's conception of law was clearly something larger than the simple recognition of rules. He viewed the formative value of the law as subsisting in the Common Law: in precedent, custom, and tradition. More than this, he regarded the law as a living process and not merely a static compilation of statutes. Coleridge emphasized the active element of interpretation through the human intercession of judges and jurors. He echoed the opinions of the Swiss jurist J. L. DeLolme in distinguishing between statute (the written law), immemorial custom (unwritten law), and the common law that mediated statute and custom.[36] This deeply historical continuity of the Common Law, which had been defined and memorialized in Mathew Hale's writings, was the underlying source of the Common Law's capacity for reasonability and mediation.[37]

The mediating component of the Common Law was that which adjusted for the particular, the individual, the contingent: in short, the human and humane qualities of the law. It was through this process of mediation that reason became manifest. Through the accumulated wisdom of custom and practice in case law, common lawyers and judges distilled principles of reason. This formulation of principle, along with the establishment of precedent, constituted an active historical voice in the law. In Coleridge's view, this active historical voice constituted a distinctive third component, alongside rules and cases, in the law of the land. It survived in reasons for judgment, where judges employed historical precedents alongside longstanding principles to interpret statutes as they applied to individual cases. These new interpretations were, in turn, incorporated into the body of law; they became custom as they changed custom.

With this process in mind, Coleridge was acutely critical of the attempt to integrate commentaries into rules and to encode precedent into a positive body of laws. With respect to the crisis of the day he wrote that the "old treason laws" were "superseded" by "the exploded commentaries of obsequious crown lawyers." Through the government's preferring a gloss by a servile judge to an accurate interpretation of the spirit of the old law, "the commentary has conspired against the text." The magnitude of this crime was such that it was as if "a vile and useless slave," legal commentary, "has conspired to dethrone its venerable master," the treason law of King Edward.[38]

Coleridge was not upholding the primacy of positive law over common law. He was arguing against the corruption of judicial process, which was the consequence of according commentary the positive force of statute. By "text," he referred not to any particular rule but to the laws of England. Coleridge maintained that where rules were drafted too complexly, in an attempt to articulate whatever "absolute" principle the government of the day required, there existed a vicious corruption of the law. His barbed reference to "exploded commentary" and "obsequious Crown lawyers" was a reformist challenge to precisely this sort of vice and corruption. Vice was often cloaked by the creation of labyrinthine and ornate embellishments. The best and most virtuous rules, Coleridge contended, were the simplest.

Coleridge construed the two acts as obfuscatory, undermining the reason of the law. Beyond elevating commentaries over rules, the prime minister had attempted to redraft the existing statutes in order to incorporate abstract principles. As Pitt attempted to destroy the clarity of the old treason laws, he overrode historical wisdom. Coleridge believed that this was a true violation of natural justice. The government's new legislation was, he believed, ahistorical rather than transhistorical. It was, as such, arbitrary in creation and unreasonable in intent. Consequently, it was as artificial and abhorrent an innovation as anything proposed by Robespierre and the Jacobin tribunals. How then to defeat the "Plotters"? Coleridge enlisted the aide of the Bristol gentlemen in a defense (and reform) of British liberty.

Coleridge aimed his critique in *The Plot Discovered* specifically at Pitt's "unconstitutional" ministerial actions. By doing so, Coleridge expressed his faith in the basic soundness of the constitutional status quo prior to 1795. While Coleridge did not shrink from invoking the names of the great republican writers of the past, his position on constitutional reform in *The Plot* diverged from more authentically "radical" opposition attacks. Coleridge's opinions, by comparison to those of Thelwall and the "Jacobins," mainly relied on a set of older Whig arguments and cannot accurately be classified in the ranks of "radical" antigovernment polemic.[39]

Coleridge's conclusions in 1795 on what was best for Britain in terms of change and reform never employed the "radical" political theory of the natural "Rights of Man and the Citizen" nor the avowal of "Liberty, Equality, and Fraternity." Indeed, he was never so heavily invested in the success of the ultrademocratic, *truly* "Jacobin" wing of the French Revolution as were those who lent their active talents towards advancing the Revolution in France itself (Paine) or to forming coherent political groups dedicated to a speedy and wide-ranging British Reform (Hardy, Thelwall).

In his earliest political writings in 1795, Coleridge had already repudiated Robespierre and the Jacobin party's murderous harnessing of the sansculottes and had additionally condemned the *relatively* moderate Dantonists and Brissotins for opening the gate for the escape of the beast of unchecked popular power. This is not to say that Coleridge utterly detested everything that had taken place in France after the Tennis Court Oath, as the flamboyant high Tory reactionaries did. Like Wordsworth, Coleridge felt elation at the "dawn" brought about by the collapse of Bourbon absolutism. The wicked empire of Bourbon despotism, after all, had been a stock villain in the loyalist Georgian polemic of Whig and Tory pamphleteers for over a century. Thus, one could without contradiction support British freedoms in the constitution as it stood (imperfectly) in 1789 and extend congratulations to the vanquishers of the lettre de cachet and other relics of Bourbon tyranny. The true falling-off from admiration for the Revolution amongst Coleridge and other Whig constitutionalists came with the steady arrival of the massacres, the breakdown of constitutional rule, and the institution of revolutionary dictatorship from 1791 to 1794.

Coleridge and other moderate constitutionalist "pro-French" thinkers had never supported such actions as the Terror, the destruction of the aristocrats as a class, or the extirpation of the French royal family. He had not turned against these policies, for he never supported them in the first place. Therefore, Coleridge's disapproval (renunciation or "recantation') did not amount to "repudiation," "treason," or "apostasy" against the "cause," so much as a righteous anger that what had begun so promisingly had derailed and utterly demolished itself. If one were to "place" Coleridge in the milieu of the French Revolution, one might position him in the environs of Lafayette, Mirabeau, and the early Feuillants, or in the ranks of the revivers of the powers of the propertied among the Thermidoreans. Given that Paine himself narrowly escaped the guillotine for the crime of excessive moderation, it is inconceivable that Coleridge would have fared very well among the true "Jacobins" in France. On the other hand, Coleridge detested the ultraroyalists who were willing to waste English lives and money in order to restore the Bourbon despotism in all its malicious and unrestrained power. Thus, in 1795 Coleridge was caught, like so many others of his generation, in the middle: he hated Jacobinism and Terror and hated Bourbonism and absolute monarchy and did not wish to see either succeed.

Indeed, it is more correct to see Coleridge's political lexicon in 1795 as not waving the republican *tricoleur* of universalist French theories but as repairing and re-erecting the old aristocratic banners of the ancient constitution and the Common Law originally sewn by the great avatars of the *these nobiliare* in France (Montesquieu), Switzerland (DeLolme), and Britain (Blackstone,

Burke). Coleridge's ideas in 1795 owed an incalculable debt to the work of the very "dough-baked Patriots" and "self-styled constitutionalists" at whom he is *presumed* to have jeered in his *Moral and Political Lecture* of 1795.[40] Coleridge by 1795 was deeply grounded in the European *these nobiliare* and appears to have accepted its central emphases on the benefits of constitutional balance (between the king, Lords, and Commons), preserving and mending the old whenever possible, and evading broad-brush statutory reform. Because of his fundamental accord with these old aristocratic, constitutionalist writers, Coleridge never ventured very far into the high-democratic and republican arguments that were made by the true "radicals" of 1795. Far from contributing to a radical or democratic republicanism newborn in 1789, his arguments in *The Plot* reflect a subtle and careful constitutionalism rooted in the works of the 1730s through the 1780s. He argued for the stabilizing balances of free opinion, "the King in parliament," and the sovereignty of law over the will either of absolute royal authority or of absolute popular authority.

Such preoccupations have long been associated, both by modern and contemporary critics, with "True" Whig ideology. The Rockinghamite "New Whig" Edmund Burke had identified these more "conservative" or classical strands of Whiggery in his *Appeal from the New to the Old Whigs*.[41] An ideology that reached back to the seventeenth century and beyond, "True" (or real or loyal) Whiggism was a variant strain of "Country" anticentralism that relied heavily on ideas of constitutional balance, moderation, and Common Law for its conception of sovereignty.[42]

Coleridge's "radical" attack on Pitt, therefore, was only as "radical" as the invective against "corruption" and "influence of the Crown" that Bolingbroke and Amhurst had used against Walpole in the 1730s *Craftsman* essays and that John Dunning had employed against Lord North in his famous "Resolution" of 1780. Like Bolingbroke and Dunning, Coleridge saw the influence of a powerful first minister expanding so quickly that it threatened to devour the theretofore independent powers of judges and lawmakers.

The Plot contributed to a defense of Whig "revolution principles" and a constitutional tradition that looked to Cicero rather than Machiavelli, Cato, or Robespierre for its model of an ideal republic. Coleridge combined in the pamphlet his conception of classical republicanism with ideas of Common Law, a system of checks and balances, and a view of history that he derived from a variety of political sources: the Tory Bolingbroke, the Old Whig Shaftesbury, the reformer James Burgh,[43] and the conservative Edmund Burke, as well as from those more "radical" specters of liberty whom he mentioned in *The Plot*: "Milton, Locke, Sydney, [and] Harrington." Coleridge believed that the works of the great republican writers of the seventeenth century such as Milton and Har-rington provided a shocking example of a set of authors formerly considered to be innocuous or even patriotic who would be branded seditious by the passage of the bills. The argument he employed in defense of British liberty was essen-tially True Whiggish or Old Constitutional Tory rather than republican in the contemporary sense. It paid heed to the moral condition of the citizenry in the republic and the problems of wealth in terms of national virtue and renovation rather than to the sorts of bills and charters of rights that confirmed the funda-mental rights of the subject, which had achieved a sort of apotheosis above the reach of Parliamentary power.[44]

The heroes of Coleridge's pantheon, it must be remembered, were not only heroes to "radicals" in the late eighteenth century.[45] The use of the mythicized "pantheon of liberty" by members of the "party of liberty" of all stripes was *not* an indication that one agreed with all of the heroes' particular deeds, *nor* that one thought that admiring sturdy republicans such as Milton made a man a republican, but that one concurred in their impassioned and stalwart defense of the chartered (or natural) rights of the subject against the incursions of tyrants. The invocations of the great shades of the heroes of lib-erty by Coleridge in *The Plot* was an effort to make such tyrants as Pitt realize that, like Robespierre, they "had a lith in their necks." They could not, he warned, run roughshod over the liberties of the people without the people striking back in defense of their liberties. To be sure, "corruption" presented certain practical, although not insurmountable, problems for the constitution. Accordingly, Coleridge sought moderate solutions in his ambitions for reform.

Practical problems of application, whether questions of revenue or the ef-ficacy of the electorate, had dogged the constitution before Pitt's attempt to destroy it. But Coleridge perceived these to be problems of misapplication and not fundamental errors of structure or principle. To use later Coleridgean ter-minology, the "Idea" of the British Constitution balanced between king, Lords, and Commons, executive, legislative, and judicial, was essentially a sound one. Only the practice of it had been warped and bent by years of cor-ruption and purchase and exchange of seats by aristocrats and Crown officers. In his assumption that the "Idea" of the balanced constitution was definitely correct despite the excrescences that had grown upon it through corruption, Coleridge again emphasized the discrepancies that existed between the ideal and the actual: the "real [ideal] world," true and pure and perfect, and the "moral [material] world," fallible and impure and imperfect.

Coleridge focused on the sicknesses of the realm that merited a moderate Parliamentary reform and derided the instances of borough-mongering and corruption which he saw as playing into Pitt's hands. Turning to what he perceived as an overwhelming bias in favor of the executive, he criticized the powers of the treasury and the seats that it controlled in the Commons through placemen, pensioners, and other Crown officials. The other practical problem was corruption, and specifically the corruption that attended elections.

In the "corruption" of Parliament, Coleridge blamed all three branches of the government. He blamed the Crown, which through the Civil List and the first minister's patronage controlled and gave out Treasury-funded seats to court and administration lackeys, placemen, and pensioners. He blamed the Lords, which owned and distributed seats in rotten boroughs to idle sons and pliant minions. He blamed the Commons, which undertook their civic duty of electing members of Parliament not with a sense of sobriety and dignity but in a roistering chaos of "the drunkenness, perjury, and murder that attend a general election." Indeed, the behavior of the common people at any given election was so bad, complained Coleridge, that "every honest man [might] wish that the lesser number of the house of commons [who were elected "freely" by voters in open boroughs and counties] were elected as [are elected] the majority (or actual legislative power) [of the House of Commons;] that is by the one hundred sixty-two peers, gentlemen, and treasury."[46]

Coleridge, unlike most of his "radical" contemporaries, was a timocrat rather than a democrat in his plans for Parliamentary reform. Even in his relatively "wild" youth, when he saw himself as blowing the tinny trumpet of sedition, he could never quite shake off his scorn for the great unwashed. During the entirety of 1795, he retained a subtle bias in favor of the responsible patrician elements of government and a suspicion of the general, more plebeian elements of the electorate. Even in his most "democratic" moments, his partly subconscious, detestation of the multitude and the mob would surface: note that he could not defend the "Majesty" of the common people in its own right, but instead cloaked it in the corporate and more decorous "Majesty" of King George. Even in his so-called "radical years" of 1794 to 1796, Coleridge regarded the "citizens," into whose hands the radicals wished to commend the spirit of the laws, as not (yet) the somber, devoted, sober-sided Roman-style people the radicals imagined them to be. In Coleridge's *Plot,* the British "citizen" was admittedly more "an antique Roman" than a Briton. Unfortunately, as of 1795 the British common man was the wrong kind of antique Roman: not the dignified, self-sacrificing, Spartan saint of the Catonian era that the "radicals" pictured him as, but rather the loutish, dole-besotted begetter of "drunkenness, perjury, and murder" at elections, the sort of Roman who had sold the imperial dignity to the highest bidder in the time of Galba. If those plebeians who already had the franchise went to the polls drunk and were swayed in their votes more by bribes and hired bully-boys than by independent thought, then how could expanding the number of voters purify the constitution?

Yet, again criticizing the constitutionalist's position, Coleridge considered Paley's defense of the propertied interest equally flawed. Paley was not so much interested in reform of process—that is, a broadening of the number of Britons eligible to vote for M.P.s—as in the reform of representation: a betterment of the quality and wisdom of the men returned as members to those seats in the Commons. Paley argued that "if men the most likely by their qualifications to know and promote the public interest, be actually returned to parliament, it signifies little who returns them."[47] Paley theorized that once such an appointment of wise men to the house had been made, the large number of the members in the Commons should diffuse and balance their interests. Furthermore, appeals to a broader consensus would do no better. "If such a number of such men," Coleridge quoted Paley as saying, "be liable to the influence of corrupt motives, what [more democratically elected] assembly of men will be secure from the same danger?" All of "the different interests" in the nation, Paley had argued, "are *actually* represented and of course the people *virtually*."[48]

Nonetheless, it should be apparent that although Coleridge was not in favor of expanded democratic franchise as a panacea, he held a great degree of scorn for the corruptions that he saw in the unreformed Parliament of his day. He was especially hateful towards those legislators whom he saw as Parliamentary mercenaries rather than as independent-thinking legislators. Coleridge's later 1801 contention, that an independent ownership of substantial property was an essential qualification for M.P.s that kept them from becoming rootless freelances who would sell their talents to the highest bidder, was already evident in *The Plot*. He noted Paley's observation that "many individuals eminent by their abilities and eloquence" that is, "in plain language, needy young men of genius," were "occasionally picked up by one party or other, presented with title or place, and then brought forwards as rhetorical gladiators for the amusement of the good people of England." "A prize or two gained at Oxford," Coleridge smirked, "sometimes proves an excellent advertisement to a young man who wants the lucrative office of an accommodating legislator."[49] Throughout his career, even in his "Tory" years, Coleridge maintained the ardor of his "Country" invective against the "needy young" entering a Parliamentary arena where they could only serve as farcical "rhetorical gladiators" and "accommodating legislator[s]." Even in 1795, Coleridge saw the ideal M.P. as a man who had property that kept him from being "needy" and thus kept him in the category of honorable men, as citizen-soldiers rather than as mercenary gladiators.

Yet even in the aftermath of the candid and sarcastic tour around Britain's corrupted and sad political circus to which he treated his audience, Coleridge believed that unreformed England was not *yet* a despotism, not in the Ottoman or the Venetian or the Jacobin senses of the word. He was prepared to pile abuse upon the various toadies and underlings who plagued the Commons, but he was not prepared to shift the blame for this condition onto the structure of property in the state or the "Idea" of the tripartite constitution or the existence of hereditary honors such as monarchy and peerage. As theatrical as Coleridge became in *The Plot*, he was never capable of reaching the height of "radical" hyperbole that would have led him to denounce the Britain of his day as a "despotic" realm. "This conclusion," he insisted, "we disavow."[50] As of 1795, Coleridge saw Britain in great danger of becoming a tyranny under Pitt, but not yet fallen into that condition.

Indeed, Coleridge thought that the constitution even in its unreformed state had most of the features it needed to represent the public will. He argued, for instance, that the voice of public opinion was intended, by virtue of the nature and structure of the *constitution*, to be listened to by the monarch and Parliament even in the unreformed state of the law and the constitution. He argued for the responsible vigilance of the men of property, and for the emphasis on property as a guarantee of incorruptibility in M.P.s. And he implied the need for a moderate and specific reform of Parliament against the encroachment of the Crown and the corruption of ministerial and aristocratic patronage. In this regard, Coleridge's 1795 speech to the Bristol gentlemen, while a rallying cry against tyranny, must be understood within the long constitutional memory of measured resistance.

It must be recalled that Coleridge was addressing men of property in his lecture at Bristol. His appeal was therefore to the independent backbencher, the honorable opposition, and those interested citizens to whom they were responsible and who through the liberty of the press made their influence felt. In short, Coleridge was addressing the enfranchised patriot of property and standing. His patriot was to be found both in the house, as a member of Parliament, and "out of doors" as a private citizen. Coleridge emphasized that there was a direct line between these different spheres of influence, between a representation both virtual and direct.

The text of *The Plot Discovered* presents a politically moderate if rhetorically impassioned Whig critique of corruption and centralization in the Pitt administration. Coleridge's constitutional criticism was neither republican nor democratic in the more extreme sense but contributed to a defense of the landed oligarchy and the propertied interest against the encroachment of an arbitrary executive. Against such an encroachment, Coleridge recognized the right and indeed the duty of responsible propertied resistance in defense of parliamentary sovereignty.

In the spirit of moderation and rational criticism, and deliberately setting himself apart from the popular radicals of the London Corresponding Society, Coleridge began his lecture with something of a disclaimer. Referring to Bolingbroke, he remarked that "true political moderation" consisted in "not opposing the interests of government *except when great and national interests are at stake.*" When the great and national interests were at stake, the citizen was bound not to overreact. He was justified only "in opposing them with such a degree of warmth as is *adequate to the nature of the evil.*"[51]

Yet Bolingbroke was very careful in his defense of resistance to emphasize that he did not advocate an ongoing right to constantly oppose government, as he believed some of Locke's adherents had done, nor did he mean to defend nonresistance and divine right as was practiced under the old King James II. Bolingbroke simply argued, as did most men of his age who were not Jacobites or High Tories, that every man had the right to resist tyranny in extremis. The question for Coleridge in 1795, as it had been for Bolingbroke before him, was how did one define the limits of abuse? What constituted tyranny? Coleridge drew a principle from Common Law in his allusion to what has been called "necessary and sufficient force." Specific and limited abuses by government that threatened the national interest were not to be met with a complete termination of the social contract and a descent into insurrection and lawlessness. Rather, government must be resisted and criticized surgically. Continuing his gloss of Bolingbroke, he asserted that "to oppose" government "upon any other ground" than true defects and emergencies was wicked. It was especially factious, Coleridge noted, "to oppose things which are not blameworthy" or "which are of no material consequence to the national Interest." Using "such violence as may disorder the harmony of government" was "certainly faction" and not to be tolerated or allowed as legitimate.[52]

Coleridge introduced several of his pivotal concerns in this passage: a national interest, the harmony of government, and the nature of faction. The emphasis upon a harmony of government was a critical component of Coleridge's conception of a limited and specific resistance. He believed that the proper sphere for criticism or resistance was through the editing and adjustment of specific conditions of abuse and mistake. These were to be considered in terms of particular instances and as they occurred. Coleridge distrusted systematic solutions to human problems, and, while he looked for universal goals, he accepted the necessity of specific means.[53] He attempted a limited and specific critique of ministerial abuses in his pamphlet and argued that members of the house must do likewise when they observed treachery in the cabinet. Resistance must be constructive; it must restore and conserve the existing framework of the constitution and not promote further dissension.

Promoting a loyal opposition, Coleridge's "patriot" had a duty to oppose those elements of government that threatened the greater structure of the constitution as an active force. Coleridge called this active structure "the harmony of government." With regard to the merits of opposition, he noted that it was "likewise faction, and faction of the worst kind," if one decided in a true crisis or case of authentic oppression "either not to oppose at all, or not to oppose in earnest where the principles of liberty are endangered."[54]

Coleridge referred to the "principles of liberty" and the national interest in the preceding passage. His "harmony of government" was the best safeguard for these principles. He argued that the constitution and the sovereignty of the law preserved individual freedom and promoted the national interest. Coleridge's conception of a national interest was as an aggregate of individual interest that did not exist as a collective or general will. In this regard, there was an individualistic rather than broadly communitarian basis to his concept of government. Coleridge suggested that an individual showed "true political moderation" if he, "with all feelings of abhorrence and with all powers of fearless argument" within his power, "gird[ed] himself up to oppose the bill for the more effectively preventing seditious meetings and assemblies."[55]

Coleridge contended that it was not books, assemblies, or public meetings but the government's own legislation that generated sedition. He argued that Pitt's legislation was a provocation to unbridled and ill-considered resistance outside the house. Coleridge informed his audience that the bill was in itself a betrayal of the constitution and the harmony of interests that the constitution was truly meant to represent. If passed, Pitt's legislation would create a seditious assembly in the cabinet as it allowed ministers to conspire against the law. Only by opposing the government's current legislation could the "true Patriot" act against faction and sedition that threatened from within. Only by preserving the legislated discourse of opinion and law could the "true Patriot" defend the constitution.

CHAPTER 4

Liberty and Law

THE PURSUIT OF liberty, like the pursuit of happiness, is a hunt in which the ostensibly sought-after quarry is almost never captured by those hunters who give chase to it. This is generally because the hunt usually dissolves into squabbles about what species of quarry is actually the most desirable and how the prizes shall be shared out. In essence, although there was in many polities of the early nineteenth century a stated desire to be "free" and to enjoy "liberty" rather than "oppression," the differing ways in which these words were used makes one wonder if taxonomically one would not be better-off discussing separate species of "freedoms" and "oppressions" rather than addressing them as if they were unified concepts. The similarity of the diction of the widespread effusions of support for "liberty" from 1801 to 1830 among the various factions in the United Kingdom concealed a vast difference between *strategies* of how to obtain that liberty, *visions* of what that liberty would look like, and *timetables* of when that liberty might be perfectly achieved, if it had not already been achieved. As John Selden pointed out in the mid-seventeenth century, the language of "liberty" was so pervasive and so poorly defined even in *his* time that would-be absolute monarchs used its lexicon to make their points on occasion. In Coleridge's own time, when the "Tories" were in truth the last fundamentalist believers in the "Whig" "Principles of 1688," this language of liberty that employed the same words for different ideas was even more baffling. In the time of the American Rebellion, Lord North had used the same sort of flowing phrases in the defense of "liberty" as had his enemy John Adams. In the years of the French Revolution, the Younger Pitt had spoken as eloquently in favor of "liberty," as had his critic Thomas Paine. Indeed, even the crustiest and most senile Tories of Coleridge's era could not have been coaxed into offering up huzzahs for "oppression," or roused into damning "liberty." They, too, believed that they were the "defenders of liberty." One cannot dismiss this similarity as the result of "mere cant." What made late Georgian Britain nearly unique among states existing from 1800 to 1850 is that discussion did not focus on whether it was a good thing to have "liberty" or not, but instead focused on how best to attain the liberty that all professed to desire.

The study of a culture such as later Georgian Britain, in which real differences in goals and methods of seekers after "liberty" are masked by the similarities in the political values and vocabularies which define them as different social and political groups, makes for a fundamentally more difficult problem than the study of a culture in which there is a true bifurcation between authoritarian and pro-liberty lexica. How can one make sense of a term that was used by so many for so many divergent and incompatible purposes?

Understanding Coleridge's political and social "science" presses us to delimit and describe the ways in which he thought about this fog-shrouded and complex issue of "liberty." Arguably, the most distinctive and independent aspects of Coleridge's political thought were to be found in his conception of liberty. His innovative views of liberty in the 1820s set him apart from the purported "Toryism" of his late career, just as his views of liberty in the 1790s separated him from the Painite radicalism with which his earliest political writings have been associated.[1] I suggest that in his analysis of liberty, Coleridge once again employed his characteristic dynamic vision of the "Idea" (in this case the "Idea" of liberty). I also wish to suggest that Coleridge offered a language of liberty that presented a chance to resolve the longstanding apparent conflict between liberty-as-private-property and liberty-as-community-equality.

In order to comprehend the magnitude of Coleridge's achievement in transcending the traditional antimonies of individualism/property and communitarianism/equality, it will be necessary to do two things. First, it will be necessary to see what a powerful chokehold this dichotomy had on the Atlantic political tradition in the early-nineteenth-century discursive world that Coleridge inhabited. Second, it will be necessary to understand that the power of those dichotomies has continued to be so great that they still shape, and even distort, modern thought on the subject.

Coleridge produced two rival theories of the Commonwealth's role in advancing freedom: Liberty-in-Private-Property and Liberty-in-Community-Equality. Coleridge's conception of "political justice" rested on his simultaneous commitment to what some have considered two contradictory visions of liberty: liberty inherent in the goals of unfettered private property, and liberty inherent in the goals of enhanced equality and community. Much of nineteenth- and twentieth-century political theory has been taken up with the issue of whether a society that maximizes the individual rights of private property holders can also maximize the social equality and rights of the community as a whole. The solutions presented by liberalism and laissez-faire placed the balance of power in the hands of liberty in the shape of *property*, presuming that the freedom to use one's own property (whether land, labor, or money) as one pleased was most likely to ensure general social freedom. The solutions of socialism and other such redistributive theories of government placed the balance of power in the hands of liberty in the form of *equality*, suggesting that true freedom was impossible unless it was recognized that the "freedom to do as one likes" was meaningless to have-nots until they were given property or the means to obtain it. These two major lines of argument were already relatively well-drawn by the early nineteenth century in the English-speaking Atlantic world. Philosophers such as Locke, Smith, and Jefferson had stated the case for private property as the agent of liberty; philosophers such as Rousseau, Paine, Spence, and Godwin[2] had suggested that equality and redistribution of property imbalances would have to take place before "true liberty" could emerge.[3]

"Liberty" is typically defined in modern political theory as either "positive" or "negative." Isaiah Berlin was the most famous exponent of this theoretical division between "negative" liberty and "positive" liberty.[4] These terms describe the relative relationship between the holder of the liberty in question, whether an individual or a group, and the commonwealth, state, or society, which is that liberty's guarantor. "Freedom from" governmental or other social restrictions on one's actions is traditionally described in terms of "negative liberty." "Freedom to" perform certain actions or to receive certain benefits that will enable the fulfillment or accomplishment of corresponding entitlements has traditionally been associated with the idea of "positive liberty." In general, the ideology of "negative liberty," with its stress on noninterference by the governors in the property of the subject, has been associated with "individualism" and with the advocates of a limited sovereign power in the community and the state (the school of Locke, Smith, and Jefferson). As a rule, the ideology of "positive liberty," with its stress on the superior claim of the social well-being of the many over the freedoms of the few, has been associated with "communitarianism" and with the advocates of an expanded sovereign power in the active institutions of community and the state (the school of Rousseau, Paine, Spence, and Godwin).

Where the competing claims of liberty in property and liberty in community conflict, a decision must be made. A polity must either choose to shift the balance of society in favor of "freedoms from" interference by the commonwealth with one's individual liberty and property, or it must elect to pursue a program of enhancing "freedoms to" provide a minimal standard of equality for the commonwealth. In either case, a dense and thorny tangle of political questions as to which of the two alternatives creates a truer or purer form of "liberty" must be hacked through.

Debates in political theory in the final decades of the twentieth century have suggested not-so-novel ways in which the competing claims of the individual and the group may be weighed in the balance to most effectively ensure the idea of liberty. As this is not a study of contemporary political theory, I will not spend much time on post-Coleridgean thinkers on the issues of property and community. Such comments as I make on modern political thought, post-1830, will only be by way of noting that the debate on liberty versus equality in property rights is no less closer to solution 170 years after Coleridge's essential writings on the subject than it was in his era. (It is also by way of suggesting that the claim of social justice and equity in community is not a modern invention, nor inherently a "radical" one, and was quite strong even during the so-called "triumph of laissez-faire"). The most widely read modern authors on the subject, Robert Nozick[5] and John Rawls,[6] confront essentially the same problem as Coleridge confronted in his thinking about property.

Obviously, then, this balancing of community and individual claims in the matter of property is a persistently insoluble question and is not an invention of the late twentieth century. These conflictive ideas of the relationship between liberty, property, and equity as determined by law and the limits of government may be usefully employed in considering Coleridge's understanding of the idea of liberty.

Coleridge perceived liberty in terms of the "individual versus community rights" divide. Liberty, for Coleridge, was a principle of action "constituted"—that is to say, created as well as delimited—by civil society and its living institutions. He insisted that the institution of private property was the foundation of civil society and of all government. He resembled the advocates of strong property rights in his belief in property as a fundamental basis of good order in the state. Coleridge did not advocate an "absolute" or "natural" right of property based on God or *lex naturis* as certain theorists, such as Locke, famously did. But he did recognize property as a weight-bearing girder essential to the construction of a free and stable society. Such an essential girder of the state could not be "torn out" and abolished by law without similar problems ensuing as had occurred when Samson had toppled pillars in the Temple of Dagon. He regarded liberty and property as complementary, rather than antagonistic, entities.

In distinction from the standard libertarian defense of property rights, Coleridge transformed property into a dynamic, organic principle. The typical defenders of liberty in individual property treated property as a mindless set of material objects, passive chips to be accumulated and traded. Coleridge's great innovation was in considering property as a living *subject*, which acted upon its owners, rather than a passive *object*, which was only acted upon by its owners.

With resemblance to certain communitarians of his day, Coleridge stressed the organic relationship of each constituent part of society to all others and did not see a strong regulatory state as an inevitable threat to liberty.[7] He saw property not only as granting certain "freedoms from" state interference with the owner's will, but as demanding and inspiring a broad set of civic duties from the propertied classes. In line with other communitarians, Coleridge advocated consistent and firm state intervention where needed rather than total laissez-faire. His writings in support of the Factory Acts in 1818 made it clear that in a conflict between absolute liberty of property and the good of the community (i.e., the health of children), he would choose community. In that conflict, he stood on the side of reducing the Lancashire mill owners' "rights" to hire whomever they wished and the parents' "rights" to vend their childrens' labour when and where they wished in favor of the general "rights" of English children as a class not to be subjected to work in hazardous circumstances.

Coleridge differed from the standard communitarians of his era because he did not insist that property weakened the cause of commonwealth and thereby destroyed liberty. Property was not invariably corrupting to Coleridge, in the way that it had been both to condemners of property rights, such as Babeuf, and defenders of "corrupt" property, such as Mandeville. He ultimately viewed property as a constructive, rather than a destructive, moral force. Coleridge refused to embrace the commonplace views of his contemporaries that property was either morally neutral or invariably socially corrupting. In his innovative theories he envisioned private property as not only a practical necessity but as a *principle for moral improvement*, as a principle of self-actualization.[8] Throughout his career, Coleridge developed ideas both of individual agency and political institutions into a Conception of the nation-state as a trusteeship founded on property, where rights and duties must always be aligned.[9]

Coleridge's Conception of liberty and his theory of property were both components of what became an institutional social theory of the state by his last great work, the treatise *On The Constitution of the Church and State* (1830). His view of the "interdependency" of property and liberty and his vision of property as a "constructive" moral force both demonstrated a strong view that a phenomenon such as "liberty" could not be studied in isolation but must be examined with an eye to its self-reflective mutuality of influence on property and morality. In other words, liberty, property, and morality were essentially linked and interdependent forces. This view contributed to what Durkheim once identified as a protosociological tradition of political analysis.[10] This protosociological tradition examined social structures as well as laws and high political phenomena in explaining the politics of a given nation or culture.

Many critics have associated the interactive and synthetic components of Coleridge's ideas of liberty and property with the post-Kantian, post-Hegelian "German phase" of his writings (1800–1817).[11] It is equally likely that Coleridge had developed his own early "protosociological" views on organic dynamism through his readings of Montesquieu and Rousseau, who included statements about climate and manners in their estimates of the validity of a nation's constitution. He may also have owed some of his vision of the interconnectedness of society to Burke. Furthermore, one may look beyond Burke to an earlier English source: Coleridge's first readings of seventeenth-century Common Law and constitutional theory.

In the seventeenth-century treatises on sovereignty and consent, duty and right, law and morality, Coleridge traced the evolution of a Natural Law philosophy that paralleled the dynamic organism of the natural world. The nature of this world, its order and its life structure, was dynamic and dialectical. Cudworth and Newton had suggested as much in their Platonist writings on physics. Blake provided a poetic echo of this view in his account of "contrariant" opposites. Coleridge developed these ideas in his own writings as a political and moral corollary of the juridical and physical implications of natural philosophy.

Although his preoccupation with duality may be traced to his earliest writings, by 1800 Coleridge had developed a theory that he termed the "Polar Tension" of opposites applicable to ideas of property and community. This "polar tension" between the diverse concerns of private interest and public welfare was a chief focus of Coleridge's political thought after his return from Gottengen.[12] It marks the beginning of a conscious effort in his journalism as well as in his philosophical and theological writings to lay down a metaphysical foundation for a comprehensive system of political thought. In other words, it constitutes the first of Coleridge's deliberate efforts to establish a statesman's science. He believed that personal attainments, such as private property, needed to be considered not sufficient unto themselves but counterbalanced by an objective community of social "goods" in the commonwealth. The corollary of this was his belief that a community interest in equality and the social welfare of all could not be established merely by government fiat but had to be the long-term result of an aggregate of individual concerns, including those of private property holders. There was no clear priority (ranking or privileging) of individual *or* community interest in Coleridge's understanding of political institutions. This tendency to reconcile rather than rank opposites distinguished Coleridge from most of his contemporaries.

For Coleridge, freedom was not meaningful as a political "Idea" outside of its temporal, material, manifestations in civil societies. He located the "existence" of the Idea of freedom not only in a superlunary realm, or in the mind of God, but in the everyday ability of an individual to act according to his will without illegitimate constraint or obstruction of that will. The Idea of liberty, therefore, was perpetually manifesting itself in quotidian affairs. Its chief and most historic expressions of itself were in the chartered "legal" rights, powers, and "possessive dominiums" of the subject.[13] For this reason, Coleridge's view of the right of property was intrinsically connected to his conception of liberty. He regarded the "freedom" of property as inseparable from the "liberty" of a subject to dispose of or possess an object.

Coleridge's conception of liberty consistently set him the problem of reconciling a broad program of freedom of the will with necessary social constraints on action. In the course of the study of that dynamic, he also outlined the interconnection of the exercise of rights and the performance of duties. In addition, he examined the problems inherent in a government founded on a propertied trust acting to secure the "liberty of the subject" and how the sanctity of private property affected the welfare of the community, which included so many propertyless individuals.

Coleridge's bravado in grasping such a hideously thorny nettle as the relation between individual rights in property and individual responsibilities to the Commonwealth and then presenting a new model that attempted to reconcile their differences was not rewarded.[14] His dualistic, dynamic model of the state, because of its refusal to privilege one side of a duality and condemn the other, has been lambasted as timid, trimming, and cowardly. Alternatively, it has been branded with the old mark of "apostasy." The charges of inconstancy and duplicity to the cause of liberty, which met him during his lifetime, have been echoed ad nauseam by later critics, and at least one of these has seen Coleridge as a compulsive liar.[15]

But is this persistent critique of Coleridge as a traitor to the cause of liberty—either through out-and-out apostasy or fuzzy-minded, neo-Hegelian trimming, which, it was held, obscured the importance of the claims of freedom over community welfare—at all merited? John Stuart Mill, who was no meager authority on questions of individual freedom within social systems, saw the "Mature Coleridge" as a persistent and eloquent friend of liberty. Mill remarked that "the Coleridgeans, far from being Tories, were *a second liberal and even radical party*, on totally different grounds than Benthamism and vehemently opposed to it."[16] Mill's quip was an important observation, because it suggested that Mill and others already recognized the degree to which Coleridge had deviated *both* from the main-stream of "Toryism" *and* from the senior tribe of the "radicals" after 1800, the "Benthamists."[17] Coleridge, Mill thought, had rescued from oblivion "truths which Tories have forgotten, and which the prevailing school of liberalism never knew."[18]

Mill's various observations on Coleridge are important not because they provide another nail to the coffin of the vision of the mature Coleridge as a pattern-book Tory. Rather, Mill's opinion on Coleridge is of value because it shows that as early as the mid-nineteenth century, the "*totally different* grounds" of Coleridge's vision of liberty had been perceived. Mill also appreciated the degree to which Coleridge had been able to revive those "truths" that had been ignored by Tories and radicals alike. Presumably, by the "truths" that Tories had forgotten, Mill meant the basis of Toryism in a reasoned defense of constitutional liberty, based on the interest in the church and the land, rather than on ultratraditionalism. Presumably, by the "truths" which the Benthamites never knew, Mill meant Coleridge's own emphasis on moral and social factors as foundational ideas that the Benthamites (or so Mill thought) had neglected.

But beyond the assertion that the Coleridgeans and the Benthamites represented differing visions either of radical Toryism or nascent liberalism, one is returned again to the problem of these classificatory labels as such. Certainly Coleridge rejected the polemic as well as the affiliatory pull of party. He believed that even so-called "Free Associations" were repressors of liberty. His lifelong political affiliation was to the defense of the independent. Such independence would sometimes produce sympathy for a leader or faction combined with hostility to their policies, while at other times suggest that a hostility to an individual or group could be tempered by an endorsement of their current political practice or action. In this regard, friendship with John Thelwall did not prevent Coleridge from attacking the program of the rights-of-man polemicists in 1796, nor did admiration for Lord Liverpool restrain Coleridge from a radical criticism of the established church in 1828.

Thus far, I have systematically attacked the old view of Coleridge as a "young radical" from 1794 to 1802. In doing so, I have largely dealt with Coleridge's doctrines in a number of seminal early works to suggest that Coleridge did not share the *ideologies* of the "radicals." I now wish to suggest that Coleridge did not entertain a "radical's" view of *institutions* either. Evidence of

Coleridge's view of "radical" organizations is important because it demonstrates cogently his view that institutions and ideas were interlocked and that bad institutions could not successfully promulgate good doctrines, nor good institutions successfully promulgate bad doctrines. It will become apparent that institutional and constitutional forms were given great priority in Coleridge's thought because to him they were not soulless operating systems but embodied transcendent "Ideas" of the state with a life and vitality of their own.

The myth of "young Coleridge" as a "radical" has yet another bar to its credibility if one recognizes that Coleridge never joined *any* of the reform societies, even the aristocratic and moderate ones. Coleridge's refusal to join these reformist and "radical" leagues was not a result of either a laziness that made him unable to put his ideas into action or of a fear of prosecution by the government. Instead, his not joining was due to a fundamental commitment to an independent mind and a critical stance, a stance that he felt obviated him from taking part in any collective action. Coleridge believed that all political societies, factional parties, and reformist clubs were coercive.[19] Because he felt that valid organizations would encourage broad and deep thought and reflection by their individual members, Coleridge denounced the groups of his own era. The political clubs and associations of the reform era outraged Coleridge in their resort to narrow party manifestoes, slogans, and rallying cries in an effort to whip up unified support and squelch dissent. In his opinion, they demolished independent thought and set up a single, stone-graven factional rhetoric in its place.[20] Coleridge also suspected the motives of many of the leading "reformers" of his time. He scornfully noted that grandstanding and behind-the-scenes deals dominated meetings that should have been open and free, that should have been governed by duty and conscience. Coleridge first exposited this antiparty view in his early, 1796 essay, "Modern Patriotism." In "Modern Patriotism," he suggested that faction and party were always at odds with the principal of liberty because they erected the fences of group-thought which penned in the free exertion of individual will in political choice.

An ideal organization, Coleridge suggested, would present its decisions as the result of a debate between individual choices. Such an organization would also respect and register the dissents of members as a sign of its regard for independence of mind. In the societies of the "Modern Patriots," Coleridge claimed to see a very different and patently false "consensus," a sham unity that a party, a society, or a club generated to standardize and homogenize the opinions of its members. In his estimate, political clubs spoke in the voice of a corporate identity that presented the opinions of a majority, or even of a few drafters of a manifesto, as "the opinions of all members," as if they had been

unanimous rather than contested or even imposed from above. Coleridge perceived a deep incompatibility of the radicals' fabricated (and self-delusional)
"united front" of a univocal collective conscience with his own goal of liberty
as the exercise of individual conscience, voice, and will.

While Coleridge thought that criticism and independence were important
in society, he did not wish to suggest that mere obstreperousness was a desirable trait in general. Indeed, to take the role of a "spoiler" in an organization
simply to annoy one's enemies appears to have been as wicked to Coleridge as
imposing one's ideas upon them. The essential work of criticism and opinion
must never be allowed to degenerate into factionalism, and opposition must always be conducted (where necessary) from a position of disagreement rather
than jealously or spite. Coleridge's vision of rights and liberties is interesting in
the context of his analysis of the threat that the careless exercise of the freedom
of association posed to the freedom of thought. In his critique of the "modern
patriots," he expressed his opinion that "free associations" such as political clubs
were as capable of destroying freedom "from below" as a repressive government was capable of destroying it "from above." Any institution, public or private, which inhibited the duties of conscience and individual opinion, he alleged, undermined the notion of right. This was the case because Coleridge
conceived of a right or liberty as an entitlement conferred through the exercise
of the duties of private conscience. Because censors and club manifestoes obstructed individual conscience, they poisoned liberty as well.

Coleridge's critique of the natural-rights tradition depended on his definition of liberties and rights as practices and as political ideas. His attack on the
unfreedom of "free associations" in "Modern Patriotism" suggests that his personal vocabulary of "liberty" and "rights" differed from that used by many of
his contemporaries. It is easy enough to see that Coleridge considered himself
to be of the general party of freedom, the line of mythologized reformers that
was so often summed up in the pat formula "Milton, Harrington, Sydney,
Locke." It is more difficult to determine how Coleridge *differed* from other
liberty-minded thinkers of his day. One of the best ways in which to differen-
tiate Coleridge from other philosophers of liberty is to examine his doctrine of
the origin and nature of rights. For although all of the "party of freedom" con-
verged in the opinion that it was a good thing to be free and a good thing for
members of a polity to have rights that protected them from oppression, they
invariably diverged when it came to the issue of whether those rights emanated from tradition, nature, god, custom, the Common Law, or some combination of those sources. They also repeatedly disagreed on whether one could
speak logically of "rights" and "liberties" as existing outside the obligations of

"duties" and the positive law and legal traditions of a historically located civil polity that had the power to enforce those freedoms.

Coleridge, for his part, appears to have rejected natural-rights philosophy. Natural-rights doctrines had claimed that rights emanated either from God or nature and could be spoken of as "existing" regardless of whether any nation past or present had ever encoded them as either statute or custom. Natural-rights theories also tended to suggest that a subject's rights were not "granted" by his being born into a specific national tradition of local freedoms, or "earned" by virtue of civic participation or performance of duty, but were "implicit" in his status as a human being. By suggesting these premises, natural-rights theorists presumed that the true rights of a Russian serf were in truth equal to those of an English lord, despite their differences in social rank, ability to exercise "civic virtue," or the different laws and customs of the empires into which they had been born.

In many ways, the natural-rights tradition, which assumed the a priori existence of an eternal and incorruptible standard of rights, one that lived above the everyday shortcomings of any particular existing government, was far more "idealistic" and overtly "Platonic" than Coleridge's own "Idealist" theory of rights. Coleridge's metaphysical concept that "Ideas" were the products of material circumstances (as well as the ends, causes, and shapers of them) meant that he could not envision an Idea which was not grounded in the historicist evolution of existing institutions in everyday life. Because of his historicism and his insistence that Ideas gained their reality from constant interaction with the material world, Coleridge parted company with the proponents of natural rights.

Indeed, Coleridge feared the claim that natural rights were conferred solely by virtue of existence, nature, or reason and regarded it as a dangerous proposition. He argued instead that rights were socially normative and civically constructed. They would always remain so and indeed *ought* to remain so despite theoretical attempts to misrepresent this reality for purposes of political advantage. If one held a certain civil right, one held it by virtue of its existence in the laws and constitutions of a particular polity in a particular age. One also held this right conditionally, as a recognition of one's performance of that right's corresponding duties. Natural-rights theory, by suggesting that rights were ultimately derived from God's will or nature, tended to imply that "law" was morality.[21]

The confusion of law with morality, a theoretical confusion implicit in the natural-rights doctrine, was at the core of Coleridge's anxiety as to the uses of this polemic. This did not mean that Coleridge was a "legal realist" who thought that morality had no place in lawmaking. Coleridge thought that law was aimed towards the "Ideal" moral telos of justice, and in this important respect he agreed with the natural lawyers. He dissented from them because they suggested that the *lex naturis* was deducible purely through ratiocination and that it required no comparative study of civilizations. Coleridge thought, in contrast, that the progress of law towards the Idea of justice could only take place within the traditions and struggles of laws and courts groping rung by rung toward the moral goal of universal justice, but that laws could never, as rules taken singly, comprehend a universal standard.

The material capacity and moral facility for individual choice and conscience were central to Coleridge's theory of liberty. This theory focused on moral and political "freedom" as dependent on the exercise of choice, and "choice" was regulated by conscience. This was not in itself a surprising or unusual move, since most discussions of "freedom," whether political (as in freedom/oppression) or theological (as in freedom/determinism), typically began with a discussion of what moral agency meant. Typical formulations of the liberty of the will in the eighteenth and early nineteenth centuries generically began with a statement of how liberty, which was usually defined with some reference to the human will, tempered and governed by conscience, was a different thing from license. License, in contradistiction to liberty, was depicted as the unfettered and unruly human will (or animal sensual instinct), the will without reference to conscience. In order to be truly free, such studies usually concluded, man must neither be in chains nor completely unleashed. He must not only be able to exercise his will without unjust hindrance from the state but must also be restricted by law or conscience from enacting his desire to do things that are unjust. Here the struggle or conflict was conceived of as an internal one, between man's baser animal self and his higher, rational, or divine self.

The suggestion that "liberty" did not mean the freedom to do whatever one pleased but meant the freedom to do as one should had been a pervasive one. Certain Nominalist theologians had suggested that even God Almighty distinguished between those deeds that were in his absolute power (*potentia absoluta*), but that he would not do because they were wicked, and those deeds that his self-imposed moral tradition (*potentia ordinata*) left him at "liberty" to perform.[22]

In his discussions of choice in politics, Coleridge assented to these standard divisions between "license" and "liberty."[23] Nevertheless, he took them to a far higher level of complexity in his writings on the role of conscience and individual choice in defining "liberty." The faculty of moral conscience, Coleridge argued throughout his career, conferred two gifts: the power to choose and its correlative, the obligation to act. There were two notable strands to Coleridge's thought on will, liberty, and conscience. The first was his assumption that the definition of a "free will" as being free to choose was inconceivable without the ability of the will to implement its choices. The second was his assertion of the principle "*du kannst, denn du sollst*": if one had the ability to perform a duty, then one had a positive obligation to perform that duty.

Note that although Coleridge was an "Idealist" philosopher, his concept of moral conscience was strictly pragmatic in its insistence that the power to choose was meaningless unless one assumed the ability to act or to implement one's choices. For Coleridge, "choice" meant not only the conceptualization but also the actualization of the individual will. "Will," understood as mere good intention, was insufficient to the realization of rights. Agency, demonstrated in action, was also required.

In consequence of this theory that liberty was evidenced only by actions, Coleridge focused on the theme of duty and its relation to agency. Rights were regularly defined as dependent not only upon the correct choice to do one's duty, but upon the actual deed of exercising that duty. It was necessary, argued Coleridge, for a citizen to exercise the choice, the "liberty," to perform his social duties before earning the "liberty" of exercising his civil rights. Only through choice, he avowed, could the entire realm of "liberty" function.

The civil "liberty" that lived through the state and its institutions depended upon two things, Coleridge claimed. First, it depended on the noninterference by the state in the ability of the citizen to think freely and to act according to his conscience so long as he did not break the laws of the land. This was a negative liberty, in that it consisted of the "subject will's" freedom from the state's obstruction of its exercise. Second, civil liberty depended upon the active work of the citizenry in not only being willing to perform their duties to the commonwealth, but also in exerting themselves to fulfil those duties. This was a point of positive liberty, in that it represented the subject's "freedom to" act civically and conscientiously as a citizen. Thus, in Coleridge's politics, the personal "liberty" of the individual will to choose and act well was integral to the general civil "liberty" of the nation as a whole. If the citizen lost the ability to reason and act well for any reason (whether from state oppression or submission to a party manifesto), then liberty would be lost in the nation at large.

The interplay of individual choice, political duty, voluntarism, and free conscience was the central concern of Coleridge's 1795 last-ditch defense of liberty of the press in *The Plot Discovered*.[24] The importance of a free press, he insisted, resided precisely in the diversity of opinion among the subjects of the realm that such a frank exchange might air. In *The Plot*, as readers may recall,

Coleridge lavished praise upon the contentious nature of political criticism, "Those sudden breezes and noisy gusts which purified the atmosphere they disturbed." To him, such "gusts" represented the all-important exertion of "liberty" of conscience by the citizenry. The passage of the two acts by Pitt would kill off this freedom of thought, putting the nation into a situation where the exercise of civic duty was "hushed to death-like silence" once "all political controversy [was] at an end." The censorship of the two acts would destroy the liberty of thought of the subject and so the liberty of action of the citizen. The new law, argued Coleridge, made the intention to think differently than the prime minister a criminal act and so all opposition and all opinion (whether polite or vulgar) incapable of exercise in action. And a will without a corresponding ability to act was not a "free" will at all, for Coleridge.[25]

Coleridge argued cogently in *The Plot* that the free exchange of information among citizens who may be described as critically minded secured liberty. Unfortunately, such a truly free polity—where the citizens willed to think and act well and were not prevented from doing so—depended for its existence on the free choice of the subjects to perform their duty of conscience. The state could play a minimal part at best in the encouragement of such civicism; states were far better at preventing citizens from undertaking bad actions than in encouraging them to perform good actions. In Coleridge's opinion, the performance of the duty of conscience, like the duties of education and enlightenment, depended far more on the active and good wills of the citizens rather than on the coercive power of the state. The genuine transformation of individual belief, he argued, occurred through the individual citizens' freely willed emulation of examples of good deeds or not at all. Coleridge appears to have defined this state of civic virtue as a polity where citizens not only did the bare minimum required to avoid punishment but exerted their liberty by doing well, performing their duties as subjects as best they could. True civic virtue and true exercise of civil liberty would not emerge as a result of homogenous-thinking associations and could not surface in a monoculture. Nor could such virtuous civicism be drummed up through the emotional power of a policy or rhetoric that targeted the base interests of a mob. Here it is useful to recall Coleridge's timeocratic distinction in *The Plot* between *public* opinion and *vulgar* opinion. Where *public* opinion was the product of a nation of individuals exercising their liberty of judgment and conscience, *vulgar* opinion was a form of slavery, for it obstructed all independent thought and therefore all independent action.

Liberty of opinion was an intrinsic component of social liberty (both negative and positive) for Coleridge. The sort of opinions that individual subjects possessed, and their consequent ability to "think well," played an important role for Coleridge in determining the degree of their ability to "act well," their civic virtue. People imbibed truth, Coleridge opined, "like insects feeding on a leaf, till it colours their whole heart."[26] If their consciences were fed on nothing, or on garbage, they could only be expected to possess a faculty of liberty that was tainted, stunted and gnarled, and impotent. Therefore, Coleridge insisted, any scheme for encouraging liberty had to begin by considering the general population's critical acumen, its autonomy of will, and its potential for exerting positive liberty in favor of the community. "That general illumination must *precede* the revolution," Coleridge asserted, "is a truth as obvious as that the vessel should be cleaned before we fill it with a clear liquor."[27] A people with unfree minds could not be liberated by an external act of "revolution," no matter how constitutionally pure or well orchestrated, because they were as yet incapable of performing the higher degree of civic duties that a freer and more democratic form of government would demand. Coleridge likened liberating a people with stunted wills by giving them a newer and better form of government to pouring a fresh bottle of good claret into a "vessel" full of dirt, mold, fungus, and insects as an effort to "improve" the bottle's capability as a decanter.

Therefore, Coleridge was faced with a dilemma. He had stated clearly that his hoped-for goal was not a world of tyranny and ignorance, but one of liberty and "general illumination." He had asserted, equally forcefully, that true freedom could only come about through the creation of an enlightened citizenry capable of handling the work of expanded liberties and expanded duties. On the other hand, he had insisted that even the best-designed governments could not force citizens into becoming autonomous moral agents and exerting their freely willed benevolence through an autarchic voluntarism. How, then, could a people become more "free" if they could not be legislated or tyrannized into that freedom, if they could not be "forced to be free," as Rousseau had suggested?

Coleridge's solution appears to have been one of "conversion by example." Throughout his career, even in the 1790s, he regarded an inwardly motivated conversion of the heart and mind as the only way to achieve the autonomy of intellect and will that he desired for all and that he believed was the prerequisite of a freer state. In his advocacy of internal, personal change as the agent of social transformation, Coleridge once more voiced his profoundly Evangelical psychology. His adoption of the wine and wineskins metaphor from the gospels, there used with reference to personal salvation, in a reference to social reform suggests that Coleridge saw the work of Evangelicalism and the work of reform as fundamentally linked. In both spheres, Coleridge implied, it was not enough to perform "good works" simply because the "law" demanded them and one obeyed. True "illumination" (Coleridge's "inner light" of the Holy Ghost in the state) would bring about a world in which subjects would undertake their duties because they had a purified intent and a clean "vessel." Such a soul-felt enlightenment could not be brought to the people by the partial and abstracted reason of an arid and desiccated philosophy. It had to be brought in joyfully, Coleridge proclaimed, and with conviction, by a vibrant, living human being: ideally someone who, although he possessed the intellect of a philosopher, was fired by "the *zeal of the Methodist.*"

This emphasis on liberty as emanating from a purified and well-willing conscience emerged in Coleridge's early polemics against Godwin. Coleridge argued that Godwin's idea of general benevolence demonstrated how little Godwin knew of true human nature.[28] Coleridge believed that Godwin's principle, which claimed moral action ought to be blind to the "fellow-feeling" inspired by family and patriotism, was too mechanistic. Godwin's paradigm failed to incorporate the variables of passion, love, familiarity, loyalty, and the contingencies of daily life that went into most people's decisions.[29] Godwin's *Political Justice*, according to Coleridge, falsely assumed a uniformity of the transmission of benevolence from person to person, through reason rather than habit or feeling. Godwin had postulated in a famously eccentric argument (which was more often ridiculed than understood) that people could extend their benevolence evenly with the help of "Reason." In his advocacy of benevolence, Godwin had made a crypto-Hartleyan claim that an "associative principle"—a sort of rationalized moral sentiment which would recognize the pain of others by mental analogy—would allow disinterested reason to lead to general benevolence. Godwin's "associative principle" explained the same phenomena as emotional theories of moral sentiments, of the sort that Adam Smith advanced, but categorized those phenomena in such a rationalistic way as to suggest that this net of analogic thinking could cover the world in a vast blanket of "fellow-thinking" rather than "fellow-feeling." But unlike Smith's enlightened self-interest, Godwin's extension of rational benevolence lacked the driver of some form of personal motivation. Those psychologists of benevolence such as Hartley and Smith, while they had not ignored association by mental analogy, had suggested that this process was weaker than the powerful sympathetic pull of habit and affection based upon sense experience and sentiment.[30]

If Coleridge was obviously discontented with Godwin's rationalism, he was even more irked by what he (wrongly) saw as Godwin's reliance on "private societies as the sphere of real utility."[31] Godwin, Coleridge alleged, had

exposited a trickle-down theory of truth which claimed that "Truth by a gradual descent may at last reach the lowest order."[32] The mistake in Godwin's
thought, argued Coleridge, was his failure to realize the magnitude of the gulf
between rich and poor, a gap which meant that "those immediately beneath"
one might be too far away to be reached by truth. "Society as at present constituted does not resemble a chain that ascends in a continuity of links," complained Coleridge. Therefore, truth had to be sent across the gap between rich
and poor by a specific messenger deputized for that purpose. Individual efforts
aimed at neighbors and familiars were not enough. "The best as well as the
most benevolent mode of diffusing Truth," claimed Coleridge, was to employ
a messenger "who[,] uniting the zeal of the Methodist with the views of the
Philosopher, should be *personally* among the Poor, and teach them their *Duties* in order that he may render them susceptible of their *Rights*."[33]

This axiom, "teach them their *Duties* in order that he may render them
susceptible of their *Rights*," was one of the most foundational pillars of Coleridge's timocratic and evangelical scheme for social reform. Coleridge's elitism is clear in this passage, as in so many others. The active partner in this enterprise was the messenger who will "teach *them*" and "render *them*" politically
competent (my italics). The "Poor" were assumed to be as yet incapable and
incompetent agents of their own reform. This form of paternalism, which denied that the poor were capable of their own self-advancement—and the accompanying distrust of the "People" in their unwashed state—is usually seen
by interpreters of the period as quintessentially a "Tory" trait. (That this was
not invariably the case can be seen by a cursory glance at similarly paternalistic comments made by timocrats of the period active in the Whig party in the
United Kingdom and of the Federalist party in the United States. As Jonathan
Clark has pointed out, what we would today consider an arrogant condescen-
sion towards the poor was the rule rather than the exception in a society
which was still unabashedly "aristocratic" in its patrician mores.[34]) It is therefore interesting to see the "young" Coleridge exhibiting his "friendship" with
the people in a way more characteristic of Hannah More or John Wesley than
of John Thelwall or the other "radicals."

Coleridge's conception of liberty relied centrally, as we have seen, on an
understanding of freedom in some perfect philosophical sense. He argued that
true freedom found expression through the performance of right action at the
behest of *individual* choice and agency. Because he defined the Idea of government as a propertied trust founded on a bonding of rights and duties, he attempted to prove that government could arbitrate the inevitable conflict between the competing free choices of individuals and group interests in the

"moral world." Throughout his writings on liberty, Coleridge consistently paired external freedom of conscience with autarchic constraint of action. Ideally, he thought, citizens would be offered the freedom by the state to do all the good that they could and be denied the opportunity to do any evil by the promptings of their "fixed principles" and consciences.

Coleridge believed that the proper concern of the state's material law dealt best with those conditions where action involved others. In contrast, private conscience did not typically "involve others"; it was a silent interior discourse of citizens in their own souls. Coleridge did not think it was the state's business to make "windows into men's souls," to borrow the epigram of Queen Elizabeth. He conceived of the limits of government's intrusive powers as the border that separated the private from the public. *Actions* that harmed or threatened other persons besides the individual could be constrained legitimately. *Thoughts* and *words*, which harmed no one but the individual who uttered them, were only restricted by tyrants. It was not the province of governments to police thoughts and words unless such words harmed another through action, as in cases of slander and libel.

It is evident that Coleridge's opinions on this point combined aspects of theories of negative liberty and theories of positive liberty and community interest. Coleridge was an advocate of negative liberty on this point inasmuch as he suggested that even noxious opinions should be left free of state interference until they resulted in some tangible wrong of a specific rather than a vague sort. His opinion that deviant thoughts were not crimes contradicted centuries of socially monist, traditional communitarian belief in continental early modern European political thought.[35] Coleridge's views also contradicted a long and well thought-of (in his time) *British* tradition of antiheterodox communitarian monists stretching from Sacheverell in 1709 to the authors of the two bills in 1795 to the last Ultra defenders of the Test Act in 1828. All of these men had argued with varying degrees of success that the state had a moral obligation, for reasons of promoting community and ensuring political survival, to punish or eliminate deviant views. Despite Britain's fragile tradition of toleration from 1689 onward, and "free speech" from 1695 onward, such ideas still held great popularity and had gained in popularity even more as a result of the backlash of the "British community" against the French Revolution.

But this defense of liberty of thought and speech was not a libertarian polemic to grant citizens the right to "think as they pleased." Coleridge conceived of his work as a defense of the positive liberty to exercise the conscience of a citizen. This freedom, he most fully conceived of as the freedom to "do" as one *ought*. The positive source of this civic duty was in the free

choice of an autarchic and righteous "Will." Contrasting the will of the citizen to the animal instinct of the mob, Coleridge advanced a theory of the
"metaphysical Will" as the basis for material political obligation.

For Coleridge, the will was the source of all moral choice. Through the
guidance of conscience, it became the agent of moral obligation and the execu-
tor of civic responsibility. Because the citizen's will either led or failed to lead to
the performance of that citizen's civic duty, Coleridge thought that the study of
human will ought to be at the core of any account of political thought. Although
he failed to convince many of the validity of the thesis that preferred the principle of "moral will" as the center of political study, he applied it rigorously to
his own thought. His aim throughout his career was to find a moral anchor for
the vicissitudes and uncertainties of political and social life. His search for "certain fixed principles," as he had described them in "A Moral and Political Lecture," forced him to look at political action through the lens of what he referred
to somewhat confusingly as "religious philosophy." This religious philosophy
was developed and explored most completely by 1825 in Coleridge's *Aids to Reflection,* which combined an account of individual spirituality with a critical
moral philosophy established on transcendental and aesthetic grounds.

CHAPTER 5

Morality and Will

COLERIDGE'S VIEWS OF political and juridical freedom must be understood in light of his underlying moral and religious philosophy. This far-reaching, metaphysical, and foundational religious philosophy was central not only to Coleridge's doctrine of the will but to his views on the importance of conscience and, through conscience, the political and social pull of duty. By "religious philosophy" then, he never meant any specific sectarian doctrinal belief. Rather, he attempted to articulate his own Schellingesque *Naturphilosophie*, with strong aesthetic and ethical components.[1] In "Elements of Religious Philosophy" from his *Aids to Reflection* of 1825, Coleridge remarked that "if there be aught *Spiritual* in Man, [then] the will must be such." This "will" was the pith at the center of Coleridge's theory of moral enfranchisement. He asserted that "*if* there be a Will, there must be a spirituality in Man."[2] Coleridge rejected the "insidious title" of "nature's noblest *animal*" because he thought it savored of the "animalising tendency" of the "Epicurean . . . philosophy." Coleridge announced that there was "more in man than can be rationally referred to the life of Nature and the mechanism of [biological] Organization," since man possessed "a will not included in this [theory of] mechanism." Indeed, it was the human will that separated the species from all others, said Coleridge: "the will is an especial and pre-eminent part of our Humanity."[3]

The preeminence of the human will was an important point for Coleridge to have made, for the simple reason that belief in "the mechanism of [biological] Organization" was waxing in influence during his career. Not only, did the eighteenth century witness a continued revival of "Epicurean" tenets—a movement which reached back at least to Gibbon—but there was an increase in models of humans as "Machines" (to use LaMettrie's title), with biologically determined urges and behaviors rather than autarchic wills.[4]

Having maintained the will as "the especial and pre-eminent part of our Humanity," and identified it as the source of our moral sense, Coleridge set out the doctrine of the existence of the moral will as the basis for all valid theories of political obligation. He saw "the distinction of moral philosophy" was that it "assume[d] a something, [the human will,] the proof of which no man can *give* to another, yet every man may *find* for himself." Coleridge thought that while the will could not be empirically proven by positive science, it was, still, perceivable by reason and even by "common sense." Indeed, the existence of the will was so self-evident to Coleridge that he scoffed, "if any man assert that he *cannot* find [his will], I am *bound* to disbelieve him. I cannot do otherwise without unsettling the very foundations of my moral nature." If one denied that one had free moral will, Coleridge argued, then he denied that anyone could have such a will. "For I either find it as an *essential* of the humanity *common* to him and me," continued Coleridge, "or I have not *found* it at all." Since the "moral will" was intrinsic to political choice, and political choice was intrinsic to the citizen's performance of his political duty in a civil society, a man who denied that he had a moral will logically implied that he could not perform his political duty. Coleridge noted triumphantly that if a citizen does not find his moral will and denies that it exists, that citizen then "excommunicates[5] himself [from the polity]. He forfeits his *personal* rights, and becomes a *Thing*: that is one who may, rightfully be *employed*, or *used* as means to an end, against his will, and without regard to his interest."[6]

Coleridge's position on the "moral will" is so vivid, so characteristically *Coleridgean* in its melodrama and hyperbole, that it demands some clarification. The true message of this fiery critique of materialist psychology must be separated from the invective. It seems relatively clear, especially given his public and consistent stance against censorship and against the Crown's making windows into its subjects' souls (and thereby punishing them for evil thoughts rather than evil deeds), that Coleridge did not mean what he said literally. One cannot imagine, for instance, Coleridge travelling about the metropolis from door to door, like Sulla, with a list of the "excommunicate[d]." One cannot envision him hunting down those materialist and "animacular" philosophers, such as Godwin and Bentham,[7] who had denied the existence of the soul and rounding them up for transportation to slavery on the grounds that their wicked doctrines had caused them to "forfeit [their] *personal* rights," and become "Things." As usual with Coleridgean invective, one must separate out the flourishes of the "tin trumpet" of momentary passion from the bass ground of consistent reason. What Coleridge *meant* in this passage was not that Bentham ought to be chained to a sugar-mill in Barbados, but that the doctrine of will-lessness and soul-lessness, while an admirable toy for the fashionable intellects, was a political impossibility. If it were true, then no one could be an effective citizen, since citizenship depended on a voluntary and informed undertaking of duty by the citizen himself.

For Coleridge, the "scheme of *Expedience*" was inevitable, "unsettling" to "all," and could have no other result but the "anarchy of Morals."[8] Within the "moral world," a world of relative value and choice, only the autarchic will made citizens capable of judging good from evil. Only the will made them capable of acting legally in the absence of probable reprisal. The coercive power of the state was not extensive enough to handle even the existing sum of vice and crime and depended largely on the daily decisions of most subjects to remain within the bounds of the law. Without individual will, that quotidian decision of the majority to obey the laws would disappear. If that occurred, no coercive power in the state, no matter how strong, could tame the "anarchy of Morals."[9]

The image of the "anarchy of Morals" was the companion-piece (*pendant*) to the image, which occurred so often in Coleridge, of the prudent, independent, critically minded citizen. The citizen and the herd animal were, for Coleridge (like Kant), incompatible. Indeed, they represented the two species of political behavior, animal (will-less) and human (will-full), a distinction that the "animalizing" Epicureans in politics had tried their best to break down.[10] The "young" Coleridge in his "radical" years implicitly justified the armed force of the law (which, in the 1790s before the innovation of police forces, could only have meant detachments from the unpopular standing army) against the madness and unreason of the mob. Indeed, the need to muzzle the animal licentiousness of the mob was a favorite subject of Coleridge's, presumably because it was the reverse image of everything he thought a human and a citizen ought to be. In reference to the plight of the poor in his discussion of property in lecture 6, "On Revealed Religion," he vouched that "*security* is required *against* the poor whilst the poor are *brutalized* into *beasts*."[11] Once more, Coleridge's self-location in this schema—"against" the "beasts," not "for" them— made it all too clear that he saw himself and his Bristol audience as a superior type of people who had a mission to preserve liberty by preventing the swinish multitude from grasping at freedom before they were mature enough to deserve it. This unselfconscious elitism (in a lecture on the "wickedness" of private property, no less!) not only distanced him from the "radicals," with whom he has so often been misclassified, it also allied him with the school of the pro-liberty but antidemocratic timocrats in France (LaFayette), Britain (Burke), and the young republic of the United States (Hamilton).

The syllogism in Coleridge's political thought appears to have run thusly: (A) Poverty has "brutalized" many of the poorest subjects of the realm to the state of "beasts." (B) Beasts, because they have no will and therefore no autarchy, cannot act as responsible citizens. (C) Ergo, the poor in their current state of brutalization are, at least for the foreseeable future, incapable of becoming citizens. Coleridge did not suggest, as did Malthus and Ricardo, that the poor were ultimately responsible for the state of their poverty. But he did consider it as a sad truth that as long as the poor persisted in their condition (a condition that Marxist social theory would later dub "immiseration:), they were doomed to be morally debased.

Both Coleridge and the radicals saw that the poor were in a sorry state in 1795. The solution that the true radicals chose was to offer the poor the gift of liberty and fuller citizenship (which was their due, anyway, according to natural rights doctrine), perhaps even offer them property to lift them from the pit, and then rest from this labor in the confidence of a satisfactory outcome. The solution which *Coleridge* chose was to postpone any calls for greater liberty and enfranchisement until the poor became more "susceptible of their rights" through moral education and evangelization, and to avoid giving them redistributed property since property corrupted as often as it uplifted. This evangelical work "among the poor," Coleridge exhorted his listeners, would "teach them their *Duties* in order that he may render them susceptible of their *Rights."* In the end, once the moral conscience of the poor had been awakened, they might have "illumination." Due to the benefits of "illumination," the poor would develop "self-will" in a different manner from that which the "animalizing" philosophers saw them as possessing. This self-will would allow them finally to undertake the duties that they had been taught. Having learnt their duties, the poor would finally be eligible for their rights. Through moral evangelism by the "philosopher" elite ("preach the gospel to the poor!") Coleridge suggested that the poor would finally progress into autarchy and citizenship.

Coleridge typically emphasized the term "personal" in his consideration of rights and duties. This would ordinarily be taken as a sign of an "atomistic individualism" that viewed the critical issue of citizens' rights as a personal rather than corporate concern. But it must not be forgotten that Coleridge's theory of "personal rights" was grounded in a moral vision that the "personal will" must be able to accomplish its duties to the "civic" Commonwealth as a prerequisite of any rights. The Coleridgean concept of a "personal right" tied social entitlement to a more tangible set of "personal" relationships than a necessarily vaguer "natural right" or "right of man" could. The concept of the personal right forged the link between Coleridge's doctrine of the will and his doctrine of rights. Coleridge's theory of will had suggested that the man of free will ought to perform his social, religious, and civic duties with autonomous diligence, from his conscience's desire to do well rather than from fear of punishment. Coleridge's theory of rights presumed that the learning and performance of these duties rendered a subject "susceptible" of the rights of a citizen. Because he saw "moral obligation" as a strong cement for society, Coleridge condemned those who had mocked it. Coleridge wrote that the neo-Epicureans who wanted to destroy the language of duty and will and morality, "denie[d] the reality of *all* moral obligation, the existence of *any* Right." Ultimately, this meant that the neo-Epicureans could not have any grounds on which to claim the respect and loyalty of others. For in traducing moral discourse they "assume [duties that] according to himself he neither is nor can be under any *obligation* to assume," and "demand [rights that] he *can* have no *right* to demand." In the end, Coleridge caviled, one had to assume that if a neo-Epicurean "uses the *words* Right and Obligation, he does it deceptively, and means only power and compulsion."[12]

This was the alternative for Coleridge. One could take the Epicurean road trod by Malthus, Ricardo, and Bentham and enter an amoral political world, a cesspit of "power and compulsion" where humans, since they were only the brutal animals they were taught to be, recognized no rights and duties and could only conceive of political obligation in crude terms of either being thrown pacifying sops of pleasure or being beaten back with lash after lash of pain. Or one could take the Coleridgean road, and enter a world where crypto-Evangelical education presumed that even the basest of men could be lifted up from the kennel, made into citizens who recognized their duties to the commonwealth and were rewarded for this service by extensive grants of rights to them as citizens. Coleridge, since he had set up the comparison so tendentiously, invariably preferred his own system of education, will, duties, and rights to what he saw as the "Utilitarian" schemes of immiseration, instinct, power, and compulsion.

Coleridge's strong focus on the will as the only solid ground on which to found a theory of political obligation was directly tied to his understandings of conscience, right reason, and duty. He argued in 1825, in *Aids To Reflection*, that the "*Christian* grounds his philosophy on assertions; but with the best of all reasons for making them—namely that he *ought* to do so."[13] Coleridge's deliberate use of "ought" was no mistake, since his theories by 1825 were even more strongly focused on themes of duty, loyalty, and obligation as imposed by a free moral will that voluntarily chose to follow a strict and transcendent moral law. The highest form of reason was, for Coleridge, the good will, which based its decisions on truth filtered through conscience. The Coleridgean will operated on similar epistemological lines as the Coleridgean reason: it was able to infer and envision that which was not always directly visible in the material world.

The intuitive and "constitutive" Ideas of good and evil, Ideas that one could discover by the faculty of reason guided by the will, composed what Coleridge called the moral law. Whereas the "moral world" was, since it was mainly material, plagued with the ambiguities of everyday contingency, the "moral law," since it was mainly "Ideal," was simpler and clearer in its emotional power, although less easy to discover in empirical detail. The moral law provided "fixed principles," principles that Coleridge increasingly defined as the sort of "assertions" which one "ought" to make, as he did in 1825. The moral law provided a solid "bottom" for action in the knowledge of good and evil, the presumption of human agency and willpower, and the elevation of conscience to an active guide for decisions.

In his "mature" work, Coleridge increasingly asserted that since the "Ideas" of goodness and duty were not analyzable in the same way that the laws of gases or falling bodies were, one had to trust to one's reason and one's common sense to provide a rationale for abjuring evil and following good. "Empirical" (or "Epicurean") efforts to study morality, since they could only comprehend sensible pleasure and pain, invariably failed to address the immeasurable roles of force of will and the influence of morality in human behavior. Coleridge suggested that his moral citizen "asserts [doctrines of morality] he can neither approve, nor account for, nor himself comprehend: [except by means of] the strongest *inducements*," such as the inducement that by following these doctrines he will be able to understand "whatever else most concerns him to understand aright." Yet Coleridge took great pains to suggest that his moral citizen, although he followed a Christian moral law that in some ways was "above" understanding (i.e., not directly provable by experiment or "Concept'), did not act in a way that was "contrary to" understanding. "His assertions," promised Coleridge, "have nothing in them of theory or hypothesis: but are in immediate reference to three ultimate facts." The first of these facts was "the Reality of the *Law of Conscience*." Coleridge claimed that the law of conscience was "a fact of consciousness."[14] The second of these facts was "the existence of a *Responsible Will* as the subject of that law." Coleridge claimed that the existence of human will was "a fact of Reason necessarily concluded from" the reality of the law of conscience. The third of these facts was "the existence of *Evil*—of *Evil* essentially such, not by accident of outward circumstances, not derived from its physical consequences, nor from any cause, [but simply evil emanating] out of itself." Coleridge argued that evil was "a fact of history interpreted by both" the real law of conscience and the human's responsible will[15]. These three postulates of Coleridge's moral system can be simplified briefly as: (1) "A Law of Conscience exists, because my consciousness tells me it does." (2) "A Responsible Will exists in all humans, because it is necessary for a Will to do good to exist if a Law of Conscience is to make any ethical sense." (3) "Some deeds are truly Evil because history shows many instances of acts of nearly pure evil, and my own conscious experience and Reason corroborate the existence of such unmitigated Evil."

We have already examined the importance of the law (or Idea) of conscience in Coleridge, as well as the crucial significance of the responsible will. It remains to consider why Coleridge devoted such attention to proving that there was some transcendental Idea of "Evil" which could not be explained away by any contextual or circumstantial rationale. For Coleridge true evil constituted some conscious effort of will, one that purposelessly and gratuitously violated the known dictates of conscience, right reason, and duty. In other words, true evil constituted some act of malice. For Coleridge, this could only be understood as a deliberate and conscious abrogation of the moral law, in which a responsible will knew what ought to be done yet did the exact opposite. Why, other than for its theological effect, was the recognition of what we might call "*irresponsible* will"—or evil—so important to Coleridge's system?

The reason why Coleridge so stressed evil is because it proved choice. Choice was central to Coleridge's theory that only the responsible will of the moral citizen demonstrated the autarchic ability to fulfil duties and enjoy rights. If one presumes a world in which all acts are universally moral, or universally amoral, then the choice to follow the moral law on the basis of conscience becomes a theoretical impossibility. For if there is no theoretical option of a deliberate error of the will, then there is no freedom of choice. It is impossible to perform a truly moral action where moral action is the only option.

By 1825, Coleridge had considered three models of moral will: one necessitarian, one deist, and one uniquely Coleridgean. The importance of this investigation of moral obligation and free will became clearer for Coleridge after 1817 as he set his view apart from the two major schools of writers who had addressed the problem of morality in human agency: the "Necessitarians" and the "Old or Pious Deists." He argued that his own conception of freedom of the will and the moral law was a departure from two prevailing errors in philosophy. The first was the necessitarian thesis of predestination, which suggested that men had no *real* freedom of the will since all things were preordained. This was the theory that had been advanced by men such as Thomas Hobbes and Joseph Priestley. The second was the deist theory that the personal God who was the traditional base of morality did not exist, but that men might be encouraged to act morally by philosophical contemplation of the "Natural Law" and the "Laws of Reason." That theory had been first advanced by the "Pious Deists" in the school of the third Earl of Shaftesbury but had been taken up in later years by their impious atheist descendants, who reckoned that if God's intervention was to be discarded, then his existence might as well be discarded at the same time. "At each of these two opposite roads (the philosophy of Hobbes and that of Shaft[e]sbury)," warned Coleridge, "I have placed a directing post, informing my fellow travellers, that on neither of these roads can they see the truths to which I would direct their attention."

Coleridge attacked the necessitarians because they treated the study of human psychology as if it were an exercise in tracing the paths of bowling balls. They "assume," Coleridge complained, "that motives act on the will, as bodies act on bodies." It did not matter whether the necessitarian was a materialist (as was Hobbes) or a devout Christian believer in the soul (as were Calvin, Edwards, and Priestley); the tendency of the school was to erase human agency and human choice from moral discourse. "Whether mind and matter are essentially the same, or essentially different" in the schemes of a particular necessitarian, Coleridge pointed out, mind and matter "are both alike [i.e., thought of by materialist and idealist types of necessitarians alike as being] under one and the same law of compulsory causation." Necessity failed because in making all action compulsory and predestined it made the decision to do good or evil irrelevant.

Having set up his first directing post condemning the road of the necessitarians as unfit, Coleridge then turned his energy "to oppose the disciples of *Shaft[e]sbury*[,] and those who[,] substituting one faith for another[,] have been well called the pious Deists of the last century."[16] Coleridge disliked the deists "because they imposed upon themselves an *idea*" of an impersonal moral law and Natural Law "for a fact" of God's personal existence. Unfortunately, noted Coleridge, although the Natural Law was "a most sublime idea indeed," and indeed "so necessary to human nature, that without it no virtue is conceivable," it was "still [only] an idea." The deists failed because their impersonal code of virtue did not provide "the strongest *inducements*, [such as the inducement that by following these doctrines he will be able to understand] whatever else most concerns him to understand aright," which Coleridge saw Christianity as offering. The deists made moral action imaginable but did not make it likely, especially for those who needed more to motivate their piety than a set of regulations for action, especially for those who needed a "Methodist" rather than a "philosopher." The second road had been marked as impassable as well.

It remained to Coleridge to suggest a third road that would avoid the mistakes of the first two. "In contradiction to their splendid but delusory tenets," Coleridge stated, "I possess a deep conviction that man was and is a fallen creature." This fallenness, Coleridge explained, was "not by acts of bodily constitution [i.e. biological]." Nor was it due to "another cause, which *human* wisdom in a course of ages might be supposed capable of removing," that is, simply like a design flaw in a machine. No, man was "diseased in his *Will*, in that Will which is the true and only strict synonym of the word, I, or the intelligent Self."[17] Because of this disease of the will, this "fallen state," both the reason and understanding are clouded, and the fallen being chooses evil rather than good and fails to perform duties. This striking use of Pauline and Augustinian language of "fallen" man, though common to most Christian soteriologies of the 1820s, was most strongly emphasized among the Evangelicals and the Methodists, with their resultant emphasis on redemption that Coleridge had also mimicked.

Coleridge did not believe that human nature, given its fallen state, was perfectible by any positive act or policy of governments and laws. A fundamental condition of the species could not be declared out of existence by an emperor's edict that, "all men were thereafter to be considered to be born virtuous rather than debased." Nor could the diseased will of all men be cured by provision of better bridges and manhood suffrage and agrarian justice. The only logical solution, claimed Coleridge, was to admit rather than deny the fallenness of the species and to use plausible means stronger than the deist's logic to redeem that fallen man into a position where he was capable of performing the duties of a citizen with a healthy rather than a diseased will.

Coleridge's solution was rather harshly Pauline and Augustinian in its alternatives. The diseased will must be cured by means stronger than "human wisdom," or it will remain sick and incapable of true virtue. One possible reading of this passage is that Coleridge, the transcendentalist, is challenging his readers to an agon, a striving of the will, in which the self would be discovered, purified, and raised from its fallen state. Such a reading would suggest that the fundamental disease of spirit underlying man's "fallen" nature was based in the denial of the weak to undertake the tasks of responsible will. Only courageous moral choice and an acknowledgment of the freedom of the human will could redress this failing. Those who allege that Coleridge was simply a thief and plagiarist from Kant typically see this doctrine as a bold-faced pastiche of the Kantian doctrine of the "good will." The problem with the "self-revising good will" reading is that it suggests that Coleridge was more like Kant (or even Emerson or Nietzsche) in his concept of the will than he actually was. For the most part, the "Kantian" thesis accords with the proto-Emerson, proto-Nietzsche theory of a self-curing soul whose own agency is sufficient to redeem it from its errors. Unfortunately, Coleridge's language in the passage suggests not the Emersonian agon of "Self-Reliance," or the Nietzschean agon of "The Will to Do, To Be, To Know," but the candid admission of defeat and incapability in the absence of divine assistance that lay at the heart of Evangelical piety in Coleridge's era. It was, perhaps, less Coleridge's "Kantian" strain than his staunch Christian piety that influenced his vision of the fallible will in society.[18]

Whether we describe Coleridge's views on the human as crypto-Kantian visions of the self-amended "good will," Evangelical views of the God-redeemed "saved will," or proto-Emersonian views of the "independent will," one thing remains certain: Coleridge posited a doctrine in which the individual human will was fallible by nature but redeemable by a combination of personal will and "transcendent" forces that he vaguely described. This theory meant that Coleridge positioned the emendation of the will—the "betterment" of the individual political agent—as the necessary and inevitable first step toward a fully developed nation of informed and autarchic citizens. Because of the primacy of his doctrine of the "fallen" man, Coleridge believed that the nation would have to take measures that would allow plebeians to develop a responsible will before allowing them to enter the forum of fully enfranchised citizenship.

The responsible will was alone capable of being an active and autarchic agent for change, because its possessor alone was capable of performing the duties that "rendered him susceptible" of his rights. Before moving on to the concept of duty as the foundation of civic life in Coleridge, it is necessary to delineate more clearly why Coleridge thought the language of rights could not be employed without simultaneously employing the language of duties. The roots of this connection rested in the centuries-old battle within the "Party of Liberty" between advocates of a system of "rights" based on "civic-humanist" and "Common Law" models, and defenders of a system of rights predicated on belief in so-called natural rights. Coleridge's standard of "susceptibility" to rights set the party of liberty as an inherently divided interest constituted by the breach between "pure civil" and "natural" theorists of rights.

Coleridge's idealist philosophy naturally conceived of the "Idea" of civil rights as transcending the quotidian and "constituting" (molding and shaping) everyday examples of these rights in the laws of varying nations. But one must not make the mistake of presuming that because Coleridge was an idealist that he had a Platonic conception that an Idea existed without reference to the quotidian material reality that it constituted. For Coleridge, it is true, the transcendent Idea of liberty as a telos was greater than the sum total of the various rights and liberties written in the laws of imperfect and only partially free states in the "material world." On the other hand, it was *simultaneously* true for him that the Idea of liberty "got its hands dirty" by constant encryption and interaction in the "material world." The constant involvement and implication of Coleridgean Ideas in everyday life had the corollary for Coleridge that in order to have status in the realm of Ideas, a would-be Idea must be truly *embodied*, to a greater or lesser degree, in the muck and mire of the "material world." Ideas, in Coleridge's *episteme*, were not incorrupt and perfect forms floating gracefully above the material world without reference to the circumstances of that world. Coleridgean idealism always stressed that it was a theoretical impossibility to posit a transcendent Idea of something—for instance, a mythological beast such as the unicorn or the manticore—that had no objective constituents in the real world. Since, for Coleridge, Ideas were the transcendent teloi of everyday experience, if a thing did not exist in everyday experience, then it could not claim status as an Idea.

In marginal notes to Sir John Walsh's pamphlet *Popular Opinions on Parliamentary Reform* (1831), Coleridge lambasted the theorists who had claimed that there were natural rights that existed only in the mind of God but were not yet rooted in current laws, customs, or recognized by any government. "A Right without a power," he scoffed, "is a right to an impossibility, i.e. an absurd Right." He added that "where nature gives the instinctive volition," "this [natural?] Will is assuredly followed by the appropriate Organization! . . . [O]f all Rights," he concluded, "the most whimsical would be the right to a non-exi[s]tant thing, which could only *exist* by the non-exercise or overwhelming of that Right."[19] Coleridge's comments on Walsh adequately display his life-long capability of becoming irate and sarcastic over what he saw as the shoddy thinking of the natural-rights theorists. This loathing of natural-rights theory was a trait that the "old" Coleridge exhibited in full flower as late in his career as 1831, but which was equally loudly displayed by the "young" Coleridge of 1796.

His conviction that to be "real," an Idea had to have existing, if imperfect, manifestations in the material world, led Coleridge to condemn the theory of natural rights. Advocates of natural rights claimed to have located a perfect telos of a transcendent right, which had no existence in everyday laws and statutes. In this sense, Coleridge argued, to claim a "natural" right that bore no relation to existing laws of any realm and that had no remedies or duties pertaining to it of the sort which were attached to rights in every known human society was illogical. One could not, argued Coleridge, rationally posit a purified and perfected form of a thing that (as yet) had no material manifestations on earth, in the way that he believed the natural-rights theorists did.

It is important to regard Coleridge's strong distaste for theories of natural rights in the context of his strong support for a broad set of civil rights and liberties, in whose support he was always vocal. A great deal of confusion has arisen in the study of writings on the subject of liberty in the years 1760 to 1830 because analysts have too often assumed that someone who condemned the doctrine of natural rights must have done so in order to advance the arbitrary powers of monarchs and other tenets of "reaction" and "counterrevolution." In the minds of too many historians of ideas who examine this period, the years around the turn of the nineteenth century were a battle between "pro-Liberty" natural-rights theorists (usually seen as founders of the liberal and radical movements of the century) and "anti-Liberty" conservatives and monarchists.

Unfortunately, as had been amply demonstrated by the studies of the civic-humanist and Common Law traditions of liberty, the "Party of Liberty" was historically divided over the issue of whether or not natural rights actually existed. In this debate, Coleridge sided with the anti-natural-rights advocates. This did not make him a "conservative," unless we wish to group the Tory "radical" Jeremy Bentham, who ungenerously called natural rights "nonsense on stilts," as a "conservative" as well. Instead, it suggested that Coleridge thought that the concretized Idea of the Common Law tradition of British civil rights and civil liberties more effectively guaranteed the maintenance and growth of liberty in the United Kingdom than did the uncodified norms of natural rights.

Natural-rights advocates believed in a *ius naturale*, which not only existed as an abstract telos but granted and guaranteed concrete, inalienable rights to all humans on the authority of God and/or nature, even if corrupt and blind laws of states on earth ignored or denied these rights at present. Natural-rights advocates typically presumed that the rights that they postulated were either God-given or nature-given. These natural rights were "gratuitous" in the sense of not being conditioned on membership in any polity except for the human race. They were "gratuitous" in the sense of not being conditioned on the "recognition" of the rights by any polity except the Godhead or nature. And they were "gratuitous" in the sense of not being dependent for their grant on the performance of any duty except for being alive. They were independent of the historic laws and freedoms of existing realms, and the net of reciprocal rights, remedies, recognitions, and duties that these "Ancient Constitutions" implied. They may or may not be considered God granted; they certainly were not dependent on community recognition.

In contrast, the civic-humanist and Common Law traditions asserted that (in the words of the old maxim) every claimed "right" must have a "remedy" in an existing court of law in the sublunary world. Also, they pointed out that every purported "right" must also encompass an accompanying, and publicly contracted rather than tacit, "duty"[20] Third, they contended that every suggested "right," in order to exist anywhere else but fairyland, must be "recognized"—that is to say, honored, even if in the breach, by at least one real-life polity.[21]

Coleridge, it is clear to all interpreters, sided with the Common Law and civic-humanist critiques of natural rights. He considered the claims of the natural-rights advocates to be subversive and potentially deadly to the cause of liberty that they had hoped to advance. He was as strong a believer in rights as they were, perhaps more so. Yet he maintained along with the critics that such rights were only valid in the historical and constitutional contexts of "remedy," "recognition," and "duty." The greatest of these, for him, was duty, for duty implicated the conscience and the responsible will that he had placed at the center of his concept of the citizen.

Not only were "civil rights" and "civic duties" distinct yet interdependent concerns, they were, in Coleridge's account of political theory, tied to the idea of "country." The argument thus far has examined Coleridge's doctrine of individual liberty, the responsible will, and the autarchic conscience, which were the foundation for his theory of the citizen. The following will examine his psychology of "individual liberty" as the basis for his vision of "civil liberty": the duties and rights that the individual exercised in a polity. Throughout his career, Coleridge sought to define the boundaries and importance of "duty" in the government of a nation and to define nation or country as the wellspring of the people as a commonwealth.

Coleridge's consistent focus on duty was a result of his lifelong study of the relationship between duties and rights in civil society. Coleridge had paired rights with duties as early as 1796, in *The Watchman*. He continued to do so up to his 1830 treatise, *On The Constitution of the Church and State*. As a rule, Coleridge never examined the question of rights except in the context of an examination of corresponding duties, and vice versa. Coleridge, throughout his long political career, argued (along with the civic-humanist and Common Law critics of natural-rights theory) that rights only existed in civil societies, in the context of an active set of institutions that could recognize those rights and provide remedies for the aggrieved in case of their violation.

Coleridge always portrayed duty as precedent to right. Once a citizen had performed his civic duties, he was granted the rights implicit within them. In Coleridge's assessment, only a fool would suggest that one might deserve or enjoy a right that was *not* maintained by a corresponding duty paired with it in a dyad. One of his earlier writings, in the *Watchman* of 1796, attacked a speech in the House of Commons in which William Windham had used the term, "a natural Right of Property."[22] Coleridge's footnote dissection of the phrase was surgically precise, but nonetheless brutal. "This sentiment" of natural rights, observed Coleridge, "is so lugged into every debate, that it has degenerated into mere parrotry." This revealing statement displayed Coleridge's exhaustion at the "degenerat[ion]" of the term into crowd-pleasing claptrap as early as the mid-1790s. It also indicated how natural-rights theory had become so popular by 1796 as to be (at least to Coleridge's perceptive eye) an anodyne, patriotic bit of verbal bunting "lugged into *every* debate" (my italics).[23]

In appendix B to *A Lay Sermon*, Coleridge wrote lucidly about the relationship between rights and duties. "Right in its most proper sense," he argued, "is the creature of law and statute. . . . Only in the technical language of the courts," he added, where it was connected to the *recognition* of that right by the court and the provision of a *remedy* by that court, "has it any substantial and independent sense." He completed his analysis by stating that "in morals, Right is a word without meaning, except as the correlative of Duty."[24] It was even so in Coleridge's political theory.

In the *Watchman* note, Coleridge implied that rights, in order to exist, had to be recognized as constituting an agreement between the citizen and the polity. All social claims and obligations, such as contracts, existed in reference to a second party. A right, therefore, could only exist in reference to something else, in this case a duty. Thus, each claim by a citizen or group of a "right" was only valid if accompanied by a corresponding "duty" that another individual, group, or the polity at large was obliged to perform in fulfillment of that compact. As the result of the duty of each individual to contribute to the aggregate of group happiness, each individual possessed a right to enjoy some measure of that happiness. The right emanated from the duty. In essay 6 of *The Friend* (1809), he asked the reader, "Can anything appear more equitable than . . . the *equality* of Rights and Duties?"[25]

In the 1796 *Watchman* note criticizing Windham, Coleridge presented his own vision of a proper category of rights as a subset of duties. He began with the aphorism that "those duties are called *Duties* which we exercise towards others." From this he drew a second aphorism that "those duties are called *Rights* which we exercise towards ourselves." The gist of this statement is actually somewhat startling: those things we normally conceive of as rights, Coleridge argued, have been mislabeled by political theorists. The proper term for them is that of the overarching set of norms to which "rights" belong, "*Duties.*" If we are to think clearly of the relationship between duties and rights, he argued, we must effectively reconceive them not as separate and independent spheres of action, but as set and subset. We would indeed be better off describing them, he implied, as "other-duties" and "self-duties."

By defining rights as a subset of duties, Coleridge's theory of citizenship leaned heavily towards duty and its fulfillment. "It is the *Duty* of each individual," proclaimed Coleridge in *The Watchman*, "to aim at producing the greatest possible happiness to the whole." Yet this aim required something beyond Roman self-sacrifice and the merely ascetic and self-effacing virtues. Indeed, Coleridge's ideas on this subject could not have been more unlike the writings of the Spartan civic humanists, who painted a vision of agrarian plainness, virtuous altruism at the expense of self, and abstemious sacrifice in the service of community. Coleridge's vision of duty was more "liberal," in the eighteenth-century sense of that word as implying both generous and pleasurable. Coleridge suggested that duty, far from requiring self-negation, was not only compatible with the "pursuit of happiness" by individual citizens, but was actually a prerequisite for it. "As the happiness of the whole is made up of the happiness of its parts," Coleridge added, "it is the *Right* of each individual to enjoy every pleasure which does not injure himself, nor lessen or render insecure the enjoyment of others."[26]

Coleridge's view that the individual had a "*Right*" to pursue happiness, in effect (to "enjoy *every* pleasure" which did not "injure himself" or "lessen" and threaten the "enjoyment" of others) foreshadowed Mill's later formulation of this classic "liberal" principle. Coleridge's vision of liberty was, perhaps, one of the most overtly *individualistically* hedonistic definitions of "duty" in the entirety of political thought up to the year he wrote it (1796).[27] It was a remarkable "move" for Coleridge to suggest that duty, which was generally conceived of in the seventeenth and eighteenth centuries as requiring grim self-denial and sacrifice of the individual to the community, was actually entirely compatible with an utterly individualistic, even self-indulgent, vision of the duty-rights of "pleasure" and "enjoyment."

Coleridge vividly developed his broad view of the liberties of the citizen in the sixth essay of *The Friend* (1809), written seven years after his alleged defection to Toryism. "Each man is the best judge of his own happiness," Coleridge maintained, "and to *himself* must it therefore be entrusted. . . . The *only* duty of the Citizen," he added, "in fulfilling which [duty] he obeys *all* the laws, is *not to encroach* on another's *sphere of action.*"[28] These passages suggest the depth of Coleridge's protoliberalism. He conceived of each citizen as having an individual "sphere of action," which suggested an atomistic social theory where one could theoretically undertake endeavors that did not impinge on any other citizen.[29] He also suggested that "each man" was the "best judge" of his "happiness," a statement that dealt a double blow to conservative "Tory" social theory. First, it privileged autonomous "happiness" as something which all citizens ought to have, an idea that conservative Tory "stations of life" theory flatly denied. Second, it implied that citizens had a prerogative to exercise autonomous judgment in matters which did not affect other citizens, which suggested that a citizen could act well without reference to the opinions of others, whereas in traditional Tory social theory, the poor and middling sorts were supposed to rely on opinions promulgated by the traditional paternalistic social net of churchmen, squires, and local worthies. If each man was the best judge of his own happiness, one might infer that the judgments of the parson, the squire, and the neighbors would have to be dethroned from the traditional sovereignty they had been granted in Tory community theory.

In this set of Coleridgean definitions of the proper sphere of individual liberty, one sees clearly the basis for Mill's claim that Coleridge, although a "conservative," represented a "second strand" of liberalism that in some ways was as expansive in its claims for the broad sphere of individual decisions allowed by the government as was the "liberal" school of thought. Mill, of course, would go farther than Coleridge and strip away the prohibition of self-injury in the name of expanded liberty. Yet the striking resemblance between the two in their discussion of the boundaries of citizen agency demonstrates even more strongly why Mill was such an avid student of Coleridge's writings.

Coleridge's proto-Millean theory of the pursuit of happiness, because it left so much latitude for the citizen to identify and pursue "every pleasure which did not injure oneself, nor lessen or render insecure the enjoyment of others," needed to anchor itself in the Coleridgean scheme of autarchic responsible will. The exercise of the duty to the self required the choice of conscience and right reason to do good rather than evil. In Coleridgean psychology it may be recalled, "choice" is only possible when the agent actually has the option of doing ill. The citizen's virtue in doing his duty only takes place if he does his duty from *volition* rather than from *compulsion*. For this reason, Coleridge saw the citizen rather than the state as the best agent for the guarantee of both self-duty and other-duty. The implication of this conception of civic agency in Coleridge's view of state and autarchy, as opposed to government and exarchy, was that Coleridge may be viewed as both a statist *and* a liberal.

Coleridge's conception of the role that the "state" should play in the lives of its citizens was ambitiously expansive by 1820.[30] One must not be misled by Coleridge's use of this ambiguous term. Coleridge used the term "state" where we might use the term "nation," to describe that network of ideas, institutions, and mores that are far greater than the coercive and administrative apparatus of "government." Broadly speaking, for Coleridge the "state" represented the forces of moral *autarchy*, and the "government" represented the forces of moral *exarchy*. Coleridge believed that the "state," since the bulk of its power was persuasive, should have broad latitude to influence the lives of citizens by example in order to lead them toward responsible will. In contrast, the government, since the bulk of its power was coercive, should not be allowed to intrude into the lives of citizens, since repeated interference would create a tyranny in which the exercise of responsible will, or any will at all, would be impossible. Thus, while Coleridge wanted a strong "state," he wanted a weak "government." Even after 1820, Coleridge asserted that those *governments* were best that prevented their citizens from harming others, but not from harming themselves. The role of the *state*, in contrast, was to supply the moral and spiritual education that would allow the citizen a reasonable chance to achieve this relatively high level of moral autonomy.

Coleridge carefully defined the limits of governmental intrusion into the lives of citizens in essay 9 of *The Friend*, written in 1809. He began by stripping the magistrate of the governor's traditional power to act as the moral policeman of the community. The power of the governor to act as guard and guide to public morals had been a basic assumption of much Tory—and even some Whig and radical—social theory. It was one of the chief contentions of communitarianism, which was based on a vision of the magistrate as providing unity, harmony, and orthodoxy to the realm, and thereby rendering it happy.[31] Therefore, Coleridge's decision to divest the magistrate of any role in making the commonwealth virtuous and serene was bold, to say the least. "The greatest possible happiness of a people," he professed, "is not according to [my] system the object of a governor." Having defined what a governor ought *not* to do, he turned to the ruler's positive duties: The object of a governor is "to preserve the Freedom of all by coercing within the requisite bounds of Freedom of each." That is to say, the government could not use the excuse of advancing the freedom of the commonwealth in order to transgress the "bounds of Freedom of each": the rights of the individual were as important as the rights of the community. The duty of government, he elaborated, "is to take care, that itself remain the sole collective power, and that all the citizens should enjoy the same Rights and without distinction be subject to the same Duties."[32] Thus Coleridge guaranteed a measure of "coercive" power to the magistrate. But he limited this magisterial power only to the provision of "the same Rights" and "the same Duties" to all citizens, regardless of their "distinction." The only time in which government could legitimately coerce and intrude was in defense of the boundaries between individuals' spheres of action. "The business of the Governor is to watch incessantly, that the State shall *remain composed of Individuals acting as Individuals*, by which alone the Freedom of all can be secured." The governor could intervene legitimately only in those cases where one subject violated the "Freedom of each. . . . *Whatever* a government does more than this [preservation of freedom]," he concluded, "comes of Evil" (my italics).

Several things are clear in this passage: First, Coleridge in 1809 did not envision the state as a single monistic community in which the goal of the governor was to enforce harmony, orthodoxy, and unity. Instead, he saw the nation as a set of autonomous individuals pursuing their own visions of happiness and deemed capable of judging for themselves what that happiness was. He theorized that the nation not only *was*, but ought to "*remain*," "*composed of Individuals acting as Individuals*." Second, he was committed to some conception of a rights/duties-based egalitarianism in the nation. Coleridge believed that all citizens should possess "the same Rights" and "the same Duties," regardless of their "distinction." Third, he disbarred government from interfering by using its coercive powers in any instances other than those necessary to prevent individuals from harming one another. Fourth, that he saw any government that went beyond its narrowly defined role as being not only ambitious but actually "Evil." The inclination to act beyond this limited capacity had been at the heart of the Jacobin hybrid monster: its lineage composed of one part Bourbon despotism and one part philosophe heartlessness. Like Frankenstein's monster, its entirety was the fruit of false science.

Although he had increasingly wide expectations of the state, Coleridge disliked most of the interventions of the government that he witnessed in his lifetime. He had a very low opinion, in particular, of those governments that had attempted to perfect mankind and to promote public happiness and virtue through frequent, coercive intrusions into the life of the citizenry. Coleridge believed that the Jacobin party in France had been the most blatant example of attempts to whip and torture a nation into being good. In appendix B of *A Lay Sermon*, Coleridge treated this problem at length. He contended that the "comprehension, impartiality, and far-sightedness of reason," if isolated from other influences ("taken singly and exclusively"), degenerated into "mere visionariness in intellect" and "indolence or hard-heartedness in morals." To

Coleridge, because the Jacobin morality was so completely based on "vision-ariness in intellect" and "hard-heartedness in morals," it quickly became de-praved. Jacobinism was for Coleridge "the science of cosmopolitanism with-out country" because it denied that a citizen might feel more strongly for fellow-Frenchmen (with whom he shared habits, beliefs, and mores) than for Tahitians, who lived on the other side of the world. Jacobinism also repre-sented the Godwinian doctrine "of philanthropy without neighbourliness or consanguinity," which presumed that one's thoughts of benevolence directed towards complete strangers would be as strong as one's feelings towards fami-ly and friends. In addition, Jacobinism represented the Spartan/Roman re-publican ideal of the citizen sacrificing his own interest for the good of the polis, taken to bloody extremes.[33]

Coleridge was especially angry at those monstrous births of communitarian civic humanism, those "impostures of that philosophy of the French Revolu-tion, which would sacrifice each [citizen] to the shadowy idol of all [the re-public of virtue]." Jacobinism for Coleridge was a freak, a horror, a "*monstrum hybridum*." One of the parents of this bastard spawn was "despotism, or the lust of rule grounded in selfishness," the sort of raw ambition which had been the chief trait of Louis XIV. The other "part" or parent was "abstract reason mis-applied to objects that belong entirely to the experience and the understand-ing"; the hyperintellectual systems of the materialist philosophes, such as LaMettrie, Holbach, and Helvetius, who treated humans as if they were ma-chines. In Coleridge's view, the "instincts" and "mode of action" of the Ja-cobin party had been in "strict correspondence" with its "origins" as a cross-breed of ambitious monarchical despotism and heartless philosophe system building. "In all places," Coleridge claimed, "Jacobinism betrays its mixed parentage and nature." The Jacobins accomplished the Bourbon despots' elitist goal of "build[ing] up government" by "applying [i.e., resorting] to the brute passions and physical force of the multitude (that is to man the mere animal),"[34] and unleashing the power of the ignorant and furious plebeian mob where the Bourbons had suppressed them. In addition, the Jacobins had replaced the il-logical and specious Bourbon system of "social privileges" with an equally il-logical and specious philosophe system of natural rights. As a result of their ad-herence to the dreams of the philosophes, the Jacobins had reconstructed "the frame of society" using the erroneous guides of "the universals of abstract rea-son." In adhering to Enlightenment schemes, argued Coleridge, the Jacobins stupidly and dangerously ignored the tried and true strategies of "positive insti-tutions," such as law courts, parliaments, and churches; "the lights of specific experience," such as the lessons of history; and "the modifications of existing

circumstances," an attitude of renovation and conservation rather than demolition of the ancien régime.[35]

Coleridge transferred several of his theories of reason and power to his criticism of Jacobin misrule. "The universals of abstract reason," he contended, if
"taken singly and exclusively," without the grounding of "the lights of specific experience," could only result in a cold and rigid "imposture." French philosophy, translated into power and application, had been just such a case of abstract reason gone wild. The French Revolution began with relatively harmless
philosophe affectations well-suited to the contained and civilized atmosphere of
the salon: "mere visionariness in intellect," "cosmopolitanism," "philanthropy"
"indolence or hard-heartedness in morals," and "abstract reason misapplied to
objects that belong entirely to the experience and the understanding." It ended
in the cold-blooded horrors of Jacobinism: "without [the fellow-feeling of a]
country," "without neighbourliness or consanguinity," relying on "the brute
passions and physical force of the multitude" in order to "sacrifice each to the
shadowy idol of all."

Coleridge's early criticisms, both of Robespierre the despot[36] and Godwin
the philosopher[37] had turned on precisely this distinction. Reason, if un-
governed by experience, sense, and understanding, was the real *monstrum hybridum.* The action of will directed by pure reason, without the softening governance of conscience and duty, invariably denied history, particulars, and
individuals. Godwin's doctrine of disinterest had suffered from this flaw. Coleridge explained his objection to Robert Southey in a letter dated 13 July 1794.
With respect to Godwin's theory of disinterested benevolence, he wrote:

> The ardor of private attachments makes Philanthropy a necessary habit
> of the soul. I love my friend—such as *he* is, all mankind are, or *might
> be!* The deduction is evident—Philanthropy (and indeed every other
> virtue) is a thing of concretion—some home-born feeling is the centre
> of the Ball, that rolling on through life collects and assimilates every
> congenial feeling.[38]

"Home-born feeling," "congenial feeling," the "ardor of private attachments," for Coleridge, were the "thing[s] of concretion." These particularities anchored reason to the data gathered in the "material world" and rooted the teleological dream of perfection in the soil of everyday reality. They
also sized up the schemes of visionaries by the measuring sticks of common
sense, intuition, loyalty, habit, custom, and other suprarational standards. In
short, they were particular, contingent, local, historical, and could not be or-

dered under the Procrustean rule of a single and patently false "science of government."[39]

The true science of government was to be found in the amalgam of theory and practice, in the legitimate and reasonable application of just principles through good institutions. It must comprise a realization of true rights through civil polity and the principles of law in conditions and relations of property. Only in this manner could Coleridge conceive of a *groundwork* for his politics of morals.

The basis for Coleridge's negative attack on the Jacobins and philosophes is clear. What remains to be explained is the positive dimension to this critique. Coleridge had demolished the hopes of those who trusted in coercive attempts of government to apply rules and policies to the project of creating a new social man. He had narrowly defined the role of government, suggesting that government's chief role was to guard the boundaries of citizens' individual rights and duties and forbid the transgression of them by any individual or other "collective power" in the state.

Given such a minimalist role for government, devoted only to maintaining equality of rights and duties, it is only logical that Coleridge praised those institutions (such as the Common Law) that he saw as mending the walls which protected each citizen from intrusion on his rights of moral autonomy and damned those innovations (such as arbitrary statute) which he saw as tearing down the walls of equal rights in the service of national security (Pitt) or community (the Jacobins). I have discussed elsewhere in this study the importance of the Common Law and of property as "constitutive" of Coleridge's vision of liberty; in the final chapter I shall speak at length of the church as another component of this vision. In each of these instances, Coleridge conceived of the role of the government and coercion to be minimal, used only to defend rights. In each of these cases, he conceived of the informal authority of the state—that great conger of law, religion, property, morals, and the Ideas of each—as plenipotentiary.

I have argued thus far the degree to which an examination of Coleridge's writings on liberty not only forces one to rethink the hackneyed "young radical"/"old Tory" dichotomy, which has persistently deformed Coleridge studies, but more importantly forces one to reconsider the meaning of the terms "liberal" and "conservative" in the first decades of the nineteenth century. These terms, as applied to British politics, of course, date from the period 1820 to 1840, and the overly punctilious might exclude them altogether from use in the evaluation of Coleridge's attitudes in 1809. However, having admitted that they are a post facto historiographical conceit, one might agree to use them because they are convenient and widely understood. Having done this, one must immediately declare that they are terms that (even when used "nonanachronistically") raise as many questions as they answer. Inasmuch as Coleridge advocated a minimal coercive apparatus for the government and a nonexistent role for the magistrate in generating virtue and community, he was an atomistic liberal. Inasmuch as Coleridge envisioned an omnipresent influence of law, property, and religion in forming the moral autarchy that he believed necessary to regulate the citizen's egalitarian pursuit of happiness, he was a communitarian conservative.

CHAPTER 6

Science and Nature

OLERIDGE'S WRITINGS AFTER the turn of the nineteenth century were elaborate and complex variations on the basic themes of politics, power, law, and morality that had been announced in his earliest publications from 1795 through 1800. Typically, "apostasy" theorists such as Thompson and Erdman have argued that Coleridge, whether through "disenchantment" or "default," "turned" in 1802 away from the radicalism of his youth to a true-blue Toryism.[1] The argument thus far has contested the apostasy theory and rejected the view that Coleridge "changed sides" in 1802 by deserting from the Jacobin ranks and treasonably skulking over to the Tory camp. Having dismissed the traditional paradigm of Coleridge's evolution from 1790 to 1830 as a false one, I have also suggested the constructive dimensions of Coleridge's intellectual development during those years as constituting more than mere refutation of government policy and conventional opposition. Coleridge's strongly historicist accounts of liberty and human agency in political life advanced original political philosophy and established the foundations of his statesman's science.

I wish in what follows to suggest that the fundamental changes that took place in Coleridge's style of thinking after 1802 focused on the scientific foundations of a basic political theory rather than on the rhetorical and ideological merits of those arguments tied exclusively to party politics. The changes in Coleridge's politics were not due to disenchantment, nor default, as Erdman and Thompson have argued, but were instead the product of a positive and expansive development of his own philosophical system. Such a change must be considered not as a "giving up" or "pulling back" into textbook Toryism, but as a rapid *forward* movement into a more technically complex and philosophically informed development of the early and largely untutored work of the 1790s.

The interdependency of the constitutional principles of liberty and property remained as central to Coleridge's late political writings as they were to his early works. But he expanded his understanding of these "constitutive ideas" by combining German idealism and his own natural-scientific study, with the changing conceptions of wealth and social organization that had been suggested by the works of the Scottish literati.[2]

Three crucial catalysts advanced Coleridge's intellectual development after 1800: encounters with the ideas of (1) the natural scientists, (2) the political economists, and (3) the German idealists. Coleridge combined these three influences into his own political theory of a science, which was, he thought, at the same time both empiricist and realist (almost Berkeleyan) in its aims and methods. Metaphysics, epistemology, and studies of nature were even more integral to Coleridge's politics after 1800 than they had been in the 1790s. Therefore, his views on politics cannot be considered, much less understood, without looking at his views on the sciences and what sorts of knowledge they ought to yield.

This encounter between Coleridge and the three schools of thought, as we shall see, was not a matter of passive absorption or of tuition at the feet of masters whose ideas he would simply copy and popularize for a British audience. Coleridge's "critical" approach to texts meant that even more than most of his critically minded contemporaries, he transformed what he read, assimilating it to his own needs.[3] As a result of this lifelong strategy, Coleridge was ill fitted to the task of discipleship. He tended to pick fault almost excessively, even in those arguments he admired. He also tended to distrust simple mathematical models of society, altering the knowledge he gained from studying them into corollaries of his own which he felt better expressed the complex, dynamic nature of political and economic change.

Due to his eclectic temperament, Coleridge could not resist the temptation to meddle and tinker with the ideas of those who influenced him. The traditional claim that Coleridge's reading of Hegel made Coleridge into a Hegelian is insufficient because it focuses on the catalyst rather than the resultant reaction. It is almost certainly closer to the truth of that encounter to assert that Coleridge's reading of Hegel "made" *Hegel* into a *Coleridgean*. Where Hegel's dialectic had three stages, Coleridge felt it necessary to add a *fourth*. This constant adaptation is characteristic of Coleridge's approach to "reading" the German transcendentalists, the natural scientists, and the political economists in the first decades of the nineteenth century.

Coleridge combined the philosophical ideas of the German transcendentalists, the natural scientists, and the classical economists in his accounts of society and order. The result of this unusual melange of disciplines was that he viewed the law, as he viewed property, in terms of the cultural and economic implications of commercial activity. Concomitantly, he saw liberty as the historically mediated consequence of the actions, collectively and individually, of people, people who were participants in a living social and political matrix.

Increasing efforts at a work of intellectual synthesis did not so much herald Coleridge's "trimming" defection from one party (Jacobin) to another (Tory) as it suggested the pervasiveness of his antiparty sympathies. If Coleridge was personally ill fitted for the party politics of the 1790s, he was even more out of place in the world of the 1800s. In the great era from 1790 to 1832 when formal political parties first gained respectability and permanence in the national life of British politics, Coleridge's increase of learning only made him more adamant about the insufficiency of party and faction to solve social problems. Coleridge's associations and ideas during these "later" years were too emphatic on the need for constant change to be conservative and too adamant on the need to maintain fundamental institutions to be radical. Because he saw the state as more than a family or a church based on the paternalism of Anglican landholders, Coleridge made himself an unfit champion for the "Tories." Because he saw the state as more than a set of gears and levers put together to extrude equal citizens and promote a mathematical vision of the greatest good for the greatest number, Coleridge made himself odious to the "radicals."

Rather than advancing a mechanical model of government, Coleridge adopted a biological model of the state. This organicism was not understood to be merely analogous to politics. Coleridge contended that it was the true, or "real," foundation of all science, whether natural or political. His reading in the German transcendentalist philosophers (Kant, Schelling, Lessing, Hegel, Schlegel) during this period is well known. Less often discussed is his equally important and, by 1800, growing fascination with the accomplishments and the limits of natural science.[4] Beginning in 1799, his scientific pursuits were fuelled by his friendship with Humphry Davy, during the course of which he involved himself in basic research of his own on nitrous oxide.[5] Coleridge was particularly interested in the metaphysical, causative underpinnings of empirical physical sciences such as chemistry, medicine, and animal physiognomy. He increasingly believed, as a result of his scientific study, that organic and somatic processes would provide not only an objective corollary in natural science but also an explanation of deep cause for his conceptions of history and society in the human sciences.

As a result of his growing preoccupation with metaphysics and natural science, Coleridge's continuing thoughts on reform focused increasingly on the use of biological metaphors of the "organism" as descriptions of the constitution of the modern state. Of course, the interlinked "organic" world of

nature was an old and shopworn metaphor for the state. A primitive organi-
cist vocabulary existed long before the scientific revolution increased understanding of how plants and bodies actually worked. The old Medieval vocabulary of the "body" politic, the "royal oak" of the state, and the
"patriarchal family" of Adam and Noah as the basis for kingship and the rule
of fathers had stressed for centuries that every part of a polity had a function
and could only be "lopped off" or taken up "root and branch" at great peril.
The difference between these older uses of organic imagery and Coleridge's
was that, for Coleridge, the use of biological metaphor was not simply to
provide an emblematic illustration of what was "nature's way," as the old or-
ganicist thought had. For Coleridge, the entirety of nature provided a model
of the complexity of dynamic relations in a system; in short, "*organization*"
was quite literally somatic function. The biological metaphor was *central* to
Coleridge's thought in a way that it would never again be central to the
work of any other British thinker until Herbert Spencer's (mis)use of Dar-
winism. The number of biological metaphors in Coleridge's work is aston-
ishing, the innovative way in which he used them to inform his political
theory even more so. This active biological (even protoecological) study of
the relations of organisms to environment had two major results. In its wake,
Coleridge expanded his belief in the centrality of property as the ground for
political power. He also refined his view of liberty as the generative and sustaining impulse behind that power.

Ironically, Coleridge's plunge into the study of organic phenomena appears to have made him less tolerant of the "scientific" approaches to politics
that were coming into vogue in the first decades of the new century. His study
of science from 1799 to 1802 appears (I infer from his writings against the
economists) to have convinced him of two things. The first was that even in
the natural sciences, but especially in the study of human behavior, excessive
simplicity in theory was a vice rather than a virtue. His writings against the political economists suggest a rejection of "Occam's Razor" with regard to biological phenomena (such as the growth of human populations) on the grounds
that no simple model could explain the complexity of interdependent systems
involving free and moral agents. The second was that any mechanical account
of physics alone was meaningless or even destructive in the absence of the
guiding hand of metaphysics and morality. For Coleridge, to assume that humanity was *Homo oeconomicus* could only mean that the species was incapable
of performing the work of *Homo sapiens*. Men who assumed this, he gathered,
could only be enemies to liberty. Coleridge's arguments against the political
economists suggested his account of nature's un-simple plan.

From his youth, Coleridge had been preoccupied with debunking what he called the "mechano-corpuscular" philosophy of Locke and Hartley. He found "mathematically" styled rationalism and strictly nominalist forms of empiricism equally faulty. In his eyes, they tended toward too-static and too-simple explanations for the complex and constantly moving web of human nature, morality, and socioeconomic change. By proposing single causes in a "frictionless" model, they failed to account for the dynamic and multicausal complexity of social relations.

The true process of social relations, Coleridge believed, was analogous to the transmutation, growth, and decay of living organisms. Just as an individual was more than the sum total of his body parts and physiological processes, so the "history" of a nation was more than the chronological list of outwardly visible causes and effects. More than the day-by-day annals of past events, history was also, as Coleridge conceived of it, simultaneously the active product and agent of the institutional structures, the functions and telos, of a people. As such, history was purposive—determined by intentions, objectives, and aspirations that might never be consciously expressed in the historical record and were certainly not listed in the annals, chronicles, and *Res gestae* of the various nations. Even the best social analysis of his day, claimed Coleridge, generalized only to the "physical" level of explaining how events happened rather than asking the "metaphysical" questions of why and to what end they took place.

A true theory of history or, for that matter, a "theory of life," had to consider the teleology (or what Coleridge conceived as the "futurity") of these processes.[6] If it ignored these in favor of cataloguing phenomena alone, it was (in Coleridge's view) doomed to be simplistic, mechanistic and reductionist. Yet, Coleridge did not believe that his focus on "futurity"—deep causes and final "ends"—meant any denigration of human freedom in history.

Coleridge was able to advocate a strong emphasis on teleology without suggesting that individuals had no role in the direction societies took. Indeed, despite his focus on deep underlying causes and distant ends, he always showed merciless hostility to determinist systems. In several cases, his rejection of a philosophical system was due to what he saw as its erasure of the human will from its model of society. In the 1790s, Coleridge had shown some enthusiasm for the account of motion and agency implicit in David Hartley's theory of association of ideas, until Hartley's belief in necessity repelled him. In 1795, Coleridge criticized Godwin's *Political Justice* for advocating both necessity and a straight-line theory of historical development that assumed inevitable progress. Coleridge disliked any theory that in defining structures and ends went so far as to "factor out" human will from their calculations altogether.

This fundamental objection fuelled Coleridge's rejection of the political economists and the utilitarians. It found its expression in a two-pronged strategy of attack against the doctrine of disinterest. In part this entailed a reevaluation of William Godwin's understanding of "disinterested benevolence." But it focused most critically on the "dismal science" of moral calculus as practiced by the Reverend Thomas Malthus. Malthus, along with Paley and Bentham, had transformed the idea of disinterest into the idea of utility. Just as Godwin began his 1796 retreat from the idea that society could be understood without reference to "the empire of feeling" and basic human attachments, the philosophy of prudence, utility, and maximand was gaining adherence.

One of the most striking turnabouts of Coleridge's mature career was his change of attitude toward Godwin. Because he disliked the idea of discarding a philosophical system in its entirety, unreflectively, Coleridge often made efforts at partial salvage. His originality as a thinker was largely a function of which pieces of the intellectual past he saved, which he rejected, and how he refitted them for his own uses. In 1796, he dismissed Godwin as "jejune in language and singular in judgement."[7] When Coleridge returned from Germany in 1801, he had altered his opinion so much as to form a close association with his old philosophical adversary.

By 1801, Coleridge conceded that his early criticisms of *Political Justice* as being excessively rationalistic and cerebral were rash. Coleridge admitted that he probably misunderstood certain aspects of it. This growing sympathy towards Godwin was perhaps the result of Godwin's own changing ideas as much as Coleridge's. Godwin published his own "recantations" in the second (1796) and third (1798) editions of *Political Justice* and had decided to stress the importance of the "empire of feeling" rather than pure disinterested benevolence. This new emphasis on emotion no doubt mollified Coleridge, who had rejected as unrealistic Godwin's 1793 model of disinterest as excluding human emotion. Unfortunately, just at the time when Godwin had relented and repented the "heartlessness" of his old system of disinterest, Coleridge found a new enemy who merited a greater degree of censure than that he had showered on Godwin in 1795. By 1802 a new theory had arisen, one which seemed to argue not only for the banishment of the advocates of the "empire of feeling" from political disputation, but for a new form of "disinterested malevolence."

In 1802, Coleridge took up the cudgel against Thomas Malthus's *Essay on the Principles of Population*. In his 1802 annotation of Godwin's *Thoughts Occasioned by the Perusal of Dr Parr's Spital Sermon*, Coleridge defended the "reconstructed" Godwin and criticized Malthus. Godwin's pamphlet was a triple reply to the Anglican divine Rev. Dr. Samuel Parr, Sir James Mackintosh, and

Rev. Thomas Malthus, who had all attacked *Political Justice* in their individual writings. Reflecting on his early objections, "in the innocence of my youth," Coleridge had great praise for Godwin's new *Thoughts*. He claimed somewhat unctuously that he "remember[ed] few passages in ancient or modern Authors that contain more just philosophy in appropriate, chaste, & beautiful diction" than Godwin's reply to Parr. He added that those passages of Godwin's "reflect equal honour on Godwin's Head and Heart. . . . I feel remorse *ever* to have spoken unkindly of such a man."[8] While Coleridge still held his objections to the first edition of *Political Justice*, he—somewhat too publicly confessing his sin—regretted underestimating Godwin's character and intellectual intentions in the letters of 1796 to Thelwall.

Coleridge's only objection to Godwin's *Thoughts Occasioned* was that Godwin had not been aggressive enough in demonstrating the immorality of Malthus's system and had been too reserved in his criticisms.[9] Coleridge, for his part, believed that the failure of Malthus's theory to link questions of morality to population was a fatal flaw in the system. Indeed, he asserted in a marginal note to his copy of Malthus, "[Malthus] is to the last degree, idle to write in this way without having stat[ed] the meaning of the words Vice and Virtue."[10] Coleridge noted that it was "Strange" "that G[odwin] should so hastily admit [Malthusian] principles so doubtful in themselves, and so undoubtedly dreadful in their consequences." Coleridge for his part asserted that "there exists no proof, & no improbability has been evinced by Malthus, that an excess of population arising from *physical* necessity has introduced *Immorality* or that morality would not in itself have contained the true, easy, and effectual Limitation." "The Whole" question, for Coleridge, was "a business of '*which is the Cause? w[hi]ch the effect?*' "[11] One could, like Malthus, assume that unchained reproduction among the poor led to crime and vice. Or one could, as Coleridge obviously did, assert that "morality . . . in itself" could function as a "true, easy, and effectual Limitation" for population growth, concluding that weak public morals were a cause of reckless procreation. Since his explanation preserved the chance for moral autonomy and exercise of independent will, Coleridge preferred his scheme to Malthus's.

Coleridge generally detested those systems that eliminated the language of virtue and morality—the "bottom" and "fixed principles" which he had spoken for in his lectures of 1795. Therefore, he rejected Malthus's deterministic theory, which claimed that "Vice" and "Virtue" were less important in determining the chastity of the poor than the supply of bread. He also heaped scorn upon the imputation that the population biology of humans was not significantly dissimilar from that of rabbits, who mindlessly increased mathematically until their food supply was exhausted and famine ensued. Malthus's assumption in the first edition of his theory—that population increase would be an uninterrupted constant—ignored or scoffed at the moral force of social censure and individual choice. Not only did these forces have a potential to adjust the progressive rate of population, but they were also the active elements in constituting morality.

Given that Malthus's theory was fundamentally immoral, argued Coleridge, any legislation predicated on his ethology would be a disaster. Coleridge lamented that "the monstrous practical sophism of Malthus" had made such rapid gains that it had "gotten complete possession of the leading men of the kingdom!" The crime which Malthus had committed in propagating "an essential lie in morals" was compounded by the scientific invalidity of the theory, making it "a practical lie in fact."[12] Bad science could only result in bad policy. Malthus's "principles" were not only "doubtful in themselves," claimed Coleridge, but were "undoubtedly dreadful in their consequences" if put into action.

Coleridge's insistence that virtue and morality must be included in all theories of statecraft meant that he was an inveterate enemy of the prudentialists and the utilitarians and the "Dismal Scientists" of economics. All three of these schools of thought were coming into vogue among segments of the governing elite from 1790 to 1820, particularly among those interested in reform. As he presented an alternate moral ground for reform that was incompatible with their theories, Coleridge saw himself as bound to attack the rising influence of these men in the state.

Coleridge believed that a fundamental sophistry lay at the bottom of the "mechano-corpuscular" theory, which he conceived as looking only at naked causes and effects without considering their rightness or wrongness. He traced the rise of this "mechano-corpuscular" error (inaccurately) in a line of descent that ran from John Locke through David Hartley, Helvetius, Adam Smith, William Paley, Jeremy Bentham, and Thomas Malthus to David Ricardo. In Coleridge's assessment, the mechanists focused only on low-level generalizations such as food production, wages, birth rates, and prices: the sort of sublunary theorizing of "hows" which resulted in what Coleridge termed "Concepts." Coleridge condemned the mechanists for ignoring and even scorning a higher realm of metaphysical Ideas. The "science of Ideas," as Coleridge often described it, not only kept the discourse of civic virtue at the center of political theory but also suggested a sociological account of political, cultural, and ethical institutions. Where the "mechanists" had only studied human activities in isolation, Coleridge considered the individual as existing in a social and political matrix composed of the complex interrelationship between the components of society. Because the mechanistic fallacy ignored the complexity of the social net by looking at its components in isolation and outside of a fundamental moral vocabulary, it was an approach that prevented accurate modeling of the forces that regulated human society and political powers. The mistake of the so-called disciples of Locke, Coleridge argued, was their attempt to confute general principles with actual occurrences, an error that led to the articulation of "half-truths which are whole errors."

The "young" Coleridge had criticized Paley's *Principles of Moral and Political Philosophy* for its emphasis on prudence over duty. He had seen Paley's prudential ethics as sliding too easily into the situational ethics of ends justifying any means, the situational ethics of Robespierre and Pitt. Coleridge also saw in Malthus and Ricardo the propagation of the false morality of prudence. They had, according to Coleridge, cloaked Paley's philosophical musings in the garb of "objective" science in order to disguise its immorality. For this reason, it was Malthus and Ricardo, rather than Sir James Steuart, Adam Smith, or the French physiocrats, whom Coleridge targeted in his attacks on political economy.

Coleridge rebuked the static view of society that he believed "the Malthusians" had taken from Smith.[13] However, he appears to have been less total in his condemnation of Smith and the early Scots economists than he was of Malthus, Ricardo, and Mackintosh. This is *presumably* because Coleridge believed that authors such as Smith had not discarded the language of virtue and moral sentiments even in their writings on matters such as the price of rope. Indeed, as has been suggested, Coleridge was keenly interested in the "practical moralism" and sociological jurisprudence that he considered central to the "Scottish philosophy."[14] Coleridge's own conception of the hidden hand or the cunning of history was a synthesis of the sociological economics of Adam Smith and other Scottish moralists with the historical and transcendentalist views of Immanuel Kant. The underlying assumption that made this conceptual union of Scottish moralism and German idealism possible was a peculiarly Coleridgean rendering of what might best be described as "Platonic empiricism."

Coleridge's searched throughout his youth for a valid alternative to the sterility and immorality of the "mechano-corpuscular" tradition.[15] He considered this "mechanic philosophy" to entail an "apostolic succession" of error from Locke to Ricardo. This search finally brought him to the writings of Immanuel Kant, perhaps as early as 1795. Although Coleridge initially disliked Kant's work because it savored too much of the materialism of Aristotle, he nevertheless believed that Kant's work had achieved the most complete philosophical system yet.

In a letter of 1820 to his philosophically minded friend James Gooden, he expressed the opinion that all philosophical perspectives were either "Platonic" or "Aristotelian." This sentiment that Platonism and Aristotelianism represent two major modes of thought is, in itself, commonplace and even trite— it appears in almost every introductory textbook in philosophy. What was unusual was Coleridge's innovative use of these traditional categories, which elevated his statement above the level of textbook platitude. Coleridge argued that there were "half a dozen things," that is, philosophical sects, that had been "nick-named" "Schools of Philosophy" in England. Nevertheless, in "the only accurate sense of the term," there were "but two essentially different Schools of Philosophy." The first was the "Platonic"; the second was the "Aristotelian." The surprise came when Coleridge revealed which thinkers he had consigned to these rival camps. Among the Aristotelians, he put the transcendentalist "Emmanuel Kant," although he suggested that Kant made "a somewhat nearer approach to the Platonic." Among the Platonists, he grouped Bacon and Leibnitz and Berkeley (the later Berkeley, "in his riper and better years"). Finally, he "pledge[d] [him]self an adherent" to Platonism, though he qualified this grant of allegiance with the characteristically Coleridgean demurral that "as every man has a face of his own, without being more or less a man, so is every true philosopher an original."[16] It goes without saying that Coleridge included himself in the category of the "true philosopher." It is of interest that as late in his life as 1820 he was still obsessed enough with the idea of individuality that he stressed that the real philosophers were "original" men like himself, unique and above categorization.

One's assessment of Coleridge's attitudes toward empiricism and idealism must be modified in the light of Coleridge's daring and bizarre taxonomy in his letter of 1820. Coleridge viewed Bacon, Leibnitz, Berkeley, and himself as Platonists. He did so despite Bacon's already having been canonized as the founding father of British empiricism and science and Berkeley's sensationalist epistemology having long been used by Hume, and others, in ways that had led to Pyrrhonism more than Platonism. Yet all of them were Platonists in Coleridge's estimation. His category of "Aristotelian" is thinner: only Kant, and Kant as a Platonically minded Aristotelian. Obviously, he saw Platonism as the broader road, one that he himself trod, and one that was superior to the "mechano-corpuscular" views of the rival school of Locke. The suggestion, then, is that Coleridge saw Platonism as a superior ground for natural science rather than an impediment to it. Hence, he "kidnapped" Bacon from the empiricist pantheon. The critical question for Coleridge concerned the way in which these thinkers combined a realist theory of Ideas, with a sense-based epistemology rooted in solid ground and respect for the study of phenomena.

Coleridge enlisted Kant into his band of worthies of Platonism as an Aristotelian who made "a somewhat nearer approach to the Platonic" than his less enlightened brethren.[17] Kant was, in his view, a Platonic sort of Aristotelian (as was Aristotle for some critics), a man who combined the technique and pursuit of science characteristic of empiricism with the depth of understanding of Ideas of the Platonist. As Coleridge observed, both the world and humanity's understanding of that world were "alike unto the law of nature." Coleridge's post-Kantian synthesis seems to have sought the best of both worlds: a combination of Aristotelianism's respect for particulars within groups and Platonism's grasp of universals as real and true things above mere categories of convenience. A true philosophy would respect particulars without denigrating universals, and vice versa, for "every man has a [particular] face of his own without being more or less a [member of the universal set of] man."[18]

Coleridge was aware that his attempt to splice together the most effective parts of the old schools was a novel work of syncretism. This was not simply the result of a personal mania for syncretism as a way of life. Coleridge did not, it will be remembered, approve equally of all syncretistic solutions. He appears to have believed, for instance, that his own revised and empirically minded brand of Platonism would avoid the errors of the Jacobins. Philosophe eclecticism, as practiced by the Jacobins, had resulted in what Coleridge had derided as a "*monstrum hybridum*," or the combination of the worst and weakest aspects of a variety of systems. Presumably, he wanted his own mix of modes of inquiry to result in an *angelicum hybridum*: a mix of the best in an eclectic range of philosophies traditionally segregated from each other. It is quite clear from his own writings around the turn of the century that Coleridge was highly aware of the novelty of his new philosophy. It was so novel, indeed, that even he could not explain it in simple terms. In a telling notebook entry of 1801, he described his new system as a "Spinozo-Kantian, Kanto-Fichtian, Fichto-Schellingian Revival of Plato-Plotino-Proclian Idealism."[19] One could hardly ask for a more candid admission of eclecticism. Like the bee in Swift's *Battle of the Books*, Coleridge seems to have seen his effort as collecting the best, harvesting the "sweetness and light" from these authors and distilling it into his own system.[20] This approach dictated his encounter with Kant. But in Coleridge's encounter with Kant's theory of ideas, Kant was cast as the Aristotelian to Coleridge's own protagonistic Platonist.

It is clear from Coleridge's own enthusiastic account of his first encounter with Kantian metaphysics that Kant was the only philosopher whose works

Coleridge could recommend that a friend take his time to read in toto. Coleridge candidly informed the philosophical tyro James Gooden that "In [Kant's writings] is contained all that can be *learnt*."[21] It is beyond doubt that Kant was one of the leading influences in Coleridge's philosophical career. Deirdre Coleman has explored, in depth, the impact that Kant's ethics had on Coleridge's political and social thought.[22] Coleridge seems to have been equally inspired by the realist metaphysics of Kant's *Critiques*. Reading both Kant's ethics and his metaphysics led Coleridge to consider new theories of human nature and historical process. In this new system, he appears to have wanted—as he had done in his redefinition of Platonism—to promote an idealist philosophy that could accomplish more or better things in the sciences than had the pure materialist tradition. In doing so, he hoped to defeat the mere mechanists who denied the reality of immaterial things such as virtue and morality.

There were, of course, only a handful of "disciples of Kant" in early-nineteenth-century Britain. Indeed, almost all that the literati of the United Kingdom knew about Kantian theories up to about 1830, they knew as a result of Coleridge's own translations, recensions, and pastiches. Thus, it was nearly impossible for Coleridge's contemporaries to evaluate the degree to which Coleridge was merely a diligent pupil and copyist of Kantian writings—a popularizer, in effect—and the degree to which Coleridge criticized, modified, and perfected those doctrines that he found in Kant's work. Even at the present time, Coleridge's adaptive recension of Kant tends to be underestimated or even condemned as plagiarism by scholars such as Welleck and Fruman[23]. Like Plato, Melancthon, and Beza, Coleridge tinkered with the "system" of the "great man" whose mantle he had inherited to such a degree that he made it truly his own and put his stamp upon it. It would be more accurate to suggest that Coleridge transmuted Kant than to say that he translated him: *traddutore traitore*. For this reason, it is a more fruitful and worthwhile enterprise to seek out Coleridge's deviations from pure Kantianism than his faithful adherences to it.

It is of crucial importance here, therefore, to discern how Coleridge differed from the continental disciples who formed the "school" of Kant. Although he considered Kant to be an omnibus philosopher who was exceptional reading for a novice like Gooden, Coleridge saw serious flaws in Kant's doctrine of how Ideas functioned in the material world.[24] Coleridge believed that Kant's system was a truly comprehensive one, but one that ultimately fell short of its goal because it did not pay enough attention to the reality of Ideas as they interacted with concepts.[25] He regretted that Kant's emphasis on analytic philosophy had caused Kant to slip into an Aristotelian and materialist bias. This Kantian "Aristotelianism" was, ultimately, the basis of Coleridge's parting of the ways with Kant. His disagreement with Kant's doctrine on the reality of Ideas was the reason why Coleridge saw himself as a true disciple of Plato, and Kant as only a true disciple of Aristotle who occasionally spoke like a Platonist.

Looking beyond the *regulative role* of ideas, which Kant had explored in such detail and with such success, Coleridge considered ideas to have *constitutive reality*. It was the essential reality of the Idea, Coleridge believed, that Kant had neglected. He instructed James Gooden that in many ways, the two schools offered the same basic tenets. Both the Aristotelian/Kantian and the Platonic/Coleridgean schools could offer their adherents "a firm faith in God, the responsible Will of Man, and Immortality." On those basic points, he saw their work as identical: "Kant will demonstrate to you, that this faith [in God, the Will, and Immortality] is acquiesced in, indeed may be confirmed by the Reason & Understanding, but grounded on postulates authorized and confirmed by the Moral being—*These* [opinions] *are likewise mine.*"[26]

The true split between the two approaches, Coleridge pointed out to Gooden, was a technically sophisticated issue not over *if* God, the will, and immortality were true, but over *how* they were true, and *how known* to be true. Coleridge did not wish to trouble his less philosophically minded friend with the technical disputes that made no pragmatic difference to a layman who only wanted proofs of nonsensory phenomena such as God. He told Gooden that the *Wegestreit* between Plato and Aristotle was "of living interest to the philosopher by profession alone."[27]

But obviously, to those who were "philosopher[s] by profession," as Coleridge certainly saw himself by this time, those very fine points that were *adiaphora* to the layman were essential and crucial points. The crux of the matter was "whether the ideas are *regulative* only as Aristotle and Kant teach, or *constitutive and actual* as Pythagoras and Plato [argue]." This difference lay at the heart of the debate. He suggested that there was no practical difference between the two systems as long as the Aristotelians stuck to the analysis of sublunary variety and held back from attacking noumenal unity. "Both systems are equally true," he informed Gooden, "if only the former [the Aristotelians] abstain from denying *universally* what is denied individually." In the end, the roads divided in the discussion of how Ideas worked. For Coleridge, "He for whom Ideas are *constitutive* will in effect be a Platonist—and in those for whom they are *regulative* only, Platonism is but a hollow affectation."[28]

To assert that Ideas "regulate" phenomena, as the Aristotelians did, was (in Coleridge's mind) to consign Ideas as mere sorters into orderly taxonomical categories. Such an approach suggested that Ideas provided a structure for being in the same way that a file clerk might provide a structure for papers. To assert as Coleridge (and those he saw as his "fellow-Platonists") did that Ideas "constitute" phenomena was a very different business. His theory suggested that ideas created and made data as well as organized it; ideas were actual creative forces above and beyond their minimal role as "sorters" of the raw material of sense impression. Widely considered, Ideas, in what Coleridge called the Platonist system, *made* events, *constituted* them.

The originality of Coleridge's interpretation of Kant lay in his invention of this doctrine of the "constitutive dynamism of transcendental ideas." Because he was a realist, Coleridge believed that the noumenal Idea undergirded the existence of all phenomena. Yet he asserted that the proclaiming of the higher reality of Ideas neither negated nor demoted the material world of sensory perception and sensory impression to the lower level of mere shadows and ghosts without any significance to true philosophy. He also stressed that *noumena* (Ideas) could, in fact, be studied and comprehended by means of empirically obtained sense-data, and that these phenomena could be organized as "conceptions." Philosophers of Ideas were not precluded from using objects of sense, which were demonstrable and sensible, as the basis for understanding the underlying reality of such objects of sense.[29] The Coleridgean "Idea" was therefore a development, through the agency of reason and understanding, of commonsense empirical data through intuition and metaphysical reason.[30] It was also an important step, one that Kant had not entirely made, towards giving Ideas a hands-on role in the generation of events and material structures. The Coleridgean "Idea" was not merely a category of convenience, as the empiricists had argued. Nor was it "higher thought," reason concealed behind the curtain of phenomena, as Kant had claimed. The Coleridgean "Idea" was a living, active thing in itself, something which formed and shaped the material world of phenomena.

The most powerful case that Coleridge made against the Aristotelians was his attack on what he dubbed "the Cult of Locke." Coleridge believed that Aristotle had been a materialist and that the epistemological basis of materialism was empirical. He regarded the method and temperament of the Aristotelian as that practiced by the botanist or the zoologist. It was, Coleridge argued, a largely taxinomical activity of filing information into pigeonholes, of dissecting and categorizing. The Aristotelian natural philosopher was, to be sure, a physicist, but one who stopped short of the search for metaphysical foundations. Such a thinker knew *how* nature worked, bemoaned Coleridge, but not why.[31] Aristotelian science and its Lockean and Hartleian and Malthusian descendants endlessly recorded and distinguished between "genus" and "phylum" but never proposed a universal theory of genesis, or a theory of what "life" meant. For Coleridge, the low epistemological ambition of materialism created problems in historiography and political theory as well as in natural sciences. Coleridge argued that antiquarianism of the Aristotelian variety was no substitute for a science or philosophy of history. The Lockean "mechano-corpuscular" philosophy considered the world to be made and acted on ("constituted") only through detectable material causes. To Aristotelian theorists, all events in history were only the product of material causes. The theories (or more properly Conceptions) that made up Aristotelian science proceeded from these materialist assumptions. Those assumptions limited the purview of Aristotlelian science to only those questions of cause that rested on things that could be sensed, catalogued, and analyzed with the naked eye. Such limited assumptions also restricted Aristotelian theory to low-range generalizations induced from the patterns evident in frequently recurring phenomena. Such was the method of Boyle and the Royal Society, of Newton, and of the English tradition in science in general. Coleridge's critique of their works was only the latest in the long line of critiques of pure empiricism stretching back to Hobbes[32] and Leibniz.[33]

Ideas, to the "Aristotelian" in Coleridge's schema, were ways of regulating our descriptions of these occurrences, but they had no higher constitutive reality. Ideas organized the sensory events in life, but they did not shape them. Coleridge objected that such a system was inadequate. Like Leibniz, he believed that until there was some synthetic or transcendental explanation of why things occurred as they did, there was no true knowledge of phenomenon, only observations and descriptions. Indeed, Coleridge characterized his own system as working in tandem with Leibniz and the "later Germans" as an attempt "to reduce all knowledge into harmony."[34]

Coleridge believed that the materialist philosophy of Aristotle and, from that tradition, the "mechano-corpuscular" philosophy of Locke and the Enlightenment had erred in obsessively creating descriptive laws while ignoring and even deriding prescriptive laws. Indeed, the success of Newtonian science in predicting and categorizing material phenomena had led to an increasing arrogance and conviction among the Aristotelian party that a science of man could be founded that was as accurate and simple as the science of falling bodies. The Aristotelians, Coleridge alleged, invented the doctrines that asserted that man was a machine, and that government was a machine, and that "fixing" states was only a matter of amassing the right data and generating the correct models for a new society. Such was the legacy of LaMettrie, of Robespierre, and now of Ricardo, Malthus, and Bentham. In a conversation with

Henry Crabb Robinson in December of 1810, Coleridge addressed both the Lockean tradition in science and its Leibnizian alternative. Coleridge, reported Robinson, "spoke, as usual, with great contempt, that is in reference to [Locke's] metaphysical work. He considered [Locke] as having *led to the destruction of metaphysical science, by encouraging the unlearned public to think that with mere common-sense they might dispense with disciplined study.*"[35] It was this very "metaphysical science," which looked above "mere common-sense" upwards towards "true sense," which Coleridge hoped to revive in the natural and especially in the human sciences.

Coleridge feared the widespread popular simplification of such Aristotelian ideas and, beyond that, dreaded the way in which empiricist ideas were appropriated and deracinated by factional interests to advance their party in the state. He saw the error of the French, as we have seen, in their insistence on using pseudoscientific theory in their attempts to reform their society rather than thinking deeply about the ends of government. This French obsession with Lockean method, Coleridge believed, was the legacy of Voltaire's Aristotelian battle against the Platonist Leibniz. Coleridge in 1810, remembered Robinson, "ascribed Locke's popularity to his political character . . . and to the nationality of the people who considered [Locke] and Newton the adversaries of the German Leibniz. Voltaire[,] to depress Leibniz, raised Locke."[36]

Coleridge returned with regularity throughout his career to his criticisms of Lockean philosophy as the chief exemplar of modern Aristotelian thought. This was not only because Locke was, in Coleridge's opinion, the most mechanistic of the empiricists, but because he had been canonized during the course of the eighteenth century as a secular saint of British liberty and of the scientific Enlightenment. It was Coleridge's belief that "Locke" the god, and not John Locke the man, had rapidly gained adherents in the United Kingdom and France who knew little of his work except that he had "disproved" the contentions of Leibniz and others that there was anything more than phenomena to be considered by science. Coleridge considered that some of the "empiricists" had produced more measured accounts of Ideas in their philosophical works. He believed this particularly in the case of Berkeley, but he also considered it true of Newton and Bacon.[37]

It was through the philosophy of Francis Bacon that Coleridge invoked a native-born English tradition of Platonic science. Among English thinkers, argued Coleridge, Sir Francis Bacon's genius (what Coleridge called the Verulamian logic) gave the best account of the world regulated by the constitutive reality of Ideas, Ideas that lay behind rather than after their empirical effect. This realism, Coleridge argued, was apparent throughout Bacon's masterwork,

Novum Organon. Coleridge concluded that Bacon's inspiration was in seeing beyond mere events to the final realities of those events. This placed him in the company of such poetic visionaries as Shakespeare and Dante. It also, despite Bacon's protests to the contrary, put Bacon in the camp of the Platonists, as far as Coleridge was concerned. Coleridge contended that "Lord Bacon, who never read Plato's works[,] thought pure Platonism in his *great* work, the Novum Organum, and abuses his divine predecessor [Plato] for fantastic nonsense which [Plato] had been the first to explode."[38] Coleridge would later describe Bacon in *Church and State* as the "British Plato."[39] These bold acts demand at least a speculative explanation.

What was Coleridge's purpose in raising the banner of Baconian science against the Lockean tradition? There were probably at least three reasons. First, Bacon had the advantage of "Englishness." Since chauvinism would inevitably rear its head in a nation's acceptance of philosophies, Coleridge would have been wise to use that effect to his benefit. Coleridge stated in 1810, as we have seen, that "the *nationality* of the people who considered [Locke] and Newton the adversaries of the German Leibniz" had helped to make the Englishman Locke more popular than the "German" Leibniz. By introducing Bacon as a substitute for Leibniz as the champion of rationalism, he may have hoped to level the playing field. With a choice between two Englishmen, the decision between rationalism and empiricism would be less likely made on the basis of "nationality" and more likely on the basis of merit. Second, he was probably duplicating a tactic that he had described in his conversation with Robinson. As he noted in 1810, "Voltaire[,] to depress Leibniz, raised Locke." Coleridge, in turn, may have aspired to use the Voltairean strategy to "depress" Locke's influence by raising Bacon. Third, Coleridge authentically believed that Bacon combined an unimpeachable commitment to experimental work—indeed, was a martyr to it—with an equally unimpeachable concern for higher concepts and the telos of science. That Coleridge viewed *Novum Organum* as an essentially Platonic work suggests much about the hybrid empiricist-Platonist view of nature and science with which he was increasingly concerned after 1816.

Coleridge has often been charged, both by modern and contemporary critics, with an unacceptable degree of mysticism and obscurantism in his philosophy. His view of Bacon as a hero for the English Platonic style in science suggests that his understanding of metaphysics and material science was not entirely divorced from questions of empirical study. He strove, instead, to form a new tradition in science that would combine the real and factual attainments of Bacon and Leibniz with their ability to rise above "Concepts" into the world of Ideas in their descriptions of nature and society. Describing society as an extension of the physical world, Coleridge regarded all political institutions as forming an objective corollary to the systems of nature. In his efforts to define this "objective corollary," Coleridge employed an approach that he described as "medico-philosophical." He extended this medico-philosophical approach to life and nature to his social and political ideas. And, as an account of power and experience, it advanced a profoundly historical understanding of change and time.

CHAPTER 7

History and Life

C OLERIDGE USED a number of self-plagiarized catchphrases to describe his view of the processes and powers, both natural and civil, that consti-tuted human experience. These included variously "the Science of the Legis-lator," "the Harmony of Government," "the Science of History," and "the Life of Nature." His understanding of the relationship between the science of the legislator and the harmony of government has already been discussed with regard to his accounts of public opinion and political and moral will. Howev-er, the underlying connections between these two formulations of political so-ciety are best understood in reference to the deepest foundation of Coleridge's famously amorphous "fixed principles": the vibrantly organic and dynamical-ly interdependent nature of history and life.

In 1816 Coleridge began the composition of his book *Hints Toward the For-mation of a More Comprehensive Theory of Life*. Because it was not on an overtly "political" subject, this work has often been omitted from the canon of Co-leridge's "political" writings. This omission is unfortunate, for it was in *Theo-ry of Life* that Coleridge outlined the metaphysical doctrines of dynamism and the interrelationship of opposites that were implicit in every one of his later works. It is no exaggeration to say that without a consideration of Coleridge's general biological theory of life, his specific theories of politics and statecraft will remain opaque. The *Theory of Life* provides the interpreter of Coleridge with a master key to the basic ideas that shaped all of his later works of the late 1810a and the 1820s. The views of politics and history that he expounded in such mature works as *The Lay Sermons* (1817), *Aids to Reflection* (1825), and, fi-nally, *On The Constitution of the Church and State* (1830) were all predicated on the conceptions of power and causation that Coleridge developed through the theory of the "objective corollary" in his *Theory of Life*.

Coleridge's conception of science had two major contentions. First, he blended the "idealist" theory of categories with the "experimental" tradition of verifiable empirical observations in order to suggest a new hybrid theory of knowledge in the sciences. This hybrid, of course, was the "Baconian" tradition in science that he wished to gain ascendancy over the "Lockean" tradition. Second, he argued that politics and historical process reflected the underlying dynamic interrelationships common to all life.

For Coleridge, history, which was as much a science as biology or astronomy, was an ideal subject matter through which to understand the ways that ideal forms structured and interacted with the material content of human societies. The question of the relationship of form to content became particularly thorny for Coleridge around 1816. After that year, he began to consider the ways in which form became content even as content became form.

Coleridge expressed this study of content-form/form-content relations in the terminology of the "objective corollary." In the pursuit of this "corollary," Coleridge put to use the terminology and concepts that he gained through his years of studying Kantian philosophy and natural science, two subjects with which (as we have seen) he had increasingly occupied his time from 1800 through 1815. After 1816, Coleridge returned to the territory of history and politics, which he had left somewhat fallow since his journalistic forays in the first decade of the new century. Throughout his peregrinations, he returned again and again to questions of social process as reflected in institutions and to the related study of teleology, or final causes. In order to understand whether an instrument, or organ, of government was effective, Colerigde argued, one must always return to the question of function or purpose. These questions were often clarified by crisis and failure, by the striking dysfunction of a system out of balance with its own life force. The years of domestic crisis that followed the British victory at Waterloo brought Coleridge to consider the body politic as dysfunctionally stressed and diseased. In his theory of a "state physiology," the strategy of treatment focused on the underlying causes of disease rather than the superficial reduction of symptom.

Coleridge's search for the objective corollary turned increasingly towards a "medico-philosophical" vocabulary by 1820. The specific event that caused him to turn his attention towards medicine and biology was the vituperative controversy between two eminent physiologists: The materialist William Lawrence, on the one side, represented the "Lockean" tradition in British medicine epitomized by John Hunter's widely accepted *Theory of Life*. The realist John Abernathy, on the other side, had impugned the "narrow rationality" of the Hunterian theory as described by Lawrence. Indeed, Lawrence both lectured and published a new textbook in physiology in order to silence Abernathy. Coleridge, sided with Abernathy and the realists. However, he thought that Abernathy had been tactically foolish in his defense of a deeper truth in medicine. He argued that so long as Abernathy clung "to certain points, so long would he lay himself open to the attacks of Lawrence and the Materialists."[1] It was Coleridge's decision to make Abernathy's case in a clearer and more consistent form that led him into the fray occupied until then only by the Georgian medical establishment.

Attempting to describe his understanding of causation with respect to the particularity of organic form and content, Coleridge wrote to J. H. Green on 25 May 1820. In this important letter, Coleridge spoke of "those facts or reflections" that were so strong as "to change belief into *insight*," and so strong as to "never lose their effect." In his consideration of "the physiological question," Coleridge had come to the conclusion that "reflections" which provided "*insight*" on a patient and on disease in general were equally important, or even more important, than the ticking-off and adding-up of the experiential "facts" in a case. He compared the true understanding of "the distinctive *sensations* of Disease" with the aridity of "a mere *perceived* correspondence of Systems with the Diagnostics of a medical book." In Coleridge's view, this central "physiological question" had been (improperly) "generally decided one way by the late most popular writers on Insanity."[2]

Coleridge's close reflection on the problem of understanding the somatic or physiological origins of madness, rather than simply diagnosing its symptoms and prescribing a standardized cure, struck to the heart of the dispute between the rival schools of physiology and psychology in the London of the mid-1810s. He entered enthusiastically into the arena of this battle over what distinguished physical sensations from mental perceptions. He considered where and how pain became anguish. He pondered the difference between pleasure and joy, asking if it were a question of kind or degree. These "deep questions" in medicine and psychology were questions that, in Coleridge's estimation, the Lockean physicians and Benthamite psychologists had failed to address.[3] They ignored these deeper questions because they treated patients as if they were simply steam engines in for repairs. Their uninventive diagnoses and remedies came only out of "a mere *perceived* correspondence of Systems with the Diagnostics of a medical book." Coleridge had insisted to Green that medicine had to be about more than crude technics of diagnostics based on physical symptoms alone. True medical research had to consider that "the efficient cause of disease and disordered action & so collectively of pain & perishing" may not be "entirely in the Organs." Medicine was more than engineering, and curing a patient was more than simply cutting open the mechanism, tossing out the defective parts, and installing new ones.

In a thought experiment involving an hypothetical (and in terms of 1816, impossible) organ transplant by an imaginary being, Coleridge pointed out to Green exactly why he thought a human being was more than the sum of its component "parts." Coleridge imagined (for the purposes of the parable) that some "other plastic spirit" could "awhile suspend" his "own proper principle of life," in effect placing him under "suspended animation." During this period of stasis, Coleridge imagined that the plastic spirit would "reconstruct my body & thoroughly repair the defective organs." Its tinkering finished, the spirit would set about "reawakening the active principle in me" and, having revived his patient from stasis, "depart." Coleridge asked Green about the net result of this "tune-up" by the plastic spirit. Coleridge's little foray into science fiction *avant la lettre* was more than an amusing tale; its simplicity concealed a difficult conundrum for Green to ponder. Would "Coleridge the patient" be *better off* or *worse off* than he was before after his gutting and refitting by the hypothetical plastic spirit?

Coleridge believed that the transplants of the afflicted organs would *not* have, as Hunterian physiology had it, "removed . . . all pain and disease." He also denied that after the meddling of the plastic spirit that he would "stand in the same state as I stood in previous to all sickness & to the admission of any disturbing forces in my nature." This was not, for Coleridge, the way human bodies worked. They were not as steam engines or other machines, where to stick in a new part was to fix the whole. "On the contrary," Coleridge suggested, "such a repaired organismus" would "be no fit organ for my Life."

Using a second parable, he compared the meddling, imaginary spirit who had operated on him to a man who owned "a *worn* lock with an equally worn key." This man, Coleridge told Green, had "exchanged" his old lock "for an equally perfect Fac Similie of the same Lock, such as it was as when it was new." Unfortunately, he still had his old key. Coleridge asked Green to consider whether "the key might no longer fit the lock?"[4] In this second parable, Coleridge underlined his earlier concern that putting fresh parts into a faulty system would only result in a continuance of the failure of that system (in this case, a human body), despite the "new parts," or even because of them.

The point here is not to consider Coleridge as an early advocate of holistic medicine or to question his (dubious) medical wisdom in denying the utility of transplants for patients with dysfunctional organs. The validity of Coleridge's somewhat eccentric gestalt theory of disease has been considered in depth elsewhere by scholars who have looked specifically at Coleridge's contributions to the medical debate of the 1810s.[5] Rather, the point here is to see the incredible degree to which his view that the sum of a system was greater than the total of its constituent parts was the cornerstone of his theory of the state. Coleridge criticized the Hunterians in *medicine* for thinking that all one had to do to cure a patient's disease was to follow a rigid "cure" set down in a book and "fix" the afflicted part without reference to the body as a whole. Coleridge criticized the Lockeans and utilitarians in *government* for imagining that all one had to do to reform a corrupted polity was to follow a universally valid policy set down in a book and to correct the corrupted institution without reference to the morality or virtue of the citizenry as a whole. In this sense, Coleridge considered his reflections on the nature of science and the body as not only relevant but essential to his study of the function of social and political interactive forces in the state.

Coleridge emphasized his vision of an integrated association between natural science, the study of history, and political science in a letter to John Hookham Frere in 1826. He presented a model of knowledge to Frere which was an "Isociles triangle." The first side of the triangle was "a philosophical spirit, and the introduction of philosophy in its objective type, among our physiologists and naturalists." The "basis" of the triangle was "dynamic Logic." The "Apex" of the triangle was "Religion." Within this schema, history was a cognate discipline of the natural sciences. "The historic *Idea*," remarked Coleridge, "is the same in Natural History (Physiognomy) as in History, commonly so called." The difference between natural science and history was only that the "idea" in each was "but polarized or presented in opposite and correspondent forms."[6] In this context, it is not surprising that Coleridge believed his theory of medical interdependency of the body in "Natural History" bore great consequences for his theory of change in "History, commonly so called." For in science and history both, the "historic *Idea*," not the simple accumulation of facts and stratagems, was the basis of true understanding. When these ideas were translated from sick human bodies to corrupt bodies politic, Coleridge's medicophysical theory of animal physiology was applied to the historic *Idea* of the state.

In the years after 1816, Coleridge's speculations on the difference between "symptoms" and "causes" in medicine led him to examine the institutional forms that might best suit the dynamics of individual action and change in politics. In the course of this work, Coleridge moved from his medicophilosophical interests of 1816 toward revised theories of action and value in the constitution of a state. He summed up these connections explicitly in a letter to his brother Edward in 1825, the year in which his *Aids to Reflection* reached print. This letter contrasted crude behaviorist psychologies with true studies of ethics, such as he considered his own efforts. Sciences which dealt only with

the "outward Deed," which included "Schemes of Ec[onom]y, social and political—such as Paley's (mistitled) *Moral* and Political Phi[loso]phy," invariably
failed to understand anything but simple stimuli and responses. What students
of behavior needed was a science of "the inward principle of responsible Action"; only an emphasis on virtue and on motive could create "the *science* of
pure Ethics."[7] Coleridge himself (modestly) hoped to provide such a science.

For Coleridge's "science of pure Ethics," it was not enough to consider the
outworks of men's characters, as did the political economists such as Malthus
and Ricardo (for whom his scorn had not significantly diminished). The inward principles of responsible action must also be considered. The "Unreformed Constitution" maligned by the utilitarians and radicals was the "worn
lock" of Coleridge's parable; the degraded virtue and agency of a people was
the "worn key." The reformers of the 1820s, to Coleridge, schemed for an
improved "Fac Similie of the same lock, better than the old lock was "when
it was new" in 1688. Unfortunately, they still had the "worn key," an immoral
and corrupt people. Such a "worn key" "might no longer fit" the bright,
shiny, allegedly more efficient new lock of reformed government.[8] Only a
pairing of politics with metaphysics, and a "science of pure ethics," maintained
Coleridge, could address "disordered action" and make the worn key of the
corrupted people new and solid so that it would fit a new lock.

In his account of the importance of the study of history and the "Historic
Idea" Coleridge advanced a working description of the relationship between
"*Structures et Evenements.*" In short, he conceived of the study of the historic
Idea as the intellectual process by which the interrelationship of lock and key,
of institutions and peoples, could be best studied. He also advocated history as
the field of study in which the "science of pure ethics" was best shown in its
applied form, the historic Idea. In both the natural and human sciences, the
development of this historic Idea was a constantly changing, living, and organic process. This master process, even when considered through the veil of
fragmentary and partial human knowledge, perpetually revealed the principle
of its working in actions, intentions, and institutions. This endeavor was the
"science of history" to which Coleridge referred in 1830 in his study of church
and state.

Coleridge wrote in his 1826 letter to Frere that the "purpose" of history
was "to exhibit the moral necessity of the [Idea of a] whole [society] in the
freedom of the component parts: the resulting chain necessary, each particular
link remaining free."[9] Most historians, complained Coleridge, were only capable of showing *either* the "big picture" of the broad sweep of social development *or* the small day-to-day details of human decisions and anecdote. In

the works of the sociological macrohistorians—a group in whom Coleridge placed "Hume, Robertson, [and] Gibbon"—the great waves of history and large-scale change were well defined, but any idea of individual will or of heroic or villainous acts having any influence on the deep course of the *longue durée* was lost. It was a masterfully rendered landscape without figures. In the works of the anecdotal microhistorians—a group in which Coleridge lumped "our old chroniclers and annalists" (presumably Bede, Geoffrey, Holinshead, Foxe, and their ilk)—the moral value of the heroes and villains was well defined, but the sense that there was any Idea of the grand development of the society, anything beyond a long parade of one thing after another, was lost. It was a cabinet of miniatures with no arch design behind their collection except for the love of detail. Coleridge later described such a view of history as "a great heap of little things."[10]

Coleridge had only found two books that both "exhibit[ed] the moral necessity of the whole [society]" and detailed "the freedom of the component parts": *The History* of Herodotus and the Hebrew Bible. True science, whether studying nature, culture, or politics, had to concern itself with the grand scheme and the detailed account at the same time. True science, claimed Coleridge, also had to reconcile the freedom of the individual in history with the "moral necessity" of deep social forces. He summed up this interaction in a phrase from his letter to Frere: "The absolute Freedom, Will both in the form of Reason and in its own right as the ground of Reason[,] is the principle of the whole in the component parts."[11] Any ethics or politics worth the name would examine this "Reason" and its foundation in the "Freedom" of the "Will." He considered the ordering moral imperatives behind human action, the "Will," to accord ultimately with living processes. Living processes, in turn, all possessed some absolute structuring principle that animated and determined them.

The state, Coleridge pointed out, operated as the most common and pervasive "structuring principle" for human social, economic, and political activity. This structuring principle was not a rigid box that (like the bed of Procrustes) forced everything put in it to conform to its own shape. The "structuring principle" was instead a living process, an "Idea, which was *itself* constantly changing due to the actions of individuals. In this context Coleridge argued that even as men made the state, the state made men. The hypothesis of a deep Idea of the state that was more profound than individual acts (and which in large part conditioned those acts) did not, in Coleridge's development of it, suggest that the process was inevitable or that human agency did not matter. Coleridge's model of the individual's agency in a social structure was a dynamic process, in which the individual's actions and intentions themselves *became* part of the determining force that had shaped his actions in the first place. Human will and action became a part of the structuring matrix of the state and helped to constitute its ultimate aim or telos. Because of Coleridge's theory of the relations of individuals to social and cultural determinants, he consistently argued that individual freedom could not be discussed without reference to social activity or common goods. It was the importance of this individualist and voluntarist principle in politics that led Coleridge to his second critique of Malthus, essentially a historical-relativist attack on pure materialism.

Coleridge thought that the political economists were determined to consider action as entirely conditioned by environment and society, without reference to intention (or the morality and virtue which the embrace of intention implied). His criticisms of Malthus's revised theory turned on such a distinction. In his marginal notes to the second edition of Malthus's *Essay On the Principle of Population*, Coleridge summed up his objections. He considered "[the] Whole question" posed by Malthus as capable of being summed up in one query: "Are Lust and Hunger both alike [in being the mere products] of physical necessity . . . independently of reason, of the Will?" He thought that Malthus's very act in daring to ask such a repulsive question brought "Shame upon our [human] Race."[12] Obviously, for Coleridge, while "Hunger" could be credited entirely to "physical necessity" and deemed "independent of reason," "Lust" could not be similarly biologized without traducing the ethics which made humans distinctive.

Malthus had himself revised his theory between 1798 and 1803 to consider the issues of moral restraint and human decision as constraints on what he had originally argued was a reproductive growth regulated only by scarcity of food. In Coleridge's eyes, Malthus had not truly revised his old errors but merely tacked on a petty exiguous doctrine of morality's effect on the birthrate as an afterthought to fend off critics. To Coleridge, Malthus's theory was still at heart immoral. In the end, Malthus simply asserted that the rise in population was an arithmetic progression that invariably outpaced the geometric advance in food production. The causes, motivations, and moral constructions of these cycles, claimed Coleridge, were still not addressed. Even the "revision," which in Coleridge's eyes "wholly confute[d] [Malthus's] former pamphlet," still stuck to too many of the old errors. Coleridge inveighed against the revised Malthus with an even greater fury than he had against the first edition: "Merciful God! Are we now to have a Quarto to teach us that great misery & great vice arises from Poverty & that these [social vices] be [only the signs of] poverty in its worst shapes. Where ever there are more mouths than loaves and more heads than grains!"[13]

Coleridge attacked Malthus's ethology for the same reason that he attacked Hume's, Gibbon's, and Robertson's histories: they presented only great sweeping material forces and ignored the morals of individuals or the influences of virtue. By doing so, Malthus and his acolytes *implied* that morals and virtues were a specious "superstructure" slapped atop the true structures of society. Only material conditions, argued Malthus and his followers, *truly* conditioned behavior. All other social phenomena were mere reflections of that deeper truth.

Coleridge wished to argue, against Malthus, that norms of morality and virtue, as Ideas, were actually part of the deep structure of social life and were as important in reckoning the likely reproductive behavior of a pair of humans as the amount of grain harvested that year. The study of society, asserted Coleridge, was not as simple as totaling up "mouths" and "heads" of the population and comparing them to the available "grains" and "loaves" produced to feed them. Coleridge argued that all moral decisions had to be understood in light of the ineffable and immeasurable work done by intentions and the will, and not solely in light of things which could be counted, such as the material consequences of "heads" and "loaves."

Indeed, Coleridge thought that Malthus's revision, in its attempt to tack on a "moral view" to an essentially immoral thesis in the first edition, was all the more wicked. For Malthus's 1798 edition at least had the courage to bracket out virtue and vice as baggage not worthy for scientific contemplation. The 1803 edition, more cowardly, hid behind a patina of "morality" to reiterate the same grotesque lies. Coleridge attacked Malthus's "Ignorance," which he demonstrated by calling his work "a moral view" but writing it "without stating what a moral view is." Indeed, Coleridge believed that the Reverend Malthus's heartless calculations were cruelest because they made economics simply a matter of utility, without any reference to the Christian values that Malthus himself was bound to propagate. "If it be immoral to kill [a] few [unimportant men] in order to get [the] population of a country capable of sustaining a 1000 times as many capable and happy men," Coleridge thundered, "is it not immoral to kill millions of infants[,] then[,] by crowded cities, by hunger and by the pox?"[14]

The crucial point that Coleridge made in his lambasting of Malthus was that all political theory was "moral" or "immoral." The attempt by Malthus and the other dismal scientists to escape the boundaries of the traditional language of virtue and vice in social policy was a failed one. A treatise on the poor that viewed them as a population no more interesting than one of rabbits was inherently "immoral" because it wrongly suggested that the starvation of "millions of infants" could be examined dispassionately as a regulative mechanism rather than as an intolerable social evil. In treating starvation and reproduction as sociobiological issues only, Malthus, asserted Coleridge, had stripped the poor of their humanity.

Coleridge's objection was that Malthus's moral calculus not only ignored broader social and ethical problems, but that it was inherently evil because it did so. Coleridge also, as has been stated, assaulted Malthus because Malthus suggested that material causes were the strongest determinant of behavior. Malthus proceeded on the deterministic assumption that overpopulation alone was the cause of all poverty and that poverty was the cause of all crime and vice. By reducing population, Malthus argued, one would decrease poverty and thereby abate crime and vice. Coleridge argued in response that there was no reason to suppose that such a causal link existed or that Malthus's projections were credible, mostly because Malthus had ignored the motivations behind vice and had made a mockery of the actual meanings of the terms "vice" and "virtue."

Paradoxically, Malthus's "immorality" was less culturally relativistic than Coleridge's own defense of the study of morality. Malthus had, in his second edition, spoken of "Promiscuous intercourse, unnatural passions, violations of the marriage bed, and improper acts to conceal the consequences of irregular connections" as "clearly" belonging "under the head of vice."[15] This meant that Malthus, whatever his opinions of the underlying *causes* of vice and the degree of *culpability* that the poor bore for succumbing to it, knew perfectly well which acts were vicious and which were virtuous. Coleridge's marginal note on that passage from Malthus relativized and historicized that argument. Where Malthus saw virtue and vice as stable constants, Coleridge saw virtue and vice as slowly emerging, historically conditioned Ideas. Coleridge condemned Malthus for speaking of morality "without having stat[ed] the meaning of the terms Vice and Virtue." Obviously, the crimes that Malthus had listed were all "vice in the present state of society." But Malthus, because he ignored the depth of the Idea of vice and virtue, had also ignored that the very definition of what was virtuous and what vicious was historically conditioned and was not universally that held by sensible parsons in late Georgian England. If he had known that "Promiscuous intercourse" was a vice in Georgian England, Malthus had conveniently forgotten that "celibacy" was an even more heinous crime in the "Patriarchal ages." "Vice and virtue," Coleridge insisted, "subsist in the agreements of the habits of a man with his reason & conscience." Coleridge stressed in his marginal note that his foray into relativism was not meant to suggest a *total* relativism that would deny that anything could be described as moral or immoral: "We mention *this* [relativity of morals in various stages of civilization] not under the miserable notion that any state of society will render these actions capable of being performed with conscience and virtue."[16]

Coleridge argued in his attack on Malthus that value in the sphere of action was something that must be gauged in terms of particular historical norms. To this he added the important qualification that virtue, although historically conditioned, was always moving towards a telos of perfection and universal relevance. Virtue meant that an agent acted "authentically" and consistently in the light of what was known in his time to be the standard of "reason" and "conscience."[17] However, while codes of conduct that related to action had to be gauged with an eye to particular circumstances, the ultimate *intention* or motivation behind human conduct looked toward a perfected human morality that was not only superior to that of the primitive "Patriarchal ages," but was also superior to the smug morality of Georgian England, which Rev. Malthus had considered the measure of all things. For Coleridge, the "cunning of history" was the final arbiter of moral value, as it alone reflected the essential dictates of reason and the will. His marginal notes condemning Malthus suggest that "reason" and "conscience" "can have but one moral guide, Utility or the virtue & happiness of other rational beings." Note that under the heading of "Utility" Coleridge included not only the "happiness" of other humans and their presumed state of being well fed with "loaves," but also added "virtue." This was an anti-utilitarian use of the principle of "Utility," for it suggested that the greatest "virtue" of the greatest number was an equally important goal as the greatest "good" or "happiness" of the greatest number.

Coleridge could never bring himself to "believe works like Malthus" which were at their "*warmest*" when they suggested "that man never will be capable of regulating the sexual appetite by the laws of reason." He also defied once again Malthus's notion "that the ★★★★★★ Lust is a Thing of physical necessity equally *with* the gratifications of Hunger."[18] In the end, Coleridge's objections to Malthus turned on his detestation for Malthus's view that human agency and volition were not as important as population biology and food supply in determining the rate of reproduction and the frequency of crimes in a society.

The parallels between Coleridge's visions of the demerits of the Hunterians in the medicophilosophical debate and the demerits of Malthus in the debate on population were striking. In both cases, he argued against carnal definitions of processes of change. For Coleridge, the Malthusians, like the

Hunterians, viewed human society in narrowly materialist terms that admitted little or no causal role for Ideas, morality, and human volition. In the case of medicine, he argued that physicians, if they truly wished to cure their patients, should think of human bodies as more than the sum of their constituent organs. In the case of statecraft, he argued that reformers, if they truly wished to reform their societies, should think of institutions such as churches and states and normative Ideas such as virtue and vice as intrinsically important to the success of their endeavors. They should not dismiss mores, as Malthus had, as irrelevant superstructures ineffective in the study of the "basic" material truths of birth and procreation and death, hunger, and satiety. Instead, they should consider those social frameworks of institutions and values as the particular and imperfect material manifestations of a much greater and more perfect telos toward which their society was travelling. This institutional framework of laws, political bodies, and mores, according to Coleridge, constantly modified itself through the actions of its constituent members. The framework also changed through constant processes of generation and evolution, competition and decay, which were as natural as the processes of growth and decay in the human body.

Coleridge viewed human societies and their moral norms as constituting fragmentary yet evolving manifestations of history, nature, and truth. As we have seen in previous chapters, Coleridge insisted that the unfortunate trend in legislative thought from 1790 to 1830 had been an increasing preoccupation with specific actions and novel methods for their own sake, as opposed to attention to constitutive principles. Most modern governments and new constitutions failed, argued Coleridge, because they legislated for particular events and evanescent contingencies rather than essential functions.

Perhaps the most forceful exposition of Coleridge's argument relating political and moral forces to natural forces came in his 1820 letter to Green. In it, Coleridge detailed an idealist model of change. Coleridge's letter to Green argued against the "system of materialism" that emphasized the study and reform of the "means" of "organization" rather than keeping its eyes on "Nature[,] or God, & Life &c. as its [end] results." Materialism, he pointed out to Green, had the advantage of banality: it offered comfort in its promise to "remove a great part of the terrors which the soul makes out for itself." It had the disadvantage of soullessness, "remov[ing] the soul too, or rather preclud[ing] [the use of] it." A social "organization," argued Coleridge, was "primarily" dependent on its clear-sightedness in defining the "result," or grand ends of the institution, in terms of nature, virtue, and other transcendental concerns.

It was "only by reaction" that a short-term goal, which Coleridge described as a "*cause*," mattered much in constitution building. Doctors could only cure their patients if they gave thought to what a truly healthy individual would be and diagnosed the various nonbiological factors that contributed to their patient's ills rather than simply troubleshooting specific ailments in that specific patient "by the book." Reformers, likewise, should focus less on the methodology and technique of reform and figure out what the general ends of government were and what government ought to aim toward being and doing. Otherwise, they would end up treating the entire endeavor as if it were a club for claret rather than the embodiment and enhancer of the morals and aspirations of an entire people. "It would be well [for physicians] to consider," Coleridge had stressed to Green, "what causes are, in this life, in which the restoration of the organization removes Disease." In most cases, Coleridge alleged, the "restoration" of the general "organization" (i.e., the organism as a whole) was more effective in "remov[ing] Disease" than the specific spot cures of a physician to various diagnosed ailments. Certainly, it was a bad idea to subject the body to a set of "new" organs if the general health was poor, just as it was a bad idea to buy a new lock if one planned on keeping the old, worn key. In the end, Coleridge informed Green, a vital, lively, and self-renewing polity, in which one could remove small stumbling blocks to its workings as the need arose, was sound. Certainly it was sounder, he asserted, than one that underwent the sort of wholesale revision of essential organs that he had imagined happening at the hands of the hypothetical "plastic spirit." "Is the organization ever restored, except as continually reproduced? And are not the *majority* of instances [of successful wardings-off of disease] cases of removal of mechanical or chemical obstructions [tumors, etc.] *from* the organization?[19] One sees again that Coleridge's discussion of disease, like his discussions of reform, pertained not to a particular organism or constitution but to a broader conception of "organization" or system.

Coleridge distinguished in his letter to Green between "restoration" of the "organization" and the "continual . . . reproduc[tion]" that brought such "restoration" about. His conception of historical progress was central to this distinction. In restoring an organic organization, an old lock could not be replaced unless a new key was bought along with it. The essential workings, the institutional forms, had to be restored and revived along with the outward institutions and rules and techniques, so that the organization could continue to evolve or develop dynamically. It was of no use to put a fresh set of lungs into a corpse. The process of reform, believed Coleridge, should reveal or unfold providentially that which was inherent in the design of all such institutions but which was as yet imperfectly realized in that specific example.

In Coleridge's scheme, each moment in history and each society was unique, although conforming to certain essential teleological forms. Such organizations actively constituted the building blocks of everyday reality—loaves of bread, people, buildings, state papers, political offices. These elements themselves participated in the evolution of the institution, the organization, or the state. Coleridge detailed the interactive nature of this process in the conclusion of his letter to Green. Writing of God, causation, and the will, he remarked, that "no power" could be "redemptive" that did not at the same time "act in the ground of the Life as one with the ground." This meant that the "power" in question must "act *in* [the individual's] Will and not merely *on* [the individual's] Will," even though it always worked simultaneously "extrinsically as an outward Power, i.e. as that which outward nature is to the organization."[20]

Coleridge's phraseology in his letter to Green evoked his recurrent theme of institutions simultaneously living inside and outside the individual citizen. He had already gone beyond the crude theories of "social control" in which the state "act[s] . . . merely *on* [the individual's] Will" and had recognized that the subject-object relationships of states and citizens were far more complex. Effective governments, although they kept their status "extrinsically as an outward Power," acted in the individual will. It was in this regard that Coleridge would argue that the state made men and that "a State like a river constitutes its own products—*subsists* in its own productive Ideas."[21]

One cannot help noticing the resemblances in the 1820 letter to Green between Coleridge's vision of the state's existence *inside* the will and the interior, heart-centered salvation doctrines of Evangelical Anglicanism. Evangelical soteriology asserted that grace working in the heart of the individual believer was stronger by far than the mere external power of the law. Compare this to Coleridge's assertion that "no power" could be "redemptive" that did not at the same time "act in the ground of the Life as one with the ground." Additionally, Coleridge saw the state as a "redemptive power." The strong undercurrents of this language in the theology of grace suggests that Coleridge was already working towards certain of the ideas and emphases of his treatise on church and state, in which the two are somewhat conflated. Evangelicalism's stress on the superiority of the religion of the heart to that of the head may have echoed in Coleridge's higher ranking of the inward reform of the moral constitution of a nation to the outward reform of its mere externals.

It will be helpful at this point to turn toward a representative instance of the application of these general principles of government and change. This will suggest not only how Coleridge saw generic processes of change working within the state but will also evince how he employed these principles to analyze and support a specific piece of legislation. Specifically, Coleridge's defense of Peel's Factory Bill provides a telling portrait of the "Tory" crusader against laissez-faire and physiocracy. By 1818, Coleridge turned his theories of progressive agency to his criticisms of specific legislation. His view of the proper role for individual agency in public life allowed him to defend Peel's Factory Acts and reject contemporary Whig arguments for a completely "free market" in labor. Coleridge maintained in his contributions to this debate that *true* liberty was best advanced on occasion by rare and specific limitations on individual freedom. It should be recalled that Coleridge's theory of liberty only allowed the government to intervene in the private sphere of "liberty to do as one liked" when an individual or group was threatening to destroy the rights of individual citizens. Thus, the Coleridgean law would not prosecute a factory owner who blasphemed (and hurt no one but himself), but could legitimately prosecute him for needlessly endangering the life of a factory worker. The factory owner's "right" to do as he pleased on his property at the mill ended for Coleridge whenever exercise of that right interfered with a worker's right to life.

Coleridge's limitations on the "free market" in labor, although they diminished liberty of individual citizens in the short view, in the long view were intended to enhance the general social and economic welfare of all. It was characteristic of Coleridge's theory of teleology that he argued that it was more important in considering the bills to see their impact on the long-term goal of liberty rather than focus on their short-term diminution of the factory-owners' particular liberties.

Coleridge published his *Two Addresses on Sir Robert Peel's Bill* in April of 1818. In it, Coleridge supported Peel's legislation to limit the hours worked by *children* in the Lancashire cotton mills. The focus of Coleridge's address was the "free labour" arguments that the M.P. for Lancashire, Lord Stanley, had advanced on behalf of the manufacturers among his constituents.[22] Coleridge identified Stanley's arguments with antique physiocratic ideas and with the more recent innovations of the political economists. Lord Stanley and his allies argued that the free market would itself create social equity and eliminate hazardous laboring conditions if the forces of the owners' enlightened self-interest and the freedom of the labor market were not hindered by intrusive law.

Coleridge expressed his concerns over the debates surrounding the bill in a letter to Henry Crabb Robinson. He sentimentally tugged at Robinson's heartstrings with maudlin images of "the poor little children employed in the

cotton factories who would fain have you in the best of their friends &
helpers," but he had the more hard-headed goal of discovering whether there
was yet any law regulating the employment of either children or adults or both
in white-lead manufacturing. A report of the Select Committee of the House
of Commons on the state of children in the cotton factories in 1816 contained
a statement by Mr. Ashley Cooper that there was such a law. Coleridge sought
from his friend "any . . . instances in which the legislature has directly, or by
immediate consequence, interfered with what is ironically called "Free
Labour.'" Coleridge used the term "Free Labour" sarcastically. He thought
the phrase the worst sort of cant because it hid the filthy truth of "soul-murder
and infanticide on the part of the rich" and "self-slaughter on that of the poor"
behind a veil of euphemism.[23]

Coleridge's appeal to Robinson for precedents was the beginning of his crusade against the factory lobby's laissez-faire arguments. He was especially eager
to suggest that although the owners allied against the bill represented themselves
as the advance guard of the forces of progress and advancing liberty and a freer
society through "free" labor, that they were in truth the stodgy defenders of a
rapidly passing and indefensible way of life. It is striking that Coleridge considered Stanley's argument and the arguments of the factory owners to be essentially conservative objections to progressive innovation. Coleridge identified the
"free market" pundits with a regressive and reactive view of legislation.

In his "Remarks on the Objections which have been urged Against the
Principles of Sir Robert Peel's Bill," Coleridge's enumerated the five major attacks made by the factory owners upon the bill. The first attack, that "children
were happier in factories," Coleridge believed could be dismissed summarily
as "nonsense." However, he suggested that the remaining four arguments held
wide support in the nation and could not be ignored. The second strand in the
owners' "objections," according to Coleridge, was "the impropriety of legislative interference with free labour." Factory owners had suggested that the
beginning of regulation of the free market in labor and wages was the first step
onto a slippery slope leading to the government's tyranny over manufacturers.
Coleridge pointed out that the mill-owners thought the acts were a "danger"
on account of their "beginning a course of innovation, without any certainty
at what point it may stop, and thus of encouraging an endless succession of
claims" for social amelioration by statute. The third contention of the owners
was that the bills would be ineffective. Coleridge described how the mill owners assaulted "the inadequacy of the [legislative] measures proposed to the removal of the [social] evil." The fourth argument of the owners was that the
bill would create an unrealistic attitude among the people; they might claim

that all of their grievances should be cured by legislation. Such an idea was in-
imical to the principle of laissez-faire. They suggested that the bill raised false
hopes "by attracting attention" to schemes for ameliorating society through
law. The factory owners claimed "the excitement of hopes" drummed up by
supporters of the bill were "incompatible with the present state of society, and
with the indispensable conditions of a commercial and manufacturing nation."
By unleashing rising tides of expectations where there had been few or none
before, the owners gathered that the bills "are calculated to increase discontent
in a greater degree than they can be expected to palliate the grievance." Their
fifth and final argument against the bill, reported Coleridge, was that a combination of the philanthropy of individual mill owners, the market forces,
which made it evident to owners that healthier workers were more productive, and a general growth of benevolence and civilization in the land would
get rid of the factory evils faster than the law could. "What can be done towards the removal of the evil can best be brought about by the master manufacturers themselves," or so claimed the manufacturers. The owners presumed
that the acts of the owners as "individuals," rather than as a class, and "the humane spirit of this enlightened age," when combined with "the consequent
growth and increasing influence of an enlightened self-interest" would lead to
better conditions for factory workers. "We may rest assured," the owners
claimed, "that the said individual [manufacturers] will gradually more and
more attempt to do what they alone can do effectually." The factory owners'
five attacks on the Peelite legislation, admitted Coleridge, were "formidable"
not so much "in themselves" but "on account of the impression they appear
to have made" among the literate public.[24]

Coleridge flatly denied that either the "enlightened self-interest" of mill
owners acting as buyers in the labor market, or the increasing "humanity" of
the "enlightened age" and the increase in sympathy for the downtrodden
would impel the owners of the offending factories to address the suffering of
the factory worker. The "individual" who Coleridge's theory posited had the
right to be the "best judge" of his own "happiness" could legitimately be re-
strained from his pursuit of that goal by a coercive government whenever he
"encroach[ed] on another's *sphere of action*" and thereby violated his prime duty
as a citizen. The magistrate had a compelling reason to hold back citizens from
doing evil to one another. It was of no import, argued Coleridge that such
evildoing might be done with the complicity of the injured party and thereby
be described by the evildoer as the "free" act of the injured.

Coleridge addressed one by one the arguments of the opponents of the bill.
First, he attacked the charges of "legislative impropriety" and of a slippery

slope towards government abridgement of liberties. "On what grounds" was this "impropriety" "presumed" asked Coleridge. It was his perception that neither "past experience" nor "the practise of the British Constitution" prevented regulations on wages, hours, and working conditions. Indeed, argued Coleridge, the "statute books" of the kingdom were "(perhaps too much) crowded with proofs to the contrary," that the government could regulate laboring conditions and prices. The "first institution, by law, of apprenticeships," Coleridge pointed out, was an "interference with free labor." The statutes on apprenticeship, which date back to the Middle Ages, contained (according to Coleridge's account) "various clauses that regulate the time, privileges, & c. of the individuals." Indeed, the ancient law went so far "in many cases," attested Coleridge, that it indulged in "controlling the power of masters, as well as the employment of the free labour of adults, however skilful, who had not been previously bound to the trade. . . . The recent regulations of the labour to be required from apprentices" in early modern times, he claimed, were "still more unfavourable to the presumption" advanced by the factory lobby that commerce in labor and wages was free and unfettered by the state before the turn of the nineteenth century.[25]

At the same time that he was one of the leading advocates of a more active role for the state in setting the standards for social and economic welfare, Coleridge retained his fundamental assumptions about constitutive principles and the importance of the common law and the ancient constitution of the realm. He still contended that new legislation was too often short sighted and superfluous, as witnessed by his remark that the statute books were "perhaps too much" filled with Byzantine regulations on labor. The law had to interfere to protect the "sphere of action" of a free subject from the intrusions of rapacious members of society such as the factory owners. Given this unpleasant necessity of adding new laws to protect the subject, Coleridge thought it best for the drafters of the bill to write the new rules to reflect existing but imperfectly developed "constitutive" principles, old developments that already had a firm foundation in precedent and the common law.

Coleridge's argument in favor of Peel's bill, therefore, was not a blank check for the activities of Tory or Whig or radical reformers to unleash their pent-up goals in a torrent of ream after ream of new legislation. The "mature" Coleridge of 1818 was no more confident of the ability of governments to mend a sick polity by the passage of new legislation than the "younger" Coleridge had been in 1809 or 1795. Coleridge appears to have persisted throughout his life in a belief that all legislation stood or fell on the basis of its grounding in ancient precedent and teleologically evaluated constitutional fitness.

Legislation that reached too high too fast was doomed to fail. (In this respect, Coleridge shared the factory lobbyists' doubt in the efficacy of mere statute built on utopian dreams. He simply thought that Peel's bill was better founded than they did.)

Coleridge insisted that since the factory lobby could not argue against the bill on the basis of precedent statute and the common law ("the *practise* of the Legislature"), their claim was even weaker when one considered it in the light of an "appeal to the *principles* and *spirit* of the British Constitution." One could only implement Stanley's policies wholesale, he argued, if one ignored the long tradition in the Common Law of labor regulation and the teleological Idea of the constitution to provide freedom to the poor. Indeed, he contended, "only under a military despotism," of the sort that would be "entitled to dispense with [the Constitution] at all times for its own purposes," could the "principle" of unregulated market forces in labor and other commerce "be even partially realized." At any rate, Coleridge thought the plans of the physiocrats and the advocates of laissez-faire would invariably result in economic as well as political disaster for the nation. Pure laissez-faire, argued Coleridge, would "reduce all classes to insignificance, [except for] those of soldiers and agriculturalists."[26] Ironically, in doing so, they would destroy and bankrupt the very factory owners and other capitalists who had hoped to use the "free" market in labor and the "Iron Law of Wages" to increase their empire of lucre.

It had certainly been the case, he asserted, that unbridled laissez-faire competition had brought despotism and doom to France. He contended that the legislative policies of the opponents of the bill constituted a move towards French principles.[27] He maintained that the "states and countries" that had been "the most prosperous in trade and commerce," and at the same time the "most remarkable for the industry, morality, and public spirit of the inhabitants," were "Great Britain, Holland, the Hanseatic & other free towns of Germany." Those states, noted Coleridge, all had one trait in common, despite their manifest differences. They all had been "governed and regulated by a system of law and policy in almost direct opposition to the so-called Physiocratic principles of modern Political Economists." The "result of their adoption in France under all the revolutionary schemes," and "with more especial predilection under the last government" of France (Napoleon's), did not tend to weaken any "doubts" in his mind of their counterproductiveness and danger.[28]

Coleridge believed that a well-regulated market in labor was a fundamental component of the authentic growth and power of commercial and manufacturing society. Civil liberty had expanded in the free states of Europe, he appears to have believed, through the medium of increasing property ownership in the nation at large. This development of a middle class or bourgeoisie advanced the principle of progression by the empowering of commercial and manufacturing interests—from shopkeeper to banker, artisan to entrepreneur. As the kinds and number and sophistication of forms of property advanced, Coleridge implied, increasingly complex forms of law were needed to determine its rights and uses. Labor, as a form of property common to all, was no different.

In his treatment of labor as a commodity whose commerce ought to be regulated as all commerce historically was, Coleridge again chained together the Ideas of liberty and property. In suppressing the "freedom" of "soul-murder and infanticide on the part of the rich" and the "freedom" of "self-slaughter on that of the poor," no true liberty (in the Coleridgean sense of the word) was lost. For just as the rich man could not use the euphemism of "free labor" to destroy the lives of his workers in deadly conditions, neither could he use the same euphemism to describe the choiceless, hunger-induced "self-slaughter of the poor." For Coleridge, rapine and suicide were not legitimate freedoms, nor worthy of protection or expansion by the state.[29] Indeed, because Peel's bill increased for the worker the "sphere of action" in which he could exercise his individual will, it could be argued that the legislation actually expanded liberty. Certainly, the bill was congruent with Coleridge's principle, expressed in *The Friend*, no. 9, and his "Remarks on the Objections" that the law existed to balance and adjust the claims of the individual against those of the community. "The *principle* of *all* constitutional law," he reminded his readers, "is to make the claims of each [citizen] as much compatible with the claims of all, as individuals, and as those of the common-weal as a whole. . . . Out of this adjustment," he concluded, "the claims of the individual first become *Rights*."[30] Those claims that could not be made compatible with the claims of "all [citizens] as individuals" as well as "those of the common-weal as a whole"—for example, child labor—could not be considered valid nor worthy of being described as rights.

The law, insisted Coleridge, regularly and unabashedly denied the rights of property owners to do as they pleased with their "property." This was especially true when that "property" had a "sphere of action" of its own as a citizen, such as a worker who had sold his labor to a mill owner. It was also true in cases of *inanimate* property, such as canals, Coleridge pointed out, if the state could make a compelling argument that unfettered exercise of the right to do as one likes with one's own property would injure the commonwealth. (One may not exercise the freedom to open one's own dike, for instance, if in doing so one would flood one's neighbors' fields and thereby ruin their crops and houses.) Canals, of course, were for the most part in 1818 in private hands.

Yet, as they were (like turnpikes) public conveniences in private trusts, the state had an interest in regulating them and preventing profiteering or unsafe operation. "Every Canal Bill," argued Coleridge, "proves, that *there is no species of property which the legislature does not possess and exercise the right of controlling and limiting, as soon as the right of the individuals is shewn to be disproportionately injurious to the community*" (my italics). Having said this, Coleridge needed to identify a palpable injury that the community suffered because of child labor and unregulated factories. Coleridge identified the injury not in the materialist terms of damage to health of the workers, but in transcendental and moral terms as "the subversion of morals." That *"contra bonus mores*, the subversion of morals, is deemed in our laws a public injury" was, Coleridge argued, an axiom of English law. He added that the principle was so widely recognized that it would be "superfluous to demonstrate."[31]

Coleridge's conception of individual freedom was tempered by considerations of injury, or harm, to the individual citizen's "self-duties" and "sphere of action." Two ideas emerge in this passage. The first is the issue of balance or "proportion." The second is the notion of public welfare. What could not be tolerated or sanctioned by law was a disproportionate injury (*"disproportionately injurious"*) and thus a "public injury" against the "common-weal." The Idea of the government, after all, as Coleridge defined it in 1809 in *The Friend*, was "to watch incessantly, that the State shall *remain composed of Individuals acting as Individuals*, by which alone the Freedom of all can be secured."[32] It was pointless to use individualist arguments such as laissez-faire to allow the continuance of conditions under which those "Individuals" were so sucked dry of vitality and were forced into such a narrow "sphere of action" that they were in effect condemned to eternal servitude without hope of remission.

Neither constitutional principle nor the Common Law could sustain the absurdly high doctrine of "personal property" that occasioned unwarranted harm or ran recklessly against the common good. Where statute contravened this principle of "commonweal," either through a positive rule or an omission in drafting, Coleridge suggested, the law had erred and needed to be mended. This, Coleridge argued, had been the presupposition behind the increased regulation of canals: private property constrained by the government. In the case of the Factory Bill controversy, "the subversion of morals" through the failure to regulate child labor and other abuses in factories, constituted a public injury. As such, it violated the principles of English law and merited response.

Coleridge's concept that broader human concerns for the commonwealth and community were explicit in the English law and Constitution was in keeping with his objections to the "mechano-corpuscular" philosophy. Such reductionist theories as those implicit in Malthusian psychology or laissez-faire economics were presumed suspect by Coleridge. Stanley saw the "free labour" problem of 1818 in terms of rational actor theory and *Homo aeconomicus*; Coleridge saw the "free labour" problem of 1818 in terms of "soul-murder," "infanticide," "self-slaughter," and "the poor little children employed in the cotton factories." Where their advocates saw the theories of Malthus and Ricardo as providing for the first time a truly scientific basis for political decision making and more efficient laws, Coleridge saw those theories as a heartless and unethical traduction of essential principles of the rights of workers *both* as "Individuals" *and* as members of a "common-weal." He insisted that general principles such as the "Iron Law of Wages" or the geometric/arithmetic dilemma of Malthusian population and food analysis "are apt to deceive us." Instead, it was far wiser to "Individualize the suffering which it is the object of the Bill to remedy." For, if one could "follow up the detail in some one case with *a human sympathy*" then "the deception vanishes."[33].

There is a proto-Dickensian aspect to much of Coleridge's writing on this subject, probably because of the similarity of his invective against the economists to the critique of Mr. Gradgrind and other products of the "Dismal Science" in Dickens's novels, but also because of his insistence that social problems can best be understood by "human sympathy" and "Individualize[d] detail in some one case" rather than columns of statistics. In his final attack on Stanley and the anti-Peel factory owners, Coleridge ridiculed the contention that reform would be best left to the good sense and humanity of the factory masters. He pointed to the actuality of industrial development and the urban factory system that underlay the prosperity and progression of British society. The purely technical progress in division of labor and increased productivity had, if anything, degenerated the human condition. Ironically, the introduction of machines into labor had not created more leisure for workers but had in fact created *more* work, so that children were drafted into the service of the factories with more frequency as mechanization increased. Coleridge declared it "notorious" that "within the last twenty years the time and quantum of the labour extorted from the children has been increasing." In light of this depredation, the degree of civilization of the United Kingdom might be questioned, however unrivalled its technical achievements might be. A nation, suggested Coleridge, might be on the rise in money, productivity, and technological sophistication, and yet be further and further from their goal of an "enlightened age" than they were before the rise of mechanical science. "The growth of the sciences among the few, and the consequent increase of the conveniences of life among the people at large," Coleridge reminded his audience, "are however, far from necessarily implying an *enlightened* age in that sense which alone applies to the case in question. . . . There are few who are not enlightened enough to understand their duties," he added, as a rebuke to the factory owners. Concluding that only those who by their actions blinded themselves to moral concerns could ignore such clear duties, Coleridge said that the majority of Britons would have to "*wink hard*" and shut their eyes to the suffering around them in doing so, "not to see the path laid out for them."[34]

Coleridge outlined a distinction between reason, duty, and conscience, in his program for the practical realities of law and social policy. He acknowledged the benefits that "progress" had brought to the different orders of society: knowledge to the elite and mass-produced and mass-consumed material comforts to the growing propertied classes. Yet this was insufficient. "Something else is wanted here," he insisted, "the *warmth* to impel and not the *knowledge* to guide" (my italics). He recalled to his readers that "the age" had been "complimented with the epithets of enlightened, humane, & c." for many years *before* the abolition of the slave trade. A speedy comparison of the two ages would, Coleridge was convinced, render into nothing the arguments of the factory owners that their own benevolence and economic self-interest would improve the conditions of their workers. "That [slave] Trade," Coleridge reminisced, was not "abolished at last by the increasing humanity, the enlightened self-interest, of the slave-owners," but by the moral outrage and indignity of those who saw beyond the profits, losses, and balance sheets for plantations into the "human sympathy" and "Individualize[d] detail in some one case." His outrage was barely concealed: "dare our Legislators even now trust to these influences [of the owners'good-will]?" especially given the feeble reaction to the worse evil of slavery? He considered "the bills passed" and "the one now before the House concerning the Slave Trade" as "the best reply."[35] Those who waited for the advocates of increased profit and productivity to ameliorate the lives of slaves and children, who resembled each other in being "property" in labor, would wait in vain.

Throughout these remarks, Coleridge lashed out at malign influences and interests. His underlying suspicions of "corrupt interests and secret influence" had only found different targets since *The Plot Discovered* and his objections to Paley's philosophy of expedience. Stanley had drawn a line of division between "sides" in his critique of the bill. On the one side, Stanley had placed the "liberal" liberty "to do with one's property as one" likes, the freedom promised by laissez-faire economics, and statistically based modern science. On the other side, Stanley had placed "conservative" meddling in individual rights, arbitrary power over citizens' property, and backwards, unscientific nescience which denied the gains of the "enlightened age." Coleridge had not honored that line.

Instead, Coleridge developed a view of progressive agency that addressed questions of both human frailty and political expedience in a complex, stratified, and diverse social world. Such a world was conditioned and advanced organically, as a living tissue of sinuous constraint and fluid agency. These living forces were best understood historically, as temporal and spatial powers of change and order, through the principles of permanence and progression as constituted in the ideas of church and state.

CHAPTER 8

Defending the Church

THE DEBATE ON the proper power relations between church and state permeated British politics and society from the Reformation through the end of the nineteenth century. The church–state conflict was a central, unavoidable, undeniable factor in national life; every political philosopher of consequence in Coleridge's time took note of it. Although British society had arguably become more secular in the course of the eighteenth century, political and social life still included the church to a greater degree than it would in the twentieth—or even the late nineteenth—century. The border disputes over the size and nature of the spheres of influence of the "spiritual" and "temporal" powers of the realm were therefore fundamental rather than ornamental issues in the years in which Coleridge wrote his political tracts. For this reason, it would have been more remarkable if Coleridge had chosen to ignore this theme of church–state relations than it is that he chose to devote such a monumental and systematic effort to revising understandings of it.

Although less violent and combative than they had been in the era of the Civil Wars, church-versus-state battles still showed themselves extremely capable, throughout Coleridge's long political career, of raising tempers and dividing the polity. The acrimonious crisis in his lifetime over subscription, toleration, relief, establishment, and ecclesiastical reform raised tempers to such a pitch that they actually inspired riots and other forms of public violence, in addition to more genteel forms of social combat, such as pamphlet wars.[1] Clergy, quite naturally, wished to preserve their prerogatives, powers, and influence in the nation against a rising tide of state meddling in the church, control that they termed "Erastianism."[2] Political reformers like Major Cartwright and John Wade, quite naturally, hoped to see the church tamed, if not declawed, and aspired to buttress their domains against the continued intrusions of a power-hungry clergy, incursions that they maligned as "Priest-craft."[3] Because he was heavily influenced, and fascinated, by the writings of sixteenth- and seventeenth-century theologians, Coleridge was able to see the deeper roots of these venomous struggles over the strength of church authority in his own time in the rancor of the two centuries that preceded the eighteenth.[4]

Both his interest in the current antagonisms of church and state and his concern with their deep roots in the seventeenth century fuelled Coleridge's investigations into church–state friction. Yet his interest was not merely scholarly. Coleridge's writings on politics, religion, and constitutional sovereignty returned again and again to the central conflict between church and state in an attempt not only to make historical sense of it, but actually to solve it, and by solving it to end it. His work, *On The Constitution of the Church and State According to the Idea of Each*, must be seen, then, as a proposal for a finish to the old warfare between church and state and a refounding of their relations on better grounds. Such a new constitution, Coleridge believed, would ensure the peace and prosperity of the temporal and spiritual dimensions of the kingdom in a way that the old, misconceived settlements of the church had not. There were three traditional positions on the balance of power in church and state that emerged, between 1550 and 1750, as efforts to sever the eccleisiopolitical Gordian knot. Coleridge considered each of these ideas in turn, concluding them to be partial solutions at best to what was an essentially constitutional question.

Seventeenth- and eighteenth-century divines and politicians had long disagreed on the limit and abuse of ecclesiastical power in the polity. Generally speaking, there were three traditional positions that one could take in this debate. The originality and innovative quality of Coleridge's solution to this ancient puzzle can only become clear if one understands the degree to which these three positions had become so standardized as to be positively ossified by Coleridge's time. The novelty of Coleridge's approach to the dilemma of church/state relations becomes clear when it is compared to the typical stances in the debate that thinkers took before his work on the topic.

The first stance was that the established church's power was currently being attacked and diminished, placing the church in danger. According to this theory, proper respect for the church's authority in the state demanded that the state recognize and protect the church's distinct status as an institution. As such, the church had the power to make laws and administer justice through its own institutions and influence secular politics and morals, as well as to pray and preach and administer Christian sacraments. This had been the opinion of all "High Churchmen," and although it traced its roots backwards to Lancelot Andrewes and William Laud, it had been expressed with particular vigor and authority in the Convocation Controversy of Queen Anne's reign, as well as by the High Churchmen of Coleridge's own day.[5]

The second stance was that the independent power of the church had always been too great, even after the gains of the Crown and Parliament in the Reformation, and that its secular authority over the affairs of the state should be diminished if not ended. Indeed, many advocates of a stronger state believed that the state had to obtain true political sovereignty over the running of the church in order to preserve social peace, that it must sustain the royal supremacy in fact as well as in name. This had been the opinion of all those called "Erastians" and had been developed with considerable style by John Jewell and Richard Hooker in past times. The doctrine of Erastianism had been further refined and expanded by Benjamin Hoadly in the reign of George I,[6] and by the "Low Churchmen" of the late eighteenth century.[7]

The third opinion was an irenic one, which attempted to end the war between church and state by suggesting that their spheres of influence were complimentary rather than contradictory. Their relation, argued this middle party, was not a zero-sum game. A strong state did not depend upon a weak church, nor did a strong church demand a weak state. The geniuses of the middle party were Edmund Gibson and William Warburton, both bishops. These men, and others like them, managed to negotiate a profitable peace with the Whig supremacy. The church gained more by assuming a stance of cooperation and professing "alliance" and peace under Warburton and Gibson than it ever had by waving the bloody banner of defiance under Atterbury and Sacheverell.

Coleridge's solution to the war between church and state is most often said to be dependent upon Warburton's "alliance" theory. In order to understand the true novelty of Coleridge's plan, it is important to place it in the context of Warburton's less satisfactory solution to the problem. By doing this, it should become clearer why Coleridge rejected Warburton's high-political solution and forged a new one of his own devising based on a deeper consideration of the purposes and goals of church and state.

Bishop Warburton's *Alliance of Church and State* (1736) attempted to settle the debate irenically by emphasizing the natural interdependency and harmony of the powers of church and state. He argued that they were, and must be regarded as, two distinct bodies with separate duties. This being the case, Warburton contended that an alliance rather than a conflict was to their mutual advantage.

For Warburton's alliance to work, the independent power of the church, as of the year 1736, would have to be maintained, or even enlarged, to make it able to stand as an equal to (rather than submitting as a vassal of) state power. Warburton believed that independent ecclesiastical power could only maintain itself if it could shake off the yoke of temporal supremacy and rise out of its chains to cooperative equality with the state. The yoke, Warbuton stressed, had not been placed maliciously. Elizabethan divines, in their attempts to weaken the high-clerical claims of papist and Puritan critics of Elizabeth's Anglican Church, had ceded too much power to the Crown and Parliament.[8] Warburton believed that the celebrated Richard Hooker in particular had forgotten the fundamental equality of the church to the state in his desire to close off the avenues of "high-church" Puritan and papist critics of the Elizabethan settlement. The "low church," or Erastian, view of church and state proposed by "the judicious Hooker" effectively gave all rights of ecclesiastical dominion over to princes. Such an arrangement, Warburton argued, unjustly tipped the balance of power towards the Crown.

It should be remembered, in the face of Warburton's able criticisms that the Erastian tradition, despite diminishing the powers of the church, did not aspire to eliminate the church from a central role in the nation. Jewell, Hooker, and even "heretical" Hoadly had all been churchmen and throughout their lives adhered to the idea of a single national church for England to which all should conform if they could do so in good conscience. They simply thought that given the church's distinctly supramundane mission, it should not be accorded a secular power in the realm comparable to that of Crown and Parliament.

Coleridge overcame the limitations of these three traditional models in order to formulate his own vision of an improved church-state relations. Although he distilled certain concepts from Warburton, such as the alliance, he was not a "Warburtonian" in the true sense of the word.[9] He borrowed from the Erastians both a vision of a strong role for the Crown and Parliament in the managing of church life—as a component in the "nationality" with which government concerned itself—and an ethos of tolerance for diversity in doctrine, as long as it was theistic. He borrowed from the High Churchmen a vision of the centrality of the church's mission in creating a just and moral nation and encouraging learning and righteousness.

Coleridge's *On The Constitution of the Church and State*, like so much of his other writing, attempted to save what was best in the traditional elements of the establishment (of which the church was a very important pillar indeed). It did so even as it admitted the necessity and desirability of change and what we might anachronistically term modernization. Coleridge desired to "reform in order to conserve" in his vision of the revivified national church. He was not so conservative as to think the church was in a perfect if tarnished form, as the High Churchmen did. Nor was he so radical as to think the church was so imperfect as to merit demolition, as the most extreme of the anticlericals did. He hoped for a solution that would retain the church's role as a moral keel for the nation funded by national wealth but that would also refound the doctrinally defined Anglican clergy as a pragmatically defined Christian-humanist clerisy. He built his conception of the constitution of church and state upon ideas of alliance, but alliance as he conceived it, in a way which Warburton never had: based upon a complex sociological model of the separate social, cultural, and political spheres of commercial independence and landed trust.[10] Coleridge's solution was, once again, an essentially scientific one. His case for devaluing political parties and religious sects as interpretative frameworks for church and state set the critical focus for the reform of the constitution on a deep analysis of structure and function.

The debate over the alliance of church and state often expressed itself, by the 1820s, in terms of the words "radical" and "conservative." The general problem of applying these labels to Coleridge has already been examined. Here, it is important to address specifically why these ideological-factional labels are less helpful to understanding the originality of Coleridge's approach than are the three ecclesiopolitical categories of High, Erastian, and alliance/Warburtonian, which are delineated in the preceding section. For Coleridge's innovations in ecclesiological theory were not strictly political; he did not think that the solution lay in putting more Whigs in place rather than Tories or in putting more Tories in place rather than Whigs. Neither were his positions doctrinal: he wrote no *Age of Reason* to mock Trinitarian doctrine, as did Paine, nor a systematic theology to defend it, as did Horne[11] or Horsley.[12] He was silent about party and dogma in his imagined church constitution, and was even antagonistic towards parties and sects as discouraging independence of mind. His self-avowed critical and antiaffiliative intellect makes him peculiarly unsuited to a schematization based on party or sect, for he despised parties and sects to an almost fanatical degree, and hoped for the national church that he envisioned to transcend rather than propagate them.

In recent writings on eighteenth-century politics and society, it has become voguish to trace all politics back to religion. Where historians once sought class as the magic formula for sorting out the complex skein of political opinions in later Georgian Britain, they now turn to religion as the great determinant of political stances. Formerly, one could trust in scratching a Tory and finding a rural landowner, and scratching a Whig and finding a city merchant.[13] But, the class-as-politics paradigm has been largely eroded by a steady stream of empirical evidence on Tory stockbrokers and Whig petty landowners. The new magic formula, therefore, has become doctrinal faith. Scratch a radical and find a Unitarian. Scratch a conservative and find a High Churchman.

In due time, no doubt, this new catch-all interpretation will also fall by the wayside, as exceptions to the rules—such as Coleridge—add up in greater and greater numbers. Coleridge seems to have been an Evangelical Unitarian in youth and a Neoplatonic (rather than Athanasian) Trinitarian in maturity and old age. At no time, therefore, even after his Plotinist reconciliation with the doctrine of the Trinity, was he a pure, orthodox Athanasian. Throughout his life, Coleridge not only developed a complex and conflicted Christology uniquely his own, but also kept a great number of heterodox and freethinkers among his friends. The fact that such a man came to believe deeply in the concept of a national church rather than a future of disestablishment and sectarian laissez-faire certainly suggests that Unitarianism and "heterodoxy" were not invariably motors for radical politics. The Unitarianism of his early years did not destine Coleridge to radicalism any more than the self-avowed deism of Lord Bolingbroke persuaded him to become a Whig.

At any rate, Coleridge's Christological opinions around 1828 are difficult to determine with any certainty. Because his vision of the church was structuralist and functionalist rather than theological, he tended to focus less in his writings on the establishment of "good doctrines" (*ortho doxa*) than he did on founding "good churches" (*ortho ecclesia*). Therefore, we might consider Coleridge in his writings on church and state as a political scientist *avant la lettre*, engaging less in the study of orthodoxy than in the study of orthoecclesiology. Unlike so many of the Trinitarian controversialists of his day, he seemed more obsessed with the proper shape and mold for the church as a vessel for bringing truth to the nation than he was concerned for the exact confessional content of the truths it would proclaim.

Because he tended to "bracket out" high doctrinal theological problems (such as Athanasian formularies of the Trinity) from his study of what made for good national churches, it is difficult to pigeonhole Coleridge's innovative proposal for a national church in the orthodox-versus-heterodox taxonomy that Jonathan Clark and other historians have found so effective as an analytical tool.[14] Indeed, it was his a-doxy rather than his heterodoxy that frightened one of the best critical readers of his treatise. Julius Hare, a professor at Cambridge in the late 1820s, described Coleridge as an "evil genius."[15] He was a "genius" to Hare because, in a way that the rival philosopher could admire, he had applied his discernment and talent to a penetrating social analysis of church and state as national institutions. He was "evil" to Hare because in a book on a "New Model" for the Christian church, he had eliminated particular discussion of the creed that the church was to confess and propagate. Hare recognized that the innovation of Coleridge's work was that it presented a constitutional model of a national church that "evacuated" or "bracketed out" analysis of the doctrinal mission of the church in favor of discussing its political and social efficacy.

This insistence on *forms* of political and ecclesiastical organization, rather than on *ideologies* of parties and sects, was what separated Coleridge as a political thinker from most of his contemporaries. Coleridge believed that a just society could be built by philosophical reflection on the deeper meanings of institutions and their ultimate purposes. He did not seek to effect change by setting up new rules, creeds, and doctrines, as the "radicals" desired. Nor did he seek to retain tradition by making fetishes and totems of prescriptive Loyalty to the old institutions without critically understanding those institutions, as the "conservative ultras" did. His search for a metapolitical "end" of churches and states separated him from those contemporaries who founded their politics either on tradition for its own sake and detestation of change, or on belief in pure political reason, natural rights, or utility. That metapolitical end was to be realized, Coleridge contended, in a new moral and cultural elite, or "clerisy." Its mission, as Coleridge conceived of it, was the preservation and custodial guardianship of the nation as a sacred and secular trust.

Coleridge concerned himself throughout his career with finding a constitutional theory that could define and preserve the political and cultural institutions that were already extant in Britain rather than with defining abstract general principles for a newly minted government. Through this effort, he developed the idea of the trust as the center of his rationale for the continued influence of landed property in a rapidly commercializing and slowly industrializing nation. His political thought increasingly focused on two major points. The first was his conception of landed property and its significance as a permanent public trust. The second was his belief that the commercial spirit was the dynamic that vivified this trust and breathed life into liberty.[16]

Coleridge envisioned the public trust as conserving and distributing nationally held (i.e., nonprivate) reserves of property. He named this reserve the "nationality." The government would hold this reserve of public lands and public funds in trust and use its income to maintain an independent cultural and intellectual elite, or clerisy. The clerisy were to be distinct from the ordained Christian clergy of the national established churches of England, Scotland, and Ireland, who would still be funded and paid either by their own rectorial freeholds and tithes or by the wages provided by a lay proprietor, another clergyman, or the Crown. The clerisy, in contradistinction, would provide a source of generic conscience and ethical guidance rather than specific political ideologies or doctrinal religion. Their mission was deliberately left vague. Coleridge hoped that the clerisy would serve as critics and public philosophers, unmasking through their skeptical gaze several baleful influences in the kingdom. The divisive influences that Coleridge expected the clerisy to erode included the narrow-mindedness of political faction, the sectarian parochialism and doctrinal infighting of confessional religion, and the rigid orthodoxy of state religion as it had been previously constituted. Such a clerisy would also provide the "democratic" and integrative motive force behind the idea of the constitution, the cultural *ecclesia*.

Coleridge's argument for preserving and refunding a national church had certain conservative resonances in a generation (1820 through 1840) that initiated intense debate on parliamentary control of church revenues, such as Irish sees, and even seriously opened discussion of disestablishment. One naturally associates attempts to strengthen the church's influence in the state with the old traditions of Laud and Atterbury, with the new influence of John Keble in his famous "Sermon Against National Apostasy," and with the young Tractarians who were fired into action by Keble's battle cry. On the other hand, the advocacy of the institution of a single national church did not in itself imply Tory High Churchmanship or Trinitarianism. Most of the republicans of the commonwealth and protectorates, after all, had called for a nationally funded and administered Puritan clergy and had approved a new national liturgy to replace the Anglican Prayer Book.[17]

Coleridge's plan differed from the national churches envisioned by the Laudians, the Kebleites, and even the old Commonwealthsmen of 1640 to 1660 in that it hoped to purify institutional forms while avoiding the issues of doctrine and confession that had so obsessed earlier churchmen. His bold invention of a national church as a doctrinally vague institutional form (unlike the Christian Church), was a break with almost every potential solution to the problem of church and state that had come before him, whether Anglican or Puritan.[18]

Where Coleridge differed from most "Tories" of his day was in his willful inattention to the battles over the Athanasian definition of the Trinity and other high-theological disputes among the clergy. Most "church and king" Tories of the 1820s defended the old doctrine-based discrimination and the Test Act as long as they could because they felt that national unity and tradition demanded that only confessing Anglicans be allowed full civil rights and participation in the state. In comparison to the typical Tory's defense of doctrine as a bar to civil participation, Coleridge was a lifelong critic of religious orthodoxy. He despised institutionalized dogma as forging shackles and chains to impede the advance of the search for truth. His vision of a national church was of a very broad church indeed, one that was most significant in its form or constitution rather than its particular doctrinal content. It is not surprising that Coleridge has been seen as a founder of the Broad Church movement of the nineteenth century.[19]

Yet his system did not aspire to create an *entirely* free market in ideas. Coleridge's church perhaps most resembles the civic religion proposed by the French Revolutionaries, in that while it made all Christian sects equally legal and ended the discriminatory preference for adherents to the old established confession, it still vocally condemned atheism and immorality and sought to inculcate ethics broadly. While the Coleridgean church absolved itself from the propagation of belief and understanding of a positive doctrinal system such as the Thirty-nine Articles or the Creed of St. Athanasius, it drew the line of ne plus ultra before atheism. Coleridge believed that such a national church, even after it had divested itself of the homogenizing influence of the traditional creeds and formularies, could be a civilizing force. As he himself described his civic religion, borrowing a phrase from the Roman poet Ovid, "*Emollit mores nec sinit esse feroes*" (It softens the manners and does not permit them to be brutal).[20] But civilization was not desirable without cultivation, and manners, while a refinement of morality, were not a substitute for morality. For this reason, landed property was the rock on which Coleridge built his national church.

It is beyond doubt that the vision of an ecclesiastical polity that Coleridge invented in *Church and State* was built on concepts of virtue, honor, and land ownership. Landed property was the foundation not only of the wealth from which Coleridge aspired to fund his clerisy, but also of the values of love of country and patriotism that he believed sprang from connection to that land. Land was not the exclusive foundation of Coleridge's constitutional theory, but land mattered for Coleridge in a way that placed it at the heart of his scheme for a new established church.

Some critics, notably J. T. Miller and John Morrow, have considered Coleridge's early writings to be neo-Harringtonian in tone.[21] Morrow has charted what he believes to be a transition in Coleridge's later writings on politics toward a language of civic humanism. This language is undoubtedly present in *Church and State*, and Morrow is quite right to emphasize it. Coleridge, however, augmented this agrarian-virtue theme with a celebration of the role of commerce in promoting civility and progress in the nation. This lionizing went well beyond the classical republican account of civic pride in the polis to cognize the more modern accounts of law and commerce that Scots moralism and the Whig skepticism had advanced.[22] Unlike most neo-Harringtonians,

Coleridge did not have the gentleman-farmer's suspicion that a rising tide of prosperity and wealth was going to hurl the kingdom into perdition. Unlike most neo-Harringtonians, he thought that the risk of the polity dying from stagnancy was as great as the risk that it would die from corruption. For Coleridge, land and commerce were both crucial parts of the body politic.

Throughout his career, Coleridge maintained that the principle of landed property was, and must be, the stable foundation of any good government. Landed property was the basis of the Common Law, and as such it was the foundation of the ancient constitution. It provided, through the Common Law and the constitution, the "fundamental liberty" of the nation. Land alone, however, was not enough to guarantee the freedom of the kingdom. Only the additional principle of a constantly growing liberty that sustained and regenerated a just and dynamic polity could bring about true freedom. "An expanding liberty," as Coleridge termed it, was the product not of the landed property which created fundamental liberty, but rather of the culture and workings of commercial urban society. The Idea of a state depended, for Coleridge, on the combined operations of both landed and commercial society. Commercial wealth, when taken alone, corrupted liberty because it left it adrift without the moral anchor that landed property provided. Landed wealth alone stagnated liberty because nothing urged it onward into new ideas and new innovations that commercial activity brought. Only an alliance of land and commerce could insure the survival of a liberty that was both fundamental and expanding.

Coleridge's political ideas are best understood in terms of decisions about the shape of active institutions, rather than as decisions about the sort of ideologies that would fill them. He saw institutions not in terms of particular doctrinal or ideological content, but as structures of power and distributors of resources that facilitated the cultural freedom and prosperity of the nation. If such institutions were effectively conceived and executed, stability for the community (authority) would coexist with the individual's capacity for self-actualization (liberty). Two principles animated Coleridge's Idea of the state: permanence and progression. Briefly stated, the forces of permanence emanated from agriculture and landed property, whereas the forces of progression flowed from moveable property and the mercantile economy. Coleridge's "binary" model of the state comprised the twin poles of land and capital, or permanence and progression .

Permanence contributed stability and continuity in Coleridge's ideal constitution. It was embodied in the one thing that did not alter as a physical base,nor diminish in social value: landed property. Land could not be made or destroyed by men, only transformed into greater or lesser degrees of productivity.[23] Land was a finite resource that was always necessary to habitation or enterprise. It was fundamental to life and survival in a way that ships and banks and shops and joint-stock companies were not. Land could not be exported, nor could it be fabricated. Its attainment and trade therefore cut, recut and shared out the pieces of a pie that was essentially fixed in size even before the first British tribes had settled in the isles. This predetermined and permanent quality of land kept its economic value relatively stable. In addition, its ownership remained relatively constant in the great landed families. The perfection of entail and primogeniture in the late seventeenth century had contributed to the establishment of landowners as (seemingly) permanent presences on the land, who had been there for generations and who would remain there for generations to come.

While land always remained a constant resource and a source of permanent presence in a locality, its status as the sole source of value in the polity changed as soon as trade appeared. Coleridge believed that there was a socioeconomic basis to culture and that the rise of trade transformed all cultures where it occurred. Commercial activity was inherently mobile and volatile. Both the sum total and the relative economic value of manufactured goods and services were in constant fluctuation. Where land, which was uncreated, perpetually stayed in the same place, goods were created and moved across counties or even oceans in search of buyers. In the eyes of early-nineteenth-century economic theorists, Commerce rode an eternally spinning wheel of fortune.[24] The winners and losers of the market place were determined by cycles of boom and bust, through periods of expansion and contraction in productivity and enterprise, by shifting patterns of consumption, by changing conceptions of wealth. Mercantile wealth, unlike landed wealth, did not tend to be handed down or entailed in the same family, and the death of the founder of a merchant house often resulted in the dissolution of the firm as a corporate entity in the state. Commerce was, therefore, especially in comparison to land, a fluid, dynamic and progressive force. It was also the basis of Coleridge's second great principle of an ideal constitution, the principle of progression.

The progressive spirit, as realized in the activities, relations, and productions of commerce and finance, was the opposite of permanence. There were times and places, Coleridge argued, in which agricultural activity was overshadowed by industry, trade, and brokerage. At such times, the social and economic realities of a nation were transformed. Cultural and moral values, political and social institutions and expectations were all reconstructed by the rise of commercial endeavor as the mainspring of a national economy. Yet

Coleridge did not see the transmogrifying power of commercial activity as a discrete and unmediated force. The progressive principle of commerce and finance was indissolubly related to the permanence of land, whether or not it desired such a relationship. Land would always remain the base for the entire economy, by virtue of its existence as the territory on which all economic activity perforce took place and by virtue of its status as the seedbed of permanent (i.e., aristocratic) cultural and social values. The rise of trade and finance, Coleridge insisted, did not *replace* the landed economy; it simply transformed and influenced it, at the same time as landed wealth exerted its tidal pull on the rising economy of trade and finance.[25]

Thus permanence and progression, once progression was born, evermore existed in "equipoise." Progression regenerated the nation and launched it forward toward its goals. Permanence counseled that power, and in doing so preserved the realm's continuity, traditions, and institutions. Together, permanence and progression formed a binary system that allowed for the dynamic growth of finance and merchant capital to be guided by the ancient and fundamental traditions of land ownership, and for land ownership to be revivified by the innovations and enterprise of commerce. This binary system, for Coleridge, was the true Idea of the nation-state.

Both Morrow and Miller conceive of Coleridge's principles of permanence and progression as suggesting a disdain for commerce and a less than critical admiration of landed values. These interpreters argue that Coleridge viewed landed society as a leash to hold back the undisciplined and dangerous beast of commercialization.[26] Those who interpret Coleridge as an heir to the country Tory "politics of nostalgia" argue that he saw aristocratic values as mainly a defensive bulwark against the onslaught of the corrosive tendencies of commercial society.[27]

Only a deep misreading of *Church and State*, however, could identify Coleridge with pure, Bolingbroke-style, Country Party nostalgia. The "Country Coleridge" is a failed paradigm because it suggests the Country "antagonism" model of the defense of landed culture against the hostile attack of moneyed men as the best analytical lens through which to read *Church and State*. Coleridge, however, did not share this "antagonism" model. Instead he saw an alliance in the relations of permanence and progression, and an unusually beneficial relationship between these two social and political forces. Where Bolingbroke and his circle tended to see landed society as a victim, under siege and barely able to hold its own, Coleridge saw it as a partner in the first phase of a long and dynamic relationship with commerce, a partnership in which land would affect commerce every bit as much as commerce affected land.

The pure Country model posited a static and reactionary role for the landed interest; Coleridge's model placed the landed interest in a dynamic and progressive role.

How could Coleridge think that landed society was "opposed" to moneyed society and yet not see the two, as the Country tradition did, as doomed to be "contrary" enemies? The answer lies in Coleridge's own technical use of those terms. Coleridge began his discussion of the Ideas of permanence and progression with an extended note of caution:

> Permit me to draw your attention to the essential difference between *opposite* and *contrary*. Opposite powers are always of the same kind, and tend to union, either by equipoise or by a common product. Thus the + and - poles of a magnet, thus positive and negative electricity are opposites. Sweet and sour are opposites; sweet and bitter are contraries. The feminine character is *opposed* to the masculine; but the effeminate is its *contrary*. Even so in the present instance, the interest of permanence is opposed to that of progressiveness; but so far from being contrary interests, they, like the magnetic forces, suppose and require each other. Even the most mobile of creatures, the serpent, makes a *rest* for its own body, and drawing up its voluminous train from behind on this fulcrum, propels itself onwards. On the other hand it is a proverb in all languages, that (relatively to man at least) what would stand still must retrograde.[28]

Coleridge argued that the forces of permanence and progression, being opposites, complemented rather than contradicted each other. He did not give formative priority to either of them. Like the head and the tail of the serpent in his example, they each depended on the other for their mutual viability. To see the principle of land as a bulwark *against* the invasion of commerce, as the early-eighteenth-century Country Party had, would have been to value permanence over progression, which Coleridge did not do. Indeed, if there was any priority of influence or intent suggested by his note on "opposing force" it was the dynamic or vibrant principle that was emphasized. For "what would stand still must retrograde." The traditionalist's view, that society ought on principle to deny efforts at change and rest confidently in its current form, was, therefore, a recipe for stasis and, through stasis, death. Coleridge chose instead to emphasize a genuine interdependency or alliance, a binary system in which each body exerted its pull and influence on the other. No living body could survive without the integrated connections of muscle and bone. Living flesh without its supportive structures was a shapeless mass of fleshy pulp. But a skeleton without the animating fluid of blood and tissue was nothing more than a dead thing, a desiccated and lifeless shell. So it was with all forces of permanence and progression. As in life, so it was in the state.

To Coleridge, commerce liberalized and regenerated land, at the same time that land tempered and stabilized commerce. Landed society was not a virtuous bulwark against the perfidy and moral vacuity of the commercial world. Coleridge did not envision an ideal state like Gulliver's Brobdingnag, nor did he hope for a Spartan paradise with commerce and towns almost non-existent and the plough and the hoe the major implements of life. Nor did he look back, as Bolingbroke had, to an idealized Elizabethan Age when commercial society "knew its place" as the subordinate to land and aristocracy.[29] Instead, he saw commerce and land as welcome and active partners in the state; both forces had a crucial role to play, and either was insufficient on its own to sustain liberty and virtue.

This model of "integrative dynamism"—what I have termed the binary system of mutual influences—was the linchpin of Coleridge's Idea of a state. Its primary object, the preservation of landed property, had to be constantly adjusted to accommodate those changing uses and understandings of the meaning and value of that property brought about by trade and finance. How did Coleridge envision this integrative system that brought about the binary equipoise between commerce and land? The answer lies in his description of the nature of the two principles and the two orders of society that sprang from them. Significantly, Coleridge began his account of the workings of church and state by explaining the benefits of land and commerce in their capacities as engines of permanence and progression.

In describing the importance and the limitations of the Idea of permanence in the principle of land, Coleridge described both landed property and landed society as a constant and stable social base, even after their transformations by emergent commerce. This constancy, permanence, stemmed not only from the durability of land as a material and concrete form of wealth, but also from the consistent status of land as a primary object of human ambition. He assumed as self-evident that landed property and the social meaning that accompanied it were desirable goals. "It will not be necessary" insisted Coleridge "to enumerate the several causes that combine to connect the permanence of a state with the land and the landed property." The desire for permanence was natural, instinctive, and deeply human. "To found a family, and to convert his wealth into land are the twin thoughts, births of the same moment, in the mind of the opulent merchant, when he thinks of reposing from his labours."[30] For Coleridge, the acquisition of landed property was the ultimate ambition of every citizen and the ultimate end of all capital accumulation. (Significantly, historians' analyses of eighteenth- and early-nineteenth-century merchants' investments have shown that Coleridge's description of British society's prejudices in favor of landed wealth were essentially correct. Most merchants in his era eventually hoped to place their earnings into what they hoped was the more lasting and estimable form of wealth, land.[31]) Land was the most desirable form of property, the most "real" estate, because it was the most immovable, the most permanent.

This permanence was important not only because it seemed to secure economic stability for the landholder, but because the ownership of immovable landed property in a given nation and locality suggested perpetual membership and participation in the politics of the "country." Beyond material wealth, land imputed both rank and history to its owners, even if they were not themselves of unusually old family; it communicated its own permanence to the person of its current possessor. The ultimate value of landed property and the final objective of all human action argued Coleridge, was cultural and social continuity. Individual experience was, he suggested, only made meaningful in its relationship to the history that inhered in the "land" and the "country." He asserted that a man "from the class of the Novi Homines" (i.e., the "new men" or nouveaux riches) altered his very nature when he purchased an estate. Coleridge felt that such a man "redeems himself by becoming the staple ring of the chain, by which the present will become connected with the past; and the test and evidency of permanency afforded."[32] In the end, only permanence could grant stability, and only stability could confer meaning. He continued his defense of landed tradition, not for its own sake, but for its inherit historical and, therefore, structural merit. "To the same principle [of permanence] appertain primogeniture and hereditary titles," maintained Coleridge, arguing that "the influence that these exert in accumulating large masses of property" was to counteract "the antagonist and dispersive forces, which the follies, vices, and misfortunes of individuals can scarcely fail to supply."[33]

One who read only that far in the treatise might be forgiven for presuming that Coleridge's *Church and State* was a pure pro-landed-culture polemic along the lines of Bolingbroke or even of Burke's "Letter to a Noble Lord."[34] For Coleridge, as for them, land represented tradition, veneration, the weight of history, the brake on excessive social change, and the best way of chaining individuals to their country and their born (or acquired) duty as aristocrats or gentry. Yet the degree to which Coleridge found landed values, taken exclusively, to be an inadequate as social forces seems clear. He acerbically noted that the entail and primogeniture existed to protect the elite from their own "follies [and] vices." Obviously, land itself did not guarantee civic virtue; it only guaranteed a greater chance at displaying it to advantage.

In the end, Coleridge stressed that permanency with nothing to modify it was insufficient for a good society. Permanency in isolation, in the style of the Spartans or Brobdingnagians, was an imperfect principle. To the stabilizing continuity of landed society, Coleridge noted, "tends the proverbial obduracy of prejudices characteristic of the humbler tillers of the soil." Such simple rusticity produced an "aversion even to benefits that are offered in the form of innovations."[35] It was clear to all Country Party theorists that the vulgar "new man" needed the integrity and virtue and permanence that investment in land offered him. Coleridge, however, knew something that they and their heirs in the second Tory party ignored. He knew that the "tillers of the soil," whether humble or noble, also needed qualities that commercial society alone could bring them: civilization, polish, enterprise, and energy. Without the leaven of commerce to make it rise, Coleridge knew, the vaunted country virtue was but a very dull lump of "proverbial obduracy of prejudices" indeed.

Coleridge delineated next the properties and advantages of the commercial spirit. The political principle of progression, or "the progression of the state, in the arts and comforts of life," was fundamentally engrained in all that could be called civilizing, as were the gifts and blessings of the commercial or competitive spirit. Where the land brought honor and virtue to the state, the towns and their commerce brought material progress, refinement, sociability, and the energy of emulation. In those ancient and medieval states where the culture of towns and trade had not yet arisen, war, raiding, and plunder had fulfilled this role. War provided a more brutal and less pleasant way of introducing new ideas and wealth to the nation than did trade. But at least it assured the circulation of the produce of the arts and sciences throughout the world and by its tempting fruit motivated plundering peoples to become civilized in their own right. Because plunder and conquest were active forms of enterprise, they were (despite their obvious crudity) preferable as instruments for the spreading of culture than were tyranny or monopoly.

That Coleridge saw more evil in monopoly and a placid pastoral tyranny than he did in the bloody havoc of conquest and raiding societies speaks volumes. It demonstrates beyond doubt that he saw the stoppage of commerce and progression as every bit as great a threat to society as the erosion of landed permanence. In considering the disaster of permanence without progression, Coleridge turned his attention to the case of Italy. The political failures of Florence and Venice provided Coleridge with the means to repudiate the pure civic-virtue theory of the classical republicans.

Incessant competition, either of merchants in civilized polities or warriors in barbaric nation-states, made adaptation and technological innovation a way of life essential to survival. The interaction and circulation of the scientific innovations produced in this ceaseless one-upmanship advanced through the avenues of emulation, greed, comparison, competition, and theft. This swirl of competitive and emulative activity invariably and unwittingly expanded civil liberty even in states, such as ancient Rome, where the rulers did not wish this increase of liberty to ensue. Coleridge argued that

the progression of a state, in the arts and comforts of life, in the diffusion of the information and knowledge, useful or necessary for all; in short all advances in civilization, and the rights and privileges of citizens, are especially connected with, and derived from the four classes of the mercantile, the manufacturing, the distributive, and the professional. To early Rome, war and conquest were the substitutes for trade and commerce. War was their trade. As these wars became more frequent, on a larger scale, and with fewer interruptions, the liberties of the plebeians continued increasing.[36]

So far, so good. But when the progressive circulation of commerce halted, liberty shrank accordingly, even in states where the ruled did not wish this decrease of liberty to take place. Coleridge ended his socioeconomic analysis of the rise and fall of liberty on the Italian peninsula with a vision of a modern Italy that, lacking in either imperial conquests or trade, languished in a backward pastoral stupor. There, a purely agricultural economy of latifundia had created a world of bucolic and picturesque oppression, whose beauty "like a garden" could not entirely obscure the repulsiveness of its stagnation, its lack of freedom. Italy "is supposed at present to maintain a larger number of inhabitants than in the days of Trajan or in the best and most prosperous of the Roman Empire. With the single exception of the ecclesiastical state [the Papal States around and including the city of Rome], the whole country is cultivated like a garden. You may find there every gift of God—only not freedom."[37]

Coleridge, unlike Harrington and Harrington's followers, asserted that a chiefly pastoral and agrarian society not based on incessant plunder, and successive wars of conquest was absolutely incompatible with freedom. Only during the old plundering days of the Roman republic in Cicero's time, or in the era of the canny, volatile, and acquisitive commercial city-states of the Italian Renaissance, did liberty prosper. The loss of all "virtue" and "liberty" in Italy, according to Coleridge, had *not* been due to her change toward an

individualistic market and merchant economy and consequent loss of common values and amateur military arts, as Machiavelli, Guicciardini, and their
English disciples had argued. Instead, Italy had lost its virtue and liberty
through her embrace of backwardness, sluggish rural peace under an absen-
tee foreign yoke, and an abandonment of the vitality of the Renaissance city
for the safety and torpor of the baroque *palazzi*. Modern Italy exemplified for
Coleridge the dangers of permanence without progression, the dangers of a
serpent that was all tail and fat and no head or muscle.

For Coleridge, an excess of Country Party values emphasizing the superiority of rural morals to urban morals, rather than a dearth of them, had strangled Renaissance *liberta*. Italy, argued Coleridge, was "a country rich in the
proudest records of liberty, illustrious with the names of heroes, statesmen,
legislators, philosophers." Its history was "alive with the virtues and crimes of
hostile parties, when the glories and the struggles of ancient Greece were acted
out over again in the proud republics of Venice, Genoa, and Florence." Because of this, "the love of every eminent citizen was in constant hazard from
the furious factions of their native city." Yet despite this, "life had no charm
out of its dear and honoured walls." So much so that "all the splendours of the
hospitable palace, and the favour of princes, could not soothe the pining of
Dante or Machiavel, exiles from their free, their beautiful, Florence." But, for
all of that, Coleridge concluded, "not a pulse of liberty survives."[38]

It was through the forced suppression of trade, Coleridge argued, that the
conquerors of Italy in the early sixteenth century had destroyed the liberties that
had flourished in the fifteenth century, even in the "tyrannies." The Hapsburgs
had brought Italy to its senescence through a conscious policy of pastoralization:

It was the profound policy of the Austrian and the Spanish courts,by
every possible means to degrade the profession of trade; and even in
Pisa and Florence to introduce the feudal pride and prejudice of less
happy, less enlightened countries. Agriculture, meanwhile, with its attendant population and plenty, was cultivated with increasing success;
but from the Alps to the Straits of Messina, the Italians are slaves.[39]

The preceding passage is both evocative and articulate in its emphasis on the
liberalizing tendencies of commerce and the stultifying tendencies of agriculture. Coleridge once again demonstrated in this analysis that permanence on
its own, without the vivifying influence of progression, naturally and in-
escapably led to "the feudal pride and prejudice of less happy, less enlightened
countries."[40]

In all of this, Coleridge's views are in alignment not with the Harringtonians, but with the proponents of skeptical Whiggery and those other defenders of commerce as a force for morally improving the nation. Coleridge's denial of the self-sufficiency of Tory and Country Party landed values has not escaped the notice of critics such as J. G A. Pocock, who have regarded Coleridge as one of the late-model expositors of an eighteenth-century skeptical Whig tradition that saw commerce in a positive light. This tradition, dating back to the "Whiggish" Tory David Hume, rejected the Country Party equation of commerce with corruption and arbitrary power. Instead, Hume and his successors stood the neo-Harringtonian argument on its head by making commerce, wealth, and civility the essential building blocks rather than the destructive wrecking balls of liberty. Indeed, Pocock, more than most, has been able to penetrate the fog of party names and cant that lies in such thick layers on the nineteenth-century political landscape. He has seen that the "Old Tory" Coleridge, like so many "Old Tories" of the second Tory party (including his old enemy Pitt), were the ideological heirs of the old "conservative" wing of the Whig party. These old-style Whigs had liked the revolutionary principles of 1688 so well that they saw little need to advance much farther forward from them. Pocock notes that Coleridge "further complicates the meaning of the word 'Tory' at a time when it was increasingly used to denote a last-ditch defender of the Whig order."[41]

Coleridge's acquaintance with the "skeptical" defenders of commerce and finance was extensive. He had read the works of David Hume, James Steuart of Goodtrees, and Adam Smith by 1811. While Coleridge rejected what he perceived to be "multitude of sophisms" in Steuart and Smith, he also maintained that their principles, though clothed in what he considered the specious pseudoscientific cant of the new economists, contained a moiety of "just and important result[s]" that were deducible from the "simplest principles of morality and common-sense."[42] Like Smith, Coleridge believed that culture and morality and political institutions were integrally related to each other by and through their historical development as social practices. As such they were intrinsically tied to a process of human order in which cities and commerce played an active and important role. This interpretation was not located exclusively in the discourse of juridical/individual rights, nor was it to be found exclusively in the vocabulary of civic-humanist/communitarian duties. Coleridge, like Montesquieu, Rousseau, and arguably Smith, viewed the state as the agent of a sociologically originated jurisprudence that comprehended the lexica of both liberty and civil rights and civic virtues and duties. David Hume and Andrew Fletcher of Saltoun had both emphasized the liberalizing and civilizing effects of urban commercial life in their considerations of the importance of local power and local communities in preserving liberty and happiness. For Hume, capital cities were "centres of law, government, culture, and . . . trade."[43]

Nicholas Phillipson has traced this idea of the commercial city as defender rather than corrupter of freedom from the unlikely sources of Fletcher and Hume to its great expositor, the skeptical Whig Adam Smith. Smith's market theory and moral philosophy were, for Phillipson, a development of earlier eighteenth-century ideas of civicism. He considers Smith a practical moralist who emphasized the quotidian role of cities and provinces in encouraging a cultured and easy civility. Smith, in perfecting this argument, deflated the bombast of the classical republican litany of melodramatic statements on how the corrupt city dwellers could only be fended off by the stoic resolve and civic virtues of the frugal and incorruptible gentry.[44] Phillipson further distinguishes Smith's views from communitarian civicism by emphasizing Smith's focus on ideas of propriety and the moral development of the individual rather than the virtue of the community at large.

Smith's civic moralism rested on ideas of moral autonomy and voluntarism. Civic moralism was an idea that seems to have been echoed in Coleridge's writings after 1816. It was founded as a riposte to the tendency in commonwealth arguments to seek "global" (i.e., societal rather than individual) amelioration and to mistrust individuals, especially those with money. In contradistinction, civic moralism proposed an idea of virtue—like that developed by Addison in the 1710s and repeated by Coleridge in the 1820s—that strove to improve the general social good of all citizens without condemning commerce or individualism as unpatriotic. Indeed, the success of the civic moralist program positively depended on the personal agency of well-intentioned persons such as "Addison's urban and urbane Christian gentleman."

The civic moralists sought to do for patriotism what the latitudinarians had done for religion: make it smoother, less strident, less rough, more comfortable with cosmopolitan culture, more sophisticated (in the good sense of the word), and more open to the possibility that well-intentioned individuals might engender change. Reed Browning gave a differnt name to this change in political style than the old dichotomy of civic-humanist and juridical rights. He described the great divide as consisting of the emulators of Cato opposed to the emulators of Cicero. According to Browning, whereas the Catonian style was strong on accusations and bluster and last stands of patriotism against tyranny and corruption, the Ciceronian style sought to reach the same goal of liberty by a less rugged road of compromise, prudence, and urbanity that recognized the difference between a government which was truly corrupt and one that was simply slovenly.[45]

Donald Winch has produced a very constructive approach to Smithian civic moralism and social anthropology. Winch's analysis clears up much of the current scholarly confusion that seems to attend the discussion of the relative influence in a given individual's political thought of the (allegedly incompatible) discourses of jurisprudence (with its guarantee of individual liberty and rights and its dependence on volition) and the civicist tradition (with its focus on community and duty and virtue as the basis for freedom). Winch believes that for Smith, the discourse of justice and rights was not incompatible with the discourse of duty and civic virtue. Refusing to privilege an exclusively materialist economic reading of Smith's use of the four stages, Winch believes that the stages described by Smith must be considered as having both economic and political meanings. The four stages in this reading become significant because they show how Smith believed that laws and governments "grew up with" rather than were "produced by" social and economic development.[46]

Using Winch's analysis of Smith as an heir to the sociological jurisprudence of Montesquieu, it becomes possible to understand Coleridge's ongoing attempt to balance or, more pointedly, to integrate socioeconomic, jurisprudential, and moral concerns into a single cohesive state theory. Commerce and virtue, liberty and law, were to be sustained by institutional equipoise. Linking commercial activity with cultural and moral development was a persistent theme of Coleridge's. Like Smith, his greatest objection to monopoly was that it was an unnatural suspension of economic and social discourse, or commerce. The suppression of trade, similar to the censorship that Coleridge had decried in 1795 as the suspension of opinion, "hushed to death-like silence" the voices of exchange.[47] In short, monopoly censored and censorship monopolized; both degraded or halted the natural interactive workings of the social and historical forces of change. Both undermined the logic and wisdom of the "science of history." Coleridge increasingly developed his theme of virtue and liberty's dependence upon commerce after 1802 and continued to refine it in his later writings through 1832. Dependent as they were on commerce in its relationship to land, liberty and virtue existed in equipoise; their spheres of influence, like those of permanence and progression, were cognized and realized in the laws and legislature of Britain.

Having considered the merits and disadvantages of both landed and commercial society, Coleridge turned to the task of considering the variety of interests that were represented by these two orders. The "subjects of the state" he divided into "two orders, . . . the agricultural or possessors of land; and the merchant, manufacturer, the distributive and the professional bodies." Both were to be legally cognized "under the common name of citizens." Coleridge had considered the benefits of commerce at some length and he had argued for the "civilizing" virtue of trade and its capacity for "expanding liberty." Landed society, for its part, brought to the task of government the need to cognize its peculiar qualities, of honor and of entitlement. Land, as a stable basis for trust, was the foundation of promise, commitment, fidelity, and, finally, law. These questions of honor and entitlement, when realized as fiduciary promise, were the foundations of all civil polities. They reflected "by the nature of things common to every civilized country," or "at all events by the course of events in this country," the underlying principles of the law. The ancient constitution, in the oldest records of the Common Law, or "in imitation of our old law books," had "subdivided" these interests "into two classes," which "we may entitle the Major and the Minor Barons." These, "either by their interests or by the very effect of their situation, circumstances, and the nature of their employment" were "vitally connected with the permanency of the state." As such, their concern was with the "institutions, rights, customs, manners, privileges" of that state, placing their power in a dynamic opposition with that of "the inhabitants of ports, towns, and cities." This latter group represented the interests of artisans and burgesses, or the manufacturing and commercial influence. They were, as such, but "in like manner and from like causes . . . more especially connected" with the dynamic or liberalizing elements of the state, "with its progression."[48] While the inhabitants of towns may contribute through their various interests to progress and liberty, it is the principle of law in the entitlement of landed society that forms the basis of the "institutions, rights, customs, manners," and "privileges" of the state. For unlike "expanding liberty," the law reflects a principle of constraint. Its efficacy and stability are a function of its history as customary right. In short, the legitimacy of the law rests on its institutional permanency.

The origins of the common law may be traced back to the laws governing land use. Those laws, which did not accord with the entitlements and privileges of landed society, had been characterized as innovative and arbitrary by seventeenth-century common lawyers who had appealed to the landed rights of baronial oligarchy against the centralizing tendencies of the Stuart Crown.[49] Rules were considered arbitrary, and therefore unjust, according to the degree of their suddenness, their unconventionality. Hale believed that "impetuousity" in law presented considerable problems for "civic ordering." He deemed unfair and inequitable those rules that abruptly violated expectations, habits of conduct, and promises.[50] In short, it was believed that arbitrary law undermined compliance as it undermined trust. Coleridge believed that "breach of trust" constituted more than a "breach of contract" or a broken promise; it was a form of dishonor. Honor touched on reputation, habit, and expectation. Coleridge associated the origins and foundations of the law with relationships that emanated from landed society. He believed this to be a matter of juridical principle as well as a historical precedent generated from the Common Law rights governing the disposition of real property.[51] Detailing and enumerating the particular interests of the separate spheres of commerce and land, Coleridge intentionally emphasized the complexity and significance of each with respect to his two principles. With particular regard to the landed interest, he depicted the possession of land as determining not just a limited "economic" interest, but an entire set of social and juridical relationships.[52] In this regard, sovereign consensus was predicated on the idea of *recht* as much as *macht*. "Right" was a power and a property.[53] It was founded on commitments, expectations, and duties.[54] Coleridge considered the idea of property to be significant not merely as the accumulation of particular wealth, but for the social, cultural, and political institutions that its specific form and usage determined. He believed that the "world order" generated by a relationship with the land was antithetical, although not contrary, to the social structures that emanated from commercial activity. The principle of permanence existed in complementary and integrative opposition to that of progression. They formed a unity when in equipoise.

    If law, landed society, and the principle of permanence existed as a structural base that generated the institutional form of the state, then, Coleridge argued, it was the dynamic of commercial activity that animated that form. Commerce was the engine; it was the catalyst or mover that generated the resolution of these opposites. Recall that in his discussion of permanence and progression as opposite not contrary forces, Coleridge had employed the image of a snake as the metaphor for his living state. Accordingly, land became the rest of the body and commerce the tail that propelled it on. "Even the most mobile of creatures," whether "the serpent" or the state, "makes a *rest* of its own body," but, sustained by the deep roots of country prosperity, the city gathers and brokers the commonwealth and, "drawing up its voluminous train from behind on this fulcrum, propels itself onwards."[55] Coleridge continued his description of equipoise as a historical process—"in a very advanced stage of civilization, the two orders of society will more and more modify and leaven each other."[56] Landed society cultivated honor; the commercial world civilized and made virtuous the landed. And what is quite clearly meant by civilized is the expansive liberty that was for Coleridge the very essence of the civic principle. Making this relationship between law and liberty, between virtue and civility, explicit Coleridge, insisted that "the necessity for external government to man is in an inverse proportion to the vigour of his self-government." Consequently, "where the last is most complete, the first is least wanted" or, most succinctly, "the more Virtue, the more Liberty."[57] Coleridge described, in sociopolitical and economic terms, the practical mechanism of this process. It was reflected in the constitution of Parliament, where "at all times the lower of the two ranks, of which the first order consists, or the Franklins, will, in their political sympathies, draw more nearly to the antagonist order than the first rank."[58]

The tendency of the gentry to ally with the merchant classes, or franklins with burghers, was the foundation of the division of the two houses.[59] With the expansion of commercial society following Britain's financial revolution of the 1690s came a consolidation and realignment of "country" interests with borough representation.[60] The integration of *both* interests was, Coleridge maintained, essential to any criteria of citizenry. Thus the landed interest is secured against corruption and the commercial order allied to the greater national interests of the state. This resolution of opposites at the parameters of interest is an inherent principle of Coleridge's Idea of the state. A property-based law and constitution would provide not only the institutional form, but also the necessary stabilizing constraint for an urban commercial cosmopolitanism marked by vitality and flux. Both created by and creating history, the constitution as an Idea, was, in Coleridge's view, the active instrument for the interrelation of particular interests and broader social relationships within the living state.

In summary, it has been argued that Coleridge considered the ideal constitutional balance between the Lords and the Commons to reflect his two formative constitutional Ideas of permanence and progression. The "major barons," or peers, represented the landed interest of permanence in the House of Lords. The "minor barons," or franklins (landowning freeholders), in combination with the burgesses, or the "moneyed interests," represented the personal and commercial principle of progression in the House of Commons. These two "estates" operated in conjunction with the church, which Coleridge (borrowing a phrase from Elizabeth I) termed the "third great estate of the realm."[61] No one of these three estates—hereditary aristocrats, commoners, or churchmen—was intended by the Idea of the constitution to exist in a state of subjugation *to*, or lordship *over*, the others. No single interest in this triad, argued Coleridge, could profit *in the long run* by grossly undermining the power of another interest. He stressed throughout his treatise that the fortunes of the three estates were not a zero-sum game in which the peers could gain permanent wealth by beggaring the commoners. It was Coleridge's contention that all three estates of the realm were involved in a common, collective endeavor in which the true enrichment of one was the enrichment of all, and the pauperization of one the pauperization of all. Systemic imbalance might lead to temporary, short-term gains for a portion of the polity but in the end would harm all, even that portion that had originally believed itself to gain by the imbalance.

If the Lords gained such power that they pauperized the commoners, then Italian-style pastoral tyranny would ensue. (Such was his warning to the landowners who defended the Corn Laws and who squelched the importation of East Indian barks in order to keep the prices of their own bark artificially high). If the commoners amassed such power that the lords were no longer a brake upon their ambitions, then the nation would lapse either into the excessive turmoil of Athenian-style demagoguery or the fossilized torpor of Venetian plutocracy. (Such was his warning to the "radical" sections of the reform movement, which believed that the lords were a superannuated institution with no use in an enlightened age). Make the church gain power at the expense of the lords and commons, and one replicated the abuses of the papal church before the sixteenth century, whose transnational scope caused it to pauperize the "nationality" of England to which it should have been devoted. (Such was his warning to the High Church, and even more so to the philopapists who wished to spend English monies to fund Roman priests). Make the lords and commons gain power at the expense of the church's "nationality," and one re-created the conditions which had led to the worst aspects of the Henrician profiteering or the acts of the Scottish Thanes in the Regency. (Such was his warning to the various parliamentary hands that were edging their way into church coffers in search of monies to appropriate for schemes social amelioration).

Throughout his neo-Polybian constitutional theory of balance in triads, such as king/lords/commons and lords/commoners/church, Coleridge consistently pointed out that all three played necessary roles of regulation, energy, and tension. Their relationship was, to use an anachronistic term, symbiotic. Coleridge believed that one who acted only from "Conceptions" rather than "Ideas" of statecraft might initially see the existence of at least one of the members of a triad as useless but would soon find that if he diminished or (even worse) eliminated that force in the triad, then the entire organism from which he had unwittingly removed a vital organ either sickened or died. The very "obstructionism" that hindered the ambition of any one segment of the state was itself a beneficial effect of the oppositions and tensions inherent to Coleridge's Idea of the state. These balances and oppositions might make governance arduous and unwieldy, but they also maintained the health and strength of the body politic, preventing it from slipping into the seizure of excessive change (unlimited progression, civic "corruption," the Athenian and Jacobin disease) or the coma of excessive tradition (unlimited permanence, civic "ossification," the Venetian and Tuscan disease). A Hobbesian-framed state in which a single sovereign instituted his decrees without let or hindrance from any other interest in the nation was an abhorrent thought to Coleridge, since he explicitly believed that the seeming "obstruction" to the will of the sovereign was actually a beneficial demonstration of his theory of progress through dialectical opposition.

Coleridge's third estate, the church, was the ultimate focus of his constitutional theory because it was the synthetic fulcrum on which the other two estates (permanence and progression) balanced. Unlike either the commons or the lords, which were composed of partial and fragmentary interests, the national church alone constituted a single *Unis Fraterum*, a brotherhood of the nation which comprehended and included all subjects of the realm.[62] In this national church, the private, individual, and free consciences of men could be cultivated and sustained by the public trust: Coleridge's national reserve of the "nationality," the state trust. Landed property may have been the "rock" on which Coleridge's national church would be built, but the clerisy that it sent out into the nation was drawn from both the landed and landless populations. The clerisy, in its emphasis on individual freedom and moral autarchy, had its roots in the "progressive" forces of commerce and civility. As such, Coleridge understood it to be an inherently "liberal" institution.

CHAPTER 9

Attacking the Doctrine

THE MORAL and progressive independence of the clerisy was one of the most "radical" components of Coleridge's *Church and State*. Their role was antithetical to the promulgation of doctrine. If the foundation of political virtue in the republic was to be secured by landed independence, Coleridge reasoned, the possibility of moral virtue could only be founded in the equally substantial and enduring spiritual property of intellectual capital. The clerisy, unlike the clergy, were avatars of moral freedom rather than keepers of the sacred flame of any particular, and necessarily exclusive, creed.

In this respect, Coleridge could not have been more unlike the classical "Tory" Anglican theorists of the eighteenth and nineteenth centuries, who saw the priest as the representative and natural ally of the lord of the manor and the squirearch in upholding tradition, order, and stability. Coleridge regarded the "person" of the parish—the member, whether ordained or lay, of his clerisy—as an engine for change in society, the representative of the "civilising instinct" and the Addisonian Christian gentility which he located in the commercial, "progressive" segment of society. The clerisy in Coleridge's scheme would not act to keep the people in their place and make them content with their humble lot, as the priests in normative Tory theory did.[1] The clerisy would instead act to rouse the people from their torpor, to "teach the [people] their duties" so as to "render them susceptible" of higher stations and responsibilities. Ancien régime Tory political theory saw the priest as a rein to hold back the wickedness and tumultuous natures of an unruly people. In contrast, Coleridge saw the cleric as a spur that would employ the traits of initiative and enterprise of the bourgeois ("the zeal of the Methodist") in the service of the learning and rapid influx of new ideas ("the doctrines of the philosopher") that were characteristic of lively and growing societies. It is true that Coleridge disliked the idea that technical learning and new science made traditional ethical "fixed principles" obsolete. But he also abhorred the High

Church idea that the Church of England had no other purpose than the narrowly sectarian one of promulgating Athanasian formularies of the Trinity, Arminian soteriology, and Laudian sacramentalism. He desired a "church" that would combine the attention to transcendent Ideas of the priest (which he saw lacking in the Malthusian scientist) with the energy and curiosity toward new learning of the humanist (which he saw lacking in the Tory rector).

This idea, that the "person" of a parish was the representative of enterprise, change, novelty, learning, advancement, and progression rather than stability, stasis, tradition, fixed confessional doctrine, holding of the line, and permanence was, in the end, what made Coleridge's theory of the clerisy most distinctive. He did not envision his clerisy as comprising dons breathing the rarified air of the cloister where they scrutinized beauty and verity away from the noise of the general public's ignoble strife. Instead, he saw them as veritable evangelists of learning, who were not only to make the people holy and wise but were also to provide them with the general store of learning and wisdom of which their civilization was capable. Where the ancient Romans had renewed and refreshed their national pool of ideas and knowledge both technical and moral by warfare and conquest, and the Europeans had kept the light of learning aflame in a dark age through the "clerks" who preserved reading and writing, Coleridge intended that the nineteenth-century English employ the nationality to fund a clerisy that would cast the net of learning, both moral and technical, but disperse the resultant bounty freely to the people at large.

Like his hero Bacon, Coleridge saw his project for the advancement of learning as a sort of "Great Instauration" that would increase the wisdom and moral sense of the realm as well as its proficiency in the arts and sciences. The Coleridgean church, because it stressed the "fixed principles" of a Christian morality that anchored study and action in ethics, was more "religious" than the Baconian instauration, despite Bacon's well-closeted "Platonism." The Coleridgean Church, because it did not see itself as dedicated to a single confessional definition of Christianity, was less "religious" than the Laudian High Church, or even the Methodists or Dissenters. The failure to recognize the "true" or "real" Idea of the English church had led to lost opportunities, broken bones, and blessed accidents. But for Coleridge, the failure of the English church and clergy also produced the promise of the national church and clerisy.

Coleridge believed that the corruptions of the English church could be traced back to "Henry's Harvest" in the 1530s and 1540s. His conception of the English Reformation was unusual in that he did not see Henry VIII as the great despoiler and ravager of the English church; rather, he regarded Henry as a king who would have been remembered "with a splendour" that "would outshine that of Alfred [the Great] . . . if he had retained the will and possessed the power of effecting, what in part, he promised to do."[2] Coleridge argued that the king had failed to protect the nationality, those "heritable lands and revenues" that had been "*Wrongfully* alienated" and "*Sacreligiously* alienated,"[3] not only from the church but from the constituent membership of that "*Unitas Fraterum*," "the potential divinity in every man, which is the ground and condition of his *civil* existence."[4] The Henrician Reformation was, in Coleridge's estimation, the great, lost opportunity of the English church and the British state.

This opportunity was almost retrieved by Elizabeth who "saw and therefore withstood the advise of her nobles who would fain have played the Scottish Thanes with the Church, & feasted on the gleanings of Henry's harvest."[5] Elizabeth, by denying the greed of the aristocrats and gentry who desired further despoliation of church lands, avoided the utter pauperization of the church that had taken place in the neighboring kingdom of Scotland under the influence of Moray and Knox. This preservation of the dignity and estate of the English church was only a brief interlude, however, argued Coleridge. The Anglican Church had first been riven by the schism between Laudian High Churchmen and Puritans and then utterly brought down by the mistakes of that "very weak king" Charles I with "a bigot for his Prime Minister [Laud]."[6] Coleridge's reconstruction of this church history revealed much about his conception of constitutional theory and indeed his understanding of the cultural and moral role of the national church. It is essential that Coleridge's distinction between the national church and the Christian church be kept in mind. His national church was "the third great estate of the realm" (or "state" in his broader use of the term). The fact that the national church of England was a confessionally Christian church was, as he pointed out, a "blessed accident."[7]

For Coleridge as for Warburton, it was theoretically possible that England might have had a successful Moslem or Jewish religion established with beneficial results. Coleridge saw England's confessional Christianity, like its Protestantism, as a superior moral system to its rivals, but as peripheral to the shape and nature of the national church. This distinction was made with even greater clarity in Coleridge's observation that, since Charles's time, "we have had *no* Church in England," only "Religion, which is a *noun of multitude*."[8] The government, in its attempts to "suppress bigotries and negative persecution," had created the "multitude and varieties of *Religions*."[9] Elizabeth's fragile *via media* had been shattered by Laud's rejection of a Broad Church based upon comprehension and irenicism and by a movement toward persecution and schism between Anglicans and Dissenters. Two disasters had resulted from this parting of the ways. First, from 1640 to 1660 the Puritan "Samson" had blindly and will-fully "pulled down" the entire edifice of Episcopacy and persecuted Laudian practices. Second, from 1660 onward, the Anglicans in revenge had persecuted the Puritans, and set them outside the boundaries of the national church by cre-ating in the 1660s the distinction between "Anglicans" and "Dissenters." This rejection of the idea of a comprehensive national church created, from the 1660s through the 1690s, the segregative system of Tests, conformities, and tol-erations. In this manner, Coleridge argued, the Church of England was "re-duced to a [sectarian Anglican] religion, in genre [was] consequently separated from the church, and made a subject of parliamentary determination."[10]

Coleridge contended that the reduction (and hence destruction) of the Church of All England to the mere sect of Anglican religion accompanied the fall of "the Samson of Puritanism." He remarked that while it was true in the case of English church history (as opposed to the Book of Judges) that "both Samson and the Philistines were . . . dragged up alive out of the ruins [of the Philistine Temple of Dagon], . . . the compound fractures were never thor-oughly reknit" after 1660.[11] Coleridge, unlike most "Tories," considered the division between Protestant Anglicans and Protestant Dissenters to have been unfortunate and unnecessary. This implies that he saw the proper affiliation of "Old" Puritan Trinitarian Dissenters—as well as the more controversial "New" Unitarian Dissenters such as Coleridge's quondam allies Jebb and Dis-ney—as within the true national church. The Samson of Puritanism was to be readmitted into a broadened national church, in recognition of his great moral power. (It is notable that in his recounting of the agon of the schism of the English church, the Trinitarian and "Tory" Coleridge cast the Dissenters in the role of Samson and the Laudians in the guise of the Philistine idolaters).

Religion was not the only splinter that Coleridge saw in the broken bones of the Anglican Church. Beyond the High Church–versus–Low Church vari-ances "expressing the aggregate of all the different groups of notions and cer-emonies connected with the invisible and supernatural," Coleridge believed that the moral, cultural, and social functions of the church had been alienat-ed.[12] His first concern, as it had always been, was the moral, social, and polit-ical importance of the amelioration of poverty. How would it be possible to "teach them their duties . . . to render them susceptible of their rights"[13] if "the poor [were] withdrawn from the discipline of the church"?[14] Indeed, the entire possibility of teaching, of the "illumination of the multitude"[15] was jeop-ardized, he argued, if "the education of the people [was] detached from the ministry of the church."[16] It was the government's intention (in its misguided belief that it was suppressing religious bigotry by secularizing schools) that "National Education [was] to be finally sundered from all religion, but speedily and decisively emancipated from the National Clergy."[17]

Coleridge believed that a moral education, as opposed to a religious one, was the principle purpose of a national church. Because he considered the church to represent far more than the deeds of those clergy ordained "in orders" and to encompass more activities than those that happened within the walls of consecrated buildings, he coined the term the "national clerisy." In the same sense that Coleridge's 1795 lectures on politics had insisted that parliamentary reform must be grounded in, or *bottom* on, certain fundamental truths, or "fixed principles," rather than simply being a set of new rules for governance, he argued in 1830 that education must be more than mere instruction in reading, writing, mathematics, and sciences. To avoid the severance of technical instruction from moral education, Coleridge suggested that "a permanent, nationalized, learned order, a national clerisy or church" be maintained. Indeed, he insisted that it was "an essential element of a rightly constituted nation."[18] He saw the national church and its clerisy as sustaining and protecting both the permanence and the progression of the nation. He concluded that the educational alternatives offered by the Anglicans and the utilitarians were equally unsatisfactory. It was clear, Coleridge argued, that "neither [Evangelical and Methodist] tract societies nor [Dissenting] conventicles, nor Lancastrian schools, nor mechanic's institutions, nor lecture-bazaars under the absurd names of universities [such as the University of London], nor all these collectively can substitute" for true education.[19] In other words neither secular nor sectarian education could serve as a substitute for moral education as moral science. Arguing as he had done in his earliest writings on politics and society, when he had enjoined the reformer to "*go preach the gospel to the poor,*"[20] Coleridge preserved in his vision of the clerisy the idea that the patricians should lead the way in moral education. This was apparent in his sarcastic dissection of utilitarian plans for "general illumination" by use of mechanics' institutes and other non–morally grounded technical programs. In 1795, he observed "that general illumination should precede the revolution is a truth so obvious as that a vessel should be thoroughly cleaned before receiving a pure liquor."[21] His view on education in *Church and State* some thirty-five years later was similarly expressed as a challenge to reformers: "So you wish for *general* illumination," he taunted, "you would spur-arm the toes of society: you would enlighten the higher ranks per ascensum ab imis," by ascension from the lowest depths.[22] Coleridge thought the instigation of a perverse and unnatural "trickle-up effect" to be absurdly misguided and ill conceived. With a possible gibe at the dismal scientists, Coleridge considered the effects of such piecemeal and ungrounded learning, statistics divorced from any moral or sociological framework. He charged these "parliamentary leaders of the Liberalists and Utilitarians" of an "attempt to popularise science," but he concluded that they (the Malthusians and Ricardians) "will only effect its *plebification*."[23]

Coleridge believed, as he had in 1795, that "religion was the only means universally efficient,"[24] and he argued in *Church and State* that "the morality which the state requires of its citizens . . . can only exist for the people in the form of religion."[25] He did not believe that all the people could be philosophers or statesmen, but he did believe that "the idea of true philosophy, or the power or habit of contemplating particulars in the unity and fontal mirror of the idea" was "indispensable" in the "rulers and teachers of a nation" for the development of "a sound state of religion in all classes."[26] The purpose of the national wealth and the national church was to provide "*in proportionate channels*" (my italics) the maintenance "of universities, and the great schools of liberal learning." (Note that Coleridge vehemently distinguished between these and "lecture bazaars under the absurd name universities.") These institutions were also charged with maintaining "a pastor, presbyter, or *parson** (*persona exemplaris*) in every parish."[27] Note that Coleridge did not favor any particular religious affiliation for this person but stressed etymologically the nature of the parson as the "representative and exemplar of the *personal* character of the community or parish; of their duties or rights, of their hopes, privileges and requisites, as moral *persons* and not merely living things."[28] He emphasized the *personal* nature of the clerisy and contrasted it to the pastoral clergy, whom he believed to be but "imperfectly" suited to their task as exemplars because their religious ordination separated them from the concerns of the community. As a result, he argued, the pastoral clergy "cannot be that which it is the paramount end and object of their establishment and distribution throughout the country that they should be."[29] For Coleridge, the "paramount end" of that establishment was that the Church should be the "sphere and gem of *progressive civilization*."[30] If this was not a sufficiently clear pronouncement of the church's moral, social and political mission, he continued, "the proper *object* and end of the National Church is civilization with freedom."[31] The role of the clerisy was to "communicate that degree and kind of knowledge to all, the possession of which is necessary for all in order to their CIVILITY."[32] Coleridge had associated civility and liberty with commercial society and the principle of progression in his criticism of the Italian history. In the context of the national church he again defined civility as "all the qualities essential to the citizen."[33] The specific role of the church in this regard was to "diffuse throughout the people *legality*," which Coleridge here defined as "a well calculated self-interest, under the conditions of a common interest determined by the common laws."[34] The national church was the vessel through which the vital forces, the "lifeblood" of liberty, might be diffused. The nation-state integrated both national church and political government in a balanced system.

Coleridge believed that like "permanence" and "progression," "cultivation" and "civilization" were forces that must exist in balance and equipoise. Although he warned that "a nation can never be too cultivated, but may easily become an over-civilized race," Coleridge was not privileging landed society.[35] Rather, he emphasized the importance of wisdom over technical knowledge. His concern that technical expertise might outstrip the moral development of mankind was not dissimilar to Einstein's later and famous dictum. Coleridge believed that the "overbalance of the landed interest" was an equally disastrous *constitutional* corruption to an excessive burgess representation in the House of Commons.[36]

Coleridge considered the need to balance permanence and progression, cultivation and civilization, wisdom and knowledge, in terms of the "organismus" of the body politic. It is very important to understand this medical imagery. Coleridge made it quite clear that an overbalance of one of his two principles was more than a lamentable corruption of the body politic; it was in fact a potentially *terminal* disease that could result in the death of that body. "The first condition, then required," he argued, "in order to a sound constitution of the Body Politic, is a due proportion of the free and permeative life and energy of the Nation to the organizing powers brought within containing channels."[37] Coleridge's first priority, his first condition of a "sound constitution," was the regulation of the nation's blood pressure, its "lifeblood" of liberty.

The significant difference between the body politic and the body natural, Coleridge argued, was that in the body politic the "permeative species of force (progression)" may be "converted into the latter [the containing or permanent]."[38] In this manner, Coleridge argued, the lifeblood of liberty became "organized and rendered a part of the vascular system, by attaching a measured and determinate political right, or privilege thereto."[39] Coleridge's permanence and progression were not counterbalanced and antithetical forces on opposing ends of a seesaw. They were, rather, essentially fluid and interdependent forces, liberty being the rushing water of a river, which, bearing silt through its *active* flow, builds its own delta, shapes its own banks, determines its own course. Coleridge had used the river image repeatedly in his discussions of law and liberty, as in his discussion of opinion and the law—throwing a "dam across the river" of "our intellectual commerce"—with regard to censorship.[40] His metaphors for political, social, and economic action frequently involved images of fluids, water or blood, which required channeling or regulation but could not be stopped up, dammed, clotted, or constricted unnaturally. Like proper systolic function, the regulation of blood flow or irrigation should be self-shaping, without hemorrhaging or flooding. The river, like the circulation of blood and the expansion of capillary function in the body, became both the source and the product. It was both the active and potential force, its own containment and rushing vitality.[41]

Returning to his medicophilosophical analysis of the state, Coleridge compared the equally catastrophic consequences of imbalances that favored *either* aristocratic or popular constitutions. Arguing that "the ancient Greek democracies, the *hot-beds* of Art, Science, Genius, and Civilization fell into dissolution from the excess of" progression, Coleridge emphasized the organic systemic imbalance which resulted from this sociopolitical "hypertension."[42] "The permeative power" from the pulse and flow of the permeative fluid, or "expanding liberty," "derang[ed] the functions, and by explosions shatter[ed] the organic structures they should have enlivened."[43] By contrast, aristocratic societies, weighted down by too much permanence, were equally doomed and thus, Coleridge argued, "the Republic of Venice fell by the contrary extremes."[44] "All political power [in Venice] was confined to the determinate vessels, and these becoming more and more rigid even to ossification of the arteries, the State, in which the people were nothing, lost all power of resistance ad extra."[45] Both arterial sclerosis and cerebral aneurysm were, in Coleridge's view, equally fatal conditions, whether for the body politic or the body natural. The Athenian strategy of innovation and novelty at any price was lethal, but it was equally lethal to pursue in reaction to this danger the Venetian strategy of stability and hierarchy at any price. Wise states would profit from their example and avoid either extreme, revivifying their permanence through an influx of progression and regulating their progression by the restraints of permanence.

Having considered at some length the dysfunction attended by the corruption and overbalancing of the landed interest, Coleridge next made the case for the necessity of commercial vitality in sustaining a vibrant polity through the principle of civilized "liberality." In his account of the Venetian oligarchy, Coleridge had compared the death of liberty to the hardening of the arteries. Passive obedience and nonresistance, old bulwarks of Tory social and political theory, were dangerous doctrines. They promoted rigid and unreflexive conventions that could not accommodate growth and change in a living system. Coleridge's late views on obedience and resistance were similar to his earliest defenses, in 1795, of the people's civil right to resist extreme tyranny as a defining component of the balanced constitution. Such a measured resistance, he argued, expressed itself through the liberty of the press, "a sovereignty resident in the people."[46] But this sovereignty must be mediated. An unrestrained popular power was, potentially, as injurious to the life of the body politic as the stultifying constraint of magnate oligarchy.

Three kinds of corruption, or "malformation[s]" are suggested by Coleridge's emphasis on the difficult but critical problem of rapid progression.[47] His first objection was to the distribution of "direct political power to the *personal* force and influence" of the people or "monied interest . . . *without* those fixed or tangible possessions, freehold, copyhold, or *leasehold*, in land, house or stock."[48] Coleridge provided his citizen the means by which the permeative force may be "organized and rendered part of the vascular system" in two ways. On a large scale, this was done by "moving into land," as he had opined in his second chapter, for "to found a family and convert his wealth into land are the twin thoughts . . . of the opulent merchant."[49] But, Coleridge suggested, even the more modest representatives of the "Commercial, Manufacturing, Distributive, and Professional classes of the community" could be integrated into the total interests of the nation through their attachment to some fixed interest; whether "freehold, copyhold or leasehold," in "land, house, or stock." It is not clear precisely what Coleridge meant by stock, but it was likely intended to denote an endowment, trust, capital investment, or estate that produced a steady income that made its owner secure and independent. The fixed interest need not be landed, Coleridge implied, but it had to elevate the owner above the pressures of economic dependency and clientage. For dependency and clientage—situations in which one tended another's stock rather than one's own—made the expression of independent political views different from those of one's employer or patron nearly impossible.

Coleridge's interest in protecting the liberty and civility of commercial society while regulating its more licentious practices (as in the case of the Factory Acts) were not traditional Country Party/civic-humanist condemnations of city-based vice and luxury as opposed to landed virtue and simplicity. They can be distinguished from authentic Country Party polemic because Coleridge's sword cut both ways: it slashed the "corruption" engendered by philistine landed men of the country as well as that generated by effete and luxurious city dwellers. Therefore, any attempt to analyze Coleridge's critique of commercial society must be considered in light of his corresponding reservations and harsh criticisms of the "over-balance of the landed interest." It is worth noting that these objections frequently occur on the same pages as his "civic-humanist" critiques of moneyed men. As an example, Coleridge pointed to the thuggish and ignorant insularity of the landed interest as evidenced by "its obdurate adherence to the jail crowding Game Laws," its narrow-minded allegiance to "the Corn Laws, [which result in] the exclusion of the produce of our own colonies from our distillereries, &c.," and its "virtuous" adherence to medieval "Statutes against Usury."[50] Coleridge saw these idiocies of the landed interest as substantial demonstrations of the strained virtue of landed trusteeship, as easily corrupted as the townsman's. Whereas the city's corruptions led the burgess to luxury, indulgence, and bribery, the squire's corruption expressed itself in pigheadedness, selfishness, and short-sightedness. The corrupt squire's slavish devotion to tradition not only damaged his own advancement, it also undermined the principles of liberty and progression in the nation at large. Furthermore, the squirearchy's defense of the old regime of laws, made by and for their pleasure, was doubly corrupting, for, Coleridge argued, it caused a "deranged . . . equilibrium of the Landed and the Monied Interests." Having weakened the state by retaining corrupt, rotten, and bad law for the sake of tradition, the landed interests' adherence to self-serving, anticivic laws also engendered a further derangement of "the balance between the two unequal divisions of the Landed Interest itself, viz., the Major Barons, or great landowners with or without title and the great body of the Agricultural community."[51] In other words, the professedly "patriotic" and "virtuous" defense of "tradition" (in the shape of the Game Laws, Corn Laws, and Usury Laws) by the landed interest was effectively a screen for the pauperization of the smallholders and tenant farmers and colonial agriculturists.

Even as the squirearchy professed to honor and protect the "country" interest, it retained laws that obstructed or even damaged the well-being of the bulk of those who actually made their livings in agriculture. Without the reviving and diversifying infusion of liberal, civil, commercial vitality, the landed interest turned in upon itself, and began to devour its own tail. The mindless ultra defense of tradition and permanence for their own sakes and the veneration of even the worst laws on the sheer merit of their age were unthinkable to Coleridge. Equally unthinkable was the idea that the landowners were so narrow-minded and unpatriotic that they would rather see their own petty, particular enterprises succeed than the nation advance as a whole. According to Coleridge, the landed great as well as the moneyed great had allowed profit and selfishness to blind them to the good of the nation. The danger of the corrupt landed great as opposed to the corrupt moneyed great, Coleridge pointed out, was that the landed great not only were selfish and corrupt but also made a virtue out of mulish adherence to custom. The landed interest, in order to maintain its hegemony over the market, suppressed or eliminated all new technical innovation that could surpass their antiquated, inefficient habits and customs. In this manner, Coleridge implied, the landed interest smothered agricultural and technical innovations with alarming regularity. In doing so, the national subsidy to the sense of the tradition and honor of the squire implicit in legislation such as the Corn Laws cost the nation increasing amounts of wealth and efficiency. Coleridge gave a mordant example of corrupt landed influence in a description of the land-man's brutal suppression of the new trade in Terra Japonica, an acacia-wood astringent from the Far East.[52] The importation of this astringent in large quantities by the East India Company would have been of particular profit and advantage to the English tanners, since it would have made the major tool of their trade, tanning solution for their vats, far cheaper than it had been when they had depended on pricey English-grown barks. However, Coleridge recounted, "a very intelligible hint" had been spread amongst "persons of known influence in Leadenhall-street," that "in the case of any such importation being allowed" by the House of Commons, "the East-India Company must not expect any support from the *Landed Interest* in parliament, at the next renewal or motion for renewal of their Charter."[53] The company, fearful for reduction of its near-dictatorial powers in India, quietly conceded the issue and stopped plans for the importation. In essence, the landowners hectored and bullied the East India men into withdrawing a product from the English market that both groups knew would make tanning cheaper and thus reduce the cost to British consumers of essential leather goods such as shoes. Coleridge objected that the tariff walls that sheltered British produce such as astringent barks and wheat were sustained not so much in the national interest, but for the pleasure and profit of the landed. The "protected" profits of the landed were paid for through each extra penny spent by the general public—often laborers on landed estates—on leather or bread that cost more than it needed to. While Coleridge suggested that some rival monopoly, that is, "the Free Merchant of good Tea" would likely retaliate against this humiliating bullying of the East India Company, his objection was raised against monopolies in general whether they be commercial or landed.[54]

Coleridge's objection to monopolists and to the overbalance of landed influence was strikingly similar to the free-market arguments that had been advanced by the Scottish economists such as Adam Smith. While Coleridge had rejected the mechanism that he believed was implicit in the works of those men "thoroughly Adam Smithed and MacIntoshed," he viewed their fundamentally cohesive, interactive, and dynamic conception of the market mechanism and its social and moral significance to be essentially sound.[55] He paid considerable homage in *Church and State* to the procommercial works of Dr. Thomas Crawfurd.[56] Crawfurd's views on trade and the significance of that trade for the moral and political development of various peoples were influenced heavily by the writings of Smith and Hume. Crawford's *History of the Indian Archipelago* recounted the despotic consequences of the singularly agrarian society of Bali, which squelched any nascent commerce in order to maintain the hegemony of landed aristocrats. Coleridge made much the same point regarding Italy in *The Friend*, in an essay that antedated Crawford's arguments by some eleven years. There, Coleridge had pointed out that the success of the Italian peasant farms and the diminution of the "corrupting" cities, instead of bringing a rise in agrarian virtue and liberty, had instead brought about tyranny and despotism.

Machiavelli had been wrong: it was not the corrupt and effete cities that had destroyed *libertá*, but rather the hardy and virtuous farms of Tuscany. For Coleridge and Crawfurd alike, cities made rather than decayed the course of liberty. Coleridge called *The History of the Indian Archipelago* "the work of a wise as well as of an able and well informed man," concluding that "it was no ordinary gratification to find, that in respect of certain prominent positions, maintained in this volume [*Church and State*] I had unconsciously been fighting behind the shield of one whom I deem it an honour to follow."[57] Coleridge quoted specifically the "prominent position" on which they agree—that "*wherever Agriculture is the principle pursuit . . . , people will be found living under an absolute government*."[58] Coleridge and Crawfurd agreed that an exclusively rural and landed "feudal" economy was resistant to the idea of the liberty of the subject and also resistant to innovation in technology and science. In an exclusively "feudal" society there was very little independence of mind because there was very little independence of any sort. Pure feudal society, Coleridge argued, was a sink of slavishness and tyranny rather than of nobility and virtue. The feudal world, because it "predestined every native of the realm to be lord or vassal," left little room for freedom or its handmaiden learning to breathe.[59] The characteristic intellectual supineness and lack of curiosity and initiative among feudal/rural people was, Crawfurd and Coleridge concurred, the result of "a people rendering themselves more tame" in order to acclimate to the narrow intellectual boundaries in which they found themselves.[60] Because it closed up most of the spaces (Coleridge actually used the very term "breathing hole[s] of hope") by which new ideas and concepts would normally enter society, Coleridge argued that pure "Spartan" feudalism strangled liberty.[61]

Coleridge's arguments for the "expanding liberty" of commercial, *personal*, "progressive" civilization cannot be viewed as exclusive political. They were fundamentally moral concerns for the *spirit* of a people, a spirit that must be fostered and not tamed. This spirit, understood as life force or moral agency, was essentially grounded in the progressive principle of liberty as a condition of moral development and spiritual growth. Coleridge did not believe that such spiritual growth was possible, as an exclusively liberal principle, without the aid of the national church and the clerisy. But without liberty, both as a ground and as a dynamic principle, as a force both active and potential in the individual moral agent, this growth was not possible at all. The clerisy would integrate this national spirit, as it "comprehended the learned of all denominations," the best not merely of all religions, but of "the sages and professors of the law and jurisprudence; of medicine and physiology; of music; of military and civil architecture; of the physical sciences; with the mathematical as the common *organ* of the preceding." "In short," Coleridge concluded, it would comprise "all the so called liberal arts and sciences."[62]

The subjects of a liberal education and the scholars who taught them and advanced them were to be drawn from the world of abstract and practical ideas; they comprised the faculties of reason and understanding as well as knowledge and experience of permanence and progression. This clerisy was to be drawn together through "PHILOSOPHY, or the doctrine and discipline of ideas" and to educate the people as citizens and moral agents "in application to the rights and duties of men in all their various relations, social and civil."[63] Through this fostering lead, the clerisy would aid the development of "the *ideal* power, in the human being," expressed in ideas that "constitute his *humanity*." Coleridge argued that "a *man* without the ideas of God, eternity, freedom, will, absolute truth, of the good, the true, the beautiful, the infinite" was only "an *animal* endowed with a memory of facts and appearances."[64]

The idea of liberty and the "progressive" spirit of humanity were the ultimate goals of civilization in Coleridge's theory of the state. The commercial class had from its "bud" in "the earliest stages of the constitution . . . conspir[ed] to the interests of the improvement and general freedom of the country."[65] During the infancy "or what we might call the minority of the burgess order [in the Middle Ages], the National Church was the *substitute* for the most important national benefits resulting from the same [the commercial class]" (my italics). Coleridge juxtaposed the interests of the church with the interests of land, arguing that the "National Church presented the only breathing hole of hope," that "the church alone relaxed the iron fate by which feudal dependency, primogeniture, and entail would otherwise have predestined every native of the realm to be lord or vassal."[66] Coleridge believed that the national church had been an ally and protector of the moneyed interests and, that while it embodied a "permanently progressive" order to preserve the "benefits of existing knowledge" and provide "the means of future civilization" it had "foster[ed] . . . the class of free citizens and burghers" and given them their first political voice in the nation.[67] In doing so, the national church embodied the actual and potential forces of permanence and progression, as it opposed (not as a contrary force) *and* synthesized (or reconstituted) the past, the present, and the future. Thus, to Coleridge the ancient constitution of England and the tradition of liberty that supported it was gained not so much by the swords of the Barons at Runnymede, but by the centuries of quiet and patient works of the priests, monks, and burghers in their cloisters and nascent towns.

Finally, Coleridge's conception of the moral and urbane citizen was most fully articulated in his description of a living person, his lifelong friend Thomas Poole. Poole stands well as an example of a learned and humane man sensible to the changing imperatives of the commercial world while retaining the sympathy, honor, and obligation that marked an attachment to country life. Coleridge could simultaneously envision Poole "in his harvest field" or in the throng of "the market . . . now in a committee-room, with the Rickmans and Ricardos of the age." Equally, Coleridge could see Pool amongst the men of science and manufacture, with "Davey, Wooleston, and the Wedgewoods" or as he often had seen him in the company of poets such as "Wordsworth, Southey, and other friends not unheard of in the republic of letters." He considered that such a man would be at home "in the drawing rooms of the rich and the noble" no less than at "the annual dinner of a village benefit society."[68] The qualities that Coleridge identified with Tom Poole were those very qualities he believed the clerisy would cultivate in the citizenry. The quality that Coleridge identified with Poole and looked for in the moral citizen was integrity, by which Coleridge expressly meant the "entirety of its being," its "*integrum et sine cera vas.*"[69]

Coleridge honored his lifelong commitment to integrity and independence in *Church and State*. Remaining until his death in 1834 "ever a man without a party," he chose neither ossified permanence nor a licentious progression; he favored neither land nor commerce. He privileged neither aristocracy nor people, prescribing neither the deadly sclerosis of oligarchic Venice nor the explosive aneurysm of democratic Athens as panacea for the body politic. This "double vision" has made him an elusive subject for those who study his political thought. If his ideas are studied in isolation from one another, then the "dynamic" relations of dyads and triads that are the heart of all his theories will be missed. In *Church and State* ("according to the Idea of Each") he attempted one final time to create a unified theory of state and society in which various institutions would be examined and criticized—not in isolation, but in their relation to all other components in the system. He also attempted to demonstrate in a more articulated form how metaphysical Ideas shaped the "real"/"moral" world of politics. In this regard, as in all others, his solution to the problem of church and state was innovative and visionary.

Coleridge's final work of political and social thought discredited the Tory dream of the clergy as the watchdogs of the landed interest. Instead, he portrayed his "clerisy" as the guardians of curiosity, initiative, intellectual freedom, and progress. As scholars they shared these values, civil and scientific, with the burgesses, the professionals, and the artisans. Coleridge thus removed his moral guardians from their older traditional role as defenders of stability, hierarchy, and precedence. Instead, he made his clerisy bold apostles of the freedom of the mind, critical investigators charged with the slow, gradual education of the peasant into the citizen. He also stood the Spartan/civic-humanist paradigm of liberty on its head, showing that cities were the cradles rather than the graves of liberty. His clerisy were not to be the defenders of an old landed *virtu*, but instead the bringers of a truer, more "liberal" vision of liberty. This more liberal liberty meant the unceasing actualization of expanding freedom *for* a people, rather than incessant sacrifice *by* them.

Regulating the Body Politic

W HETHER HIS IDEAS found expression in pamphlets, public lectures, or private letters, Coleridge pursued one singular and unified objective in all of his political works from 1795 to 1830. This lifelong goal was to produce a comprehensive and systematic theory of the social state as a living matrix, a matrix that in its best forms would sustain and promote the idea of individual freedom. With that in mind, I have emphasized that Coleridge's metaphysics and the "medico-philosophical" language of his political and social thought were central components of a larger politico-ethical system. His Idea of the state, therefore, must be viewed as an extension of both his moral philosophy and the "theory of life" that it rested on.

Coleridge argued that life was a dynamic matrix, an integrative system of structures and animate will. Morality was a consequence of that will as it acted in the world. Beyond this, history itself was a force of animate and purposive power; the material contents of the past, directed by the *Idea*, both constituted and regulated the future. This premise, both historicist and idealist in its implication, was the groundwork for all of Coleridge's writings on the condition of man in human society. As a consequence, his political thought must be understood as a contiguous extension of his cultural, moral, religious, aesthetic, and ultimately social views of experience. In the light of the fundamental continuity and inherent progression of Coleridge's intellectual development from 1795 to 1830, in light of "the growth of the poet's mind," it is difficult to legitimately sustain the case for "apostasy." People need not recant to change.

It will be recalled that the "Moral and Political Lecture" of 1795 was published the same year as an "Introductory Address." More than an introduction to the *Conciones,* the "Address" was an introduction to what was to be Coleridge's enduring belief—that politics and morals must be considered as distinctive but fundamentally integrative forces. He articulated this view most completely in his final work of political theory, the 1830 constitutional treatise,

On Church and State. Church and State was a dissertation on morality and state-craft, education, law, and constitutional theory, ranging far beyond its ostensible grounding in the dispute on church–state relations. The essence of that relationship was the mediation between political and moral freedom. All of Coleridge's statements on reform, on law and society, rested on the idea of liberty. Although this liberty may have been inadequate as a condition of public virtue without the stabilizing influence of land, it was, nonetheless, the essential component of the private morality upon which all virtue was ultimately conditional. It was the initiating point of departure for any discussion of civil society. In short, there was no republic without virtue and no virtue without liberty. For without liberty, morality was impossible, and without morality, conscience and duty were meaningless.

Coleridge believed that the active institutions of the state, notably the constitution of government, the national church, and the law, provided the living regulative vessels and organs of the nation or the realm. As such, they constricted, regulated, and advanced the "permeative fluid" of society. Liberty was the "permeative fluid." It was the "progressive idea" and it was concretized or, to use one of Coleridge's terms, made "corporific," in the active mechanisms (or, more appropriately, the living processes) of transaction, exchange, intercourse, discourse, opinion, and commerce. Coleridge regarded this process as osmotic or fluid rather than discretely or atomistically contractual. This understanding also extended to the relationship between virtue and morality, and it was one component of his doctrine of opposites. Such opposition could be detected in the workings of the Common Law.

The Common Law, through the honor of landed society, regulated virtue, while the church and commercial endeavor regulated morality. Liberty promoted morality. Coleridge saw these two great interests of the state as mutually sustaining each other in a close symbiosis. For this reason, he favored neither land nor commerce, permanence nor progression, oligarchy nor democracy, Venice nor Athens. A systemic imbalance in either direction (the ossification of Venetian oligarchy or the mass politics and eventual demagoguery of Athenian democracy) would be equally fatal; sclerosis and aneurysm both resulted in death.

For Coleridge, the language of liberty and the language of virtue were not at war with one another; they were, on the contrary, essential to each other. Therefore, to understand Coleridge's late and radical contention that commerce provided an expanding liberty, it is necessary to understand that his conception of "liberty" was quintessentially moral. Liberty of the subject was sustained by freedom of conscience. Voluntarism, as the duty prescribed by the moral law of reason, was the foundation of the just republic. This fundamental principle had been the basis of his early defenses of the liberty of the press and, equally, was at the heart of his later criticisms of monopoly, old corruption, and his corresponding defenses of commercial society. "Those sudden breezes and noisy gusts"[1] of opinion, which he later called "our intellectual commerce,"[2] were at the heart of a healthy political constitution. The matter of regulation of this body politic, a statesman's rather than physician's science.

Coleridge's early political writings were preoccupied with questions of moderation and balance. His central argument in *Church and State*, some thirty-five years after the Bristol lectures, was for institutional "equipoise" and the systemic balance of the ideas of permanence and progression. Landed society and the Common Law provided the principle of "permanence," as both were themselves principles of historical continuity. The Common Law revealed essential truths of morality in a way that statute never could because Common Law represented cumulative wisdom and so transcended the prejudices of immediate interests. The Common Law had *time* enough to generate and evolve ideas that were more than "half-truths." It had *time* to instill and promote (but also to reflect) ideas of virtue, honor, and justice. It regulated through habit, promoting virtue by example.

The vessels of regulation also evolved and grew over time, accommodating the ebb and flow of freedom, adapting to the systolic pressure of the "permeative fluid." In this way the instruments of government, the increasing complexity of the bureaucracy, and the broadened comprehensions of the law could be tuned to the changing needs of society. They could be reformed to accommodate the shifting rhythms of a mass culture in a market economy as it grew and contracted, as its balance of interests moved from land to commerce and on, perhaps, to a renewed but irrevocably transformed use of the land. Coleridge's "permeative fluid" was freedom, represented materially as action, opinion, exchange, or trade. In this sense, Coleridge believed that it was the growth of the body from infancy to maturity that allowed the organism to become most completely what it is.

Coleridge believed that the *ultimate* (long-term) rather than the *medial* (short-term) goal of politics and society was the evolution of a state that could most perfectly foster the freedom of individual, developing conscience and will. Liberty was, for Coleridge, the absolute precondition for the moral advancement of the human spirit. Perfected humanity was the ultimate telos of human existence. His providential philosophy of history was animated by freedom, if sustained by certain teleological ideas. These ideas, or goods, "concretised" themselves in historical institutions such as the national church, the Common Law, and the constitution. In the case of his idea of progression, the "moneyed interest," the constitutional representation was the House of Commons.

The legislative role of Parliament in creating statute was regulated by the Lords but emanated from the Commons. The civil law developed with greater complexity as the forces of commercial transaction rapidly progressed, necessitating a greater complexity of regulation. The "rights" of landed property were more perfectly sustained by the Common Law. Either of these forces of permanence and progression risked corruption if its influence was "overbalanced." Coleridge criticized monopoly equally with laissez-faire policies. He argued for factory acts *and* against the monopoly of the East India Company. He did not regard his ardent support for the Scottish civil servant and "free-trader" Dr. Thomas Crawfurd as contradicting his defense of Peel's factory legislation and his attack on the doctrine of the "free-market in labour." In this regard, Coleridge's belief that the liberty of commerce must not be interpreted as the license of commerce mirrored his fundamental view that the legislator must only coerce within the "requisite bounds of each."

Liberty was not merely political for Coleridge: it was the fundamental moral principal that animated and structured all human experience and historical agency. The idea of liberty had been mediated throughout history by structures that stabilized, harnessed, and lent a progressive continuity to that fundamental human principle. These structures, or institutions, were in turn transformed by that animating and "permeative fluid" that they (more and less at various times) contained. They were forces of nature as much as law, of physics as much as politics. They must be understood as science. The statesman, then, becomes a calculator of political and moral force as a physicist unraveling the mysteries of natural force or as a physician diagnosing the hidden ailments of the body, in this case the body politic. The concepts of "natural philosophy" and the "law of nature" were extended in their implications, by Coleridge, not as metaphors and analogies of political life, but as offering direct and unified explanation of the deepest causes and conditions of the social and political world as somatic function.

A commitment to the idea of liberty, in all of its physical and moral manifestations, is the hallmark of an intellectual career that can never be understood as fragmentary and never reduced to simple questions of factional allegiance or sectarian affiliation. Coleridge's political thought culminated in a genuinely synthetic social and juridical state theory;, one that attempted to reconcile moral freedom with social and political justice and to elevate the art of the politician to the science of the statesman.

Abbreviations are used throughout these notes for the titles of works by Coleridge. They are explained in the list of abbreviations and in the bibliography.

Introduction. The Politics of Reputation, or, the Myth of a Modern Apostate

1. *CS*, 7–8; also in *W*, "Modern Patriotism," (1796), 98–100; *EOT*, "Men and the Times," 1:424; *EOT*, "Party Worst Faction" 2:380.

2. See Southey to Charles Danvers, 15 June 1809. Southey's response to Coleridge's own rejection of the Jacobin label was: "It is worse than folly, for if he was not a Jacobine [sic], in the common acceptation of the name, I wonder who the Devil was. I am sure I was, am still, and ever more shall be." *New Letters of Robert Southey*, ed. Kenneth Curry, 2 vols. (New York and London: Columbia University Press, 1965) 1:511.

3. John Stuart Mill, *Autobiography*, 4th ed. (London: Longmans, Green, Reader & Dyer, 1874), 90.

4. J. G. A. Pocock, "Cambridge Paradigms and Scotch Philosophers: A Study of the Relations Between the Civic Humanist and the Civil Jurisprudential Interpretation of Eighteenth-Century Social Thought," in *Wealth and Virtue: The Shaping of Political Economy in the Scottish Enlightenment*, ed. Istvan Hont and Michael Ignatieff (Cambridge: Cambridge University Press, 1983), 243.,"

5. As he considered law more than "mere statute," Coleridge also held, by 1814, the state to be something greater than government alone. See *EOT*, 2:381.

6. For a discussion of providentialism in Kant's moral philosophy and philosophy of history see J. B. Schneewind "Autonomy, Obligation, and Virtue," in *The Cambridge Companion to Kant*, ed. Paul Guyer (Cambridge: Cambridge University Press, 1992), passim.

7. Coleridge uses these terms (often interchangeably) to describe the dynamic principle of historical change as it is mediated by "certain fixed principles," certain formative ideas or structures. In this sense, Coleridge believed that there was a philosophy or science of history, a cunning of reason that would "out," or a providence that was

manifest. The science of the legislator inhered in the recognition of reason in the common law, or, as Mansfield described it, "the law was only reason made manifest."

8. For a discussion of the legal and commercial implications of a sociological jurisprudence, see David Lieberman, "The Legal Needs of a Commercial Society: The Jurisprudence of Lord Kames," in *Wealth and Virtue*, ed. Michael Ignatieff and Istvan Hont (Cambridge: Cambridge University Press, 1987), 203–34. Also see David Lieberman, *The Province of Legislation Determined* (Cambridge: Cambridge University Press, 1990); for a further discussion of Kames see chaps. 7 and 8.

9. John Stuart Mill, "Coleridge," in *Mill on Bentham and Coleridge,* ed. F. R. Leavis (London: Chatto and Windus, 1950; reprint, Cambridge: Cambridge University Press, 1980), 167.

10. For a discussion of Coleridge's impact on the Victorians and the nature of his conservatism, see Crane Brinton, *English Political Thought in the Nineteenth Century* (London: Benn, 1933), 74–86. Also see James Dykes Campbell, *Samuel Taylor Coleridge* (London: MacMillan, 1894); and C. H. Wilkenson, "Some Early Editors," in *Coleridge: Studies by Several Hands*, ed. Blunden and Griggs (London: Constable, 1934), 97–109.

11. Donald Greene, *Samuel Johnson's Politics*, 2nd ed. (Athens: University of Georgia Press, 1990). See 13–21 for a discussion of Johnson and Toryism. Green's account of the Whig Samuel Johnson has quite recently been challenged by Jonathan Clark, who suggests that beyond a tendency toward Toryism, Johnson had substantial Jacobite sympathies. See J. C. D. Clark, *Samuel Johnson: Literature, Religion and English Cultural Politics from the Restoration to Romanticism* (Cambridge: Cambridge University Press, 1994); and for a full account of the controversy, see Jonathan Clark and Howard Erskine-Hill, eds., *Samuel Johnson in Historical Context* (Basinstoke: Palgrave, 2002).

12. Brinton, *English Political Thought in the Nineteenth Century*, 74–86.

13. Mill, *Mill on Bentham and Coleridge*; also see Mill, *Autobiography*.

14. T. H. Green, *The Political Theory of T. H. Green*, ed. and intro. John R. Rodman (New York: Appleton-Century-Crofts, 1964). See Rodman's introduction for a discussion of the "Germano-Coleridgian School." Also one of the first to consider Coleridge as a political philosopher of consequence was J. H. Muirhead, who, in addition to his 1930 study *Coleridge as Philosopher* (London: Allen & Unwin 1930), associated the "Germano-Coleridgian School" with the development of British Liberalism in both *The Platonic Tradition in Anglo-Saxon Philosophy* (London: Allen & Unwin, 1931), and his own earlier assessment of Green, *The Service of the State: Four Lectures on the Political Teaching of T. H. Green* (London: John Murray, 1908).

15. William Hazlitt, *The Examiner*, ed. Charles Lamb (1816), reprinted in J. de J. Jackson, *Coleridge: The Critical Heritage* (London: Routledge and Kegan Paul, 1970), no. 59, 205–9.

16. Hazlitt and DeQuincy contributed to a series of editorial attacks on the Lake Poets in general and Coleridge in particular under the sponsorship of Francis Jeffrey and *The Edinburgh Review*. Hazlitt's lengthy attack on Coleridge appeared in the re-

view in August 1817 (28: 488–515); see Jackson, *Coleridge: The Critical Heritage*, no. 75, 295–324. For a more complete discussion of Coleridge and Jeffrey, see Paul M. Zall and David Erdman, "Coleridge and Jeffrey in Controversy" *Studies in Romanticism* 14 (winter 1975): 75–83.

17. Affiliation or membership in a social or intellectual coterie has in one study of Coleridge's political thought been used as a substitute for party, faction, or formal membership in a political society. See Nicolas Roe, *Wordsworth and Coleridge: the Radical Years* (Oxford: Oxford University Press, 1988), 18–19.

18. Norman Fruman, *Coleridge: The Damaged Archangel* (London: George Allen and Unwin, 1972).

19. The issue of Coleridge's plagiarism has long been the source of scholarly controversy. While the "borrowings," so meticulously rooted out by Fruman and, most famously, by Rene Wellek in *Emmanuel Kant in England* (Princeton, N.J.: Princeton University Press, 1931), challenge both the originality of Coleridge's philosophical ideas and his intellectual integrity, Kathleen Coburn has emphasized the critical and synthetic use which Coleridge made of those from whom he "borrowed." For a discussion of the "plagerism controversy," see Thomas McFarland, *Coleridge and the Pantheist Tradition* (Oxford: Clarendon Press, 1969), 1–52.

20. E. P. Thompson, *The Making of the English Working Class* (London: Victor Gollancz, 1961), 176 for "apostasy," 343 for "disappointed radicalism."

21. Raymond Williams, *Culture and Society, 1780–1950* (London: Chatto and Windus, 1960), 12–17.

22. Marilyn Butler, *Romantics, Rebels, and Reactionaries: English Literature and Its Background, 1760–1830* (Oxford: Oxford University Press, 1981). For a more measured account see Butler's introduction to *Burke, Paine, Godwin, and the Revolution Controversy* (Cambridge: Cambridge University Press, 1984), 114–115, although Butler persists in calling all opposition critics and reformers "radicals."

23. See Michael Fischer, "Marxism and English Romanticism: The Persistence of a Movement," in *Romanticism Past and Present* 6, no. 1 (1982): 364–401. Also, for a Gramscian account of Coleridge, see Peter Allen, "S. T. Coleridge's *Church and State* and the Idea of an Intellectual Establishment," *Journal of the History of Ideas* 46 (1985): 89–106.

24. Marilyn Butler suggests that "at this time it would be a pity to read Blake as though he were single-handedly the author of his own text. The corporate author is the urban sub-class which emerged through its opposition to Britain's national policy." *Romantics, Rebels, and Reactionaries*, 43.

25. For a discussion of recent cultural historicist readings of Coleridge, see Raimonda Modiano, "Historicist Readings of the Rhyme of the Ancient Mariner," in *Samuel Taylor Coleridge and the Sciences of Life*, ed. Nicholas Roe (Oxford: Oxford University Press, 2001), 271–296; and on the problems of Marxist Historicism, see Kelvin Everest "Coleridge's Secret Ministry: Historical Reading and Editorial Theory," in *Samuel Taylor Coleridge and the Sciences of Life*, 297–319.

26. John Cannon, *Parliamentary Reform, 1640–1832* (Cambridge: Cambridge University Press, 1973), passim, and especially the chapter "Reformer's Nightmares," 116–143.

27. H. T. Dickinson, *Liberty and Property: Political Ideology in Eighteenth-Century England* (Oxford: Basil Blackwell, 1977), see 7–8 and passim. Also, for a discussion of "Radical Ideology in the 1790s," see chapter 7, 232–269.

28. J. G. A. Pocock, *The Machiavellian Moment: Florentine Political Thought and the Atlantic Republican Tradition* (Princeton N.J.: Princeton University Press, 1977). Also see Pocock, "The Ancient Constitution Revisited" (1986) in *The Ancient Constitution and the Feudal Law* (Cambridge: Cambridge University Press, 1957; updated ed., Cambridge: Cambridge University Press, 1987). See 343 and 351 for a discussion of Henry Neville as "Neo-Harringtonian" and the links between Harrington and the "good old cause."

29. Caroline Robbins, *The Eighteenth Century Commonwealthsmen* (Cambridge, Mass.: Harvard University Press, 1959).

30. C. B. Macpherson, *The Political Theory of Possessive Individualism from Hobbes to Locke* (Oxford: Clarendon Press, 1962), 94–152.

31. Bernard Bailyn, *The Ideological Origins of the American Revolution* (Cambridge, Mass.: Harvard University Press, 1967).

32. Most recently in John Morrow's *Coleridge's Political Thought: Property, Morality, and the Limits of Traditional Discourse* (London: MacMillan, 1990); but perhaps first articulated in J. T. Miller's *Ideology and Enlightenment: The Political and Social Thought of Samuel Taylor Coleridge* (New York: The Garland Press, 1988).

33. R. J. White, *The Political Thought of Samuel Taylor Coleridge: A Selection* (London: Jonathan Cape, 1938).

34. *The Collected Works of Samuel Taylor Coleridge*, Bollingen Series 75, 14 vols. (London and Princeton, N.J.: Routledge and Kegan Paul and Princeton University Press); *Lay Sermons*, vol. 6 of the *Collected Works*, ed. R. J. White (1972; abbreviated *LS* in references).

35. *Essays on His Times in The* Morning Post *and The* Courier, ed. David V. Erdman, 3 vols. (1978; abbreviated *EOT* in references).

36. John Colmer, *Coleridge: Critic of Society* (Oxford: The Clarendon Press, 1959); and Coleridge, *Collected Works*, vol. 10, *On The Constitution of the Church and State According to the Idea of Each* (1976; abbreviated *CS* in references).

37. In addition to her prodigious work as general editor of the *Collected Works*, Coburn also produced and edited three sets or two volumes of *The Notebooks of Samuel Taylor Coleridge*, ed. Kathleen Coburn, 4 (of 6) vols. (London: Routledge and Kegan Paul, 1957; abbreviated *CN* in references). She was also responsible for the publication and editing of the *Philosophical Lectures* (London: Pilot Press, 1949).

38. Roberta Brinkley, *Coleridge and The Seventeenth Century* (Durham N.C.: Duke University Press, 1955), passim, and especially "The Old Divines," 125–392.

39. Nicholas Roe, *Wordsworth and Coleridge: The Radical Years*, 3–4, 18–19. Roe bases his assessment of Coleridge's "radical" youth on two less than satisfactory arguments: a narrow equation of political radicalism and rational dissent that ties Coleridge's political views directly to his Unitarian acquaintances; and a radical membership by "association" rather than direct membership in any of the reform societies. Roe contends that as Coleridge had radical friends and associates in the years from 1794 to 1796, he undoubtedly shared their political views.

40. John Morrow, *Coleridge's Political Thought*.

41. John Morrow acknowledges the extent to which Coleridge recognized the distinctions between landed and commercial property and the different social and political significance of these. However, Morrow contends that Coleridge's institutionalism rested on the cultural and political significance of landed property. His conception of the Coleridgian principles of permanence and progression sets the "cultivating" force of landed property as a bulwark against the morally corrupting tendencies of commercial wealth. He discounts any principle of commercial civil moralism in Coleridge's political theory, arguing instead for the persistence of civic humanism in "Church and State." See Morrow *Coleridge's Political Thought*, 157–58 and passim.

42. See Alan Ryan, *Property and Political Theory* (Oxford: Blackwell, 1984), 1–13, for a discussion of the political significance of different theories of "property." Ryan makes a particular distinction regarding the instrumentalist-utilitarian English tradition from Locke to Mill and the continental "self-developmental" tradition most completely articulated in Kant. These two different approaches to property as a political idea suggest different moral and legal implications for property as a political institution.

43. R. J. White, *The Political Thought of Samuel Taylor Coleridge*, 1.

44. Most notably in Richard Tuck, *Natural Rights Theories* (Cambridge: Cambridge University Press, 1979).

45. Ibid., 141 n.; and J. G. A. Pocock, "Cambridge Paradigms and Scottish Philosophers," 235–52, especially 249.

46. Donald Winch, "Adam Smith's 'enduring particular result': A Political and Cosmopolitan Perspective," in *Wealth and Virtue: The Shaping of Political Economy in the Scottish Enlightenment*, ed. Michael Ignatieff and Istvan Hont (Cambridge: Cambridge University Press, 1987), 253–70. With respect to the "science of legislation," see 256–58. Winch is not persuaded by Nicholas Phillipson's account of "Adam Smith as Civil Moralist," in *Wealth and Virtue*, op. cit., 179–202, but does consider the moral and economic discourses in Smith to be complementary rather than contradictory aspects of a broader sociological jurisprudence. See Winch, 263.

47. For a discussion of "Addisonian propriety," moral autonomy, and civility as they related to commercial property, moral virtue, and urban society, see Nicholas Phillipson, "Adam Smith as Civil Moralist" in *Wealth and Virtue*, op. cit. 179–202, especially 199.

48. Coleridge, *LS*, 168.

49. This is a "dynamic" as opposed to a "dualist" or static "monist" conception of reality. Kathleen Coburn has consistently emphasized the "dynamic" nature of Coleridge's philosophy. See Coleridge, *Philosophical Lectures*. She argues that the *Lectures* support J. H. Muirhead's early recognition of Coleridgian dynamism with reference to Coleridge's use of Kant's philosophy, describing Coleridge's allegiance to the "critical way" of the Kantian theory of knowledge in spite of his rejection of its dualism in favor of a "dynamic theory." See J. H. Muirhead, "Metaphysician or Mystic," in *Coleridge: Studies by Several Hands*, ed. E. Blunden and E. L. Griggs (London: Constable, 1934).

50. For a detailed account of Coleridge's interest in the theological and juridical aspects of Richard Hooker's *Laws of Ecclesiastical Politie* see Dierdre Coleman, *Coleridge and "The Friend," 1809–1810* (Oxford: The Clarendon Press, 1988), chap. 6, "Hooker and Burke: The Conservative Tradition," 107–31. Also see Coleridge, *TF*, 2:26, 150; *M*, 2:1131–46.

51. It is likely that Coleridge had read Montesquieu's *L'Esprit des lois* prior to and in preparation for his 1795 lectures at Bristol. His analysis of constitutional balances and the separation of powers in "The Plot Discovered" uses very similar language to F. Messeres's 1781 translation of book 11, chap. 6.

52. Direct evidence for Coleridge's early reading of DeLolme is inconclusive. However, he had read James Burgh's *Political Disquisitions* in preparation for *The Plot Discovered*. Burgh borrowed and quoted freely from the most esteemed comparative constitutionalists of his day and had placed a particular emphasis on DeLolme's *English Constitution* and its discussions of the constitutional significance of a free press. Thus, one may confidently speak of Coleridge as having at the very least read a representative sample of DeLolme as filtered and distilled through Burgh's selections. See J. L. DeLolme, *The Rise and Progress of the English Constitution*, 2 vols., ed. A. J. Stephens (London, 1838), book 2, chap. 12.

53. Charles LeGrice recalled how Coleridge had memorized all of Burke's speeches and would perform highlights *"viva voci"* when they were boys at Christ's Hospital. See Charles Valentine LeGrice, "Recollections of Christ's Hospital," in *Elia Essays Which have appered under their signature in the London Magazine* (London: Printed for Taylor and Hessey Fleet Street, 1823). Coleridge wrote a sonnet to Burke in 1793 and described Burke as "Keen and Far-sighted" as late as 1809 (Coleridge, *TF*, 2: 21).

54. Mill, *Mill on Bentham and Coleridge*, 3.

55. Along with Newman, John Keble, Edward Pusey, and Hurrell Froude, had all been members of Oriel College Oxford. Keble preached his sermon "National Apostasy Considered" in July 1833. The Tractarians, especially Froude, were influenced by Coleridge's arguments for establishment in *CS*. Froude and Newman also expanded aspects of Coleridge's educational and cultural theories, particularly the idea of a "Clerisy." See Newman's *The Office and Work of Universities* (London: Longmans, 1856).

56. Carl Sanders's *Coleridge and the Broad Church Movement* (Durham, N.C.: Duke University Press, 1942) notwithstanding. Also, for a discussion of the "liberal" dimensions of this movement, see Duncan Forbes, *The Liberal Anglican Idea of History* (Cambridge: Cambridge University Press, 1952).

57. Mill, "Coleridge," in *Mill on Bentham and Coleridge*, 68–112.

58. Isaiah Berlin makes the classic distinction between positive liberty, or the "freedom to," and negative liberty, or the "freedom from." Berlin is dubious about the coherence of the concept of positive liberty, an idea defended more recently in the writings of Charles Taylor and John Rawls. See Berlin, *Four Essays on Liberty* (New York: Oxford University Press, 1970), chap. 3, "Two Concepts of Liberty," 122–34.

59. These terms have been more recently clarified by Taylor in "Cross-Purposes: The Liberal-Communitarian Debate," in *Liberalism and the Moral Life*, ed. Nancy Rosenblum (Cambridge, Mass.: Harvard University Press, 1989), 159–82.

60. See this volume, chapter 2.

1. Romantic Radicalism

1. David Erdman and E. P. Thompson have emphasized the role of Napoleonic imperial expansion and the failure of the Peace of Amiens as critical factors in Coleridge's "political realignment" after 1802. See Thompson, "Disenchantment or Default? A Lay Sermon," in *Power and Consciousness*, ed. Conor Cruise O'Brien (London: London University Press, 1969), 149–81. Lewis Patton's introduction to his edition of *The Watchman* for the Bollingen series (1970) charts the "retrenchment" to the passage of the two acts of 1795. See Coleridge, *W*, xxxvi–xli. Joseph Cottle had accused Coleridge of a very early "defection" from radicalism in his *Early Recollections, Chiefly Relating to the Late Samuel Taylor Coleridge* (London, 1837). Patton sets Cottle's judgment against Cottle's own late and embittered resentments toward the lake poets.

2. Marilyn Butler refers specifically to the *levée en masse* that in English society formed around the defence of "John Bull." See *Romantics, Rebels, and Reactionaries: English Literature and its Background, 1760–1830* (Oxford: Oxford, University Press, 1981), 4.

3. Crane Brinton, *The Political Ideas of the English Romanticists* (London: Oxford University Press, 1926).

4. Brinton, *Political Ideas*, 66.

5. McFarland argued directly against the "apostasy thesis" as regards the radical years in an unpublished paper, "Coleridge and Jacobinism," delivered at All Souls College, Oxford, November 1986.

6. J. G. A. Pocock, ed., *Virtue, Commerce, and History* (Cambridge: Cambridge University Press, 1985), 291–92.

7. Thompson, "Disenchantment or Default," 193. Thompson, of course, locates the "apostasy" as taking place in 1802, after the Peace of Amiens.

8. Pocock also acknowledges the complexity and ambiguity of Coleridge's (as opposed to Southey's) appropriations of this language.

9. Jonathan Mendalow, *The Romantic Tradition in British Political Thought* (London: Croom Helm, 1986), 14.

10. See E. P. Thompson, *The Making of the English Working Class* (London: Victor Gollancz, 1961), 363.

11. Here I mean "myths" not in the sense of lies, but in the sense of stories of any sort (whether true or false) whose evocative power earns them a place as famous commonplaces *(loci communi)* in the literature or folklore of a group or nation.

12. E. P. Thompson, *The Making of The English Working Class*, 109. An earlier articulation of the "romantic apostacy" argument came from A. Dicey according to Harold Beeley, "The Political Thought of S. T. Coleridge," in *Studies by Several Hands*, ed. Edmund Blunden and E. L. Griggs (London: Constable, 1934), 151–75. This interpretation has survived so effectively as to have recently surfaced (in the form of an aside) in Linda Colley, *Britons: Forging the Nation, 1707–1837,* (New Haven, Conn.: Yale University Press, 1992), 312–13. For a careful discussion of Thompson's impact on later historical accounts of "romantic radicalism," see Nigel Leask, *The Politics of the Imagination in Coleridge's Critical Thought* (Basingstoke: MacMillan, 1988), 12–17.

13. Meyer H. Abrams, *Natural Supernaturalism* (London: Oxford University Press, 1969), chap. 1.

14. The implied linkage of conservative political ideology with such phenomena as decreased testosterone and male pattern baldness will invariably please some readers of Abrams more than others. One may be excused for presuming that major political ideas are predicated on more than the degree to which a political theorist is a "burned out case" who has learned that since he cannot win, he should not try.

15. For a discussion of the middle ground of the reform party and its changing relation to the antiwar faction, see J. E. Cookson, *The Friends of Peace* (Cambridge: Cambridge University Press, 1982); and, by the same author, *Lord Liverpool's Administration, 1815–1822* (Hamden, Conn.: Archon Books, 1975), 40–47.

16. For instance, music, botany, mathematics. See the entry in the *OED.*

17. J. C. D. Clark, *Our Shadowed Present: Modernism, Post-modernism, and History* (London: Atlantic Books, 2003), 221–22. Also see Clark, *English Society, 1688–1832: Ideology, Social Structure and Political Practice During the Ancien Regime* (Cambridge: Cambridge University Press, 1985), 289–313. Also see the revised edition, *English Society, 1660–1832: Religion, Ideology and Politics during the Ancien Regime* (Cambridge University Press, 2000), for an expanded consideration of the nature of radicalism during the revolutionary period.

18. H. T. Dickinson, *British Radicalism and the French Revolution, 1789–1815* (Oxford: Basil Blackwell, 1985), 8.

19. Ibid., 9.

20. Of the "British Jacobins," Dickinson writes "these radicals made advances in organization, extended their membership further down the social scale, advanced more revolutionary aims, and developed new means of achieving their objectives"

(ibid., 9). With regard to the radicalism of the petitioning movement, Frank O'-Gorman is cautious, suggesting that it had been instrumental in strengthening the cohesion of the Rockingham party. Its utility in this respect may be viewed as a sign of the movement's appeal to mainstream Whig interests. He argues that "given the absence of political consciousness and political organization in the country at large, it would be unwise to regard the petitioning movement of 1769 as a spontaneous eruption of freeholder's indignation." See O'Gorman, *The Rise of Party in England* (London: George Allen and Unwin, 1975), 242.

21. Gunther Lottes, "Radicalism, Revolution, and Political Culture: An Anglo-French Comparison," in *The French Revolution and British Popular Politics*, ed. Mark Philp (Cambridge: Cambridge University Press, 1991), 79.

22. With reference to the "continued discourse of the preceding decade [with regard to] universal suffrage, equal representation and annual parliaments as a restoration of the constitution." Lottes, "Radicalism, Revolution, and Political Culture," 83.

23. For a discussion of the philosophical and transhistorical rather than contextual approach to political theory, see Richard Ashcraft, *Revolutionary Politics and Locke's "Two Treatises of Government"* (Princeton, N.J.: Princeton University Press, 1986), 3–5. For a contemporary example of this approach as activism rather than scholarship consider Christopher Hitchens, writing in *The Nation* (September 1993), about a protest for which he had been imprisoned in his student days, recalling how he and his fellow-prisoner Raphael Samuel spent their jail time discussing the way in which E. P. Thompson's lecture on Enclosure and Common Lands, which they had attended before the protest, had stirred them into action through raising their sense of connection with the great working-class radicals of the past.

24. John Dinwiddy, "Interpretations of Anti-Jacobinism," in *The French Revolution and British Popular Politics*, ed. Mark Philp (Cambridge: Cambridge University Press, 1991), 41.

25. Thomas Philip Schofield, "Conservative Political Thought in Britain in Response to the French Revolution," *The Historical Journal* 29 (September 1986): 604.

26. Ibid., 604.

27. Coleridge, *On The Constitution of the Church and State: According to the Idea of Each* (London, 1830). Reprinted as vol. 10 of the Bollingen series, and references to this edition are abbreviated *CS* in the text and notes.

28. See Albert Goodwin, *The Friends of Liberty* (Cambridge, Mass.: Harvard University Press, 1979), chap. 7, 208–67, and chap. 8, 291–308. Also see Carl Cone, *The English Jacobins* (New York: Scribner and Sons, 1968).

29. In reference to Coleridge's 1795 pamphlet *The Plot Discovered or an Attack Against Ministerial Treason* reprinted in *Lects. 1795*.

30. Goodwin, *Friends of Liberty*, introduction.

31. Coleridge's own challenge to his critics was: "I defy my worst enemy to shew [sic], in any of my few writings, the least bias to Irreligion, Immorality, or Jacobinism." *The Friend* no. 2 (8 June 1809); *TF*, 2: 25.

32. Coleridge quoted Milton (sonnet 12: 11–12): "License they mean when they say Liberty! For who loves that must first be wise and good." See *EOT*, 2: 380n2.

33. Coleridge frequently referred to "half-truths" as the most dangerous form of lie. As early as "A Moral and Political Lecture" (1795), Coleridge used this term, but he expressed it most succinctly in his advertisement for *On The Constitution of the Church and State According to the Idea of Each* (1830) where he lamented "a world of power and talent wasted on the support of half truths, too often the most mischievous, because least suspected of errors." *CS*, 2.

34. For a detailed consideration of the romantic phenomenology of fragmentation and decay, see Thomas McFarland, *Romanticism and the Forms of Ruin* (Princeton, N.J.: Princeton University Press, 1981), 1–5.

35. Coleridge, *LS*, 63–64.

36. Despite Coleridge's Unitarian experiment, he retained a strong Anglican bias predicated on an Evangelical soteriology. He declined an offer of the Unitarian pulpit, described his *"Confessio Fidei"* as *"negative* Unitarianism" in a letter of 26 July 1802 (see *CL*, 2: no. 447; 820), and dedicated an early poem, "The Fall of Robespierre," to Mrs. Hannah Moore. See James Dykes Campbell, *Samuel Taylor Coleridge* (London: Macmillan, 1894), 35.

37. Coleridge's early concern with atheism was not its denial of any particular positive creed, but as a manifestation of infidelity. In the case of Godwin, Coleridge considered this failing to suggest a "faithless" cynicism which allowed "reason" to sacrifice "feeling." In this context, Coleridge remarked to Thelwall, "it is not atheism which has prejudiced me against Godwin, but Godwin who has prejudiced me against Atheism." See *CL*, 1: no. 133. Mark Philp has argued, on the subject of Godwin's irreligion, that Godwin's loss of faith in 1788 was addressed to organized religion rather than the belief in God. For this reason, Philp believes that we should be wary using the term atheist with respect to Godwin's religious belief. See Mark Philp, *Godwin's Political Justice* (Ithaca, N.Y.: Cornell University Press, 1986), 34. Coleridge, in contrast, was troubled by Godwin's "faithlessness."

38. See *CL*, 1: no. 33 (8 February 1794) for a strong suggestion of evangelical conversion. Also, Coleridge's writings after 1796, while critical of religious enthusiasm, suggest an awareness of the Clapham sect. Coleridge wrote to Cottle on 27 May 1814, "It is no small gratification to me, & that I have seen and conversed with Mrs. H. More—she is indisputably the *first* literary female, I ever met—in part no doubt because she is a Christian" (*CL*, 3: no. 933).

39. John Morrow, *Coleridge's Political Thought: Property, Morality, and the Limits of Traditional Discourse* (London: MacMillan, 1990), 2–7.

40. *The Monthly Magazine* 48 (1819): 204.

41. Leo Strauss, *Persecution and the Art of Writing* (Chicago: University of Chicago Press, 1988). Also, compare Coleridge's warning against "half-truths" and insistence on "the critical way," to Strauss's observation that "we know that there cannot be *the* simply true substantive view, but only a simply true formal view; that

formal view consists in the insight that every comprehensive view is relative to a specific perspective, or that all comprehensive views are mutually exclusive and none can be simply true." From "What is Liberal Education?" in *Liberalism Ancient and Modern* (New York: Basic Books, 1968), 8.

42. William Hazlitt, Joseph Cottle, and Robert Southey have done the most to advance this view. Hazlitt was Coleridge's most vicious and competitive critic, Cottle a bad poet and neglected publisher, and Southey a bitterly disappointed friend. See Richard Holmes, *Coleridge: Early Visions* (London: Hodder & Stoughton, 1989), 366–70. Also see J. R. de J. Jackson, ed., *Coleridge: The Critical Heritage* (London: Routledge and Kegan Paul, 1970).

43. Robert Southey to Charles Danvers, 15 June 1809, *New Letters of Robert Southey*, ed. Kenneth Curry (New York and London: Columbia University Press, 1965), 1: 511.

44. Lewis Patton, introduction to *Lectures, 1795: On Politics and Religion*, by Coleridge, vol. 1 of *The Collected Works of Samuel Taylor Coleridge*, Bollingen Series 75 (London and Princeton, N.J.: Routledge and Kegan Paul and Princeton University Press, 1971), xxxii (*Lects. 1795*).

45. Coleridge to Sir George Beaumont, 1 October 1803, *CL*, 2: no. 522; 999.

46. Coleridge and Southey wrote *The Fall of Robespierre* together. It contained a dedication to Hannah More (which is suggestive of the moderate and evangelical ambitions of this dramatic poem) and was published (Cambridge, 1794) by Benjamin Flower.

47. Coleridge to George Coleridge, 6 November 1794, *CL*, 1: no. 69; 125; italics mine.

48. Ibid.; my italics.

49. Coleridge presumably knew that whereas the antireform Peace Party hated the war because they felt it drove down the economy to a point where the rabble might cry out for French-style reforms, he himself hated it because it allowed Pitt to use the claim of "national emergency" to institute broad-reaching, unconstitutional powers in the same manner that he believed Robespierre had. In this case, Coleridge's antiwar stance and that of the antireformers were, although they shared the same ends, constructed from quite different assumptions about the danger the war presented to the constitution.

50. See Isaac Kramnick, "On Anarchism in the Real World: William Godwin and Radical England," *American Political Science Review* 66 (1972): 114–28.

51. Perez Zagorin, *The Country and the Court* (New York: Columbia University Press, 1969); Zagorin, "Two Cultures? Rhetoric of Court and Country in the Early Seventeenth Century," in *Origins of the English Civil War*, ed. Conrad Russell (London: MacMillan, 1973); J. R. Jones, *The First Whigs* (Oxford: Oxford University Press, 1961); Isaac Kramnick, *Bolingbroke and His Circle: The Politics of Nostalgia* (Cambridge, Mass.: Harvard University Press, 1968); J. G. A. Pocock, *The Machiavellian Moment: Florentine Political Thought and the Atlantic Republican Tradition* (Princeton N.J.: Princeton University Press, 1977).

52. John Morrow, *Coleridge's Political Thought*, 12.

53. *Lects. 1795*, 5.

54. Edmund Burke, *Reflections on the Revolution in France and on the Proceedings in Certain Societies in London Relative to that Event* (5th ed., 1790; reprint, ed. and intro. Conor Cruise O'Brien, Harmondsworth: Penguin Books, 1969), 37.

55. *Lects. 1795*, 293.

56. This is not the case with political theorists, however; Noel O'Sullivan devotes a chapter to Coleridge in *Conservatism* (London: JM Dent, 1976).

57. John Sterling, John Stuart Mill, Frederick Denison Maurice, and Thomas Carlyle all regarded Coleridge as an original and disturbing talent, as I suggest in the introduction.

58. Donald Greene's study of Samuel Johnson's politics, for instance, takes another famous "Tory" and shows him to have held principles which were essentially "Whiggish" but mediated by a mistrust of party politics and an inherent skepticism about the motives of "patriots" and innovators. See Greene, *Samuel Johnson's Politics*, 2nd ed. (Athens: University of Georgia Press, 1990). The resemblances between Coleridge and Johnson as writers of similarly skeptical temperaments, have been explored by Lawrence Lipking in his review of the final volume of Rene Wellek's *History of Criticism*. It is as least certain that those political writers who liked to think of themselves as inveterate critics were often bad partisans in political battle: they tended to take apart the clichés and cant of politics rather than spread them as gospel.

59. John Stuart Mill, *Autobiography*, 4th ed. (London: Longmans, Green, Reader & Dyer, 1874), 71.

60. Isaiah Berlin, *Four Essays on Liberty* (New York: Oxford University Press, 1970), xliv.

61. Dierdre Coleman argues that Coleridge was drawn to Kant's thought because "he saw, mirrored there, his own dualistic conception of man." See Coleman, *Coleridge and "The Friend," 1809–1810* (Oxford: The Clarendon Press, 1986), 137; G. N. G. Orsini, *Coleridge and German Idealism* (Carbondale: Southern Illinois University Press, 1969), 57–171 passim, esp. 137.

62. Coleridge called them "Plotinists rather than platonists." See STC, *Philosophical Lectures*, ed. K. Coburn (London: Pilot Press, 1949), 317. Orsini observes that Coleridge read and took notes from Cudworth in 1796. Cudworth held a doctrine of a priori but rejected innate ideas, observing in *The True Intellectual System of the Universe: The First Part: Wherein All the Reasons and Philosophy of Atheism is Confuted; and its Impossibility Demonstrated* (London, 1678), 2d ed., 2 vols. (London: Thomas Birch, 1743), that "our human mind hath other cognitions or conceptions in it, the ideas of intelligible natures and essences of things, which are universals, and by and under which it understands singulars." Orsini, *Coleridge and German Idealism*, 64–65.

63. R. F. Brinkley argues that Coleridge considered most of the essential principles of Kantian logic to have existed in English seventeenth-century philosophy. With particular regard to the idea of synthetic unity and trichotomy, she details Co-

leridge's debt to Lord Bacon's *Novum Organum* and Richard Baxter's *Methodus The-ologiae*. See Roberta Brinkley, ed., *Coleridge on the Seventeenth Century* (Durham N.C.: Duke University Press, 1955), 109–21.

64. *Hints Towards the Formation of a More Comprehensive Theory of Life* was written by Coleridge in 1816, largely dictated to J. H. Green. It was not published until after Coleridge's death in 1834.

65. See Norman Fruman, *The Damaged Archangel* (London: George Allen and Unwin, 1972).

66. For example: from Locke conceptions of natural law, from Hartley the doc-trine of association, and from Godwin the centrality of right reason, duty, and con-science. Deirdre Coleman ascribes Coleridge's preoccupation with duty to the in-fluence of Kant's *The Metaphysic of Morals*. However, an earlier source is Godwin's *Political Justice*.

67. Here and throughout the chapter, when I have referred to Coleridge's own technical use of the terms "Idea" and "Conception," I have capitalized these terms. This typographical convenience will serve to alert the reader that in those cases where the terms are capitalized, the words are used in that sentence in their pecu-liar meaning in Coleridge's own unusual philosophical lexicon, as opposed to their general meaning in twentieth-century philosophical or political thought.

68. "The moral world" is a term to which Coleridge frequently returns, but which first appears in "Lecture Six on Revealed Religion" delivered at Bristol in 1795. Coleridge used the term "realworld" to describe the ideal world of Platonic forms, as opposed to the "moral world" of contingencies and relative value.

69. Also argued in *Biographia Literaria* (*BL*), *Church and State*, and *Logic* (*L*).

70. Coleridge's own distinction between the school of Aristotle or materialism and the school of Plato and the idealists may be viewed as a gross simplification of the many discourses of a "dialectical" history of philosophy. However, it was his contention that all men belonged (ultimately) to one or the other of these two fun-damental schools. He considered himself to be a Platonist, Locke and the "adherents of the mechano-corpuscular fallacy" to be Aristotelian, materialists. See *CL*, vol. 2, letters to Wedgewood on Locke.

71. *Aids to Reflection*, ed. Derwent Coleridge (1825, reprint, London: E. Mox-ton, 1854), also ed. J. B. Beers, Bollingen Series 9 (London and Princeton, N.J.: Routledge and Kegan Paul and Princeton University Press, 2003); and *The Confes-sions of an Inquiring Spirit* (London: George Bell and Sons, York Street, Covent Gar-den 1848), 88. Coleridge in his psychology of faculty appears to have drawn freely from Kant's categories of time and space. Coleridge's "constitutive" theory of ideas bore striking similarities to the Kantian categories of time and space. In both theo-ries, the categories were assumed to be transcendent *as categories* in the ideal realm, but conceived of as imminent *in their particular execution* in the material realm. The constitutive power of the idea was objectively but contingently real. This Colerid-gian vocabulary of perception versus abstract thinking was made more sophisticated

by Coleridge's encounter with Kant but was in truth born earlier of Coleridge's first encounters with Cambridge-Platonist theories such as "plastic nature."

72. *CS*, 11.

73. Archibald Foord, *His Majesty's Opposition, 1714–1830* (Oxford: Clarendon Press, 1964). See the chapter "Parties and Creeds in the Age of Fox and Grey, 1782–1830" for Foord's most complete discussion of the imergance of an oppositional dynamic in politics, 439–51.

74. *CS*, 12.

75. Thomas McFarland argues for the pervasiveness of a language of fragmentation in *Romanticism and The Forms of Ruin*, 5.

76. *CS*, 12–13.

77. White remarked that "if we dismiss Coleridge's metaphysics, we shall understand neither the origin nor the true nature of his political ideas." R. J. White, *The Political Thought of Samuel Taylor Coleridge: A Selection* (London: Jonathan Cape, 1938), 11.

78. Muirhead describes Coleridge's idea of the state in Augustinian terms: "Coleridge regarded all actual constitutions, including that of his own country as temporary and imperfect embodiments of an 'idea' that was slowly revealing itself on earth, if not as a city of God, at any rate as a society of seekers after him." John Muirhead, *Coleridge as Philosopher* (London: Allen & Unwin 1930), 194.

79. Although, Jerome Christensen and Raimonda Modiano agree with Michael Fischer's contention that "when Coleridge chooses metaphysics over politics, he is not choosing between evasion and power, but between two kinds of power," in Fischer, "Coleridge and Politics," *Studies in Romanticism* 21, no. 3 (1981): 457–60.

2. Attacking the State

1. Coleridge continued to develop this theme after 1795, as his favorable reference in 1799 to Hume's arguments against the "Euthenasia of the Constitution" demonstrates (*EOT*, 1:26).

2. See E. Thompson, *The Making of the English Working Class* (London, Victor Gollancz, 1961), 234, for a further account.

3. Viz the assassination plots against Charles II (1683) and William III (1696). In France, Damiens's attempt on the life of Louis XV was politically significant beyond its immediate dangers.

4. For example, William III at the Boyne in 1690, or George II at Dettingen in 1743.

5. For general "high" estimates of the loathing for the king among the populace in 1795 and 1796, see studies such as: Malcolm Ian Thomis and Peter Holt, *Threats of Revolution in Britain, 1789–1848.* (London: Macmillan, 1977); and Thompson, *The Making of the English Working Class.* Also, c.f., Ian Christie, *Stress and Stability in Late-Eighteenth-Century Britain: Reflections on the British Avoidance of Revolution* (Oxford: The Clarendon Press, 1985).

6. See Albert Goodwin, *The Friends of Liberty* (Cambridge, Mass.: Harvard University Press, 1979). Also see Edmund Burke's *Letter to a Noble Lord* (London, 1796), which was a venomous indictment of fashionable democratic fervor among nobles.

7. Treasonable and Seditious Practises Act (1795), S.L. xi. 561, 36 Geo. 3, c. 7.

8. Seditious Meetings Act (1795), S.L. xi. 564, 36 Geo. III, c. 8.

9. *Lects. 1795*, xxi

10. Earl of Lauderdale, Speech to the House of Lords, 17 November 1795, *Parliamentary Register*, Lords, vol. 43, 222.

11. Richard Brinsley Sheridan, Speech to the House of Commons, 17 November 1795, *Parliamentary Register*, Commons, vol. 43, 224.

12. *Lects. 1795*, 259.

13. For a discussion of Pitt's wars, both domestic and foreign, against Jacobinism, see Albert Goodwin, *The Friends of Liberty*; Holland Rose, *Life of William Pitt*, (London: G. Bell and Sons, 1923); and John Ehrman, *The Younger Pitt: The Reluctant Transition*, vol. 2 of *The Younger Pitt* (Stanford, Calif.: Stanford University Press, 1983). John Derry takes the coalition with the Portland Whigs as evidence of genuine concern by government for matters of domestic security. See Derry, *Politics in the Age of Fox, Pitt, and Liverpool: Continuity and Transformation* (New York: St. Martin's Press, 1990), 87, 94–96.

14. *Lects. 1795*, 288

15. *Lects. 1795*, 314.

16. Ibid.

17. Ibid.

18. Ibid.

19. Bolingbroke, *The Craftsman The Craftsman*, nos. 1–511, 5 December 1726—17 April 1736 (London: R. Franklin, 1731–1737); but most particularly James Burgh's *Political Disquisitions* (London: Dilly, 1774) and its discussion of legislative corruption.

20. William Blackstone, *Commentaries on the Laws of England*, book 1, chap. 7, paraphrasing Montesquieu, *Esprit des Lois*, 11:6: "Were the judicial power joined with the legislative, the life, liberty and property of the subject would be in the hands of arbitrary judges, whose decisions would then be regulated only by their opinions, and not by any fundamental principles of law." See also William Paley, *The Principles of Moral and Political Philosophy* (London: R. Faulder, 1785), book 7, chap. 8.

21. *Lects. 1795*, 62.

22. Ibid., 61.

23. Ibid., 300.

24. The "Ancient Constitution" had traditionally been traced back to (freely mythologized) Saxon times; arguments based on it tended to say that the constitution was perfect in primitive times but had been corrupted by the "Norman Yoke" after 1066 and only restored partially in 1688. In contrast, the "Revolution Principles" were, it was freely admitted, to be newly founded in the "Balanced

Constitution" of king, Lords, and Commons after 1688. The Country Party opposition used the myth of the ancient constitution to claim what they argued were
the rights of freeborn Englishmen as preserved by the Common Law and the history of constitutional practice and amendment born in the days of King Alfred. Sir
Robert Walpole and the Whig establishment scornfully responded that the ancient
constitution was a font of oppression rather than liberty. Walpole's polemicists
borrowed arguments that absolutist royalist Tory scholars in the reign of King
Charles had used to discredit Whig images of "ancient liberty"; they argued that
there was no real liberty under the feudal law, in which the king was the font of
all law and all justice through "his" Parliament and "his" courts. Only the 1688
settlement, the 1689 Bill of Rights, and the 1701 Act of Settlement had created a
truly "free" Britain where the Parliament and the courts were not merely dogs-
bodies deputized to enact the king's Norman prerogative.

25. *Lects. 1795*, 307.

26. Ibid.

27. *Lects. 1795*, 301.

28. Ibid.

29. Except in the case of Scotland, which sent fifteen "representative peers" to
represent the entire nobility of Scotland.

30. *Lects. 1795*, 307

31. Ibid., 308–9. Coleridge also cited the pamphlet *The State of Representation of
England and Wales, delivered to the Society, the Friends of the People, associated for the purpose of obtaining a Parliamentary Reform, on Saturday the 9th of February 1793* (London,
1793), which reported that "162 return 306 out of 513 Members." Also cited in *Lects
1795*, 273n3. See also R. G. Thorne, ed., *The House of Commons, 1790–1820*, 5 vols.,
History of Parliament Series (London: Secker & Warburg, 1986).

32. *Lects. 1795*, 307.

33. Ibid.

34. Ibid., 225.

35. Ibid.

36. See Thomas Paine's letter to the Marquis de Lafayette, 9 February 1792, as
printed before the preface of part 2 of *The Rights of Man*: "The only point upon
which I could ever discover that we differed was not as to principles of Government,
but as to time. For my own part, I think it equally as injurious to good principles to
permit them to linger, as to push them on too fast. That which you suppose ac-
complishable in fourteen or fifteen years, I may believe practicable in a much short-
er period." Paine, *The Rights of Man*, 1791–1792; reprint, ed. and intro. Eric Foner
(London: Pengiun Books, 1975), 151.

37. *Lects. 1795*, 295.

38. Coleridge was increasingly interested in the interdependency of rights and
duties. While he considered both to be essential, neither was to be taken singularly
as alienable from the other. See *W*, 122.

39. *Lects. 1795*, 289.

40. Ibid., 296.

41. Ibid.

42. Ibid..

43. Pitt's speech of 12 Jun 1781, see *Parliamentary Register*, Commons, vol. 20, 564; *Lects. 1795*, 64.

44. Coleridge commented that "the great and good Dr. Jebb foresaw his [Pitt's] Apostacy." *Lects. 1795*, 64–65.

45. Ibid.

46. Ibid., 289.

47. Ibid.; my italics.

48. Ibid.

49. Ibid.

50. Ibid.

51. Ibid.

52. Ibid.

53. Ibid., 291.

54. Ibid., 296.

55. Ibid., 297.

56. J. L. De Lolme, *The Constitution of England; or an account of the English Governemnt*, ed. William Hughes (London, 1771, 1834).

3. Defending the Constitution

1. Coleridge refers here to Thelwall; *Lects. 1795*, 297.

2. See *Lects. 1795*, *Conciones ad Populum*, "Introductory Address," 33.

3. Coleridge would later expand on this in works on logic, specifically addressing the vacuity of Hartleyan association in *BL*, 1: chaps. 6 and 7. For a contemporary insight, see *CN*, 1:22.

4. See *BL*, 1:173 on imagination and fancy. Also see *Logic*: "the happiest illustration of the act of the intuitive imagination and its close connection with its product . . . I have seen in the *ephemerae* and other minute and half-transparent insects who exceeding velocity of motion actually present to our eyes a symbol of what Plotinus meant when . . . he says her [Nature] contemplative act is creative and one with the product of her contemplation." *L*, 74.

5. *L*, 219.

6. Coleridge derived the concept of "plastic nature" from his reading of Ralph Cudworth's *The True Intellectual System of the Universe: The First Part: Wherein All the Reasons and Philosophy of Atheism is Confuted; and its Impossibility Demonstrated* (London, 1678); 2nd ed., 2 vols. (London: Thomas Birch, 1743). In addition to his interest in Newton and More, Coleridge's Platonism had been nurtured through his Greek studies at Cambridge. He uses the image of plasticity in his 1797 poem "The

Aeolian Harp." For a complete discussion, see most recently Ian Wylie, *Young Coleridge and the Philosophers of Nature* (Oxford: The Clarendon Press, 1989).

7. J. A. W. Gunn, *Beyond Liberty and Property: The Process of Self-Recognition in Eighteenth-Century Political Thought* (Kingston, Ont.: McGill-Queen's University Press, 1983), 271.

8. *General Evening Post* 5655 (9–11 June 1770), as cited in J. A. W. Gunn, *Beyond Liberty and Property*, 278.

9. *Lects. 1795*, 297.

10. Ibid., 298.

11. Ibid., 312. Later, in *The Friend* (1809), Coleridge compared the flow of public opinion in society ("our intellectual commerce") to the flow of water in the River Thames. Both opinion and the river must follow a reasonable course and not be allowed to recklessly overflow its banks and endanger life, but neither must be dammed off entirely out of fear of such overflow. To build a dam of gagging laws across the river of information and opinion, Coleridge asserted, would be "to render its navigation dangerous or partial." To "render the press ineffectual" would make "the law odious," by using as "materials the very banks [of reasonable regulation] that were intended to deepen [opinion's] channels and guard against its inundations" (*TF*, 66).

12. *Lects. 1795*, 289.

13. Ibid.

14. Here the phrase "*quasi*-independently" must be stressed and emphasized. The great constitutional struggles of the seventeenth century had *modified* rather than *destroyed* the medieval theory of the king as font of all law and all justice. The major changes were limits rather than abrogations of royal influence. The Crown, as of 1795, still had the right to summon, dismiss, and prorogue Parliament at will—although tradition since 1689 went against such an act—and the king still legally possessed an indisputable veto over legislation, which had not been used since Queen Anne's time. The Crown also retained the right to appoint judges to what were still theoretically the "royal" common law courts, although after 1689 it had to appoint them for a term of good behavior rather than as long as they pleased the Crown by their decisions. The Crown also had a constitutionally impeccable right to suspend habeas corpus in emergencies, thus circumventing the typical operation of the laws. See Alexander Hamilton, *The Federalist Papers*, ed. Charles Rossiter, intro. Charles R. Kessler (New York: Signet, 2003), no. 69.

15. *Lects. 1795*, 289.

16. *Lects. 1795*, 288.

17. Ibid.

18. Ibid.

19. Ibid.

20. David Lieberman, *The Province of Legislation Determined: Legal Theory in Eighteenth-Century Britain* (Cambridge: Cambridge University Press, 1989), 55.

21. See Lieberman, *The Province of Legislation Determined*, 125, citing Blackstone, "City of London and the Dissenters," as reported in Philip Furneaux, *Letters to the Hon. Mr. Justice Blackstone, concerning his Exposition of the Act of Toleration . . . in his Celebrated Commentaries of the Laws of England*, 2d ed. (London, 1771), 278; my italics. David Lieberman points out the presence of universalizing Natural Law arguments in Blackstone's *Commentaries*, despite Blackstone's explicit commitment to a particular historical analysis of the Common Law as based on custom rather than morals. Lieberman suggests that Sir Edward Coke's defence of the right of Common Law courts to overturn unreasonable statute, as argued in Bonham's case, posed some theoretical difficulties for Blackstone. Blackstone's own belief in the supremacy of Parliament to make law was at odds with Coke's implication that Common Law courts (guided by intuitions of reason and natural justice) served as a font for judicial review. Yet, as Lieberman has observed, "Blackstone when faced with the challenge of an unreasonable act of parliament reverted to his concept of sovereignty, rather than his natural law precepts." In this regard, while Blackstone placed the ultimate magisterial power within the workings of a balanced constitution, he considered that the judiciary and the jury had significant capacity to both "find" and "make" law.

22. Coleridge was familiar with the presumptions of this pro–Common Law parliamentarian tradition through his readings of James Burgh's *Political Disquisitions* in preparation for the composition of *The Plot*.

23. Blackstone had presented a famous paradox to his readers involving the sovereignty of Parliament. Blackstone had claimed that in order for the "sovereignty" of Parliament to be meaningful, it had to be undeniable and irresistible by lesser authorities; that courts and citizens and colonies could not be allowed to pick and choose which laws they thought it would please them to obey and which they would rather ignore. This absolute sovereignty raised the moral question of what would happen if Parliament became palpably unjust and began passing laws that everyone agreed were Caligulan in nature.

24. *M*, 3:231.

25. *Lects. 1795*, 288.

26. Coleridge's association of the social and political power of the jury with opinion was one that he developed more completely in *The Friend* (1809). He believed by then, fourteen years after writing *The Plot*, that the difficult distinction between vulgar and popular opinion, between liberty of the press and seditious libel, was to be found in the spirit of rational freedom. This spirit he likened to the "universal menstrum sought for by the old alchemists." This spirit of rational freedom "diffused and bec[a]me national in consequent influence and control of public opinion, and in its most precious organ, the Jury" (*TF*, 66).

27. Coleridge would expand on this later, in a work on logic, specifically addressing the vacuity of Hartleyan association in *BL*, vol. 1, chaps. 6 and 7. For a contemporary insight see *CN*, 1:22.

28. Coleridge emphasized this form of conspiracy again in *The Friend* (no. 5, 14 September 1809): "Shame fall on that Man, who shall labour to confound what reason and nature have put asunder. . . . Shame fall on him, and a participation of the infamy of those, who misled an English Jury to the murder of Algernon Sydney!" (*TF*, 67).

29. *Lects. 1795*, 116. Coleridge was defending the Mosaic dispensation, but his question was unintentionally applicable to the radical-reform platform.

30. Ibid., 175; my italics.

31. Ibid., 285.

32. Ibid.

33. Ibid.

34. Ibid.

35. This distinction and its implication for the Natural Law foundations of Common Law is discussed by David Lieberman, *The Province of Legislation Determined*, 38. Lieberman considers Thomas Wood's invocation of Coke's dictum that "nothing that is contrary to Reason is consonant to Law" in Coke, *Institutes of the Laws of England* (n.p., 1720 ed.), 4.

36. J. L. DeLolme, *The Rise and Progress of the English Constitution*, ed. A. J. Stephens (London, 1838) see esp. vol. 2, chaps. 3 and 4, 820–835. The evidence for DeLolme's influence on Coleridge is inconclusive but extremely suggestive. Coleridge never directly mentioned DeLolme by name in any surviving papers or writings, but obviously Coleridge was deeply grounded in the study of European constitutionalist thought in general, and those treatises on the British constitution in particular. DeLolme's work was widely excerpted and quoted in the reviews and magazines of Coleridge's youth, and the Swiss theorist was among the commonly read authors that a young man beginning a study of the British polity might have been expected to know. Lewis Patton has not only suggested that Coleridge had read the famous work of DeLolme by the mid-1790s but surmises that Coleridge referred to DeLolme in his praise of the unnamed "Constitutionalists . . . not without their use" in the *Moral and Political Lecture* of 1795 (Patton also includes Adam Ferguson and Burke in this; *Lects. 1795*, 8–9n). DeLolme's distinction between unwritten law and common law considered separately the historical weight of precedence and the active process of deciding. Decisions, as they were made by judges and juries, created new law.

De Lolme identified the Common Law as a principle governing the "law of descent, different methods of acquiring property, various forms of rendering contract valid" (*The Rise and Progress of the English Constitution*, 634–636). He believed that in England these agreements had been settled by custom and practice from "time immemorial" and that they were held not to be superseded by the imposition of Roman law in the high Middle Ages. Whether these conventions actually reached back to the laws of Alfred was less important to seventeenth-century common lawyers and eighteenth-century "constitutionalists" than that the conventions had been established, refined, and maintained though the continuity of their practice over time.

37. "The strength and obligation and the formal Nature of a Law, is not upon account that the Danes, or the Saxons, or the Normans brought it in with them, but [that] they became Laws, and binding in this kingdom by virtue of their being received and approved here." Gerald Postema quotes and discusses Hale's idea of historical continuity thus: "the principles of Common Law are not themselves validated by reason; but they are the products of a process of reasoning fashioned by the exercise of the special, professional, intellectual skills of the Common lawyers over time[,] refining and coordinating the social habits of a people into a coherent body of rules." Gerald Postema, *Bentham and the Common Law Tradition* (Oxford; Oxford University Press, 1986), 7, and chap. 1, passim. Common Law judges, such as Coke, attempted to push decisions past the literal terms of particular statute when the law seemed to violate the unwritten law and the principles of the Common Law, which were reflected in statutes taken as a whole.

38. *Lects. 1795*, 286.

39. John Morrow argues that Coleridge's moral view of reform did not distinguish him from the more atheistic radical reformers like Godwin, Paine, and Thewall. While these writers did emphasize the need for education and enlightenment, I would still argue that their more active intentions must be contrasted with Coleridge's almost obsessive voluntarism, and this among other things does significantly distinguish their views from his. See Morrow, *Coleridge's Political Thought*, chaps. 1 and 2.

40. *Lects. 1795*, "A Moral and Political Lecture," 9. It is not at all certain, however, to whom Coleridge referred in his use of this invective. The Bollingen editor has hypothesized that it might have been DeLolme, Blackstone, and others like them, but Coleridge himself did not say. Given the balance of Coleridge's arguments in the essay, a more likely suggestion would be those party flacks and parliamentary adventurers who "trimmed" for the purposes of political self-advancement.

41. Mark Goldie emphasizes the "radical" origins of the True Whig ideology in "The Roots of True Whiggism, 1688–94," *History of Political Thought* 1, no. 195 (1980): 195–236. J. G. A. Pocock, however, points to the utility, for out-of-power Tories from 1689 onwards, of True Whig arguments against standing armies, public credit, and executive centralization and privilege. Pocock is also concerned with the ambiguity of late-eighteenth-century transformations and applications of these ideas, most notably in the survival of the "common-law mind" in Edmund Burke's prescriptivism. See Pocock, "The Ancient Constitution Revisited," in *The Ancient Constitution and the Feudal Law* (Cambridge: Cambridge University Press, 1957; updated ed., Cambridge: Cambridge University Press, 1987) *Disquisitions* from the Bristol Library. See George Whalley, "The Bristol Library Borrowings of Southey and Coleridge, 1793–8," *The Library*, 5th ser., 5 (September 1949): 114–31.

44. Thelwall's republicanism, or Paine's, suggested a more plebeian than patrician res publica; one that valued the contribution of the artisan over the aristocrat. Isaac Kramnick sites a fundamental shift in seventeenth- and eighteenth-century conceptions of work and leisure as contributing to the changing republican ideal. Coleridge entertained a more Aristotelian view of these things. See Isaac Kramnick, *Republicanism and Bourgeois Radicalism: Political Ideology in Late-Eighteenth-Century England and America* (Ithaca, N.Y.: Cornell University Press, 1990), 2, and on Paine chap. 5, passim.

45. The "Whig" Horace Walpole, after all, had hung in his home two great icons of English liberty: the Magna Carta and the death warrant of King Charles I, and one would be mad to suggest that Walpole ever wanted to see the reign of King George ended by the guillotine or that he would have freely given up Strawberry Hill to be used as a part of an agrarian reform scheme to give land to the landless. The "Tory" James Boswell sent Pasquale de Paoli a case of books that included the works of Harrington and other Commonwealthsmen, but in the 1790s also contributed money to a monument to the slain Louis XVI. Boswell's father Lord Auchinleck boasted to Samuel Johnson that the execution of Charles I in 1649 had "made kings gar [recognize that] they had a lith [a joint] in their necks," yet was a loyal and indefatigable servant of the Georgian state until his death and a loyal "Hanoverian" Whig.

46. *Lects. 1795*, 308–9.

47. Ibid.

48. Ibid., 310; my italics.

49. Ibid., 311. Coleridge was likely referring to George Canning, the distinguished Whig hopeful who disappointed his friends and served under Pitt. Canning had won the chancellor's prize for Latin verse in 1789.

50. Ibid., 312.

51. Ibid., 261; my italics.

52. Ibid. Coleridge draws from Burgh, *Political Disquisitions* (London: Dilly, 1774), 3:440–41 (var.), quoting Bolingbroke's *Remarks on the History of England*.

53. This is reminiscent of Burke's pragmatism, as described in Halevy in *The Growth of Philosophic Radicalism* (London: Faber & Faber, 1934, 1972), 157–58.

54. *Lects. 1795*, 261.

55. Ibid.

4. Liberty and Law

1. This association has been made most recently in Nicholas Roe, *Wordsworth and Coleridge: The Radical Years* (Oxford: The Clarendon Press, 1988).

2. Mark Philp points out that Godwin changed his views on forced redistribution, violence, revolution, and so on in the 1796 edition of *Political Justice*. Defending property rights as a means of preserving the liberty of private judgments required Godwin to reconstruct the redistributive significance of *Political Justice*, book 4, chap.

8. See Philp, *Godwin's Political Justice* (Ithaca, N.Y.: Cornell University Press, 1986), 82, 137.

3. Not all advocates of equality argued for state intervention and a political redistribution of land or wealth. But those more "Jacobin" reformers associated (erroneously) with Gracchus Babeuf did argue for the need for redistribution through state reform rather than market forces. For a discussion of Thomas Paine's use of a redistributive taxation or "ground rent" to the community in *Agrarian Justice*, see Gregory Claeys, *Thomas Paine's Social and Political Thought* (Boston: Unwin Hyman, 1989), 197–203. Thomas Spence may be considered the most "aggressive" redistributionist of the British Jacobins. See "Pig's Meat," "The Real Rights of Man," and "The End of Oppression" in *The Political Works of Thomas Spence*, ed. H. T. Dickinson (Newcastle upon Tyne: Avero, 1982).

4. Isaiah Berlin, *Four Essays on Liberty* (New York: Oxford University Press, 1970), xliv–l. Berlin identifies Coleridge, in particular, as an exemplar of the "positive" theorists who associate freedom with the "positive" activities of institutional forms of life, growth, and so on.

5. Robert Nozick, *Anarchy, State, and Utopia* (Oxford: Basil Blackwell, 1974), 164. Robert Nozick has argued that liberty is secured most effectively by the recognition of individual entitlements with regard to property, a possessive, individualist theory of justice. Nozick's theory may be considered representative of a late form of the argument that runs from Locke through Mill to Nozick himself. Nozick's is largely a "negative" vision of liberty: a freedom from the encroachment of the "nanny" state intervening in the guise of a higher community welfare.

6. John Rawls, in contrast, has considered justice and ultimately liberty to be most effectively secured by equity and fairness, by a distributive egalitarian theory of justice. Rawlsian theory is the late form of the argument from Paine to Marx to Rawls himself. Rawls's is generally a "positive" vision of liberty: an assertion of the state's benevolent role as advancer of the goals of equality and community. Rawls, *A Theory of Justice* (Oxford: Oxford University Press, 1971).

7. Coleridge had read Rousseau's *Discourse on Inequality* in preparation for his political lectures of 1795. Dierdre Coleman has discussed Kant and Rousseau's influence on Coleridge in some detail in *Coleridge and "The Friend," 1809–1810* (Oxford: The Clarendon Press, 1988). See 146–54 for a discussion of reason, freedom, and *The Social Contract*. For a further discussion of the political significance of property in Kant and Rousseau see Alan Ryan, *Property and Political Theory* (Oxford: Basil Blackwell, 1984), chaps. 2 and 3.

8. See Alan Ryan's discussion of "Kant and Possession" in *Property and Political Theory*, 74–90.

9. The alignment of rights and duties was an idea which can be traced back to Godwin's *Political Justice* and was explored by Coleridge in the lectures of 1795.

10. See Emile Durkheim, *Montesquieu and Rousseau: Forerunners of Sociology*, trans. Ralph Manheim (Ann Arbor: University of Michigan Press, 1960), 26.

11. Beginning with Elie Halevy's *The Growth of Philosophic Radicalism* (London: Faber & Faber, 1934, 1972), 158; and Crane Brinton's *English Political Thought in the Nineteenth Century* (London: London: Benn, 1933), 74–86, this theme has resurfaced with such frequency as to become a commonplace of romantic historiography. See also G. N. G. Orsini, *Coleridge and German Idealism* (Carbondale: Southern Illinois University Press, 1969); Raimonda Modiano, "Historicist Readings of the Rhyme of the Ancient Mariner," in *Samuel Taylor Coleridge and the Sciences of Life*, ed. Nicholas Roe (Oxford: Oxford University Press, 2001) 271–296; Thomas McFarland, *Coleridge and the Pantheist Tradition* (Oxford: The Clarendon Press, 1969); Rene Wellek, *Immanual Kant in England* (Princeton, N.J.: Princeton University Press, 1931); Richard Holmes, *Coleridge: Early Visions* (London: Hodder & Stoughton, 1989); Marilyn Butler, *Romantics, Rebels, and Reactionaries: English Literature and its Background, 1760–1830* (Oxford: Oxford University Press, 1981); and, most recently, Nigel Leask, *The Politics of Imagination in Coleridge's Critical Thought* (Basingstoke: MacMillan, 1988); and Coleman, *Coleridge and "The Friend."*

12. Coleridge explores this in his own work on logic. His first critic was Alice Snyder, who noted a pervasive polarity of logic in her studies of Coleridge's *Logic*. See in particular Snyder, ed. *S. T. Coleridge's Treatise on Method* (London: Constable, 1934);and Snyder, *The Critical Principle of the Resolution of Opposites as Employed by Coleridge*, Contributions to Rhetorical Theory, no. 9 (Ann Arbor: University of Michigan Press, 1918; reprint, Folcroft, Penn.: Folcroft Press, 1970). The most recent consideration of Coleridge's attempt to reduce all knowledge to one system through a "logosphilosophy" may be found in Mary Anne Perkins, *Coleridge's Philosophy: The Logos as Unifying Principle* (Oxford: The Clarendon Press, 1994).

13. For a discussion of the evolution of rights with respect to changing ideas of faculties, capacities, uses, and possessions, see Richard Tuck, *Natural Rights Theories* (Cambridge: Cambridge University Press, 1979), 16–17.

14. While most political thinkers of the eighteenth century addressed the conflict between private rights and public duties, they tended to privilege one "side" or the other of the individual/community rights divide. For Godwin, the emphasis was placed on duties, for Paine on rights, but for Coleridge it was a right/duty bond that he articulated in terms of the language of self-duties/other-duties or, as Mill would later have it, self-regarding and other-regarding rights. It is significant, however, that Coleridge prefers the language of duty to the language of rights. In this regard, his philosophical debt to Godwin was enduring.

15. See Norman Fruman, *Damaged Archangel* (London; George Allen and Unwin, 1972) for a complete discussion of Coleridge's plagiarism and alleged deceptions. Fruman argues for the possibility that Coleridge was "cunning and deceitful, at times treacherous, vain and ambitious of literary reputation, dishonest in his personal relations, an exploiter of those who loved him, a liar." These claims have been countered by Thomas McFarland in *Coleridge and the Pantheist Tradition*, (Oxford: Clarendon Press, 1969), 4–27.

16. John Stuart Mill, *Mill on Bentham and Coleridge*, ed. F. R. Leavis (London: Chatto and Wyndis, 1950; reprint, Cambridge: Cambridge University Press, 1980), 77; my italics.

17. Mill rejected the image of Coleridge as a Tory. Sardonically, Mill asked if "any Tories" had "ever attend[ed] [Coleridge's] Thursday evening sessions," suggesting that they would have found as many offensive ideas as congenial ones in his speeches; see John Stuart Mill, *Autobiography*, 4th ed. (London: Longmans, Green, Reader & Dyer, 1874). He reinforced this conjecture in his essay "On Coleridge," asserting that Coleridge's "far reaching remarks and tone of general feeling [was] sufficient to make a Tory's hair stand on end" (*Mill on Bentham and Coleridge*, 77).

18. Mill, *Mill on Bentham and Coleridge*, 167: "We do not pretend to have given any sufficient account of Coleridge: but we hope we may have proved to some, not previously aware of it, that there is something both in him, and in the school to which he belongs, not unworthy of their better knowledge. We may have done something to show that a Tory philosopher cannot be wholly a Tory, but must often be a better Liberal than Liberals themselves; while he is in the natural means of rescuing from oblivion truths which Tories have forgotten and which the prevailing schools of Liberalism never knew."

19. This, of course, is not immediate proof of his not being a radical. Godwin, who was a true radical, also despised groups because he thought they were coercive. Like Godwin, Coleridge considered party affiliation of any kind to be coercive. For Coleridge's most complete discussion of the problem see ,*The Friend*, essay 5, "On the Errors of Party Spirit or Extremes Meet." *TF*, 1:205–22.

20. This is another opinion he shared with Godwin, who also took a dim view of party associations and clubs.

21. Coleridge's conception of the a priori conditions of the "good will" is again a somewhat Kantian one, in this sense the "moral law" is the law inside the subject that *governs* conscience. However, the idea that the will is the preeminent part of man's humanity, and that the will is more than reason or conscience alone, is a more Coleridgian twist to this idea. Conscience and reason, through duty, allow us to live more or less in accordance to the moral law.

22. God's will and man's will operate with similar imperatives with respect to questions of freedom and *dominium*. See a discussion of Jean Gerson on rights theory and theology in Richard Tuck, *Natural Rights Theories* (Cambridge: Cambridge University Press, 1979) 26–31.

23. Coleridge made this distinction clearly in an editorial in *The Courier* of 29 September 1814, which deprecated "Party Confedericies in *any* form . . . [and] all 'Swearings-in,' all initiatory pledges and mysteries of membership, as factious and disloyal." His 1832 manuscript notes expands on this theme: "the assertion of *Rights* unqualified by and without any reference to Duties, a vague Lust for Power for & counterfeit[ing] the love of Liberty" (*EOT*, 2:380). Quoting Milton in a poem he continued, "Licence they mean, when they cry Liberty!" (Sonnet 12, line 11).

24. *The Plot Discovered or an Attack Against Ministerial Treason* first appeared in December of 1795 and is collected in *Lects. 1795*.

25. *Lects. 1795*, 42.

26. Ibid.

27. "Introductory Address," in *Lects. 1795*, 43; my italics.

28. Godwin differed from Hartley, who conceived of benevolence as a principle that was extended through associations of thought and habits of action.

29. Referring to Godwin, *An Enquiry Concerning Political Justice, and Its Influence Concerning General Virtue and Happiness*, 2 vols. (London, 1793), 1:207: "He that begins with an appeal to the people may be suspected to understand little of the true character of the mind. . . . Human affairs through every link in the chain of necessity are harmonized and admirably adapted to each other. As the people in the last step in the progress of truth, they need least preparation to induce them to assert it." Coleridge wrote a note: "Political wisdom sewn by the broadcast not dibble." *CN*, 1:116.

30. For a discussion of Coleridge's reliance on Hartley, see Patton's introduction to *Lects. 1795*, lix–lxiii. Also, on the weakness of imitable perfections in human beings, see Coleridge's tacit criticism, in lecture 3, of Hartley's *Observations on Man, His Frame, His Duty, and His Expectations*, 2 vols (London, 1749), 2:169. "How could mean and illiterate persons excel the greatest geniuses, ancient and modern, in drawing a character?" (*Lects. 1795*, 162). For Smith's account of association and faculty psychology, see Adam Smith, *Theory of Moral Sentiments* (London, 1759), facsimile edition, ed. A. L. Macfie and D. D. Raphael (Oxford: Oxford University Press, 1976).

31. In fact, Godwin was not a great advocate of private societies. Like Coleridge, he considered them destructive of "right reason, conscience and duty." See Godwin, *An Enquiry Concerning Political Justice*, 3:247. Also see Don Locke, *A Fantasy of Reason: The Life and Thought of William Godwin* (London: Routledge and Kegan Paul, 1980), 2–11.

32. Coleridge paraphrasing Godwin, *Political Justice*, 1:207: "Human affairs through every link in the chain of necessity, are harmonized and admirably adapted to each other. As the people form the last step in the progress of truth, they need least preparation to induce them to assert it." See Coleridge's comment cited in note 29, above.

33. *Lects. 1795*, 43.

34. J. C. D. Clark, *English Society, 1688–1832: Ideology, Social Structure, and Political Practice During the Ancien Regime* (Cambridge: Cambridge University Press, 1985), 30.

35. Typically, social thought of the period held that a "pure-thinking" polity would be polluted by religious and political deviants, who were as dangerous to the souls of a nation's citizens as a plague carrier was to their bodies. The state, advocates of censorship argued, had a compelling interest to quarantine or obliterate carriers of infectious ideas. Indeed, the state was put in danger to such a degree by er-

ratic or heterodox ideas that it was in the state's interest to seek out such deviants and silence them in order to restore unity of thought and thereby return domestic tranquillity.

5. Morality and Will

1. Coleridge's dependence on Schelling during this period was striking. Natural philosophy, or the science of nature, was an integrative aesthetic whole for both philosophers. Moral value was assumed to be consonant with this aesthetic and was to be understood in organic terms. The spiritual or religious impulse in man was a manifestation of this natural aesthetic but was not a matter of specific doctrinal religions. See Coleridge, *Aids to Reflection*, ed. Derwent Coleridge (1825; reprint, London: E. Moxton, 1854), also ed. J. B. Beers, Bollingen Series 9 (London and Princeton, N.J.: Routledge and Kegan Paul and Princeton University Press, 2003), 1–4.

2. Ibid., 88.

3. Ibid., 88–89.

4. Coleridge seems to have had first hand knowledge of Epicurus, having brought home from Malta a list of papyri excavated and unrolled at Herculaneum (now University of Toronto, VCL S MS F 14.15); see *CN*, 2:410; *CS*, 82 n. From the papyri at Herculaneum, Johann Conrad Orelli had published fragments of Epicurus, *De natura*, from books 2 and 11 at Leipzig in 1818 (*TT*, 1:203.). However, Coleridge relied more heavily upon the writings of Lucretius for his account of the atomistic philosophy of the Epicurean system, while his broader use of "Epicureanism" in lecture 6 of *Philosophical Lectures*, ed. K. Coburn (London: Pilot Press, 1949), he took from Tenneman.

5. This language of "excommunication" is in itself significant, since it returns us once again to Coleridge's strong and persistent use of Anglican and Evangelical imagery in his works.

6. *Aids to Reflection*, 89–90.

7. See James E. Crimmins, *Secular Utilitarianism* (Oxford: The Claredon Press, 1990), 271: "Bentham was both a moral atheist, who sought to disprove the utility of an immortal soul and in an afterlife of rewards and punishments, and an ontological atheist, who denied the existence of God and of a life beyond the world of material reality."

8. *Aids to Reflection*, 90; also see note 1, above.

9. Attention should be drawn to the Kantian flavor of Coleridge's language in the preceding passages. Deirdre Coleman has argued persuasively for Coleridge's dependence on Kant, specifically the *Metaphysic of Morals*, as have G. N. E. Orsini and Rene Wellek. See Dierdre Coleman, *Coleridge and "The Friend," 1809–1810* (Oxford: The Clarendon Press, 1988), 140–43; G. N. G. Orsini, *Coleridge and German Idealism* (Carbondale: Southern Illinois University Press, 1969); and Rene Wellek, *Immanuel Kant in England* (Oxford: Oxford University Press, 1971).

Wellek argues against the originality of Coleridge's idealism and contends that Coleridge had plagiarized large portions of Kant, Fichte, Lessing, and Schelling. This
theme is expanded by Norman Fruman in *Coleridge: The Damaged Archangel* (London: George Allen and Unwin, 1972), and discredited by a series of articles by
Thomas McFarland.

10. Coleridge considered the "disciples of Locke" to be the animalizing Epicureans of his age. He meant Bentham, Malthus, Ricardo and the new Utilitarian
school of political economy. See *CL*, 2:701, February 1801 to Josiah Wedgewood:
"When the fundamental principles of the new Epicuren school were taught by Mr.
Locke, and all the doctrines of religion and morality, forced into juxta-position [*sic*]
& apparent combination with them . . . " See also the Locke letters to Wedgewood
for Coleridge's most complete discussion of Locke's legacy, *CL*, 2: nos. 381–85.

11. *Lects. 1795*, 225; my italics.

12. *Aids to Reflection*, 90.

13. Ibid., 91.

14. This seems backwards, as if Coleridge or his printer got the sequence re-
versed. It seems more likely that Coleridge meant to say that (1) a conscious will was
provable by common sense—Descartes's *Cogito*, in effect—and that (2) one might
through reason deduce a moral law of conscience to govern it. However, I have
cited the sentence as it appears in the source.

15. *Aids to Reflection*, 91.

16. Coleridge added that they were called the "pious" deists "in order to distinguish them from the Infidels [atheists] of the present age, who *persuade* themselves,
(for the thing itself is not possible) that they reject all faith."

17. *Aids to Reflection*, 92.

18. It is irrelevant here whether Coleridge was an Unitarian, since that denom-
ination continued to be a professedly "Christian" church, based on professedly
"Christian" ideas of the necessity of God's grace and the validity of personal repentance for sin, long after its schism from the Trinitarian churches. Even though it rejected the Athanasian definition of the Godhead, early-nineteenth-century Unitarianism retained a "Christian" soteriology despite its severance from the Trinitarian
mainstream of the Dissenting and Anglican Churches from which it was born.

19. Sir John Walsh, Bart. M.P., *Popular Opinions on Parliamentary Reform*, 4th ed.
(London: James Ridgeway, 1831). Original marginal notes by Coleridge on Walsh,
Popular Opinions, 9.

20. For instance, the right to petition the Crown for redress of grievance was
matched by the Crown's *publicly acknowledged* duty to listen to such petitions. There
was, in contrast, no "right" to speak to the king at any hour of the day one pleased,
because the Crown had never *publicly acknowledged* such a "right." Note that the existence or nonexistence of a "right" for such advocates had less to do with the sa-
voriness of the action than its legal pairing with a duty,

There were many things that were "good to do," or "good not to have done to one," that were not encoded in "rights." The line which separated "good things to have happen or not happen to one" (or "wicked and virtuous deeds") from "rights" per se was that "rights" always, without exception, existed in dyadic pairings with corresponding duties. One representative rights-duties dyad was the coupling of the right not to be assaulted with the duty not to assault, a duty backed up by the long arm of the law and its "remedies."

21. For instance, A's informal and one-time grant to B of a free passage across his property could not be redefined by B as a perpetual "right" of travel across those lands whenever he pleased unless there was a statute or set of cases that suggested that the one-time grant conferred such extended rights.

22. The phrase appeared in William Windham's speech to the Commons in a debate on the Game Laws on 4 March 1796; see *W*, 122.

23. There were, however, more careful critics of the concept of rights at either end of the rhetorical spectrum. Godwin had argued for duty, Burke for custom, and Bentham for the positive law.

24. *LS*, 64.

25. Ibid.; my italics. The full quotation without elision reads, "Can anything appear more equitable than the last proposition, the equality of Rights and Duties?"

26. *W*, no. 111, 17 March 1796, 122. Coleridge concluded his harangue with a personal barb against Windham. "This Wyndham is a professed imitator of Mr. Burke, whom he resembles as nearly as a stream of melted lead resembles the lava from Mount Vesuvius." Coleridge's early admiration for the conservative Whig Burke was not obscured by party affiliation: nor, it would seem, was his contempt for the reformer William Windham. Coleridge's assessments of politicians tended to be individual rather than ideological, even in that most partisan year of 1796.

27. One exempts utilitarianism as representing a communitarian theory of hedonism; in the cited principle, the greatest good of the greatest number. Note that Coleridge's vision of the "pursuit of happiness" is atomistic as long as it does not impinge on the rights of the agent himself and of others to be free from harm.

28. *TF*, essay no. 9, 12 October 1809, 2:130–31.

29. The idea of independent and autonomous spheres of action around each citizen is, of course, anathema to communitarian political thinkers, who have traditionally argued that both action and inaction have palpable effects on the community; there is, for them, no such thing as "minding one's own business," since the common good is the business of all.

30. Coleridge conceived of "the state" as incorporating all the institutional functionaries of social and political life. It was in this sense larger than "government," which pertained to those law creating institutions of Crown, Lords, and Commons. See *CS*, ch.1.

31. See William Lamont, *Godly Rule* (London: MacMillan, 1969).

32. *TF*, essay no. 9, 12 October 1809, 2:130–31.

33. *LS*, 63–64.

34. Perhaps a swipe at La Mettrie, author of the extreme materialist book *L'homme machine* (Man [is] a machine).

35. LS 64.

36. See Coleridge and Robert Southey, *The Fall of Robespierre*, book 1 (Cambridge: Banjamin Flower, 1794); also *Lects. 1795*, 35.

37. On Godwin's "disinterest" and emotional naivete, see Coleridge to John Thelwall, 13 May 1796, *CL*, no. 127, 1:215.

38. Coleridge to Robert Southey, 21 October 1794, CL, no. 65, 1:114; Coleridge's italics.

39. Volney had stated that "the science of government is the science of oppression." Coleridge used this passage frequently when denouncing the rigidity of abstract French principle in politics. See *Lects. 1795*, 183; *EOT* 3:211.

6. Science and Nature

1. E. P. Thompson and David Erdman argue that the significant break in Coleridge's ideas, his conservative retrenchment, dates from the *Morning Post* articles, which attacked Napoleon, British isolation, and the peace of Amiens. See David V. Erdman, "Coleridge as Editorial Writer," in *Power and Consciousness*, ed. Conor Cruise O'Brien and William Dean Vanech (London: University of London Press, 1969), 183–201; and E.P. Thompson, "Disenchantment or Default? A Lay Sermon," op. cit., 149–81.

2. *Hints Towards the Formation of a More Comprehensive Theory of Life* was dictated by Coleridge to Dr. James Gilman from 1816. It is likely that this short work was largely completed that year, however it was not published until after the deaths of both Coleridge and Gilman. It was first printed in London with an introduction by a Dr. Seth Watson M.D., by John Churchill Ltd., 1868. Watson's own prefatory remarks include the observation that "while C considered the 'unity of human nature' to include the body and the soul, that 'Life pertained only to the body.' But C continued 'Life' was not restricted to the body but was a term also applicable to the irreducible basis chemistry and the various forms of crystals" (8). Coleridge's own remarks suggested that he viewed "Life" as a physical but generative and active force. It was a "power" which acted in three different capacities: "in magnetism it acts as a line," "in electricity as a surface," and in "chemistry as a solid" (20). Coleridge's intention was to more completely define the principles that had been touched upon by Hunter and Abernathy and that contested a narrowly atomistic or corporeal view of the life of the body and, correspondingly, the life of nature.

3. This is not to say that other readers of the time were not capable of critical and independent readings; this was obviously the case. It is simply to suggest that Coleridge read critically *to an even greater degree than was common in his era*, because

he made a fetish of his "independence" from factions, parties, and schools of thought.

4. For a detailed account of Coleridge's scientific preoccupations, see Levere, "Coleridge, Chemistry, and the Philosophy of Nature"; and Levere, *Poetry Realized in Nature*. Also see Wylie, *Young Coleridge and the Philosophers of Nature*.

5. Coleridge had an earlier interest in medicine dating back to his "blue-coat" days at Christ's Hospital. During his school years he would often slip away to watch anatomy dissections at Guy's Hospital in London. His brother Luke was a surgeon and would allow Coleridge to accompany him on his hospital rounds in 1788. During this time Coleridge read "all the surgical and medical books he could procure." See James Dykes Campbell, *Samuel Taylor Coleridge* (London: MacMillan, 1894), 12.

6. Coleridge was particularly indebted to Schelling's *System of Transcendental Idealism* (1800) for his conception of "foresight." Charles DePaolo discusses Coleridge's theory of history and "futuricity," or a history of higher purpose directed to some providential and apocalyptic vision in *Coleridge: Historian of Ideas* (Victoria, B.C.: English Literary Studies, 1992), 20–27.

7. Coleridge to John Thelwall, 13 May 1796, *CL*, no. 127, 1:212–14.

8. Marginal notes to William Godwin's *Thoughts Occasioned by a Perusal of Dr Parr's Spital Sermon* (London, 1801). Coleridge's notes likely date from 1802 and are annotations in preparation for Robert Southey's review; see *M*, 2:848. Also, see previous note.

9. Godwin had argued that "the safety of the world can no otherwise be maintained, but by a constant and powerful check upon this principle [of unlimited population]. This idea demands at once [the reconsideration of] many maxims which have been long and unsusceptibly received into the vulgar code of morality, such as, that it is the duty of princes to watch for the multiplication of their subjects, and that a man or woman, who passes the term of life in a condition of celibacy, is to be considered as having failed to discharge one of the principle obligations they owe to the community. On the contrary it now appears to be rather the [case that a] man [who] rears a numerous family, that has in some degree transgressed the consideration he owes to public welfare" (Godwin, *Thoughts Occasioned*, 62).

10. Thomas Malthus, *An Essay On the Principle of Population and a View of its Past and Present Effects On Human Happiness* (London: J. Johnson, 1803). Coleridge's marginal note is in the British Library, C.44.g.2 and reprinted in *M*, 3:11.

11. *M*, 3:11.

12. To William Godwin, 29 March 1811, *CL*, no. 819, 3:315.

13. Kathleen Coburn observed, in her editions of the notebooks, that "of Adam Smith Coleridge never had a good word to say" (*CN*, 3:4267n). However, Coleridge's persistent attack on Smith and "Scotch Philosophers" was largely a way of rebuking political economy and its prudential moral calculus. There is much of *Wealth of Nations* and *Theory of Moral Sentiments* to be found in Coleridge's account of commercial society and the value of "progression."

14. For a discussion of "practical moralism" and the idea of propriety, see Nicholas Phillipson, "Adam Smith as Civic Moralist," in *Wealth and Virtue: The Shaping of Political Economy in the Scottish Enlightenment*, ed. Istvan Hont and Michael Ignatieff (Cambridge; Cambridge University Press, 1983), 179–202. Coleridge rejected Paley's "prudentialism" but was always looking for the "kernel to the shell" in moral philosophy or, as he framed it, "Legality precedes Morality."

15. Coleridge frequently identified this phrase with the philosophy of Locke and his eighteenth-century followers.

16. Coleridge to James Gooden, 14 January 1820, *CL*, no. 1223, 5:13.

17. The most complete characterization of Coleridge's philosophical synthesis may be G. N. G. Orsini's who emphasizes Coleridge's debt to Kant and the neo-Platonists in *Coleridge and German Idealism* (Carbondale: Southern Illinois University Press, 1969), 266–68 and passim.

18. Coleridge to James Gooden, 14 January 1820.

19. Ibid., and *CN*, 2:2784.

20. It is often forgotten that Jonathan Swift had made a stern and satirical use of the term "sweetness and light" in the comparison of the spider and the bee in the relatively obscure *Battle of the Books* before Matthew Arnold's better-known borrowing (and maudlin abuse) of the term in Arnold's far more influential *Culture and Anarchy*. *Culture and Anarchy* was directly influenced by Coleridge as well as by "Coleridgeans" such as F. D. Maurice.

21. Coleridge's acquaintance with the Kantian system, it should be stressed, was not slapdash or secondhand. He had read most of Kant's major works in the original German. Coleridge argued from the time of his first contacts with Kant that Kant's philosophy, taken as a whole, was virtually a complete system. He began his studies with the *Groundwork*, moving on afterwards to the *Critiques*. He recalled himself as having "enquired after the more popular works of Kant" and then "read them with delight." He "then read the prefaces to several of his systematic works, as the *Prolegomena* & c." He continued to be impressed: "here too [in these prefaces] every part, I understood, & that nearly the whole, was replete with sound and plain tho' bold and novel truths to me." He described his method of approaching Kant as "follow[ing] Socrates['s] Adage respecting Heraclitus—All I understand [of Heraclitus's philosophy] is excellent; and I am bound to presume the rest is at least worth the trouble of trying whether it be not equally so." While he was able to recommend Kant almost without qualification to a friend, he added that he did not extend this carte blanche to lesser authors. He "by no means recommend[ed] . . . an extension of [James Gooden's] philosophical researches *beyond* Kant" (Coleridge to James Gooden, 14 January 1820; my italics).

22. Deirdre Coleman, *Coleridge and "The Friend," 1809–1810* (Oxford: The Clarendon Press, 1988), 132–63.

23. See the introduction to this volume.

24. One cannot help wondering if Coleridge's suggestion that Kant's writings might provide his friend Gooden with a simple and comprehensive introduction to a doctrine of life was some sort of elaborate practical joke. Kant is still celebrated for his comprehensive address of most important questions, but he has never had a reputation as an *easy* road into philosophy. One longs to discover the degree of frustration and perplexity into which Gooden may have been plunged by his friend's advice to read all of Kant.

25. It is again useful to remind oneself of Coleridge's distinction between Ideas and concepts. Ideas were pure forms and structured reason; concepts existed in the understanding and were sensible renderings of Ideas rather than the things themselves. See *CS*, 12–13.

26. Coleridge to James Gooden, 14 January 1820, 13; my italics.

27. Ibid.

28. Ibid.; my italics.

29. This is similar to Kant's argument that the *ding an sich* could not be directly experienced as *noumena*.

30. The psychological implications of Kantian metaphysics are discussed at length by Gary Hatfield in "Empirical, Rational, and Transcendental Psychology: Psychology as Science and as Philosophy," in *The Cambridge Companion to Kant*, ed. Paul Guyer (Cambridge: Cambridge University Press, 1992), 200–227. See also J. Michael Young, "Functions of Thought and the Synthesis of Intuitions," in Guyer, op. cit., 101–22.

31. Coleridge does acknowledge that Platonism is inherent in some of Aristotle's own writings. Where teleology, poetics, and ethics are considered in light of some ultimate good, Coleridge was sympathetic. But he rejected uses of Aristotle's philosophy that over-emphasized man's animal nature in a manner that was narrowly materialistic or Epicurean. See Coleridge, *Philosophical Lectures*, ed. K. Coburn (London: Pilot Press, 1949) 176–78.

32. See Steven Shapin and Simon Schaffer, *Leviathan and The Air-Pump: Hobbes, Boyle, and the Experimental Life* (Princeton, N.J.: Princeton University Press, 1985), for an excellent discussion of how natural philosophers such as Hobbes decried the rise of experimental science among Boyle and the Royal Society men.

33. In general, the entirety of Leibniz's published correspondence with Samuel Clarke, which critiqued Newtonian philosophy, is one of the best and most reasonable discussions of this problem in the sciences.

34. *TT*, 2:312.

35. Henry Crabb Robinson, *Reminiscences and Correspondence of Henry Crabb Robinson*, ed. Thomas Stadler, 3 vols. (London: Macmillan, 1869), 1:163; my italics. Robinson's additional comments on Locke, though not germane to the central argument of this chapter, are of interest. He noted that Coleridge "praised[Bishop] Stillingfleet as Locke's opponent[;] he ascribed Locke's popularity to [Locke's] political

character[,] being the advocate of the new [Williamite/Hanoverian dynasty] against the old [Stuart] dynasty, to his religious character as a Christian [believer in Jesus as the Messiah/Savior], though but an Arian—for both parties, the Christian against the skeptics and the liberally-minded [Arians and Socinians] against the orthodox [Trinitarians], were glad to raise his reputation. . . . " Stillingfleet had, of course, entered into a lengthy debate with Locke on certain subjects broached in Locke's *Essay on Human Understanding*. Much of Stillingfleet's ire was directed at the fact that Locke's materialism seemed to undermine arguments for the existence of the Holy Trinity. One might consider him in the long scientific realist tradition from Hobbes to Leibnitz to Coleridge.

36. Ibid.

37. Coleridge's sympathies for Berkeley stemmed from his defense of the Existence and, in this regard, his extreme idealism. Coleridge was less impressed with reductive phenomenalism as a metaphysical system.

38. Robinson, *Reminiscences and Correspondence*, 1:163.

39. Coleridge, in describing the "Idea" in *Church and State*, wrote, "that which, contemplated *objectively* (*i.e.* as existing *externally* to the mind), we call a LAW; the same contemplated *subjectively* (*i.e.* as existing in a subject or mind), is an idea. Hence Plato often names ideas laws; and Lord Bacon, the British Plato, describes the Laws of the material universe as the Ideas in nature. Quod in natura *naturata* LEX, in natura naturante IDEA dicitur" (*CS*, 5) The reference to Bacon is: "These are the true marks of the Creator on his creation, as they are impressed and defined in matter, by true and exquisite lines" (*Novum Organum*, 1:124. Quoted in the original Latin by Hartley Nelson Coleridge: "that which in *created* nature is called a law, in creative nature is called an idea." *Natura naturata* denotes the world of phenomena, of materialized form, apprehended, according to Coleridge, by the understanding; *naturata naturans* denotes nature as the essence, the creative idea of the world, grasped only by reason. For Coleridge's discussion of Plato and Bacon, see *TF*, 2:467–68; also see Alice D. Snyder, ed. *S. T. Coleridge's Treatise on Method* (London: Constable, 1934), 37–51. As early as June 1803, Coleridge planned to show that the "Verulamian Logic" was "bona fide" to the same degree as the Platonic. See Coleridge to William Godwin, 4 June 1803, *CL*, no. 504, 2:947; and Alice D. Snyder, *Coleridge On Logic and Learning* (New Haven, Conn: Yale University Press, 1929; reprint, Folcroft, Penn.: Folcroft Library Editions, 1973), 65–66.

7. History and Life

1. Coleridge to C. A. Tulk, 12 January 1818, *CL*, no. 804, 4:1096. Coleridge attempted to distil this "philosophy" in his own *Theory of Life*, which he had substantially written or dictated by November 1816. In it he engaged with the dispute between William Lawrence and John Abernathy (see *CL*, 1186). In 1814 Abernathy had published *An Enquiry into the Probability and Rationality of Mr. Hunter's Theory of*

Life. This interpretation of the writings of John Hunter was attacked by Lawrence in his course of lectures at the Royal College of Surgeons in 1815 and published as *An Introduction to Comparative Anatomy and Physiology* in the following year. For a complete discussion of the controversy see Alice D. Snyder, *Coleridge On Logic and Learning: With Selections from the Unpublished Manuscripts* (New Haven, Conn.: Yale University Press, 1929; reprint, Folcroft, Penn.: Folcroft Library Editions, 1973), 16–25, 31–32. Kathleen Coburn has considered Coleridge's preoccupation with his "Theory of Life" in her edition of *The Philosophical Lectures* (1949). See lecture 12 and two "Monologues" that Coleridge dictated to his philosophical class in 1822, published posthumously in *Fraser's Magazine* in November and December 1835. See also J. H. Muirhead, *Coleridge as Philosopher* (London: Allen & Unwin, 1930), 118–36; and Craig W. Miller, "Coleridge's Concept of Nature," *Journal of the History of Ideas* 25, no. 1 (January–March 1964): 77–96.

2. Coleridge to J. H. Green, 25 May 1820, *CL*, no. 1235, 5:47.

3. Coleridge criticized the "political economists" (*LS*, 211), the "doctrine of utility"(*TF*, 1:425), and the "catechistic Bentham"(*EOT*, 3:261) with consistent vitriol. Whether he did justice to Bentham's actual ideas is less significant than the extent to which Coleridge considered the "mechanists, utilitarians, Benthamites, and modern Jacobins" as carriers of a common disease: like Malthus they were the purveyors of a "dreadful popular sophism"(*M*, 6).

4. Coleridge to Green, 5:47.

5. Trevor Levere, *Poetry Realized in Nature: S. T. Coleridge and Early-Nineteenth-Century Science* (Cambridge: Cambridge University Press, 1981). Levere's primary interest is on the significance of the medicophilosophical writings for Coleridge's theories of chemistry.

6. Coleridge to John Hookham Frere, 6 June 1826, *CL*, no. 1532, 6:583.

7. Coleridge to Edward Coleridge, 15 July 1825, *CL*, no. 1476, 5:; my italics.

8. Coleridge to Green, 5:47.

9. Coleridge to Frere, 6:583.

10. *TT*, 2:212.

11. Coleridge to John Hookham Frere, 6 June 1826, *CL*, no. 1532, 6:583.

12. Marginal note in the preface of Thomas Malthus, *An Essay on the Principle of Population, or, A View of its Past and Present Effects on Human Happiness* (London: J. Johnson, 1803), vii.

13. Marginal note in ibid.

14. Marginal note in ibid., 6.

15. Marginal note in ibid., 11.

16. Ibid.

17. I here employ the term "authentic" in the sense in which it has been used in twentieth-century existentialist ethics.

18. Ibid.

19. Coleridge to Green, 5:47.

20. Ibid.

21. Ibid.

22. Edward Smith Stanley, later thirteenth Earl of Derby, M.P. for Lancashire, argued that the bill would interfere with the natural law of labor supply. It passed as An Act for the Regulation of Cotton Mills, 59 Geo. III, c. 66, in 1819.

23. Coleridge to Henry Crabb Robinson, 3 May 1818.

24. Coleridge to Henry Crabb Robinson, 3 May 1818. "Remarks on the Objections which have been urged Against the Principles of Sir Robert Peel's Bill," in *Two Addresses on Sir Robert Peel's Bill* (London: April 1818; reprinted for private circulation, ed. and intro. Edmund Gosse (Hampstead: T. J. Wise, 1913), 17. Also, Coleridge to Henry Crabb Robinson, 3 May 1818.

25. Ibid., 18.

26. Ibid., 20.

27. When Coleridge described France, he referred of course not to the restored Bourbon monarchy and its aristocratic Catholic and *ultraroyaliste* revanchism. He referred rather to the darkest and most bloody of the years of the French Revolution and to the principles of the Jacobins and the mechanistic philosophes. Given the atmosphere of renewed British repression of "Jacobin" and "radical" activity in the United Kingdom in the years 1817 through 1819, this insult was doubly affronting to the factory owners. It was no great pleasure for a manufacturer to be lumped in with the Jacobins at any time; it must have been doubly humiliating in 1818.

28. "Remarks on the Objections," 19.

29. One of the traits which separates Coleridge's liberalism from Mill's is the latter's higher intolerance for self-inflicted harm. Coleridge suggested that the state might intervene to prevent self-damage.

30. "Remarks on the Objections," 19.

31. Ibid. Note that Coleridge's espousal of *contra bonus mores* reasoning in law, because it licensed the government to define what is in the best interest of public morals, seems to contradict his typical timidity about allowing the government any power to intrude into individual beliefs that affect no one else. The principle that he cites could have been used as handily, perhaps more handily, to justify either censorship of the sort exercised in 1795 or strict laws demanding adherence to the Anglican Church.

32. *TF*, 2:131.

33. "Remarks on the Objections," 25; my italics.

34. Ibid., 26.

35. Ibid.

8. Defending the Church

1. The Gordon Riots of 1780 were an anti-Catholic agitation. See I. R. Christie, *Wars and Revolutions: Britain, 1760–1815* (Cambridge Mass.: Harvard University Press,

1982), 40. Coleridge would have been more directly familiar with more recent Church and King Riots at Birmingham in 1791.

2. Examples from the 1780s and 1790s include Samuel Horsley and George Horne, but the most eloquent defense of the powers and prerogatives of the Church would come from the Tractarian debates of the 1830s, Keble's 1833 "Sermon on National Apostasy" being the most influential. Also see Jonathan Clark, *English Society, 1688–1832: Ideology, Social Structure, and Political Practice During the Ancien Regime* (Cambridge: Cambridge University Press, 1985); rev. ed.. *English Society, 1660–1832: Religion, Ideology, and Politics During the Ancien Regime* (Cambridge: Cambridge University Press, 2000), 382.

3. John Wade's *The Black Book: or Corruption Unmasked* (1820) was critically important in exposing the corrupt distribution of livings in the Anglican Church during the eighteenth century.

4. Coleridge returned with great regularity and attention to Hooker's *Of the Lawes of Ecclesiasticall Politie* (1593). For a complete discussion, see Dierdre Coleman on Coleridge's use of Hooker, Burke, and "the Conservative Tradition" in *Coleridge and "The Friend," 1809–1810* (Oxford: The Clarendon Press, 1988), 108–17. With regard to Coleridge's use of "the old divines," notably Robert Leighton, upon whom Coleridge based his *Aids to Reflection*, see Roberta Brinkley, ed., *Coleridge on the Seventeenth Century* (Durham N. C.: Duke University Press, 1955), 125–375 passim.

5. For a complete discussion, see G. V. Bennett, "Conflict in the Church," in *Essays in Modern Church History*, ed. G. V. Bennett and J. D. Walsh (Oxford: Oxford University Press, 1966), 155–74. Also see Roger Thomas, "Comprehension and Indulgence" in *From Uniformity to Unity, 1662–1962*, ed. Geoffrey F. Nuttal and Owen Chadwick (London: SPCK, 1962), 189–254.

6. Benjamin Hoadly, attempting to secure church loyalty to the Crown and block Jacobin resistance in his 1715 sermon "On the Kingdom of Christ," had, according to John Hunt, virtually delivered the church "bound and Gagged" to the state. Ironically, the attempt of the High Churchmen to censure, discipline, and silence Hoadly led to the infamous "Bangorian Controversy," a dispute so loud that it had caused George I to suspend the Convocation. Thus, in an attempt to flex the muscle of the church's Parliament, the High Church party accidentally led to the amputation of its legislative arm, the Convocation. For a detailed account of the Hoadly controversy, see John Hunt, *Religious Thought in England*, vol. 3 (London: Strahan and Co., 1873), 30–47.

7. Coleridge's admiration for Richard Watson, Bishop of Llandaff, as an exemplar of this "Low Church" party, can be traced back to 1796. He contemplated an arrangement of Watson's arguments in *An Apology for the Bible; in a series of letters addressed to T. Paine, Author of the Age of Reason, Part the Second, being an investigation of true and fabulous theology* (1796) in facing columns against Paine's own. See Coleridge to Rev. John Edwards, 20 March 1796, *CL*, no. 112, 1:193.

8. The use of the terms high-clerical and Puritan as synonyms may seem jarring. But, after all, the great Scottish Presbyterian theologian Andrew Melville had as great a concept of the powers of churchmen over kings as did the Anglican William Laud. What mattered was that both papists and Puritans in Hooker's time claimed a "higher power" than the state, an authority which would allow them as churchmen to obey or disobey the Crown and Parliament as they felt God wanted them to do rather than as the monarch demanded.

9. See A. W. Evans, *Warburton and the Warburtonians* (London: Oxford University Press, 1932; reprint, New Haven, Conn.: Yale University Press, 1972) for a discussion of a group of thinkers whose relationship to Warburton was more truly that of disciples.

10. John Colmer, in his introduction to the Bollingen edition of *Church and State*, assesses Coleridge's view of Warburtonian alliance thus: "It epitomized the spirit of bland eighteenth century equipoise and enabled the Church to retain its popularity as a compromise between the two extremes of Popery and Puritanism. So mechanical and utilitarian a concept of the constitutional balance made little appeal to Coleridge" (*CS*, xxxiv).

11. The Right Rev. George Horne considered himself a Tory, wrote a sermon on the "Christian King," and "ascended the ladder of Oxford patronage" to become Chaplain in Ordinary to George III and, under Pitt's patronage, Bishop of Norwich. See James J. Sack, *From Jacobite to Conservative: Reaction and Orthodoxy in Britain, c. 1760–1832* (Cambridge: Cambridge University Press, 1993), 115–17. Also see George Horne, *The Works of George Horne: To which are prefixed Memoirs of his Life, Studies and Writings by William Jones*, ed. William Jones (London, 1809).

12. Samuel Horsley, Bishop of Rochester, spoke out in favor of abolition, defending it against charges of Jacobinism. See Horsley, *Speeches in Parliament of Samuel Horsley, Late Bishop of St. Asaph* (London: C. J. & G. Rivington, 1830), 196–97. James Sack identifies Horsley as one of a group of "High Churchmen" who actively worked for abolition and the "reformation of principles" that Wilberforce's antivice campaign championed. Horsley's career, like Coleridge's, is suggestive of the broadness and the political and doctrinal complexity of the High Church party in the late eighteenth century. Horsley, who was attacked by his enemies as the Laud of the eighteenth century, preached for the comprehension of Calvinists and Arminians. See Horsley, *The Theological Works of Samuel Horsley* (London: Rees, Orme, Brown, Green & Longman, 1830), 6:124–25.

13. For example, Isaac Kramnick, *Bolingbroke and His Circle: The Politics of Nostalgia* (Cambridge, Mass.: Harvard University Press, 1968).

14. Notably James Bradley, "Whigs and Non-Conformists: 'Slumbering Radicalism' in English Politics, 1739–89," *Eighteenth Century Studies* 9 (1975): 1–27; and Robert Hole, *Puplits, Politics, and Public Order in England, 1760–1832* (Cambridge: Cambridge University Press, 1989).

15. See Owen Chadwick, *The Victorian Church* (New York: Oxford University Press, 1966), 544.

16. In chapter 9 of *Church and State*, Coleridge refers to the state as the "NATION dynamically considered . . . (in power according to the spirit, i.e. as an *ideal*, but not the less *actual* and abiding, unity)" (*CS*, 77).

17. See Claire Cross, "The Church in England, 1646–1660," in *The Interregnum: The Quest for Settlement 1646–1660*, ed. G. E. Aylmer (London: MacMillan, 1982), 99–120.

18. See Coleridge, "The Idea of The Christian Church," in *CS*, 113–28. N.B.: "The Christian Church is not a KINGDOM, REALM, (*royaume*), or STATE, (*sensu latiori*) of the WORLD" (114). This vision of a Christian church whose doctrinal kingdom is not of this world may owe something to Hoadly's thoughts on the same topic in the 1710s.

19. For a discussion of the liberal dimensions of Coleridge's conception of a national church and its subsequent impact on Arnold, Hare, Carlyle and F. D. Maurice, see C. R. Sanders, *Coleridge and the Broad Church Movement* (Durham, N.C.: Duke University Press, 1942), 56–71.

20. Ovid, *Epistulae ex Ponto*, 2.2.6.

21. John Morrow, in *Coleridge's Political Thought: Property, Morality, and the Limits of Traditional Discourse* (London: MacMillan, 1990), 64–65, has recently argued both for traditions of civic humanism and country-party ideology in Coleridge's political thought, particularly in the period from 1799 through 1802. He points out "that Coleridge had read Toland's edition of Harrington's *Works* which included *The Art of Law Giving*, but [that] there is nothing of this period to indicate Coleridge's response to Harrington's defense of national churches." Also see Morrow, *Coleridge's Political Thought*, 67–72.

22. Coleridge's account of progress must be distinguished from the Florentine civic-humanist model as advanced by Hans Barone and others in its account of the moral consequences of commercial freedom.

23. Coleridge did not give much thought to the exceptions to this rule in drained fens and polders, which in a sense were newly "created" lands. At any rate, except in the Netherlands, such "new" lands were inconsequential in comparison to the fixed sum of extant dry land. He also appears to have ignored colonialism and empire building as a means of expanding the available land on which a nation could establish permanence, although he could hardly have failed to consider this in regard to Ireland and the Irish peers after the Union of 1801.

24. An image that William Hogarth had used to criticize the nascent stock market during the Bubble crisis. Despite the fact that a farmer could be as easily wiped out and forced to sell his land by a series of bad harvests as a merchant could be bankrupted by a series of sunken ships, eighteenth- and nineteenth-century society held on to its prejudice which viewed land as "stable" and commerce as "volatile," in the face of much evidence to the contrary.

25. Compare this to economic models that stressed the complete and total replacement of "feudal" economies and values by "bourgeois" economies and values. On balance, Coleridge's theory better accounts for what Arno Mayer and others have described as the "Persistence of the Old Regime" in nineteenth-century Europe than does Marx's.

26. While Miller states the case in the extreme, Morrow is more measured in his account of "the country Coleridge." Arguing that "Country Party language retained a lasting place in Coleridge's political theory," he concludes that Coleridge argued in *Church and State* that there was an inevitable tendency "for the spirit of commercialism to infiltrate and erode the paternalistic and aristocratic ethos associated with landed property," and that "Coleridge was impressed mainly by the political benefits of commerce; he did not accept claims about its wider moral significance" (*Coleridge's Political Thought*, 157).

27. Isaac Kramnick identified this yearning for the good old days of agricultural and aristocratic hegemony in the works of Lord Bolingbroke and the first Tory party and its Country allies. See Isaac Kramnick, *Bolingbroke and His Circle*. To Kramnick's credit, he noted that Bolingbroke and other Country Party thinkers admired trade on an "Elizabethan" model of ships and goods but were most suspicious of the new economy of stocks and credit and debt that had sprung up in King William III's reign.

28. *CS*, 24.

29. Bolingbroke's philo-Elizabethanism is dealt with admirably in Kramnick's *Bolingbroke and his Circle*. Bolingbroke contended that the Elizabethan commercial classes had kept to producing solid, visible manufactured goods, engaged in "bluewater" trading instead of engaging in stocks and speculation, and—best of all—had refrained from the social climbing and estate buying which were the sport of the eighteenth-century "moneyed men."

30. *CS*, 24–25.

31. See, among others, Paul Langford, *A Polite and Commercial People* (Oxford: Oxford University Press, 1989); Lawrence Stone, "Social Mobility in England 1500–1700," *Past and Present* 33 (1966): 45–48; E. P. Thompson, "Eighteenth-Century Society: Class Struggle Without Class," *Social History* 3 (1978): 133–65; and Thompson, "Patrician Society, Plebeian Culture," *Journal of Social History* 7 (1974): 382–485.

32. *CS*, 25.

33. Ibid.

34. See Ross J. S. Hoffman and Paul Levack, eds., *Burke's Politics: Selected Writings and Speeches of Edmund Burke on Reform, Revolution, and War* (New York: Alfred A. Knopf, 1949; reprint, New York: Alfred A. Knopf, 1970), 526.

35. *CS*, 25.

36. Ibid., 26.

37. Ibid.

38. Ibid.

39. Ibid.

40. It is perhaps not too speculative to suggest that Coleridge's choice of words here may have meant to dig at Burke's defense of aristocratic "prejudice" and "prescription" in his writings.

41. J. G. A. Pocock, "The Varieties of Whiggism from Exclusion to Reform," in *Virtue, Commerce, and History: Essays on Political Thought and History, Chiefly in the Eighteenth Century* (Cambridge; Cambridge University Press, 1985), 292: "A Tory in the post-Burkean sense might be one who sternly maintained that an established clergy was needed to preserve both moral and cultural discipline, but he would have to believe in the conjunction of the clergy with the landed aristocracy and gentry in order to qualify as a conservative. If he did not, he might remain a Tory, but would tend to become a radical."

42. "What solemn humbug this modern Political Economy is!" (9 March 1833, *TT*, 1:348). "I have attentively read not only Sir James Steurt & Adam Smith; but Malthus and Riccardo—and found (i.e. I believe myself to have found) a multitude of sophisms but not a single just and important result which might [not] far more conveniently be deduced from the simplest principles of morality and commonsense." Coleridge to J. T. Coleridge, 8 May 1825, *CL*, 5:442. Coleridge was particularly critical of Malthus and Ricardo and drafted a note against Ricardo; see *CN*, 4:5330.

43. For a detailed account of the association of commerce, culture, and freedom, see Nicholas Phillipson, "Adam Smith as Civic Moralist," in *Wealth and Virtue: The Shaping of Political Economy in the Scottish Enlightenment*, ed. Istvan Hont and Michael Ignatieff (Cambridge: Cambridge University Press, 1983), 196.

44. Ibid., 179, 197.

45. Reed Browning, *Political and Constitutional Ideas of The Court Whigs*, (Baton Rouge: Louisiana State University Press, 1982).

46. Donald Winch, "The Burke-Smith Problem and Late-Eighteenth-Century Political and Economic Thought," *Historical Journal* 28, no. 1 (1985): 231–47.

47. *Lects. 1795*, 289. For a discussion of Coleridge's view of the "sudden breezes" of public opinion, see chapter one of this volume.

48. *CS*, 26–27.

49. Kevin Sharpe describes a growing concern as to the uncertainty produced by juridical innovation in late-sixteenth- and early-seventeenth-century England. See "History, English Law, and the Renaissance," in *Politics and Ideas in Early Stuart England* (London: Pinter Publishers Ltd., 1989), 174–181, esp. 179 for a discussion of the importance of feudal tenure for English law.

50. For a discussion of Hale's view with respect to the Common Law, convention, and compliance, see the chapter "Law, Social Union, and Collective Rationality," in Gerald Postema, *Bentham and the Common Law Tradition* (Oxford: The Clarendon Press, 1986), 77–80.

51. Coleridge had admitted in a notebook entry of May 1810 that Common Law rights connected to property were of greater authority than statute. They existed as a foundation for law—"an undoubted principle of the common-law of England which I most cheerfully admit to be of far higher authority than any particular Statute can be, and so constitutional" (*CN*, 3: no. 3836 18.240). This follows on a note with regard to Locke's extrapolation of a natural right to property through the conjoinment of labor with nature. Coleridge found the assertion of a natural right by virtue of this fact "ridiculous." But he did think there was an important argument to be made on moral grounds as a corollary of Locke's argument: "Truly ridiculous as Locke's notion of founding a right of Property on the sweat of a man's brow being mixed with the soil, yet taking it as a mere metaphor . . . it is both true & Important. . . . Closely connected with this argument but of far greater and more undoubted authority, is the necessity of individual action to moral agency, of an individual sphere to individual scheme of action, and of property to this—That without which a necessary end cannot be realized, is itself necessary—therefore, lawful" (*CN*, 3: no. 3835 18.239).

52. Again, from Coleridge's extended note on Locke: "That a man who by an act of his mind followed by the *fact* of bodily usufructure has impropertied an object, a spot of land for instance, has combined it with many parts of his being—his knowledge, memory, affections, a sense of right, above all—and that this field is not to him what it is to any other man" (*CN*, 3: no. 3835 18.239).

53. For a discussion of *ius* as *facultas* and *dominium*, see Richard Tuck, *Natural Rights Theories* (Cambridge: Cambridge University Press, 1979), 24–27.

54. See chapter four for Coleridge's conception of rights as dependent on duties.

55. *CS*, 24.

56. Ibid.

57. 15 June 1833, *TT*, 1:387. Also in a letter of about the same time, Coleridge wrote, regarding the manumission of slaves, "the true notion of human freedom— viz. that control from without must ever be *inversley* as the Self-government or control from within" (*CL*, 6:940).

58. *CL*, 6:940

59. See Pocock, *Virtue, Commerce, and History* (Cambridge: Cambridge University Press, 1985), 103, for a discussion of the changing meaning of "polis" and "burg" as loci for citizenship.

60. See Pocock's introduction to *Three British Revolutions: 1641, 1688, 1776* (Princeton, N.J.: Princeton University Press, 1980), 13–15.

61. *CS*, 42.

62. *CN*, 3:4058, 4418.

9. Attacking the Doctrine

1. "Tory theory" in this context refers to the hierarchical ancien régime described by Jonathan Clark as "Anglican, aristocratic and monarchial." Roy Porter

describes the Tory order as a world where priests were the nobility's agents of social control, while H. T. Dickinson emphasizes the doctrine of nonresistance, divine right, and indefeasible inheritance as the distinguishing features of what he describes as the "Tory ideology of order." See Clark, *English Society, 1688–1832: Ideology, Social Structure, and Political Practice During the Ancien Regime* (Cambridge: Cambridge University Press, 1985), rev. ed.. *English Society, 1660–1832: Religion, Ideology, and Politics During the Ancien Regime* (Cambridge: Cambridge University Press, 2000), 6–7; Roy Porter, *England in the Eighteenth Century* (London: Allen Lane, 1982), 76–80, Dickinson, *Liberty and Property: Political Ideology in Eighteenth Century England* (Oxford: Basil Blackwell, 1977), 21–24.

2. *CS*, 52.
3. Ibid.
4. Ibid.
5. *CN*, 3:4456.
6. Ibid., 4458.
7. *CS*, 55.
8. Ibid., 61.
9. Ibid.
10. Ibid..
11. *CN*, 3:3541.
12. *CS*, 61.
13. *Lects. 1795*, 49.
14. *CS*, 61; my italics.
15. *Lects. 1795*, 634.
16. *CS*, 61.
17. Ibid.
18. Ibid., 69.
19. Ibid.
20. *Lects. 1795*, 44.
21. *W*, 9.
22. *CS*, 69.
23. Ibid.
24. *Lects. 1795*, 44.
25. *CS*, 69.
26. Ibid., 70
27. Ibid., 71.
28. Ibid., 71.
29. Ibid., 53.
30. Ibid., 53; my italics.
31. Ibid., 54.
32. Ibid.
33. Ibid.

34. Ibid.
35. *CS*, Ibid., 49.
36. Ibid., 91.
37. Ibid., 85.
38. Ibid., 86.
39. Ibid.
40. *TF*, 2:67.
41. See ibid. for a discussion of "circulation" and "irrigation" with reference to the blood and water metaphors in Coleridge's discussion of "Taxes and Taxation."
42. *CS*, 86.
43. Ibid.
44. Ibid.
45. Ibid.
46. Ibid., 86–87.
47. Ibid., 87.
48. Ibid.; my italics.
49. Ibid., 25.
50. Ibid., 90.
51. Ibid.
52. Terra Japonica is derived from the wood of *acacia catecha* and is naturally high in astringents. Coleridge's friend Sir Humphry Davy had analyzed and discovered a tannin content in the Terra Japonica of up to 55 percent.
53. *CS*, 93.
54. Ibid., 94.
55. *CN*, 1:308n.
56. Crawfurd was a Scots physician trained in Edinburgh who became an Army doctor in the Northwest Provinces of India, a noted orientalist, a radical candidate in England, and an author of pamphlets on India and free trade. Crawford produced a number of pamphlets in addition to the *History of the Indian Archipelago*, 3 vols. (Edinburgh: A. Constable, 1820), including one specifically on "Free Trade and the East India Company" (1819). He advocated a liberalization of the East India Company monopoly and a diversification of colonial interests into the territories that would allow colonists to purchase land and to more closely ally their interests with the Indian people.
57. *CS*, 89.
58. Ibid.
59. Ibid.
60. Ibid.
61. Ibid.
62. Ibid., 46.
63. Ibid., 47.
64. Ibid., 47.

65. Ibid., 72.
66. Ibid.
67. Ibid.
68. Ibid., 92.
69. Ibid.

Conclusion. Regulating the Body Politic

1. *Lects. 1795*, 289.
2. *TF*, 2:67.

BIBLIOGRAPHY

Manuscript, Primary, or Printed Sources

Blackstone, William, *Commentaries on the Lawes of England*. 4 vols. Oxford: The Clarendon Press, 1765–69. Facsimile ed., intro. Stanley N. Katz. Chicago: University of Chicago Press, 2002.

Bolingbroke, Henry St. John. *The Craftsman*. Nos. 1–511, 5 December 1726–17 April 1736. London: R. Francklin, 1731–1737.

Burgh, James. *Political Disquisition*. London: Dilly, 1774.

Burke, Edmund. *Letters to a Noble Lord*. London, 1796.

——. *Reflections on the Revolution in France and on the Proceedings in Certain Societies in London Relative to that Event*. 1790. Reprint, ed. and intro. Conor Cruise O'Brien. Harmondsworth: Penguin Books, 1969.

Coleridge, Samuel Taylor. *Aids to Reflection*. Ed. Derwent Coleridge. 1825. Reprint, London: E. Moxton, 1854. *See also under The Collected Works of Samuel Taylor Coleridge*.

——. *Animae Poetae*. Ed. E. H. Coleridge. London: Heinemann, 1895.

——. *The Collected Works of Samuel Taylor Coleridge*. Bollingen Series 75. 14 vols. London and Princeton, N.J.: Routledge and Kegan Paul and Princeton University Press:

Vol. 1. *Lectures, 1795: On Politics and Religion*. Ed. Lewis Patton and Peter Mann. 1971 (*Lects. 1795*).

Vol. 2. *The Watchman*. Ed. Lewis Patton. 1970 (*W*).

Vol. 3. *Essays on His Times in the* Morning Post *and the* Courier. Ed. David V. Erdman. 3 books. 1978 (*EOT*).

Vol. 4. *The Friend*. Ed. B. Rooke. 2 vols. 1969 (*TF*).

Vol. 6. *Lay Sermons*. Ed. R. J. White. 1972 (*LS*).

Vol. 7. *Biographia Literaria*. Ed. James Engell and W. Jackson Bate. 2 books. 1983 (*BL*).

Vol. 9. *Aids to Reflection*. Ed. J. B. Beer. 1993.

Vol. 10. *On The Constitution of the Church and State*. Ed. John Colmer. 1976 (*CS*).

Vol. 12. *Marginalia*. Ed. George Whalley. 2 vols. 1984. Vol. 3, ed. George Whalley and H. J. Jackson, 1992 (*M*).

Vol. 13. *Logic*. Ed. J. R. de J. Jackson. 1981 (*L*).

Vol. 14. *Table Talk*. Ed. Carl Woodring. 2 vols. 1990 (*TT*).

——. *The Complete Poetical Works of Samuel Taylor Coleridge*. Ed. E. H. Coleridge. 2 vols. Oxford: The Clarendon Press, 1912.

——. *The Complete Works of Samuel Taylor Coleridge*. Ed. W. G. T. Shedd. 7 vols. New York: Harper Brothers, 1958.

——. *Confessions of an Inquiring Spirit*. First edition, ed. and intro. H. St. J. Hart, 1840. 3rd. ed. and intro. J. H. Green and notes by Sara Coleridge. London: A. & C. Black, 1853. Reprint, 1956.

——. *Grounds of Sir Robert Peel's Bill Vindicated*. Three drafts, 16 pages. Huntington Library, Manuscripts. HM 12122.

——. *Letters of Samuel Taylor Coleridge*. Ed. E. L. Griggs. 6 vols. Oxford: The Clarendon Press, 1956–71 (*CL*).

——. Notebook, 1799–1834. 754 pages. Huntington Library, Manuscripts. HM 8195.

——. Notebook, 1826–1832. 196 pages. Huntington Library, Manuscripts. HM 17299.

——. *The Notebooks of Samuel Taylor Coleridge*. Ed. Kathleen Coburn. 4 (of 6) vols. London: Routledge and Kegan Paul, 1957 (*CN*).

——. *On The Constitution of Church and State*. Ed. John Barrell. London: J. M. Dent and Sons Ltd., 1972.

——. *Philosophical Lectures*. Ed. K. Coburn. London: Pilot Press, 1949.

——. *Poems on Various Subjects*. London: J. Robinson and J. Cottle, 1796.

——. *Two Addresses on Sir Robert Peel's Bill*. London, April 1818. Reprinted for private circulation, ed. and intro. Edmund Gosse. Hampstead: T. J. Wise, 1913.

——. *Hints Towards the Formation of a More Comprehensive Theory of Life*. With James Gillman. 1816. Intro. Seth Watson. London: John Churchill Ltd., 1848.

Coleridge, Samuel Taylor, and Robert Southey. *The Fall of Robespierre*. Cambridge: Benjamin Flower, 1794.

Cottle, Joseph. *Early Recollections, Chiefly Relating to the Late Samuel Taylor Coleridge*. London, 1837.

Crawfurd, John. *History of the Indian Archipelago*. 3 vols. Edinburgh: A. Constable, 1820. Facsimile ed., 3 vols., London: Frank Cass and Co., 1967.

Cudworth, Richard. *The True Intellectual System of the Universe: The First Part: Wherein All the Reasons and Philosophy of Atheism is Confuted; and its Impossibility Demonstrated*. London, 1678. 2nd ed., 2 vols. London: Thomas Birch, 1743.

DeLolme, J. L. *The Constitution of England; or an account of the English Governemnt*, ed. William Hughes. London, 1771, 1834.

——. *The Rise and Progress of the English Constitution*. 2 vols. Ed. A. J. Stephens. London: John W. Parker, 1838. Facsimile ed., 2 vols., New York and London: Garden Press, 1978.

Furneaux, Philip. *Letters to the Hon. Mr. Justice Blackstone, concerning his Exposition of the Act of Toleration . . . in his Celebrated Commentaries of the Laws of England.* 2d ed. London: Thomas Cadell, 1771.

Godwin, William. *An Enquiry Concerning Political Justice, and Its Influence Concerning General Virtue and Happieness.* 2 vols. London: G. G. J. and G. Robinson, 1793. Facsimile ed., 2 vols., Oxford: Woodstock Books, 1992.

———. *Thoughts Occasioned by a Perusal of Dr Parr's Spital Sermon.* London, 1801.

———. *Uncollected Writings.* Ed. J. W. Markin and B. R. Pollin. Gainesville, Fla.: Scholars Facsimiles, 1966.

Green, J. H. *The Spiritual Philosophy: Based on the Teachings of the Late Samuel Taylor Coleridge.* London: MacMillan, 1865.

Hamilton, Alexander. *The Federalist Papers.* Ed. Charles Rossiter, intro. Charles R. Kessler. New York: Signet, 2003.

Hartley, David. *Observations on Man, His Frame, His Duty, and His Expectations.* 2 vols. London, 1749. 3rd ed., London: Joseph Johnson, 1791. Reprint, Poole: Woodstock Books, 1998.

Hooker, Richard. *Of the Lawes of Ecclesiasticall Politie.* Preface, books 1–4. 1593. Reprint, ed. Georges Edelen. Cambridge, Mass.: Harvard University Press, 1977.

Horne, George. *The Works of George Horne: To which are prefixed Memoirs of his Life, Studies and Writings by William Jones.* Ed. William Jones. London, 1809.

Horsley, Samuel. *Speeches in Parliament of Samuel Horsley, Late Bishop of St. Asaph.* London: C. J. & G. Rivington, 1830.

———. *The Theological Works of Samuel Horsley.* 9 vols. London: Rees, Orme, Brown, Green and Longman, 1830.

Kant, Immanuel. *The Critique of Pure Reason.* Trans., ed., and intro. Wolfgang Schwartz. Aalen, Germany: Scientia Verlag, 1982.

———. *Metaphysics of Morals.* Ed. and intro. Mary Gregor. Cambridge: Cambridge University Press, 1991.

LeGrice, Charles Valentine. "Recollections of Christ's Hospital." In *Elia Essays Which have appered under their signature in the London Magazine.* London: Printed for Taylor and Hessey Fleet Street, 1823.

Malthus, Thomas. *An Essay on the Principle of Population, or, A View of its Past and Present Effects on Human Happiness.* London: J. Johnson, 1803. Containing unpublished marginal notes by Coleridge, British Library, C.44. g.2.

Montesquieu. *Esprit des lois.* Book 11, chap. 6. Trans. and presented in a single edition by Francis Maseres. London: White & Payne, 1781.

Paine, Thomas. *The Rights of Man.* 1791–1792. Reprint, ed. and intro. Eric Foner. London: Pengiun Books, 1975.

Paley, William. *The Principles of Moral and Political Philosophy.* London: R. Faulder, 1785.

———. *Reasons for Contentment.* London: R. Faulder, 1793.

Parr, Dr. Samuel. *Metaphysical Tracts by English Philosophers of the Eighteenth Century*. London: Edward Lumley, 1837. Reprint, New York: Olms, 1974. London: Routledge/Thoemmes Press, 1992.

———. *Works of Samuel Parr*. 8 vols. London: Longmans, 1826.

Robinson, Henry Crabb. *Reminiscences and Correspondence of Henry Crabb Robinson*. Ed. Thomas Stadler. 3 vols. London: Macmillan, 1869.

Rousseau, Jean Jacques. *The Social Contract*. 1762. Reprint, ed. and trans., G. D. H. Cole. London: Everyman's Library, 1955.

Smith, Adam. *Theory of Moral Sentiments*. London, 1759. Facsimile edition, ed. A. L. Macfie and D. D. Raphael. Oxford: Oxford University Press, 1976.

Southey, Robert. *New Letters of Robert Southey*. Ed. Kenneth Curry. 2 vols. New York: Columbia University Press, 1965.

Spence, Thomas. *The Political Works of Thomas Spence*. Ed. H. T. Dickinson. Newcastle upon Tyne: Avero, 1982.

Walsh, Sir John, Bart. M.P. *Popular Opinions on Parliamentary Reform*. 4th ed. London: James Ridgeway, 1831.

Secondary Sources

Abbey, Charles John. *The English Church and its Bishops, 1700–1800*. 2 vols. London: Longmans, Green and Co., 1887.

Abbey, Charles John, and John H. Overton. *The English Church in the Eighteenth Century*. London: Longmans, Green and Co., 1878. 2d ed., rev. and abridged, 1887.

Abrams, Meyer H. "Coleridge and the Romantic Vision of the World." In *Coleridge's Variety: Bicentenary Studies*, ed. John Beer, 101–33. London: MacMillan, 1974.

———. *The Mirror and the Lamp*. New York: Oxford University Press, 1953.

———. *Natural Supernaturalism*. London: Oxford University Press, 1969.

Allen, Peter. "Morrow on Coleridge's *Church and State*." *Journal of the History of Ideas* 49 (1988): 485–89.

———. "S. T. Coleridge's *Church and State* and the Idea of an Intellectual Establishment." *Journal of the History of Ideas* 46 (1985): 89–106.

Ashcraft, Richard. *Revolutionary Politics and John Locke's "Two Treatises of Government."* Princeton, N.J.: Princeton University Press, 1986.

Ashton, Rosemary. *The German Idea: Four English Writers and the Reception of German Thought, 1800–1860*. Cambridge: Cambridge University Press, 1980.

———. *The Life of Samuel Taylor Coleridge: A Critical Biography*. Cambridge, Mass.: Blackwell Publishers, 1996.

Bailyn, Bernard. *The Ideological Origins of the American Revolution*. Cambridge, Mass.: Harvard University Press, 1967.

Barfield, Owen. *What Coleridge Thought*. Middletown, Conn.: Wesleyan University Press, 1971.

Barth, J. Robert. *Coleridge and Christian Doctrine*. Cambridge, Mass.: Harvard University Press, 1969.

Beeley, Harold. "The Political Thought of S. T. Coleridge." In *Studies By Several Hands on the Hundredth Anniversary of His Death*, ed. Edmund Blunden and E. L. Griggs, 151–75. London: Constable, 1934.

Bennett, Gareth Vaughn. "Conflict in the Church." In *Essays in Modern Church History in Memory of Norman Sykes*, ed. Gareth Vaughn Bennett and John Dixon Walsh, 155–74. London: Adam and Charles Black, 1966.

Berlin, Isaiah. *Four Essays On Liberty*. New York: Oxford University Press, 1970.

———. *Herder and Vico*. New York: The Viking Press, 1976.

Blunden, E., and E. L. Griggs, eds. *Coleridge: Studies by Several Hands*. London: Constable, 1934.

Bongie, Laurence L. *David Hume: Prophet of the Counter-Revolution*. Oxford: The Clarendon Press, 1965.

Boulger, James D. *Coleridge as Religious Thinker*. New Haven: Yale University Press, 1961.

Boulton, James. *The Language of Politics in the Age of Wilkes and Burke*. London: Routledge and Kegan Paul, 1963.

Bradley, James. "Whigs and Non-Conformists: 'Slumbering Radicalism' in English Politics, 1739–89. *Eighteenth Century Studies* 9 (1975): 1–27.

Brinkley, Roberta, ed. *Coleridge on the Seventeenth Century*. Durham, N.C.: Duke University Press, 1955.

Brinton, Crane. *English Political Thought in the Nineteenth Century*. London: Benn, 1933.

———. *The Political Ideas of the English Romanticists*. London: Oxford University Press, 1926.

Brown, P. A. *The French Revolution in English History*. Oxford: Frank Cass, 1918.

Browning, Reed. *Political and Constitutional Ideas of The Court Whigs*. Baton Rouge and London: Louisiana State University Press, 1982.

Brooks, Linda. *The Menace of the Sublime to the Individual Self: Kant, Schiller, Coleridge, and the Disintegration of Romantic Identity*. Lewiston, N.Y.: Edwin Mellon Press, 1995.

Burrow, J. W. *Whigs and Liberals: Continuity and Change in English Political Thought*. Oxford: The Clarendon Press, 1988.

———, ed. *Wilhelm Von Humboldt: The Limits of State Action*. Cambridge: Cambridge University Press, 1969.

Butler, Marilyn. "Godwin, Burke, and *Caleb Williams*." *Essays in Criticism* 32 (1982): 237–57.

———. *Romantics, Rebels, and Reactionaries: English Literature and its Background, 1760–1830*. Oxford: Oxford University Press, 1981.

———, ed. *Burke, Paine, Godwin, and the Revolution Controversy*. Cambridge: Cambridge University Press, 1984.

Calleo, David. *Coleridge and the Idea of the Modern State.* New Haven, Conn.: Yale University Press, 1966.

Campbell, James Dykes. "Coleridge on Quaker Principles." *The Athenaeum* 3438 (16 September 1893): 385–86.

———. *Samuel Taylor Coleridge.* London: MacMillan, 1894.

Cannon, John. *Parliamentary Reform, 1640–1832.* Cambridge: Cambridge University Press, 1973.

Chadwick, Owen. *The Victorian Church.* New York: Oxford University Press, 1966.

Christiansen, Jerome. *Coleridge's Blessed Machine of Language.* Ithaca, N.Y.: Cornell University Press, 1981.

———. "Once an Apostate Always an Apostate." *Studies in Romanticism* 21 (Fall 1982): 461–64.

Christie, I. R. *Myth and Reality in Late-Eighteenth-Century British Politics, and Other Papers.* Berkeley: University of California Press, 1970.

———. *Stress and Stability in Late-Eighteenth-Century Britain: Reflections on the British Avoidance of Revolution.* Oxford: The Clarendon Press, 1985.

———. *Wars and Revolutions: Britain, 1760–1815.* Cambridge, Mass.: Harvard University Press, 1982.

Claeys, Gregory. *Machinery, Money and the Millennium.* Princeton N.J.: Princeton University Press, 1987.

———. *Thomas Paine: Social and Political Thought.* Boston and London: Unwin Hyman, 1989.

Clark, J. C. D. *English Society, 1688–1832: Ideology, Social Structure, and Political Practice During the Ancien Regime.* Cambridge: Cambridge University Press, 1985. Rev. ed.. *English Society, 1660–1832: Religion, Ideology, and Politics During the Ancien Regime.* Cambridge: Cambridge University Press, 2000.

———. *The Language of Liberty, 1660–1832: Political Discourse and Social Dynamic in the Anglo- American World.* Cambridge: Cambridge University Press, 1994.

———. *Samuel Johnson: Literature, Religion, and English Cultural Politics from the Restoration to Romanticism.* Cambridge: Cambridge University Press, 1994.

Clark, Jonathan, and Howard Erskine-Hill, eds. *Samuel Johnson in Historical Context.* New York and Basingstoke: Palgrave, 2002.

Cobban, Alfred. *Edmund Burke and the Revolt Against the Eighteenth Century: A Study of the Political Context and Social Thinking of Burke, Wordsworth, Coleridge, and Southey.* London: George Allen and Unwin, 1929.

———. *The Debate on The French Revolution, 1789–1800.* London: Nicholas Kaye, 1950.

Coburn, Kathleen. "Coleridge and Restraint." *University of Toronto Quarterly* 38 (1968–69): 233–47.

———. *Experience Into Thought: Perspectives in the Coleridge Notebooks.* Toronto: University of Toronto Press, 1979.

———. "Poet Into Public Servant." *Transactions of the Royal Society of Canada,* 3d ser., 54 (1960): 1–11.

——. *The Self-Conscious Imagination*. London: Oxford University Press, 1974.

Cohler, Anne, Basia Miller, and Harold Stone. *Montesquieu: The Spirit of the Laws*. Cambridge: Cambridge University Press, 1989.

Coleman, Deirdre. *Coleridge and "The Friend," 1809–1810*. Oxford: The Clarendon Press, 1988.

Colley, Linda. *Britons: Forging the Nation, 1707–1837*. New Haven, Conn., and London: Yale University Press, 1992.

Colmer, John. *Coleridge: Critic of Society*. Oxford: The Clarendon Press, 1959.

——. "Coleridge and Politics." In *Writers and Their Background: S. T. Coleridge*, ed. R. L. Brett, 244–70. London: G. Bell, 1971.

Cone, Carl. *The English Jacobins: Reformers in Late Eighteenth Century England*. New York: Scribner and Sons, 1968.

Cookson, J. E. *The Friends of Peace*. Cambridge: Cambridge University Press, 1982.

——. *Lord Liverpool's Administration: The Crucial Years, 1815–1822*. Hamden, Conn.: Archon Books, 1975.

Courtney, C. P. *Montesquieu and Burke*. Oxford: Basil Blackwell, 1963.

Crimmins, James E. *Secular Utilitarianism*. Oxford: The Clarendon Press, 1990.

Cross, Claire. "The Church in England, 1646–1660." In *The Interregnum: The Quest for Settlement, 1646–1660*, ed. G. E. Aylmer, 99–120. London: MacMillan, 1972. Revised ed., 1974.

Deen, Leonard W. "Coleridge and the Radicalism of Religious Dissent." *Journal of English and Germanic Philology* 61 (1962): 496–510.

DePaolo, Charles. *Coleridge: Historian of Ideas*. Victoria, B.C.: University of Victoria Press, 1992.

Derry, John. *Dr. Parr: A Portrait of the Whig Dr. Johnson*. Oxford: Oxford University Press, 1966.

——. *Politics in the Age of Fox, Pitt, and Liverpool: Continuity and Transformation*. New York: St. Martin's Press, 1990.

Dickinson, H. T. "Benjamin Hoadley, 1676–1761: Unorthodox Bishop." *History Today* 25 (1975): 348–55.

——. *British Radicalism and the French Revolution*. Oxford: Basil Blackwell, 1985.

——. *Liberty and Property: Political Ideology in Eighteenth-Century England*. Oxford: Basil Blackwell, 1977.

Dietze, Gottfried. *Liberalism Proper and Proper Liberalism*. Baltimore: Johns Hopkins University Press, 1985.

Dinwiddy, J. R. *Bentham*. Oxford: Oxford University Press, 1989.

——. *From Luddism to the First Reform Bill*. Oxford: Basil Blackwell, 1986.

——. "Interpretations of Anti-Jacobinism." In *The French Revolution and British Popular Politics*, ed. Mark Philp, 38–49. Cambridge: Cambridge University Press, 1991.

——. *Radicalism and Reform in Britain, 1740–1850*. London: The Hambledon Press, 1992.

Durkheim, Émile. *Montesquieu and Rousseau: Forerunners of Sociology*. Trans. Ralph Manheim. Ann Arbor: University of Michigan Press, 1960.

Duffey, Eamon. "Primitive Christianity Revived: Religious Renewal in Augustan England." *Studies in Church History* 14 (1978): 287–300.

Edwards, Charles S. *Hugo Grotius The Miracle of Holland: A Study in Political and Legal Thought.* Chicago: Nelson-Hall, 1928.

Eisenach, E. J. "Hobbes on Chuch and State and Religion." *History of Political Thought* 3 (1982): 215–43.

———. *Two Worlds of Liberalism: Religion and Politics in Hobbes, Locke, and Mill.* Chicago: University of Chicago Press, 1981.

Ehrman, John. *The Younger Pitt: The Reluctant Transition.* Vol. 2 of *The Younger Pitt.* Stanford, Calif.: Stanford University Press, 1983.

Erdman, David V. "Coleridge as Editorial Writer." In *Power and Consciousness*, ed. Conor Cruise O'Brien and W. D. Vanech, 183–201. London: University of London Press, 1969.

———. "Coleridge on Coleridge: The Context (and Text) of His Review of 'Mr. Coleridge's Second Lay Sermon.'" *Studies in Romanticism* 1 (Fall 1961): 47–64.

Evans, A. W. *Warburton and the Warburtonians.* London: Oxford University Press, 1932. Reprint, New Haven, Conn.: Yale University Press, 1972.

Everest, Kelvin. *Coleridge's Secret Ministry: The Context of the Conversation Poems, 1795–1798.* Brighton: Harvester Press, 1979.

———. "Coleridge's Secret Ministry: Historical Reading and Editorial Theory." In *Samuel Taylor Coleridge and the Sciences of Life*, ed. Nicholas Roe, 297–319. Oxford: Oxford University Press, 2001.

Fisch, M. H. "The Coleridges, Dr. Prati, and Vico." *Modern Philology* 61 (August 1943: 111–22.

Fischer, Michael. "Coleridge and Politics." *Studies in Romanticism* 21, no. 3 (1981): 457–60.

———. "Marxism and English Romanticism: The Persistence of a Movement." *Romanticism Past and Present* 6, no. 1 (1982): 364–401.

———. "Morality and History in Coleridge's Political Theory." *Studies in Romanticism* 21 (Fall 1982): 457–60.

Flathman, Richard E. *The Philosophy and Politics of Freedom.* Chicago: University of Chicago Press, 1987.

Fletcher, F. T. H. *Montesquieu and English Politics, 1750–1800.* London: Edward Arnold and Co., 1939.

Fontana, Biancamaria. *Rethinking the Politics of Commercial Society.* Cambridge: Cambridge University Press, 1985.

Foord, Archibald. *His Majesty's Opposition, 1714–1830.* Oxford: Clarendon Press, 1964.

Forbes, Duncan. *The Liberal Anglican Idea of History.* Cambridge: Cambridge University Press, 1952.

———. "Natural Laws and the Scottish Enlightenment." In *The Origin and Nature of the Scottish Enlightenment*, ed. R. H. Campbell and A. S. Skinner eds., 186–204. Edinburgh: Edinburgh University Press, 1982.

Ford, Jennifer. *Coleridge on Dreaming: Romanticism, Dreams, and the Medical Imagination*. Cambridge: Cambridge University Press, 1998.

Freeman, Michael. *Edmund Burke and the Critique of Political Radicalism*. Oxford: Basil Blackwell, 1980.

Fruman, Norman. *Coleridge: The Damaged Archangel*. London: George Allen and Unwin, 1972.

Fulford, Tim. *Romanticism and Masculinity: Gender, Politics, and Poetics in the Writings of Burke, Coleridge, Cobbett, Wordsworth, DeQuincy, and Hazlett*. New York: St. Martin's Press, 1999.

Gascoigne, John. *Cambridge in the Age of the Enlightenment: Science, Religion, and Politics from the Restoration to the French Revolution*. Cambridge: Cambridge University Press, 1989.

Goldie, Mark. "The Roots of True Whiggism, 1688–94." *The History of Political Thought* 1, no. 195 (1980): 195–236.

Goodwin, Albert. *The Friends of Liberty*. Cambridge, Mass.: Harvard University Press, 1979.

Graham, Walter. "The Politics of the Greater Romantic Poets." *Publications of the Modern Language Association* 36 (1921): 60–78.

Green, Thomas Hill. *The Political Theory of T. H. Green*. Ed. and intro. John R. Rodman. New York: Appleton-Century-Crofts, 1964.

Greene, Donald J. *The Age of Exuberance: Backgrounds to Eighteenth-Century English Literature*. New York: McGraw-Hill, 1970.

———. *Samuel Johnson's Politics*. 2nd ed. Athens: University of Georgia Press, 1990.

Gunn, J. A. W. *Beyond Liberty and Property: The Process of Self-Recognition in Eighteenth-Century Political Thought*. Kingston, Ont.: MacGill-Queen's University Press, 1983.

———. *Politics and the Public Interest in the Seventeenth Century*. Toronto: University of Toronto Press, 1969.

Guyer, Paul. *The Cambridge Companion to Kant*. Cambridge: Cambridge University Press, 1992.

Halevy, Elie. *The Growth of Philosophic Radicalism*. London: Faber & Faber, 1934. Reprint, 1972.

———. *The Liberal Awakening, 1815–1830*. Vol. 2 of *A History of the English People in the Nineteenth Century*. London: Ernest Benn, Ltd., 1926.

Hancock, A. E. *The French Revolution and the English Poets*. 1899. Reprint, New York: Kennikat Press, 1967.

Haney, David P. *The Challenge of Coleridge: Ethics and Interpretation in Modern Philosophy*. University Park, Penn.: Penn State University Press, 2001.

Hart, H. L. A. *The Concept of Law*. Oxford: Oxford University Press, 1961.

———. *Essays On Bentham*. Oxford: Oxford University Press, 1982.

Hatfield, Gary. "Empirical, Rational, and Transcendental Psychology: Psychology as Science and as Philosophy." In *The Cambridge Companion to Kant*, ed. Paul Guyer, 200–227. Cambridge: Cambridge University Press, 1992.

Hay, Carla. *James Burgh: Spokesman for Reform in Hanoverian England.* Washington, D.C.: University Press of America, 1977.

Hazlitt, William. *The Examiner.* Ed. Charles Lamb. 1816. Reprinted in *Coleridge:The Critical Heritage,* ed. J. de J. Jackson, 205–9. London: Routledge and Kegan Paul, 1970.

Hedley, Douglas. *Coleridge, Philosophy and Religion: Aids to Reflection and the Mirror of the Spirit.* Cambridge: Cambridge University Press, 2000.

Hewitt, Regina. *The Possibilities of Society: Wordsworth, Coleridge, and the Sociological View of English Romanticism.* Albany, N.Y.: State University of New York Press, 1997.

Hirschberg, D. R. "The Government and Church Patronage in England, 1660–1760." *Journal of British Studies* 20, no. 1 (1980): 109–38.

Hoffman, Ross J. S., and Paul Levack, eds. *Burke's Politics: Selected Writings and Speeches of Edmund Burke on Reform, Revolution, and War.* New York: Alfred A. Knopf, 1949. Reprint, New York: Alfred A. Knopf, 1970.

Hole, Robert. *Pulpits, Politics, and Public Order in England. 1760–1832.* Cambridge: Cambridge University Press, 1989.

Holmes, Richard. *Coleridge: Darker Reflections.* London: Harper Collins, 1998.

———. *Coleridge: Early Visions.* London: Hodder & Stoughton, 1989.

Hont, Istvan, and Michael Ignatieff, eds. *Wealth and Virtue:The Shaping of Political Economy in the Scottish Enlightenment.* Cambridge: Cambridge University Press, 1983.

Howard, Claud. *Coleridge's Idealism.* Boston: The Gorham Press Inc., 1978.

Hulliung, Mark. *Montesquieu and the Old Regime.* Berkeley: University of California Press, 1976.

Hunt, John. *Religious Thought in England.* Vol. 3. London: Strahan and Co., 1873.

Jack, Malcolm. *Corruption and Progress.* New York: AMS Press, 1989.

Jackson, J. R. de J., ed. *Coleridge: The Critical Heritage.* London: Routledge and Kegan Paul, 1970.

Jones, J. R. *The First Whigs.* Oxford: Oxford University Press, 1961.

Kennedy, William F. *Humanist Versus Economist:The Economic Thought of Samuel Taylor Coleridge.* Berkeley: University of California Publications in Economics, vol. 27, 1958.

Knights, Ben. *The Idea of the Clerisy in the Nineteenth Century.* Cambridge: Cambridge University Press, 1978.

Kramnick, Isaac. *Bolingbroke and His Circle:The Politics of Nostalgia.* Cambridge, Mass.: Harvard University Press, 1968.

———. "On Anarchy in the Real World: William Godwin and Radical England." *American Political Science Review* 66 (1972): 114–28.

———. *Republicanism and Bourgeois Radicalism: Political Ideology in Late-Eighteenth-Century England and America.* Ithaca, N.Y.: Cornell University Press, 1990.

Lacey, Michael J., and Knud Haakonssen. *A Culture of Rights.* Cambridge: Cambridge University Press, 1991.

Langford, Paul. *A Polite and Commercial Society*. Oxford: Oxford University Press, 1989.

Lamont, William. *Godly Rule*. London: MacMillan, 1969.

Lapp, Robert Keith. *Contests for Cultural Identity: Hazlitt, Coleridge, and the Distresses of the Regency*. Detroit: Wayne State University Press, 1999.

Laprade, W. T. *Public Opinion and Politics in Eighteenth-Century England*. New York: MacMillan, 1936.

Larkin, Paschal. *Property in the Eighteenth Century*. Dublin: Cork University Press, 1930.

Leask, Nigel. *The Politics of Imagination in Coleridge's Critical Thought*. Basingstoke: MacMillan, 1988.

Levere, Trevor. "Coleridge, Chemistry, and the Philosophy of Nature." *Studies in Romanticism* 16, no. 3 (Summer 1977): 349–80.

———. *Poetry Realized in Nature: S. T. Coleridge and Early-Nineteenth-Century Science*. Cambridge: Cambridge University Press, 1981.

Lieberman, David. "The Legal Needs of a Commercial Society: The Jurisprudence of Lord Kames." In *Wealth and Virtue: The Shaping of Political Economy in the Scottish Enlightenment*, ed. Istvan Hont and Michael Ignatieff, 203–34. Cambridge: Cambridge University Press, 1983.

———. *The Province of Legislation Determined: Legal Theory in Eighteenth-Century Britain*. Cambridge: Cambridge University Press, 1989.

Locke, Don. *A Fantasy of Reason: The Life and Thought of William Godwin*. London: Routledge and Kegan Paul, 1980.

Lottes, Günther. "Radicalism, Revolution, and Political Culture: An Anglo-French Comparison." In *The French Revolution and British Popular Politics*, ed. Mark Philp. Cambridge: Cambridge University Press, 1991.

Lowes, John Livingston. *The Road to Xanadu*. Boston: Houghton Mifflin, 1927.

Macpherson, C. B. *The Political Theory of Possessive Individualism from Hobbes to Locke*. Oxford: The Clarendon Press, 1962.

McFarland, Thomas. "Coleridge and Jacobinism." Unpublished paper delivered at All Souls College, Oxford, November 1986.

———. *Coleridge and the Pantheist Tradition*. Oxford: The Clarendon Press, 1969.

———. *Romanticism and the Forms of Ruin*. Princeton, N.J.: Princeton University Press, 1981.

Mendalow, Jonathan. *The Romantic Tradition in British Political Thought*. London: Croom Helm, 1986.

Mill, John Stuart. *Autobiography*. 4th ed. London: Longmans, Green, Reader & Dyer, 1874.

———. *Mill on Bentham and Coleridge*. Ed. F. R. Leavis. London: Chatto and Windus, 1950. Reprint, Cambridge: Cambridge University Press, 1980.

Miller, Craig W. "Coleridge's Concept of Nature." *Journal of the History of Ideas* 25, no. 1 (January–March 1964): 77–96.

Miller, J. T. *Ideology and Enlightenment: The Political and Social Thought of Samuel Taylor Coleridge*. New York: The Garland Press, 1988.

Milsom, S. F. C. *Studies in The History of Common Law*. London: The Hambledon Press, 1985.

Mitchell, L. G. *Charles James Fox*. Oxford: Oxford University Press, 1992.

Modiano, Raimonda. "Historicist Readings of the Rhyme of the Ancient Mariner." In *Samuel Taylor Coleridge and the Sciences of Life*, ed. Nicholas Roe, 271–96. Oxford: Oxford University Press, 2001.

Morrow, John. *Coleridge's Political Thought: Property, Morality, and the Limits of Traditional Discourse*. London: MacMillan, 1990.

———. "The National Church in Coleridge's *Church and State*: A Response to Allen." *Journal of the History of Ideas* 47, no. 4 (1986).

Muirhead, J. H. *Coleridge as Philosopher*. London: George Allen and Unwin, 1930.

———. "Metaphysician or Mystic." In *Coleridge: Studies by Several Hands*, ed. Edmund Blunden and E. L. Griggs. London: Constable, 1934.

———. *The Platonic Tradition in Anglo-Saxon Philosophy*. London: Allen & Unwin, 1931.

———. *The Service of the State: Four Lectures on the Political Teaching of T. H. Green*. London: John Murray, 1908.

Newman, John Henry. *The Office and Work of Universities*. London: Longmans, 1856.

Nozick, Robert. *Anarchy, State, and Utopia*. Oxford: Basil Blackwell, 1974.

Oakshott, Michael, *Rationalism in Politics*. London: Methuen, 1962.

O'Gorman, Frank. *Edmund Burke*. Bloomington: Indiana University Press, 1973.

———. *The Rise of Party in England*. London: George Allen and Unwin, 1975.

Orsini, G. N. G. *Coleridge and German Idealism*. Carbondale: Southern Illinois University Press, 1969.

O'Sullivan, Noël. *Conservatism*. London: J. M. Dent, 1976.

Pangle, Thomas. *The Spirit of Modern Republicanism*. Chicago: University of Chicago Press, 1987.

———. *Montesquieu's Philosophy of Liberalism*. Chicago: University of Chicago Press, 1973.

Perkins, Mary Anne. *Coleridge's Philosophy: The Logos as Unifying Principle*. Oxford: The Clarendon Press, 1994.

Perry, Seamus. *Coleridge and the Uses of Division*. Oxford: Oxford University Press, 1999.

Phillipson, Nicholas. "Adam Smith as Civil Moralist." In *Wealth and Virtue: The Shaping of Political Economy in the Scottish Enlightenment*, ed. Istvan Hont and Michael Ignatieff, 179–202. Cambridge: Cambridge University Press, 1983.

Phillipson, Nicholas, and Quentin Skinner. *Political Discourse in Early Modern Britain*. Cambridge: Cambridge University Press, 1993.

Philp, Mark. *Godwin's Political Justice*. Ithaca, N.Y.: Cornell University Press, 1986.

———, ed. *The French Revolution and British Radical Politics*. Cambridge: Cambridge University Press, 1991.

Pocock, J. G. A. *The Ancient Constitution and The Feudal Law*. Cambridge: Cambridge University Press, 1957. Updated ed., Cambridge: Cambridge University Press, 1987.

——. *Barbarism and Religion.* 2 Vols. Cambridge: Cambridge University Press, 1999.

——. "Cambridge Paradigms and Scotch Philosophers: A Study of the Relations Between the Civic Humanist and the Civil Jurisprudential Interpretation of Eighteenth-Century Social Thought." In *Wealth and Virtue: The Shaping of Political Economy in the Scottish Enlightenment,* ed. Istvan Hont and Michael Ignatieff, 235–52. Cambridge: Cambridge University Press, 1983.

——. *Language, Politics, and Time.* London: University of Chicago Press, 1960. 2nd ed., 1989 .

——. *The Machiavellian Moment: Florentine Political Thought and the Atlantic Republican Tradition.* Princeton N.J.: Princeton University Press, 1977.

——. "The Varieties of Whiggism from Exclusion to Reform." In *Virtue, Commerce, and History: Essays on Political Thought and History, Chiefly in the Eighteenth Century,* by J. G. A. Pocock. Cambridge; Cambridge University Press, 1985.

——. *Virtue, Commerce and History: Essays on Political Thought and History, Chiefly in the Eighteenth Century.* Cambridge: Cambridge University Press, 1985.

——, ed. *Three British Revolutions: 1641, 1688, 1776.* Princeton, N.J.: Princeton University Press, 1980.

Pocock, J. G. A., and Richard Ashcraft. *John Locke.* Los Angeles: Williams Andrew Clark Memorial Library, 1980.

Porter, Roy. *England in the Eighteenth Century.* London: Allen Lane, 1982.

Postema, Gerald. *Bentham and the Common Law Tradition.* Oxford: Oxford University Press, 1986.

Pym, David. *The Religious Thought of Samuel Taylor Coleridge.* New York: Harper Row Publishing, Inc., 1979).

Rapaczynski, Andrzei. *Nature and Politics: Liberalism in the Philosophies of Hobbes, Locke, and Rousseau.* Ithaca, N.Y.: Cornell University Press, 1987.

Rawls, John. *A Theory of Justice.* Oxford: Oxford University Press, 1971.

Richter, Melvin. *The Political Theory of Montesquieu.* Cambridge: Cambridge University Press, 1977.

Rielly, Patrick. *Leibniz.* Cambridge University Press, 1988.

Robbins, Caroline. *The Eighteenth-Century Commonwealthsmen.* Cambridge, Mass.: Harvard University Press, 1959.

——. *Two English Republican Tracts.* Cambridge: Cambridge University Press, 1969.

Roe, Nicholas. *Wordsworth and Coleridge: The Radical Years.* Oxford: Oxford University Press, 1988.

——, ed. *Samuel Taylor Coleridge and the Sciences of Life.* Oxford: Oxford University Press, 2001.

Rose, J. Holland. *Life of William Pitt.* 2 vols. Vol. 1, *William Pitt and The Great War, 1791–1806* (1911). Vol. 2, *William Pitt and the National Revival* (1911). London: G. Bell and Sons, 1923.

Rosenblum, Nancy. *Another Liberalism: Romanticism and the Reconstruction of Liberal Thought.* Cambridge, Mass.: Harvard University Press, 1987.

Ryan, Alan. *J. S. Mill.* London: Routledge and Kegan Paul, 1974.

———. *Property and Political Theory.* Oxford: Basil Blackwell, 1984.

Sack, James J. *From Jacobite to Conservative: Reaction and Orthodoxy in Britain, c. 1760–1832.* Cambridge: Cambridge University Press, 1993,

Sanders, C. R. *Coleridge and The Broad Church Movement.* Durham, N.C.: Duke University Press, 1942.

Schneewind, J. B. "Autonomy, Obligation, and Virtue: An Overview of Kant's Moral Philosophy." In *The Cambridge Companion to Kant,* ed. Paul Guyer, 309–41. Cambridge: Cambridge University Press, 1992.

———. *Moral Philosophy from Montaigne to Kant.* Cambridge: Cambridge University Press, 1990.

Schofield, Thomas Philip. "Conservative Political Thought in Britain in Response to the French Revolution." *The Historical Journal* 29 (September 1986): 601–22.

Scott, I. R. "From Radicalism to Conservatism: The Politics of Wordsworth and Coleridge, 1797–1818." Ph.D. diss., University of Edinburgh 1987.

Seed, John. "Gentlemen Dissenters: The Social and Political Meaning of Rational Dissent in the 1770s and 1780s." *Historical Journal* 28 (1985): 299–325.

———."Jeremiah Joyce, Unitarianism, and the Vicissitudes of the Radical Intelligentsia in the 1790's." *Transactions of the Unitarian Historical Society* 17 (1981): 97–108.

Shaffer, E. S. *"Kubla Khan" and the Fall of Jerusalem.* Cambridge: Cambridge University Press, 1975.

Shapin, Steven, and Simon Schaffer. *Leviathan and The Air-Pump: Hobbes, Boyle, and the Experimental Life . . . Including a Translation of Thomas Hobbes,* Dialogues physicus de natura aeries *by Simon Schaffer.* Princeton, N.J.: Princeton University Press, 1985.

Smith, Olivia. *The Politics of Language, 1791–1819.* Oxford: Oxford University Press, 1984.

Snyder, Alice Dorothea. *Coleridge on Logic and Learning: With Selections from the Unpublished Manuscripts.* New Haven, Conn.: Yale University Press, 1929. Reprint, Folcroft, Penn.: Folcroft Library Editions, 1973.

———. *The Critical Principle of the Resolution of Opposites as Employed by Coleridge.* Contributions to Rhetorical Theory 9. Ann Arbor: University of Michigan Press, 1918. Reprint, Folcroft, Penn.: Folcroft Press, 1970.

———, ed. *S. T. Coleridge's Treatise on Method.* London: Constable, 1934.

State, Stephen A. "Text and Context: Skinner, Hobbes, and Theistic Natural Law." *Historical Journal* 28 (1985): 27–50.

Strauss, Leo. *Liberalism Ancient and Modern.* New York: Basic Books, 1968.

———. *Persecution and the Art of Writing.* Chicago: University of Chicago Press, 1988.

Sultana, Donald. *Coleridge in Malta and Italy.* oxford: Basil Blackwell, 1969.

Sykes, Norman. *Church and State in England in the Eighteenth Century.* Oxford: Oxford University Press, 1962.

Taylor, Charles. "Cross-Purposes: The Liberal-Communitarian Debate." In *Liberalism and the Moral Life*, ed. Nancy Rosenblum, 159–82. Cambridge, Mass.: Harvard University Press, 1989.

Thomas, Roger. "Comprehension and Indulgence." In *From Uniformity to Unity, 1662–1962*, ed. Geoffrey F. Nuttal and Owen Chadwick, 189–254. London: SPCK, 1962.

Thomis, Malcolm Ian, and Peter Holt. *Threats of Revolution in Britain, 1789–1848*. London: Macmillan, 1977.

Thompson, E. P. "Disenchantment or Default? A Lay Sermon." In *Power and Consciousness*, ed. Conor Cruise O'Brien and William Dean Vanech, 149–81. London: London University Press, 1969.

——. "Eighteenth-Century Society: Class Struggle Without Class." *Social History* 3 (1978): 133–65.

——. "Hunting the Jacobin Fox." *Past and Present* 142 (February 1994): 94–140.

——. *The Making of the English Working Class*. London: Victor Gollancz, 1961.

——. "Patrician Society, Plebeian Culture." *Journal of Social History* 7 (1974): 382–485.

Thorne, R. G., ed. *The House of Commons, 1790–1820*. 5 vols. History of Parliament Series. London: Secker & Warburg, 1986.

——. *The Romantics: England in a Revolutionary Age*. Suffolk, UK: Merlin Press, 1997.

Taft, Barbara. *Absolute Liberty*. Hamden Conn.: Archon Books, 1982.

Tuck, Richard. *Natural Rights Theories*. Cambridge: Cambridge University Press, 1979.

Tully, James. *Pufendorf*. Cambridge: Cambridge University Press, 1991.

Turk, Christopher. *Coleridge and Mill*. London: MacMillan, 1989.

Wellek, Rene. *Immanuel Kant in England*. Princeton, N.J.: Princeton University Press, 1931.

Whalley, George. "The Bristol Library Borrowings of Southey and Coleridge, 1793–8." *The Library*, 5th ser., 5 (September 1949): 114–31.

White, Reginald James. *The Political Thought of Samuel Taylor Coleridge: A Selection*. London: Jonathan Cape, 1938.

Wilkenson, C. H. "Some Early Editors." In *Coleridge: Studies by Several Hands*, ed. Edmund Blunden and E. L. Griggs, 97–109 (London: Constable, 1934).

Willey, Basil. "Coleridge and Religion." In *Writers and Their Backgrounds: S. T. Coleridge*, ed. E. Brett, 221–43. London: G. Bell, 1971.

——. *The English Moralists*. London: Chatto and Windus, 1964.

Williams, Raymond. *Culture and Society, 1780–1950*. London: Chatto and Windus, 1960.

Winch, Donald. "Adam Smith's 'Enduring Particular Result': A Political and Cosmopolitan Perspective." In *Wealth and Virtue: The Shaping of Political Economy in the Scottish Enlightenment*, ed. Istvan Hont and Michael Ignatieff, 253–70. Cambridge: Cambridge University Press, 1983.

——. *Adam Smith's Politics*. Cambridge: Cambridge University Press, 1978.

——. "The Burke-Smith Problem in Late-Eighteenth-Century Political and Economic Thought." *Historical Journal* 28, no. 1 (1985): 231–47.

——. *Malthus*. Cambridge: Cambridge University Press, 1992.

——. *Riches and Poverty*. Cambridge: Cambridge University Press, 1995.

Winstanley, D. A. *The University of Cambridge in the Eighteenth Century*. Cambridge: Cambridge University Press, 1922.

——. *Unreformed Cambridge*. Cambridge: Cambridge University Press, 1935.

Woodring, Carl. R. *Politics in the Poetry of Coleridge*. Madison: The University of Wisconsin Press, 1961.

Woolfe, Paul. *Kant's Psychoanalytic Theory*. Cambridge, Mass.: Harvard University Press, 1980.

Wylie, Ian. *Young Coleridge and the Philosophers of Nature*. Oxford: The Clarendon Press, 1989.

Young, J. Michael. "Functions of Thought and the Synthesis of Intuitions." In *The Cambridge Companion to Kant*, ed. Paul Guyer, 101–22. Cambridge: Cambridge University Press, 1992.

Zagorin, Perez. *The Country and the Court*. New York: Columbia University Press, 1969.

——. "Two Cultures? Rhetoric of Court and Country in the Early Seventeenth Century." In *Origins of the English Civil War*, ed. Conrad Russell. London: MacMillan, 1973.

Zall, Paul M., and David Erdman. "Coleridge and Jeffrey in Controversy." *Studies in Romanticism* 14 (Winter 1975): 75–83.

Zwicker, Stephen, and D. Hirst. "Rhetoric and Disguise: Political Language and Political Arguments in 'Absolom and Achitophel.'" *Journal of British Studies* 21 (1981): 39–55.

INDEX

Abernathy, John, 152–53
Abrams, Meyer H., 14–15, 228n14
abstract principles, 35, 83
Adams, John, 92
agency, 2, 126; of individual in social structure, 32, 108, 157–58; relation to duty, 103–4, 262n51
Age of Reason (Paine), 179
agon, 119–20
Alliance of Church and State (Warburton), 177–78
alliance theory, 178–80, 187–88
American revolutionaries, 6, 56, 59, 61, 92
anachronistic vocabulary, 16, 18
ancient constitution, 2, 6, 9, 44, 63, 84–85, 184, 214, 235–36n24; defense of, in *The Plot,* 73–74; independence of executive and legislative branches, 51–53; labor regulation and, 168–71; orders of citizens, 54, 195–96. *See also* constitution
Andrewes, Lancelot, 176
Anglican Church, 178, 203–4, 248n18
Answer to the Nineteen Propositions (Charles I), 56
anticlericalism, 19, 22
antireformists, 25–26
apostasy thesis, 4–6, 12, 14–15, 24, 227n5, 228n12
Appeal from the Old to the New Whigs (Burke), 85
apprenticeship, 168
aristocracy, 44, 55–56, 196, 198

Aristotelianism, 141, 142–48, 233n70, 253n31
Arnold, Matthew, 252n20
artisans, 59
Athanasianism, 180, 182, 248n18
atheism, 22, 118, 230n37, 248n16
Athens, 208, 214
audience, 12–13

Bacon, Francis, 142, 148–49, 152, 202
Bailyn, Bernard, 6
barons, 44, 196
Battle of the Books (Swift), 143, 252n20
Beaumont, George, 24
behaviorist psychologies, 155–56
benevolence, 26–27, 107–8, 129–30, 138, 246n28
Bentham, Jeremy, 10, 112, 115, 122, 140, 247n7, 255n3
Benthamites, 99
Berkeley, George, 142, 148, 254n37
Berlin, Isaiah, 31, 94, 227n58, 243n4
Bill of Rights (1689), 53–55, 236n24
biological metaphors, 135–36, 163, 174, 207–9, 217. *See also* medico-philosophical approach
Blackstone, William, 52, 76, 235n20, 239nn21, 23
body politic, 57, 136, 152, 184, 207
Bolingbroke, Henry St. John, 26, 44, 51, 55, 85, 90, 180, 260n29; property, view of, 186, 188, 189